Lecture Notes in Computer Science   9831

Commenced Publication in 1973
Founding and Former Series Editors:
Gerhard Goos, Juris Hartmanis, and Jan van Leeuwen

More information about this series at http://www.springer.com/series/7409

Andrea Kő · Enrico Francesconi (Eds.)

Electronic Government and the Information Systems Perspective

5th International Conference, EGOVIS 2016
Porto, Portugal, September 5–8, 2016
Proceedings

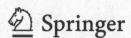 Springer

Editors
Andrea Kő
Corvinus University of Budapest
Budapest
Hungary

Enrico Francesconi
Institute of Legal Information Theory
   and Techniques
Florence
Italy

ISSN 0302-9743   ISSN 1611-3349 (electronic)
Lecture Notes in Computer Science
ISBN 978-3-319-44158-0   ISBN 978-3-319-44159-7 (eBook)
DOI 10.1007/978-3-319-44159-7

Library of Congress Control Number: 2016947194

LNCS Sublibrary: SL3 – Information Systems and Applications, incl. Internet/Web, and HCI

Printed on acid-free paper

This Springer imprint is published by Springer Nature
The registered company is Springer International Publishing AG Switzerland

Preface

The 5th International Conference on Electronic Government and the Information Systems Perspective, EGOVIS 2016, took place in Porto, Portugal, during September 5–8. The conference belongs to the 27th DEXA Conference Series.

The international conference cycle EGOVIS focuses on information systems and ICT aspects of e-government. Information systems are a core enabler for e-government/governance in all its dimensions: e-administration, e-democracy, e-participation, and e-voting. EGOVIS 2016 brought together experts from academia, public administrations, and industry to discuss e-government and e-democracy from different perspectives and disciplines, i.e., technology, policy and/or governance, and public administration.

The Program Committee accepted 22 papers from recent research fields such as open data and government cloud, identity management and e-government architectures, innovation, open government, intelligent systems, and semantic technologies applications. Beyond theoretical contributions, papers cover e-government experiences from all over the world; cases are presented from Europe and South America.

These proceedings are organized into eight sections according to the conference sessions.

We were honored that the keynote speeches, hosted this year by EGOVIS, were given by three leaders in the e-government field from academia and the public sector: Prof. Ronald Traunmuller of the University of Linz, one of the pioneers in e-government studies, discussed the information system perspective in e-government research and development. Attila Péterfalvi, President of the National Authority for Data Protection and Freedom of Information in Hungary, gave an overview of the transparency of public functions and public funds in Hungary. Finally, Prof. András Gábor from Corvinus University in Budapest addressed the problem of security governance, in particular for public sector services with regard to the social components of trust.

The chairs of the Program Committee wish to thank all the reviewers for their valuable work; the reviews raised several research questions that were discussed at the conference. We would like to thank Gabriela Wagner for the administrative support and assisting us in the scheduling.

We wish our readers a pleasant and beneficial learning experience and we hope that the discussion between researchers will continue after the conference contributing to building a global community in the field of e-government.

September 2016

Enrico Francesconi
Andrea Kő

Organization

General Chair

Roland Traunmüller   University of Linz, Austria

Program Committee Co-chairs

Enrico Francesconi   Italian National Research Council, Italy
Andrea Kő   Corvinus University Budapest, Hungary

Honorary Chairs

Wichian Chutimaskul   King Mongkut's University of Technology, Thailand
Fernando Galindo   University of Zaragoza, Spain

Program Committee

Luis Álvarez Sabucedo	Universidade de Vigo, Spain
Jaro Berce	University of Ljubljana, Slovenia
Francesco Buccafurri	Università degli Studi Mediterranea di Reggio Calabria, Italy
Alejandra Cechich	Universidad Nacional del Comahue, Argentina
Wojciech Cellary	Poznan University of Economics, Poland
Wichian Chutimaskul	King Mongkut's University of Technology, Thailand
Flavio Corradini	University of Camerino, Italy
Vytautas Cyras	Vilnius University, Lithuania
Joan Francesc Fondevila Gascón	Universitat Pompeu Fabra, Spain
Enrico Francesconi	Italian National Research Council, Italy
Ivan Futo	National Tax and Customs Administration, Hungary
András Gábor	Corvinus University of Budapest, Hungary
Fernando Galindo	University of Zaragoza, Spain
Francisco Javier García Marco	University of Zaragoza, Spain
Stefanos Gritzalis	University of the Aegean, Greece
Henning Sten Hansen	Aalborg University, Denmark
Christos Kalloniatis	University of the Aegean, Greece
Nikos Karacapilidis	University of Patras, Greece
Evangelia Kavakli	University of the Aegean, Greece
Bozidar Klicek	University of Zagreb, Croatia
Ah Lian Kor	Leeds Beckett University, UK

Hun-yeong Kwon	Korea University, South Korea
Andrea Kő	Corvinus University Budapest, Hungary
Christine Leitner	Centre for Economics and Public Administration Ltd. (CEPA), UK
Herbert Leitold	E-Government Innovation Center EGIZ, Austria
Marian Mach	Technical University of Kosice, Slovakia
Peter Mambrey	University of Duisburg-Essen, Germany
Mara Nikolaidou	Harokopio University of Athens, Greece
Javier Nogueras	University of Zaragoza, Spain
Monica Palmirani	University of Bologna, Italy
Aljosa Pasic	Atos, Spain
Andrea Polini	UNICAM, Italy
Reinhard Posch	Technical University of Graz, Austria
Aires J. Rover	Federal University of Santa Catarina, Brazil
Christian Rupp	Federal Chancellery of Austria/Federal Platform Digital Austria, Austria
Erich Schweighofer	University of Vienna, Austria
Hatem Ben Sta	National University of Ireland Galway, Ireland
Ella Taylor-Smith	Edinburgh Napier University, UK
Raissa Uskenbaeva	International University, Kazakhstan
Julian Valero	iDertec, University of Murcia, Spain
Costas Vassilakis	University of the Peloponnese, Greece
Gianluigi Viscusi	EPFL - CDM -CSI, Switzerland
Christopher C. Wills	Caris Research Ltd., UK
Frank Wilson	Interaction Design, UK
Robert Woitsch	BOC Asset Management, Austria
Chien-Chih Yu	National ChengChi University, China (Taiwan)

Additional Reviewers

Stavros Simou	University of the Aegean, Greece
Evangelos Gongolidis	University of the Aegean, Greece
Nikos Argyropoulos	University of Brighton, UK
Maria Sideri	University of the Aegean, Greece
Angeliki Tsochou	Ionion University, Greece
Prokopis Drogkaris	ENISA, Greece
Agustina Buccella	GIISCo, University of Comahue, Argentina
Andrés Flores	GIISCo, University of Comahue, Argentina

Abstracts of Invited Talks

Transparency of Public Functions and Public Funds - Controversial Actions in the Field of Transparency of Public Funds in Hungary

Attila Péterfalvi

Hungarian Data Protection and Freedom of Information Authority
peterfalvi.attila@naih.hu

Abstract. As clearly stated by the Hungarian Constitutional Court: 'without being monitored by its citizens, the state becomes an unaccountable and unpredictable machine, and this is especially dangerous because a non-transparent state represents an increased threat to constitutional rights'.

The freedom of information is one of the most sensitive rights in a democracy, because the political forces always would like to follow their own trend to communicate their vices and virtues. In opposition they urge a larger publicity, whereas as governing force they prefer to communicate according to their own perceptions.

Since the constitutional revolution of 1989, there were two governmental periods when the legislation opened more transparency on national assets: the first one was in 2003 when the left-wing coalition adopted the "Glass pocket Law", the second one was the right-wing coalition in 2012, when by the constitutional revolution, the Fundamental Law itself decrees the transparency on national assets.

The new Hungarian Fundamental Law in its preamble – called NATIONAL COMMITMENT AND BELIEF – proclaims that "true democracy exists only where the State serves it citizens and administers their affairs justly and without abuse or bias".

In Hungary the fundamental right of freedom of information has to react to the new/old functions of the State. The wide spread of State Owned Enterprises (SOEs) gave a new perspective of publicity of data in connection of financial data of these enterprises.

On one hand the legislation widened the FOI with the new constitution, what gives a quite strong basis of freedom of information:

- first of all, the Fundamental Law declares the right to know as a fundamental right,
- in addition, it creates the national constitutional foundations of transparency of public funds, of public property.

Till nowadays SOEs fall under the more or less the same transparency regulations as public bodies. According to the 2007 CVI Act on State Ownership, the State may acquire (or dispose of) assets in order to: (1) execute State functions; (2) fulfil societal needs; and (3) realise government economic policy goals. In practice, some rationales for state ownership that have been put forward, in addition to the "general public interest" have included energy security, delivering country-wide, affordable mail services (the Hungarian Postal Service Co.) or fulfilling cultural facilitation functions (the Hungarian National Film Fund).

State-Owned Enterprises filled a gap in the publicity of public funds. A body or person that is vested with powers to manage or control State property shall be treated as a person or body exercising public functions pursuant to the act on access to information of public interest. According to the Hungarian legal background, with the help of the Constitutional Court's interpretation, a body or person that is vested with powers to manage or control State property shall be treated as a person or body exercising public functions pursuant to the act on access to information of public interest.

This wide sense of public body motivated that our Authority gave recommendation on the borders of business secret and freedom of information. Our conclusion was that these state-owned business players – within strict conditions – could justify the secrecy of their management data, but they have to provide enough data to the public to control the use of the national assets.

This wide sense of transparency of public funds motivated the legislature to modify sectoral laws to "rationalize" the FOI. For example, in 2014 Hungarian lawmakers have voted to classify some data in contracts on the expansion of the Paks II nuclear power plant for 30 years. The Paks II Act classifies all data and contracts related to the planned €12.5 billion ($14 billion) expansion of the Paks II nuclear power plant by Russia, for 30 years. In March 2016 the Hungarian Parliament approved new disclosure exemptions for the state-owned postal service and for foundations established by the National Bank of Hungary. In Mai 2016 the 2017 Central Budget Act modified the Act CXXII of 2009 on the More Economical Operation of State-Owned Enterprises nondisclosure protections of data relating to the assets, functioning and contracts of state companies involved in activities such as central data acquisition and telecommunications management could be exempted from Freedom of Information (FOI) laws for up to 30 years.

Furthermore, the central and principal budgetary transparency, and the state's (new) quasi business functions, there is a quiet significant importance of transparency of political parties' finances. The FOI legal literature always tried to find real solution to legislature to find the way to wide transparency of parties finances.

To summarize the most overall theme of transparency of the state and fight against the corruption is the notion of public function, public funds. What are the borders of public functions and business sector, can we treat he same way the SOEs in monopoly and the traditional public bodies etc.?

The IS Perspective in E-Government Research and Development

Roland Traunmüller

Johannes Kepler Universität Linz, Altenbergerstraße 69, 4040 Linz, Austria
traunm@ifs.uni-linz.ac.at

Abstract. Five years ago DEXA established a Conference line under the name of EGOVIS as to underscore the importance of the Information Systems view. Obviously, the Information Systems aspect plays a pivotal role in the whole field of E-Government Research and Development. The term denotes the study of organizational systems with a specific reference to information and the complementary networks of hardware and software. It comprises a quite broad scope and thus addresses a breath of themes ranging from a strategic and design focus to managerial and operational questions. Accordingly, the IS Perspective induces a holistic and comprehensive approach for E-Government R&D. In addition it helps to comprehend and improve a series of actual and novel innovations. The contribution outlines first general merits of the IS perspective and consequently moves to discussing some recent challenges. Respective themes comprise Collaboration Features, Mobile Government, Open Government and Modelling Approaches.

Trust or Security – Stakeholders' Responsibility

András Gábor

Corvinus University of Budapest
andras.gabor@uni-corvinus.hu

Abstract. Security is one of the most often used term in the world of ICT. It is very likely, security and in a closer look the information security is an important phenomenon. The total expenditure on information security in 2015 was estimated by Gartner to 75.4 billion USD, 4.7 % growth compared to 2014 spending.

Demand for security goes back in time well before the age of ICT, somehow in parallel with the level of vulnerability. Vulnerability is the likelihood of losing something what is in our possession, nevertheless if we worked for it, or inherited it. The likelihood of losing something depends on the variety and extent of threats. Occurring a negative event which effects individuals, organisation, physical objects, processes, etc. in a bad way often call risk. Risk management takes into account the risk with the likelihood of occurrence and how serious is the consequence of the bad event. This way the weighted risk stands in front of the security measurements. Security measurements tend from the very simple physical solutions (e.g. fences) through the logical level solutions (e.g. authentication) up to the strategic level security governance.

If we raise the question, how much money is worthwhile to send on security, in order to minimize the vulnerability (=the potential loss), the answer is easy and simple. The spending on security is justified up to the level where cost of security is still a little bit less or maximum equal to the value of the potential loss. This is the answer to the question, if… we are fully in aware of the value of every property what we have. But how can we translate the value of every property on monetary tools? Anyhow.

From the angle of threat-types, they can be grouped in several groups. In the following we focus on the information security, only. The scale starts from blocking the use of an information system, information service (Denial of Service, DOS), through spamming, alteration of data, identity thieves, money flow diverting, industrial espionage up to destroying data. As a consequence, there are effective financial losses, e.g. if an outgoing invoice file is destroyed, the company cannot claim money from its customers. Beside of financial losses, important know-how can be transferred to the competitor, which may create indirectly financial losses. On the level of individuals personal or very special personal (e.g. health status) can be stolen and misused. These and similar problems encourages the ICT managers increasing the level of security, but the calculation of the needed level is in a grey zone, since no exact information of the monetary sum of potential losses.

The problem is even more complex, because due to national security, anti-cyberterrorism, budgetary reasons (tax offices), competition law (anti-trust, anti-cartel actions), and many other community reasons there is a social need for "legal backdoors" in properly secured information systems, the state is eagerly needs the data of its enterprises and citizens. Without questioning the rationality of data inquiry of the state, it raises extra security, data privacy issues.

Back to the original question, what is the sufficient extent of security spending or effort?

The usual approach is the weighted risk analysis (risk likelihood x impact), based on the foreseeable potential loss is a reliable basis, what kind of efforts are justified in order to spend on security.

Behind of the vulnerability and threats (risk) and the security measures in most of the cases work strategies. Strategy means in this case properly defined goal or goals (to block services, to get secret or hidden information, etc.) and procedures aiming to reach the goals. On the other hand, security management has the opposite goals and the suitable procedures. Game theory addresses typically similar problems, therefore it is worthwhile to investigate whether game theory can be applied in the security domain. From game theory angle this is an equilibrium problem, especially if we take into consideration its dynamical character.

Having a deeper look into goals and strategies, we find, the goals are relatively more stable, while strategies changes frequently. The reason of variety of strategies partly explained by the fast changing technology, partly is due to the different social environment. Social engineering as a separate industry branch has developed on the ground of social components of the security. Having analysed and decomposed the social environment we found the trust as one of the most effective factor. Trust on the contrary of "hard" (=well-defined) security procedure, is a "soft" concept.

Trust by a very general definition is a set of beliefs, according to which interacting other parties are benevolent. Trust has different interpretation in psychology, in sociology, in social psychology, in economics, in philosophy. Many other concepts are linked to the concept of trust, like reliance, trustworthiness, stereotypes, values and value sharing, - the list is quite long. From security point of view, the social psychological interpretation looks the most relevant. From this approach trust is a common belief in a given community (society, or the effected part of the society) which is based on the combination of shared values and expectations. The recent Panama offshore case highlight the complexity of trust issue. The Panamian law firm Mossack Fonseca offered services for shell corporations for tax evasion, money laundry and many other illegal actions. After leaking the list of its customers, investigating journalists published several very delicate issues, pushing governments to act. From the point of view of the law firm the leakage created a big security problem (an employee was the highest risk factor, as always), however this security breach fits very well to high priority social and ethical values, and apart from the interested parties the belief of citizens in justice, order, in other words trust is strengthened. The list of positive and negative examples is endless.

Trust therefore can be reformulated also as strategy, in the sense of expectations and procedures. Expectations strongly correlates to the shared values and the variety of the priority order of values, less variety of priority orders, stronger the effect of the values on the procedures. Procedures are very much linked to the actions which may follow the negative effect of trust ("being betrayed", disappointment, losing confidence). In the above example, publicity which will push governments to rethink regulations.

At this point there are different situations, different players, and different strategies, both on the security and trust "side". What is interesting at which point the prevention break-into actions (=security measures) will be in equilibrium with the actions-to-do (strategies) based on social-economic-individual requirements (=trust)? We believe the security and trust phenomenon can be approached, investigated through seeking the equilibrium among them.

Plenty of research issues arise, just to mention one which equilibrium concept fit better: Nash equilibrium or Pareto? How to operationalize strategies behind of trust? What can be taken into account as payoff? How to cope with the global character of the virtual world and the geographically diverse communities, hence trust (components, level) geographically, sociologically diverse nature?

Despite of the plenty open questions, one conclusion already can be drawn: the good security governance should address not only the advanced technical, technological solutions but should be open to the trust issues, security strategy must be based also on the socio-components of the trust.

Contents

Intelligent Systems in E-Government

E-Government Research and Intelligent Systems

E-Government Cases - Data and Knowledge Management

Identity Management in E-Government

E-Government Cases - Legal Issues

Estonian e-Residency: Benefits, Risk and Lessons Learned

Taavi Kotka[1(✉)], Carlos Ivan Vargas Alvarez del Castillo[2], and Kaspar Korjus[3]

[1] Department of Informatics, Tallinn University of Technology,
Akadeemia tee 15A, 12618 Tallinn, Estonia
taavi.kotka@gmail.com
[2] RaulWalter LLC, Rüütli 11, 10130 Tallinn, Estonia
carlos.vargas@raulwalter.com
[3] Enterprise Estonia, Lasnamäe 2, 11412 Tallinn, Estonia
kaspar.korjus@gmail.com

Abstract. Why did Estonia create e-Residency? e-Residency project challenges traditional notions of residency, citizenship, territoriality, and globalization—with potentially profound implications for social theories of the state and citizen networks in the modern era. This paper examines the foundations of the project within the broader context of the Estonian e-state and discusses the main actors and components involved in the creation and functioning of e-Residency. It presents and assessment of the initiative's benefits and risks to society. Finally, the paper concludes by exploring the broad implications of e-Residency for conventional understandings of the nation state.

1 Introduction

This paper explores Estonia's innovative e-Residency initiative, an ambitious project launched in 2014 that, for the first time, enables people from anywhere in the world to become digital residents of another nation. Like other pioneering developments in the Estonian "e-state," the e-Residency project challenges traditional notions of residency, citizenship, territoriality, and globalization—with potentially profound implications for social theories of the state and citizen networks in the modern era.

The study has both theoretical and policy-oriented objectives. Theoretically, it applies the principle of "flat" ontology, drawing from the Actor Network Theory perspective, to elucidate the workings and potential impact of e-Residency. At a policy level, the analysis provides the reader with the necessary information to understand the functions and aims of e-Residency, as well as the business possibilities that it offers. Moreover, the paper will discuss lessons and insights that will help practitioners identify and unlock the transforming potential of this new policy instrument of the e-state for other nations.

The paper has three sections. Firstly, it examines the foundations of the project within the broader context of the Estonian e-state and discusses the prime agents involved in the creation and functioning of e-Residency. Secondly, it assesses the initiative's benefits and risks to society. Finally, the paper concludes by exploring the broad implications of e-Residency for conventional understandings of the nation-state.

© Springer International Publishing Switzerland 2016
A. Kő and E. Francesconi (Eds.): EGOVIS 2016, LNCS 9831, pp. 3–15, 2016.
DOI: 10.1007/978-3-319-44159-7_1

2   Background and Origins of e-Residency

Why did Estonia create e-Residency? [1] The initiative's point of origin was the ambitious ideal of recruiting "10 million e-Estonians," which was conceived by three people: Taavi Kotka (a co-author of this publication), Siim Sikkut, and Ruth Annus. This principle emerged from the priorities established by the Digital Agenda for Estonia 2020, in which the Estonian Cabinet prioritized the aim of increasing Estonia's international recognition in digital affairs as follows [2, p. 3]:

> *"Estonia will start offering its secure and convenient services to the citizens of other countries. Virtual residence or e-Residence will be launched, meaning that Estonia will issue non-residents with electronic identity in the form of digital ID cards. The aspiration for Estonia is to become as re-known [sic] for its e-services as Switzerland is in the field of banking."*

The concept of e-Residency was then submitted for approval to the Estonian Parliament, where it received unanimous support. In spring 2014, the "10 million e-Estonians" [3] idea was sent to the Estonian Development Fund, which was organizing a competition for the "Best Development Idea 2015." E-Residency received immediate attention and won a twelve-month development grant. The e-Residency website and subscription list went viral through social media channels. In this way, the project attracted substantial international attention even before the Estonian government began promoting it. Indeed, positive coverage by the international media (e.g. BBC World News, The Guardian, The Economist, ABC News (Australia), Wired UK) was a crucial factor in the project's acceptance within Estonian society. By 1 December 2014, Estonia had recruited its first e-resident (Edward Lucas of The Economist). Animated by these early successes, the Estonian Cabinet soon after this held a second meeting to decide the future of the project. A seven-member team was assigned to run the project beginning in April 2015 (see Table 1 for an extended list of key actors in the project), led by Kaspar Korjus (Programme Director).

By May 2015, Estonia had launched e-Residency as an internationally accessible "beta" initiative. Henceforth, physical visits to Estonia were no longer required in order to apply for e-Residency. Rather, following a thorough background check, the applicant could visit any of thirty-eight foreign embassies from New York to Tokyo, identify herself with her passport, provide biometric data, and pick up the e-Residency eID card. Although the application process thereby became easier, obstacles to the conduct of business and other activities remain. For example, in order to open a bank account or to sell shares in a company, e-residents must travel to Estonia to meet with bank officials or notaries.

In July 2015, the Cabinet held a third meeting on e-Residency, which resulted in a resolution to adapt major legislation, processes, and e-services in order to facilitate the conduct of business activities in Estonia. As of August 2015, e-Residency remains in a public beta phase, meaning that everyone is invited to apply for residency and to help the Estonian government by providing feedback that will help the organizers tailor it to users' specific needs. In short, Estonia is developing e-Residency in the spirit and manner of a start-up enterprise: the launch and methods of improvement have been swift and institutionally nimble.

Table 1. Main roles of the key actors in the e-Residency project

Key actor	Role/Description
Authors of Digital Agenda for Estonia 2020	Government document from November 2013 which first discussed the e-Residency initiative
Estonian Development Fund	Organised the competition that initially promoted and funded the "10-Million E-Estonian" concept
7-member team at Enterprise Estonia	Facilitates the administration of the e-Residency project and coordinates with cooperating public, private, and non-profit sector partners.
The Board of E-Residency	Supervises the strategy, goals, and budget of the project proposed by the 7-member team
Cabinet	Supervises the strategy, goals, and budget of the project proposed by the Board
eID	Access key for e-residents to the digital world
X-Road	Estonian data-exchange layer enabling secure internet-based data exchange between public and private sector information systems
Estonian Police and Border Guard	Monitors the application process for e-Residency cards, conducts background checks on applicants, and issues cards to Estonian embassies and consulates, which will issue the eIDs to e-residents.
Information System Authority (RIA)	Coordinates and safeguards the development and administration of the national information system
Ministry of the Interior	Develops legislation regarding e-Residency applications and processes
Ministry of Economic Affairs and Communications	Manages the public-sector IT budget and formulates decisions on how to invest in applications
Ministry of Justice	Develops legislation regarding the business environment
Ministry of Finance	Develops legislation regarding the financial aspects of e-Residency and reviews its compliance with the law
Ministry of Foreign Affairs	Holds face-to-face meetings with applicants, takes their fingerprints, and issues e-Residency start-up kits

So far, the initiative has met with great success in growing the number of users. On December 2014, the Cabinet agreed to aim for 2,000 e-residents by the end of 2015, meaning that, on average, 8 e-residents per working day would have to apply

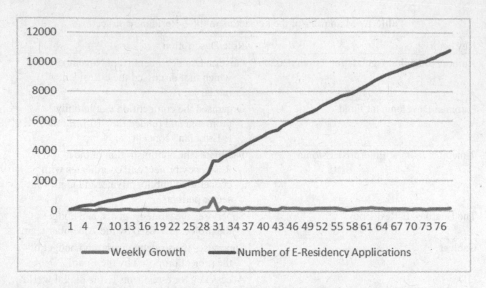

Fig. 1. Weekly growth in e-Residency applications

successfully. As of May 2016, there have been 10,353 applications (see Fig. 1 for weekly growth in E-Residency applications), of which 9,768 (94 %) resulted in e-Residency; 394 (4 %) are still in process; 136 (< 2 %) were denied. Thus, the initial goal of 2,000 applicants was exceeded by 128 % within just three quarters. Through May 2015, there were 15 applications per day. Since the launch of the online application form on 13 May, 43 applications have been submitted daily. If this trend continues, by the end of 2016 there will be approximately 14,000 e-residents—far exceeding initial recruitment goals.

Before the application became available online, most e-residents came from Estonia's neighboring countries, because applicants had been required to visit Estonia twice in order to complete the process. As of May 2016, however, the top 10 countries for applicants (see Fig. 2) are Finland, with 2,029 applications (20 % of the total); Russia, 935 (9 %); the United States, 680 (7 %); Ukraine, 580 (6 %); Italy, 551 (5 %); Germany, 462 (4 %); United Kingdom, 387 (4 %); Latvia, 351 (3 %); the India, 321 (3 %); and Netherlands, 305 (3 %). Recently, the online application platform has witnessed a surge in applications from the developing world. Since its inception, 284 Estonian companies have at least one e-resident shareholder. Additionally, the e-Residency network contains 20,069 active e-mail subscribers.

3   Benefits and Risks of e-Residency

The practical consequences of e-Residency for citizens and for the Estonian state are not yet entirely known; they will, however, create possibilities for the project's continued expansion or failure. Following is an assessment of the project's benefits and risks. It is based on interviews with 29 experts and key actors highlighted in Table 1 and feedback

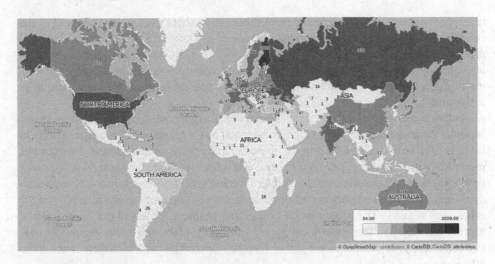

Fig. 2. Geographical distribution of e-residency applications (as of May 2016)

from 529 early e-residency applicants, which was coded, organized and structured for a summary presented in following subsections.

We argue that the positive practical consequences of e-Residency for Estonia and its citizens significantly outweigh the risks associated with the initiative; nevertheless, these risks are real and merit serious attention—particularly among policymakers in nations who may consider adopting similar measures in the future.

Although, as we argue, e-Residency is best perceived as a sort of governmental start-up, some benefits have already emerged for three types of non-governmental stake-holders: e-residents, the private sector, and the Republic of Estonia as a whole.

3.1 Benefits for e-Residents

Why do people become e-residents? The answer is simple and compelling. E-residents can currently access and use the following services online:

- Establish and administer a company;
- Conduct all their banking;
- Declare taxes;
- Digitally sign contracts and other documents;
- Access international payment service providers.

We can divide e-residents into three groups: visitors to Estonia; virtual businesses; and "fans," or the community of e-residents who are motivated by personal considerations. Visitors to Estonia include diplomats, academics, even some tourists—all of whom now and again physically live in Estonia for a short period of time.

Because present-day Estonia is a fully digitized nation, life without a digital identity can be challenging—indeed, it is almost inconceivable. As e-residents, diplomats no longer have to carry and sign invoices to obtain VAT returns; with the digital signature feature, this process can be conducted in seconds via email. Guest lecturers or researchers can now sign contracts from other universities even before arriving in the country. And visitors, during their stay in Estonia, can use the e-Residency card in local pharmacies to collect prescriptions; at libraries to take out books; or as a discount card in local supermarkets. Because every e-resident possesses a unique identity number, many digital services available to legal residents and citizens are also available to e-residents.

Individuals working in virtual businesses constitute the second group of e-residents. Mainly, these are people from neighboring countries who already have investments in Estonia. Before the era of e-Residency, changing a company's email address, for example, required visiting a notary, paying for postal and other fees, and waiting at least one week before the new information was entered into the Estonian business registry. Now, e-residents can go online and perform all of these functions—in a matter of seconds—via the e-business registry. The same ease of conducting business applies to tax filings, annual report submissions, shareholder meetings, and many other obligatory business tasks. E-Residency, in brief, makes the life of foreign shareholders and managers much more efficient.

It is important to note that the virtual business environment also includes entrepreneurs and freelancers from outside the EU, especially in the developing world. These people face huge challenges in today's changing global business environment, challenges for which Estonian e-Residency could be a solution. It is likely that in the coming years there will be many more self-employed freelancers whose lifestyle is more mobile, whose customers hail from various different countries, and whose services are sold via e-commerce channels. These trends put traditional nation states in a position that, instead of creating a business friendly environment for residents and citizens, holds them back from growing their businesses. Today's global citizens prefer to avoid the confines of national borders, face-to-face meeting requirements, and double taxation by governments. E-Residency provides the opportunity to run location-independent international businesses while keeping administrative costs to a minimum. Ownership and control of a company remains fully with its founders, without any need to hire and correspond with local directors as businesses must do in typical financial offshore centers such as Panama and the Cayman Islands. E-Residency offers individuals in the developing world a particularly useful set of business opportunities and advantages. First, for reasons of political or economic instability in their countries of origin, such individuals may struggle to gain trust in Western business circles, complicating the search for partners and customers abroad. Estonia, in contrast, is firmly embedded within the EU legal framework, which offers e-residents from developing countries a basis on which to build the same level of trust as residents elsewhere in the Western world. Second, many developing countries are plagued by significant levels of bureaucracy, travel restrictions, and sometimes unstable political climates, which make it very difficult to seize long-term competitive advantages. Third, the general level of Internet access in much of the developing world is low; furthermore, even countries with a comparatively broad level of Internet access may not offer standard digital services, such as online payment providers. Therefore, businesses in these countries cannot accept international payments—hence they cannot sell their services or products via online channels. Selling digital services exclusively in local markets greatly hampers the potential for business development.

The solution to these problems is simple: as Estonian e-residents, these business owners can establish and manage a trusted EU company online; open an Estonian bank account and transfer money online; gain access to trustworthy Estonian payment provider services; and sign contracts, tax declarations, and administrative filings online. While these functions provide particular advantages to e-residents in the developing world, they also allow all e-residents the chance to run location independent international businesses—the ultimate freedom of mobility—while at the same time keeping the administrative costs to a minimum. This, then, is the ultimate goal of Estonia's e-Residency project with respect to businesspersons: to unlock the entrepreneurial potential of every world citizen.

But why choose Estonia as a basis for residency—of any kind—in the first place? First, Estonia offers a strong social and infrastructural basis for aspiring entrepreneurs. According to a 2014 study by Freedom House, Estonia ranks second in the world in terms of Internet freedom [4].

In addition, in 2015, a study by the Heritage Foundation and the Wall Street Journal ranked Estonia first among EU member states in economic freedom [5]. Second, the country has a transparent flat-rate tax system with 0 % income tax on businesses for profits that are reinvested domestically.

A third group of e-residents consists simply of the project's community of fans—that is, individuals who join for personal reasons, not to conduct business. According to a study conducted by the e-Residency operators, 35 % of subscribers fall into this group. These individuals may be politically or ideologically minded and perceive e-Residency as a mechanism to protest against or subvert the controls of governments that are repressive of Internet freedom, press freedom, and other civil and political rights. Herein, then, lies an essential underlying premise of the e-Residency project: people everywhere resent ever-increasing restrictions in both their personal and professional lives. They do not want to choose between privacy and security—they want both. And this is exactly what e-Residency offers.

One reason why Estonians have one of the highest levels of government-citizen trust in the world is that the advanced state of Estonia's ICT infrastructure strikes a reasonable balance between user security and privacy, on the one hand, and convenience of lifestyle, on the other. E-residents find that their eIDs offer an extra layer of identity, one that is superior to those conferred by their parent states of origin, which are confined by geographic frontiers and severely limited by legal restrictions and cumbersome bureaucracies. There is a natural pool of prospective e-residents—from both the industrialized and the developing worlds—among people who are oppressed by their territorial home nations. E-residents from these nations may now enjoy a new level of belonging to an emergent, transparent, and privacy-first globalized world. For this group, the decision to become e-residents is a fundamental choice to break free from conventional restrictions of citizenship and territoriality. One cannot choose one's country of birth; one may not even be able, realistically, to choose one's country of physical habitation; but now, regardless of these two constraints, one can always choose a country of *digital* residence.

3.2   Benefits for Private Sector Entities

Another important group of e-Residency stakeholders comprises partner companies that offer services to existing e-residents. These partners generally fall into the following groups: authentication plug-in service providers, new eID service start-ups, corporations in need of optimizing internal business processes, and customer support organizations. E-Residency is not just a service; it is also a *platform*. The Republic of Estonia is just one party that offers services to e-residents, such as establishing a company or accepting digital signatures. But any third party can offer these (and many other) services as well, because all the necessary tools for organizations to implement e-Residency services are publicly available on the web.

Authentication plug-in service providers integrate Facebook-like login buttons that allow e-residents to enter their web sites. This feature is extremely useful for service providers who need to ensure that the other party is who she claims to be. Also, e-Residency is the first government issued transnational digital identity whose authentication procedures are treated as equivalent to face-to-face encounters. Hence, enabling e-Residency login makes sense for those who want to replace the requirement for face-to-face meetings with a digital form of authentication. This can be especially useful for financial service providers who need to follow very strict regulatory frameworks.

In addition to financial service providers, there are entirely new emerging business areas, such as virtual currencies, e-health, and the sharing economy that require this level of trust on the Internet. For e-residents, this trust is backed up by the Estonian government rather than by comments, likes, or shares on a website.

The second group of private sector partners consists of entrepreneurs who are inventing new services using eID platform functions, such as verification of signed document authenticity. The services of new start-ups may range from encrypted video-conferencing to safe file storage to data verification services.

A third type of partner consists of corporations that can optimize their internal processes using the e-Residency platform. Every employee, associate, or client of these corporations can use e-Residency cards to access internal information systems where activities can be encrypted, logged, signed, and traced. This opens new possibilities for outsourcing some internal infrastructure and maintenance costs to the Estonian government. This feature is particularly useful to businesses in the fields of logistics, construction, trade, shipping, and other industries.

A fourth partner consists of customer support service providers. There are thousands of new e-residents that need support of various kinds, such as legal, business, or accounting advice, which may not be obtainable with the eID. E-residents are highly valuable customers because of their innovative approach to international markets and their readiness to submit to strong, continuing background checks by Estonian authorities. Such partners are key stakeholders in the e-Residency project, because the Estonian government could not possibly offer all of these business services itself.

3.3 Benefits for the Republic of Estonia

Estonia is the third main beneficiary of e-Residency. From its very beginning, questions have arisen about why Estonia is running this project. What, then, are the benefits for Estonia and Estonians?

In spring 2014, when the discussion on e-Residency began, the main rationale for undertaking the necessary legislative changes was that these changes would facilitate business activity for foreigners who had some connection with Estonia. Previously, for example, if an Estonian company had at least one foreign shareholder, then everybody in the group not only had to sign contracts and attend board meetings in person, but occasionally also had to meet physically with governmental agencies. This resulted in higher administrative costs for both the companies and the government. In addition, the Estonian diaspora was the second target market; e-Residency was recognized as a tool to maintain closer relations with them.

So, while the initial benefits of e-Residency for Estonia were mainly related to increased efficiency in both the public and private sectors, the "10 million e-Estonians" idea refocused this aim in a way that sought to enable location-independent businesses for businesspeople outside the EU. This pivot has also made the government redefine the business value of e-Residency for the state. The most obvious revenue model would be tax collection from companies. Yet for many reasons the government has not taken this route. To begin with, in many cases taxes are payable to the country where the business value is created or where most of the board is situated; if Estonia, too, were to tax these businesses, then the companies would likely reject e-Residency because of the prospect of double taxation. A second reason why the Estonian government did not consider direct taxation as a revenue model for e-Residency is more straightforward: the government never planned to become a tax haven for businesses to optimize earnings.

For Estonia, the ultimate business purpose of e-Residency is to build stronger relations with different nations worldwide. If entrepreneurs from Ukraine, for example, can utilize e-Residency to build international businesses, sell services abroad, receive credit card payments, and pay their taxes in Kiev, then the project would increase Ukraine's GDP. And it would do so in a short period, compared to the amount of time needed for traditional economic boosters, such as education reform, and without necessitating any investment by the Ukrainian government. Instead, Ukraine can simply leverage Estonia's existing platform to boost its own economy. Therefore, instead of directly collecting taxes from e-residents' companies, Estonian companies can offer them services and bring new foreign money and investment to the country (e-residents pay for bank accounts, credit cards, tax and legal advice, physical address providers, and many other services).

With a current pool of 10,000 e-residents, the resulting income may not yet be substantial, but it will grow if the long-term goal of recruiting tens of thousands—or even millions—of e-residents is attained. As long as Estonia continues its policy of tax exemption and so long as it enables people all over the world to grow their businesses within their own countries, it is simply a matter of time before a large number of people becomes interested in this new initiative. Furthermore, in the coming years there will be 1 billion new Internet users [6]. Forty percent of the U.S. workforce alone will consist of freelancers [7]. As people become more digitally connected—and thus, in principle, more mobile—the necessity for location-independent business platforms will only grow.

In sum, the main reason why Estonia seeks to expand e-Residency's reach is to increase the country's economic size—not through direct taxation levied upon e-residents, but through the extra income generated by Estonian companies that offer products and services (e.g., bank accounts, postal services, legal and tax advice) to them. There are, moreover, secondary reasons why Estonia is building the e-Residency project. As a result of the initiative, the country has garnered sustained positive media attention with no marketing costs. This attention by itself can, in the long run, increase foreign trade investment, tourism, and export business. If and when Estonia has signed up millions of e-residents worldwide, then arguably the resulting new economic relationships may increase Estonia's national security by, for example, fostering "soft" ties to people abroad, which may help to deter future conflicts or generate increased international support should Estonia find itself in a conflict. One other intangible benefit of e-Residency for Estonians is the simple matter of national pride: the feeling that through the initiative the country is positively influencing international relationships and businesses. Much of the emphasis in the country's transition following the collapse of the Soviet Union was on internal rebuilding; now e-Residency can help Estonia project its transitional successes to the external world.

3.4 Risks

Having reviewed the benefits that may ensure e-Residency's continued growth and durability, we now proceed to discuss the factors that might imperil the project. The analysis would not be complete without considering the potential for these risks.

What are the risks? How does the government tackle them? What returns on investment are required to overcome the inherent limitations of existing political, financial, and business boundaries? These questions, which have inspired much of the international interest in the project, are difficult to answer: how can one identify or manage risks when the final outcomes and implications of e-Residency are not yet clearly understood? Moreover, for national security reasons, the Estonian government does not publish its official risk analyses. Despite these obstacles, the discussion below will illustrate some of the risks by drawing from current experience and publicly available data.

One risk is political: the governmental consistency required to sustain funding and legislative priorities across different coalitions of power may erode. A new governing coalition would not necessarily end the project, but for this kind of multi-actor initiative to work, many different government agencies must be committed to its success. The main political challenge, then, is to sustain the project's relevance to the governing coalition (whatever it be), thus ensuring that the necessary mandate to expand the project endures, while at the same time preserving the project's independence from any particular political or governmental grouping so that the project attracts support across the domestic political spectrum.

Another important risk relates to public relations and communications, both in Estonia and internationally. E-Residency was launched without a clear business model or end-goal in sight. In today's start-up world, the concept of using a technological platform to build a global "user base" is more common in business than in an entity such as a nation-state. The key to success is striking the right balance of involvement among Estonian citizens and global e-residents and remembering that the investor in the e-Residency project is the Estonian taxpayer. Moreover, the project needs to face the external challenges of managing unrealistic expectations.

Technological risks are also a concern. Possible abuse of the eID is the greatest threat, because the security of users' identity is the chief prerequisite of e-Residency. In addition to thorough background checks, capturing and analysis of biometrics, and face-to-face meetings with trained authorities, Estonia should also consider establishing a single infrastructure for all users that is optimized for the prevention and detection of misuse. In principle, this is possible: like residents and citizens, every foreigner leaves a digital fingerprint on every activity she conducts with the eID.

There are further technological risks in the threat of cyberattacks, which might threaten the stability of the eID platform that is necessary to scale up the project to over ten million users. Despite numerous security precautions, in April 2007 Estonia suffered a massive cyberattack that was reportedly perpetrated by politically-motivated Russian hacktivists angered by the Estonian government's relocation of a Soviet war monument from the center of Tallinn. The attacks prompted one of the most important strategic adjustments in Estonian and European security doctrine. Today, the protection of digital services and databases is of paramount importance to national security. Within this new security culture, Estonia has become a pioneer in the area of cyber defence, as illustrated by the establishment, in 2008, of the NATO Cooperative Cyber Defence Centre of Excellence in Tallinn. The e-Residency project reinforces this perception by sending a clear message to the world: Estonia is so confident about its technical e-government platform that it is not afraid to make it publicly available to everybody everywhere.

In sum, e-Residency opens up a whole new realm of debate about the opportunities for and challenges to national security in the digital era. Existing risk analyses suggest that e-Residency will not generate new critical risks to government functions; however, the risks could scale up if they are not adequately addressed by policymakers. Instead of trying to face these challenges in isolation or in secrecy, Estonia has opted to confront them in a spirit of public scrutiny and open discourse. Anyone from anywhere in the world is invited to identify, solve, and learn from the risks associated with e-Residency.

4 Conclusions

Estonia is the first country to offer a transnational digital identity. The implications of this move are difficult to foresee, because the world has never before experienced this level of trust in the implementation of the e-state. When users obtain digital identities, they cease to be random users and become real beings. Without a physical passport, one is not trusted to travel across countries; similarly, on the Internet one cannot be trusted without a secure digital identity. The chief implication of a secure transnational digital identity is that it makes possible a world in which every Internet user possesses a trustworthy digital persona. Several trends in this regard can already be noted. For example, e-Residency reduces the need for middle-level controls or institutions that reduce the risk of fraud in business. In addition, the project increases the pool of people who can comfortably interact with each other across national borders, thus boosting the development of peer-to-peer services within the so-called sharing economy.

These trends mean that governments could in principle adopt the habits of client-oriented service providers—just like the private sector—in order to keep citizens, residents, and non-resident clients satisfied. No government can afford to lose its resident- and citizen generated expenditures to other governments. Nor can any government afford to "sell" its services only to local residents. In the digital era, economies of scale in the management of information systems are enormous; achieving these economies requires that the system architectures are uniform—whether they serve one million national citizens or one billion e-residents. This trend paves a way for the emergence of *Country as a Service (CaaS)* concept.

These ongoing developments of the e-state present both positive and negative implications for the security and welfare of nation-states. Governments that do not partake in digital initiatives or that experience losses because of them might perceive these trends as a plan to "steal" their residents and citizens, producing political and economic tensions. But as this study has suggested, the emergent digital single market might also enhance interstate cooperation in new ways. The joint Estonian and Finnish X-Road project represents a promising case in this respect [8].

More fundamentally, the e-Residency project may lead to the redefinition of the nation-state itself. Perhaps individual identity should be based less on one's place of physical birth or residence and more on intangible values and senses of belonging. In time, the e-Residency project may radically alter the perception of belonging so that it is no longer anchored to the territorial nation-state. In this way, e-Residency challenges prevailing theories of the state.

4.1 Further Research

These developments open up a new field of enquiry in the study of government, government technology and public administration (see [9] for Estonia's policy and legal environment analysis for e-Government services migration to the public cloud). The options for academic research on e-Residency are vast. Future studies may analyze questions such as:

- What will life will look like in 2018, after regulation to expand the use of electronic identification and trust services in the EU (eIDAS) has been enforced? [10]
- What would be the political and legal implications if the EU changed its policy so that every Estonian e-resident could also become an EU e-resident?
- If secure transnational digital identities became widely adopted in the coming decades, what would the implications for nation-states be?
- If e-Residency is adopted and applied by more countries, would one be able to choose multiple countries of digital residence?

Each of these questions begets opportunities for interdisciplinary collaboration. Research on the sociology, political science, public administration, computer science, and international relations of the e-state is necessary to understand the broader implications of the e-Residency project and how it will affect citizens, governments, politics, and indeed the very future and meaning of the nation-state in the digital era.

Acknowledgments. This work draws from unpublished material in the doctoral dissertations of Taavi Kotka and Carlos Ivan Vargas Alvarez del Castillo. It has been previously made online as a working paper [11] in Cyber Studies Working Paper Series of University of Oxford. Authors would like to thank Lucas Kello and Innar Liiv for feedback to early versions of the manuscript.

References

1. Kotka, T., Liiv, I.: Concept of estonian government cloud and data embassies. In: Kö, A., Francesconi, E. (eds.) EGOVIS 2015. LNCS, vol. 9265, pp. 149–162. Springer, Heidelberg (2015)
2. Ministry of Economic Affairs and Communications: Digital Agenda 2020 for Estonia, Tallinn (2013). https://www.mkm.ee/sites/default/files/digital_agenda_2020_estonia_engf.pdf
3. Kotka, T.: 10 Million 'e-Estonians' by 2025! Tallinn (2014). https://taavikotka.wordpress.com/2014/05/04/10-million-e-estonians-by-2025/
4. Kelly, S., Earp, M., Reed, L., Shahbaz, A., Truong, M.: Tightening the Net: Governments Expand Online. Freedom on the Net 2014. Freedom House, Washington, D.C. (2014)
5. Heritage Foundation: Country Rankings: World and Global Economy Rankings on Economic Freedom. 2015 Index of Economic Freedom. Heritage Foundation, Washington, D.C. (2015)
6. Internet Live Stats: Number of Internet Users (2015). http://www.internetlivestats.com/internet-users/
7. Kvovhko, E.: The Online, Freelance, Globalizing World of Work. Techonomy, March 2014. http://techonomy.com/2014/03/online-freelance-globalizing-world-work/
8. Pau, A.: Finland and Estonia on Joint X-Road Starting November. Postimees, Tallinn (2015). http://news.postimees.ee/3264073/finland-and-estonia-on-joint-x-road-starting-november
9. Kotka, T., Kask., L., Raudsepp, K., Storch, T., Radloff, R., Liiv, I.: Policy and legal environment analysis for E-government services migration to the public cloud. In: Proceedings of the 9th International Conference, ICEGOV 2016, Montevideo, Uruguay, 1–3 March 2016, pp. 103–108. ACM Press (2016)
10. The European Parliament and the Council of the European Union: Regulation (EU) No. 910/2014 of the European Parliament and of the Council on Electronic Identification and Trust Services for Electronic Transactions in the Internal Market and Repealing Directive 1999/93/EC. Official Journal of the European Union, July 2014
11. Kotka, T., Vargas, C., Korjus, K.: Estonian e-Residency: redefining the nation-state in the digital era. University of Oxford, Working Paper Series – No. 3, pp. 1–16, September 2015

Proposal for Implementing the EU PSI Directive in Serbia

Valentina Janev$^{(\boxtimes)}$, Vuk Mijović, and Sanja Vraneš

Mihajlo Pupin Institute, University of Belgrade, Belgrade, Serbia
{valentina.janev, vuk.mijovic, sanja.vranes}@pupin.rs

Abstract. The Linked Data approach, based on principles defined back in 2006 and best practices for publishing and connecting structured data on the Web elaborated by ICT experts, can play an important role in the domain of semantic interoperability of government services. Therefore, this paper explores the technical aspects and challenges of implementation of the revised European Directive on the Public Sector Information (2013/37/EU) emphasizing the role of Linked Data approach for improved interoperability and re-use. Referring to state-of-the-art approaches in EU member states, the paper proposes a framework for implementing the PSI Directive in Serbia.

Keywords: Linked Data · Public Sector Information · Best practices · Policy implementation · Interoperability

1   Introduction

The Directive on the re-use of Public Sector Information (known as the 'PSI Directive', 2013/37/EU) [1], which revised the Directive 2003/98/EC and entered into force on the 17th of July 2013, provides a common legal framework for a European market for government-held data (public sector information). It is created around two key pillars of the internal market: transparency and fair competition. It focuses on the economic aspects of re-use of information rather than on the accessibility of information to citizens. Member States were obliged to transfer the Directive into their national legislation by the 18th of July 2015. However, the transposition of the revised PSI Directive into the national legislations across Europe has not been completed yet (see Table 1, document "Open Data: Commission launches infringement cases", 2015).

The PSI Directive is a legislative document and it does not specify any technical aspects of its implementation. Article 5, point 1 of the PSI Directive, for instance, says '*Public sector bodies shall make their documents available in any pre-existing format or language, and, where possible and appropriate, in open and machine-readable format together with their metadata. Both the format and the metadata should, in so far as possible, comply with formal open standards.*' Therefore, in July 2014, the Commission published guidelines (see "Guidelines on recommended standard licences...", 2014) [2] related to licenses (encouraging the use of open licenses), datasets (asking for availability, quality, usability and interoperability of 'high-demand' datasets) and charges where Commission preferred the least restrictive re-use regime possible i.e. limited any charges to the marginal costs incurred for the reproduction, provision and

© Springer International Publishing Switzerland 2016
A. Kő and E. Francesconi (Eds.): EGOVIS 2016, LNCS 9831, pp. 16–30, 2016.
DOI: 10.1007/978-3-319-44159-7_2

Table 1. PSI Directive related documents

Year	Type	Title of documents retrieved from the European commission
2003	Policy	DIRECTIVE 2003/98/EC OF THE EUROPEAN PARLIAMENT AND OF THE COUNCIL from the 17th of November 2003 on the re-use of public sector information. Official Journal of the European Union L 345/90
2010	Policy	Improving semantic interoperability in European eGovernment systems, ISA Action 1.1
2011	Comm.	Open data An engine for innovation, growth and transparent governance, COM(2011)882
2013	Policy	DIRECTIVE 2013/37/EU OF THE EUROPEAN PARLIAMENT AND OF THE COUNCIL from the 26th of June 2013 amending Directive 2003/98/EC on the re-use of public sector information (2013, June 23). Official Journal of the European Union L 175/1
2013	Policy	Regulation (EU) no. 1316/2013 of the European Parliament and of the Council from the 11th of December 2013 establishing the Connecting Europe Facility. (2013, December 2013)
2013	Analysis	Orientation paper: research and innovation at EU level under Horizon 2020 in support of ICT-driven public sector. EC Digital Agenda news. (2013, May 22)
2014	Policy	Guidelines on recommended standard licences, datasets and charging for the reuse of documents (2014/C 240/01). Official Journal of the European Union C240/1-10 24.7.2014
2015	News	Open Data: Commission launches infringement cases due to the late transposition of the revised PSI Directive in 17 EU Member States. European Commission. (2015, September 23)
2015	Analysis	Study on the Impact of Re-use of Public Data Resources - Creating Value through Open Data
2015	Analysis	Open Data Maturity in Europe. (2015)

dissemination of documents. The Commission has also facilitated the roll-out of *open data infrastructures* under the Connecting Europe Facility (see Table 1 "Regulation no. 1316/2013.", 2013).

This paper primarily refers to the technical aspects related to the implementation of the Directive, especially the issues that directly or indirectly contribute to the semantic interoperability of open data. Analysing the PSI Directive and other documents published by the European Commission so far (see Table 1), elements can be identified e.g. policies and legislation, software tools and platforms, selection of data for publication/dataset criteria, charging, techniques for opening data, organizational issues, formats, re-use, persistence, data quality issues, documentation of open data and data discoverability [3], that led also to the following research question:

• What do we need for PSI Directive Implementation, efficient data sharing and PSI re-use?

• How does the Linked Data Approach facilitate the PSI Directive Implementation?

The paper is organized as follows. Section 2 further explains the contextual background and justifies the research interest in the Linked Data technologies.

Section 3 presents the findings from analysis of the SHARE-PSI Case Studies on PSI Directive implementation. Section 4, using as an example Serbia, presents an elaboration of actions needed for transposing the PSI Directive in national settings.

2 Contextual Background

2.1 The "Interoperability Solutions for European Public Administrations" Programme

Since 1995, the European Commission has conducted several interoperability solutions programmes, in which the last one i.e. the "Interoperability Solutions for European Public Administrations" (ISA) shall be active during the next five years (2016–2020) under the name ISA[21]. The holistic approach (G2G, G2C, G2B) foresees four levels of interoperability, namely, legal, organizational, semantic and technical interoperability. In the period 2010–2015, the ISA recommendations were oriented more towards implementation of G2G services. However, the goal of ISA[2] is to pay more attention to the end-users outside the public administration i.e. citizens and businesses. The effectiveness of the programme and also the implications of EU Directives and policies on national ICT systems is constantly observed and measured by the Commission itself (e.g. the *National Interoperability Framework Observatory* activity) and/or with the help of independent consulting companies. Thus, in the report *"Open Data Maturity in Europe"* (see Table 1), that contains evaluation of the maturity of national policies promoting Open Data as well as an assessment of the features made available on national data portals, three different maturity levels have been identified: Beginners, Followers and Trend Setters. One of the conclusions in this report is that there is a substantial difference between the EU28+ and the candidate countries (Bosnia and Herzegovina, Albania, Serbia, Kosovo, Montenegro and Turkey) in terms of the Open Data Maturity.

2.2 e-Government Case Study

In this case study we present the process of integration of the Open Data from Serbia in EU data space. In order to use uniform solutions for accessing and re-using data coming from different publishers, the user (see right of the Fig. 1) will need standardized services to access the data (e.g. through a CKAN catalogue), as well as descriptions of the data. The ISA programme foresees using the JOINUP repository as storage of descriptions of schemes used in the datasets, as well as services that enable access/retrieval of data.

The main question that we want to answer is: *What do we need for efficient data sharing and re-use of statistical datasets?*

---

[1] http://ec.europa.eu/isa/isa2/.

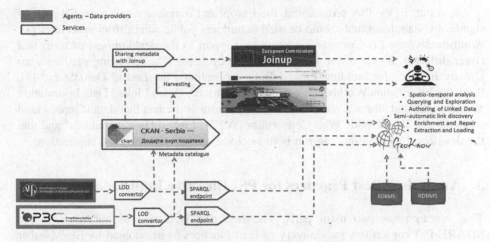

Fig. 1. Integrating public data from Serbia in EU data space

Other questions that appeared during our work on this Case Study are:

- Is it possible to fuse heterogeneous data and formats used by different publishers and what are the necessary steps? Are there standard approaches/services for querying government portals?
- What is the quality of the data/metadata, i.e., do we have a complete description of the public datasets? Does the publisher make track changes on data and schema level? Is the publisher reliable and trustful?

In order to make the use of open data more efficient and less time-consuming, the standardized approaches and tools are needed. Therefore we have explored the potentials of the Linked Data approach.

2.3 Linked Data Approach for Sharing Data

The Linked Data principles were defined back in 2006 [4]. Nowadays the term Linked Data is used to refer to a set of best practices for publishing and connecting structured data on the Web [5]. These principles encourage using URIs as names for things, typed links to other URIs and a simple graph-based data model for publishing structured data on the Web – the Resource Description Framework (RDF). Linked Data approach has been adopted by an increasing number of data providers over the past five years, leading to the creation of the global data space that contains many billions of assertions - the Linked Open Data cloud[2]. The government data represent a big portion in this cloud [6].

---

[2] http://lod-cloud.net.

As a part of the ISA programme, the European Commission has accepted a set of standard vocabularies that should be used in building public administration services [7]. Additionally, the EU Commission provides support to the development of tools that cover different aspects of the Linked Data life cycle [8]. The following platforms are already in place for building Linked Data applications: the *Linked Data Stack*[3] [9], fluidOps Information Workbench[4], Graphity Platform[5], Ontos Linked Data Information Workbench[6] and others. Common to these platforms is the fact that data is represented by using the World Wide Web Consortium (W3C) "Linked Data" standards[7] and that the developed applications can run both as cloud services or enterprise applications.

3   Analysis of Best Practices for PSI Directive Implementation

This research has two main parts. The first part is related to our work in the SHARE-PSI consortium and delivery of Best Practices to be adopted by EU Member states (see the middle layer of Fig. 2, Activities in a form of chevron). The second part is connected with our experience of developing tools for publishing statistical data in the Linked Data format (see the bottom layer of Fig. 2, Activities in a form of chevron). These two research activities are interrelated, because the experience gained in developing and testing Linked Data tools in Serbia has been proposed for approval and acceptance in the SHARE-PSI Best Practices collection[8] (see the middle layer of Fig. 2, icon with oval form).

3.1   SHARE-PSI Best Practices

Financed by the EU Competitiveness and Innovation Framework Programme 2007–2013, in the last two years, the SHARE-PSI project partners[9] were involved in the analysis of the PSI Directive implementation across the Europe. The network is composed of experts coming from different types of organizations (government, academia, SME/Enterprise, citizen groups, standardization bodies) from many EU countries. Through the series of five public workshops organized within the project in 2014 and 2015, the experts were involved in (1) presenting and discussing EU policies and case studies; and (2) consensus building on best approaches for implementing the PSI Directive. As a result, a collection of Best Practices was established as valuable sources of information for public authorities and businesses. As agreed on the beginning of the project, SHARE-PSI documents addressed the organizational and policy issues, while technical issues of PSI implementation were elaborated by the W3C Data on the Web

---

[3] http://stack.linkeddata.org/.

[4] http://www.fluidops.com/information-workbench/.

[5] http://graphityhq.com/technology/graphity-platform.

[6] http://www.ontos.com/products/ontosldiw/.

[7] http://www.w3.org/2013/data/.

[8] https://www.w3.org/2013/share-psi/bp/.

[9] http://www.w3.org/2013/share-psi/.

Working Group[10]. As a result, just few SHARE-PSI Best practices directly or indirectly referred to the Linked Data technologies.

As a part of this research we report on our findings and conclusions related to the use of Linked Data approach across EU.

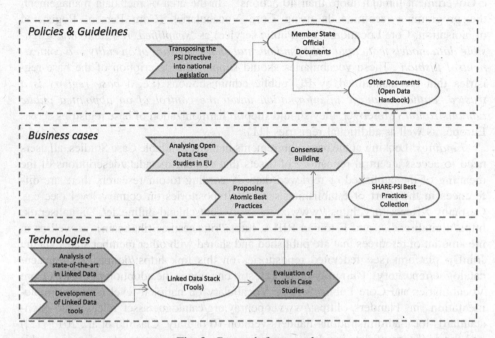

Fig. 2. Research framework

3.2 Findings Related to Metadata Management

The most common definition of metadata is "data about data." Metadata, or structured data about data, improves discovery of, and access to such information. Metadata management can be defined as "as a set of high-level processes and tools for structuring the different phases of the lifecycle of structural metadata including design and development of syntax and semantics, updating the structural metadata, harmonisation with other metadata sets and documentation". Analysing the metadata management requirements and existing solutions in EU Institutions and Member States, the authors [10] have found that 'activities around metadata governance and management appear to be in an early phase'. The effective use of metadata among applications, however, requires common conventions about semantics, syntax, and structure. Hence, the RDF can be used for this purpose taking into consideration that it enables the encoding, exchange, and reuse of structured metadata. Examples of W3C metadata vocabularies

---

10 http://www.w3.org/TR/dwbp/.

are considered for adoption in future government services are RDF Data Cube Vocabulary, Data Catalogue Vocabulary, Organization Vocabulary and others.

Re-using ISA Vocabularies for Semantic Asset Repositories: The ISA programme supports the development of tools, services and frameworks in the area of e-Government through more than 40 actions[11]. In the area of metadata management, the programme recommends using Core Vocabularies (Core Person, Registered organisation, Core Location, Core Public service) as '*simplified, re-usable and extensible data models that capture the fundamental characteristics of an entity in a context-neutral fashion*'. These vocabularies should support the description of the base registries that are maintained by EU public administrations (i.e. *a base registry is a trusted, authentic source of information under the control of an appointed public administration.*) Moreover, they should support harmonization of base registries across Europe, as well as additional registries [11].

Findings: Looking at the user requirements in many available Case Studies, all users need to access a central repository of assets that contain metadata/descriptions of the meaning of the published or retrieved data. According to our research, there are differences in the effort of establishing semantic repositories on country level (see e.g. Germany XRepository, https://www.xrepository.deutschland-online.de/, Digitalisér.dk, http://digitaliser.dk/, and Estonian RIHA, https://riha.eesti.ee/riha/main), as well as in the amount of resources that are published and shared with other member states via the JoinUp platform (see federated repositories on this link https://joinup.ec.europa.eu/catalogue/repository). Currently in the EU, still ongoing is the adoption of the ISA Core Vocabularies and Core Public Service Vocabulary on national level (see e.g. implementation in Flanders, https://www.openray.org/catalogue/asset_release/oslo-open-standards-local-administrations-flanders-version-10 or Italy, Ciasullo et al., 2015 [12]) and the exchange of data inside a country (see e.g. Estonian metadata reference architecture, http://www.w3.org/2013/share-psi/workshop/berlin/EEmetadataPilot).

Federation of Data Catalogues: The DCAT-AP is a specification based on the Data Catalogue vocabulary (DCAT) for describing public sector datasets in Europe. Its basic use is to enable cross-data portal search for data sets and make public sector data better searchable across borders and sectors. This can be achieved by the exchange of descriptions of datasets among data portals. There are two extensions to this vocabulary: GeoDCAT-AP[12] is an extension for describing geospatial datasets, dataset series, and services, while StatDCAT-AP[13] aims to enhance interoperability between descriptions of statistical data sets within the statistical domain and between statistical data and open data portals.

Findings: Nowadays, an increasing number of EU Member States and EEA countries are providing exports to the DCAT-AP or have adopted it as the national interoperability solution. The European Data Portal[14] implements the DCAT-AP and thus

---

[11] http://ec.europa.eu/isa/ready-to-use-solutions/index_en.htm.

[12] https://joinup.ec.europa.eu/asset/dcat_application_profile/asset_release/geodcat-ap-v10.

[13] https://joinup.ec.europa.eu/asset/stat_dcat_application_profile/.

[14] http://www.europeandataportal.eu/.

provides a single point of access to datasets described in national catalogues (376,383 datasets retrieved on January 5th 2016). The hottest issue regarding federation of public data in EU is the quality of metadata associated with the national catalogues [13].

3.3 Findings Related to Prioritization of Datasets

The categories of data that should be made public are recommended in the PSI guidelines. It is also recommended that "the responsible public authorities assess in advance, preferably with feedback from the relevant stakeholders, which data sets should be released as a priority". In Norway, for example, the public administration introduced the Traffic Light System [12] as a way of increasing the understanding of the value of open data within the public sector. In Czech Republic, through a transparent process, the authorities conducted supply/demand and legislation analysis [15].

As a result of "Prioritization of datasets" exercises that were conducted in many EU countries, questions have been raised related to the true understanding of the term "Open Data", the mechanisms that ensure continuous publication of the data (including updates of the datasets), the quality of the published data and the possibility to improve the quality with the users feedback, the impact of the "Open Data" on the users performance (the possibility to develop new businesses) and the types of end users.

Findings for geospatial data: Geospatial data including postcodes, national and local maps (cadastral, topographic, marine, administrative boundaries, etc.) is a category of the highest priority ("Guidelines on recommended standard licences, datasets and charging", 2014) along with other high-value datasets such as earth observation and environment, transport data, statistical data, company and business registers. From the Linked Data approach viewpoint, an alternative to the public administration sources are the crowdsourced efforts such as the OpenStreetMap, https://www.openstreetmap.org, or its Linked Data version, the LinkedGeoData, http://linkedgeodata.org/. Spatial information from these sources can be used to create geographic visualisations of the available data. Along with many benefits of opening geospatial data that influence the development of different smart mobile applications, during the SHARE-PSI Workshops, representatives from EU countries discussed as well the unintended consequences of Open Data Publication especially related to the geographic information. Some countries, such as Germany, have indicator levels for aggregation of geographic information. Therefore, risk assessment ("Unintended Consequences", 2015) and value-based prioritization of Government Data prior to publishing is needed [16].

Findings for statistical data: Statistical data are often used as foundations for policy prediction, planning and adjustments, having a significant impact on the society (from citizens to businesses to governments). Linked Data paradigm has opened new possibilities and perspectives for the process of collecting and monitoring socio-economic indicators as well as real-time events. By linking the available information e.g. coming from the Statistical Office with geo-coordinates and/or polygons, the powerful intelligent services have been proposed, see the *Intelligent fire risk monitor based on Linked Open Data* [17].

4   Re-using SHARE-PSI Best Practices

The question that we would like to answer here is related to the adoption of the SHARE-PSI Best practices e.g. by countries that have not implemented them yet. As an example, we will take Serbia that has been an associated EU country since 2012.

Example: The main political driver for Open Data in Serbia is the Ministry of Public Administration and Local Self Government. The Ministry has recognized that open data needs to be a prominent part of the next Open Government Partnership Action Plan[15] [16]. The Serbian e-Government Strategy (Directorate for Electronic Government, 2015) [19] for the period 2015–2018 foresees implementation of the PSI Directive, where the eUPRAVA portal[16] is a central point of access to e-services for all Serbian citizens (G2C), businesses (G2B) and employees (G2G) in public administration. Currently, more than 500 services are available on the portal, and about 130 bodies has announced their services there. Analysing the applicability of the SHARE-PSI Best Practices (that have been implemented in several EU countries) in Serbia, we mapped the SHARE-PSI recommendations with the actual Action Plan for implementation of the eGovernment Strategy 2015–2016 (see Table 2). Two types of actions can be distinguished: related to organizational issues (ORG) and technology oriented actions (TECH).

4.1   Organizational Challenges

One of the SHARE-PSI Best Practices indicates that "… it is not sufficient to just make the data open, i.e. simply making data available to the public isn't enough to make that data useful." [21]. This report, as well as other open data advocates [22] point out the need to establish an *Open Data Ecosystem* that will enhance coordination between public and private sector in PSI re-use and will ensure that data publishers are listening to all stakeholders and interested parties. Instead of looking on the PSI Directive in a top down manner (a mandatory action), *Open Data Ecosystem* concept calls for a bottom-up approach to implementation of an open data program. Therefore in Table 2, based on the SHARE-PSI Best Practices, we propose Actions to be considered for implementation in Serbia in the next period.

4.2   Technological Challenges

According to our analysis, the greatest challenge in implementing the PSI Directive in Serbia will be to open and express the description (metadata) about the available data/services on the eUPRAVA portal or elsewhere, in a compliant machine-processable format as is required for federation with other EU portals. Technical requirements for federation include [20]:

---

[15] http://www.opengovpartnership.org/country/serbia.
[16] http://www.euprava.gov.rs/.

Table 2. Challenges related to Open Data in Serbia (ORG/TECH), their linkage to SHARE-PSI recommendations [21] and status of activities in June 2016

Establish an Open Data Ecosystem, Develop and Implement a Cross Agency Strategy	
ORG	A crucial role in the implementation of Serbian open data program (Zylstra, 2015) is establishment of an Open Data Working Group (ODWG). It is envisioned that key stakeholders are represented in the group. Based on the Action Plan [19], activities should be further specified in details and responsibilities should be clarified e.g. an open data official can be designate in each agency *Status:* Envisioned in the Strategy [19], first activities during 2016
TECH	The ODWG will need a technical infrastructure for managing meetings/notifications and storing documentation
Identify what you already publish	
TECH	This inventory building activity can be performed automatically or semi automatically. It is also part of the National Interoperability Framework (NIF) where an asset repository will be build *Status:* NIF was adopted in 2014, but no inventory of public datasets exist [23]
Enable feedback channels for improving the quality of existing government data	
TECH	Data publisher could extend the existing services and collect different feedbacks from end users. *Status:* Feedback is collected by e-mail
Encourage crowdsourcing around PSI	
ORG	In order to improve civil engagement, different promotional activities that raise awareness should be run. *Status:* First such activities in 2015 [24]
TECH	Government can develop new services/applications that enable integration of crowdsourced and public data
Support Open Data Start Ups	
ORG	Policies needed that envision e.g. incentives for start-ups *Status:* Different activities coordinated by the Ministry of Economy
TECH	Data that will be used in innovative applications should be open *Status:* Some of them open on the publisher site
Dataset Criteria, Publication Plan, Categorise openness of data	
ORG	Additional acts needed that specify the criteria for 'high-value datasets' and help government to understand which datasets to prioritize for publication
Publish overview of managed data	
TECH	Automatic services needed for extracting and publishing the metadata *Status:* Under development
Establish Open Government Portal for data sharing, Develop a federation tool for open data portals	
TECH	eUPRAVA portal could follow the best practices reported in other EU countries
Standards for Geospatial Data	
TECH	The Geodetic Authority, responsible for national geodata infrastructure, should extend the existing processes to meet inter-governmental demand (i.e. EU INSPIRE guidelines). *Status:* National framework for geodata exist since 2010 [25]

(Continued)

Table 2. (*Continued*)

Enable quality assessment of open data	
ORG	Additional acts needed that will specify the use of open licenses and vocabularies for describing datasets. *Status:* Does not exist in the moment of analysis
TECH	Quality assessment tools and services needed *Status:* Few tools exist [26]

Table 3. Specific examples of tools, datasets and applications

Tool	Interlinked datasets	Scenarios/Benefits
RDF Validation Tool [26]	Statistical indicators on different domains retrieved from different national institutions, see http://rs.ckan.net/ or demo http://geoknow.imp.bg.ac.rs/ESTA-LD	Validation of quality of metadata, enrichment of datasets with metadata definitions and improving the interoperability of datasets according to ISA standards [30]. The tool is available for download at https://github.com/GeoKnow/DataCubeValidation
ESTA-LD [27]		Building visualizations on top of interlinked data, analysis of social-economic indicators, identification of trends The tool is available for download at https://github.com/GeoKnow/ESTA-LD
GEM [28]	Open data retrieved from publicly available sources	Motive-based search, route planning, exploration of open data. The tool is available for download at https://github.com/GeoKnow/GEM
Mobile SCD [29]	Private and public resources	Tracking suppliers, orders, and shipments and interlinking private data with public resources (weather stations, news feeds, etc.). See video at http://geoknow.imp.bg.ac.rs/mobile-scm/videos/

- Access to the harvested sites (login account or CKAN-API, FTP)
- DCAT Application Profile (DCAT-AP) for the government open data portal that will enable exchange of descriptions of datasets in eUPRAVA with other portals, as well as aggregation of and search for datasets across data portals in Europe

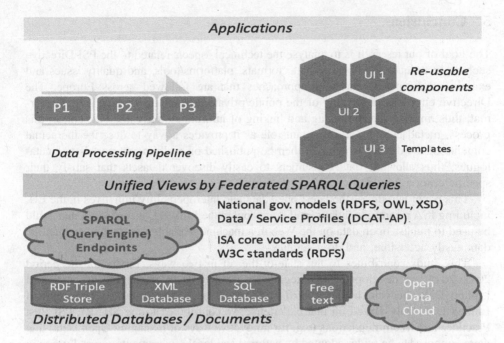

Fig. 3. Simplified illustration of integration of Linked Data tools

- Establishment of a Semantic Asset Repository and interlinking it with the JoinUp platform (Publication of the core vocabularies, code lists, INSPIRE metadata for geospatial data, etc.).

Once this metadata layer is established, innovative services that interlink datasets from different domains (e.g. statistical data with environmental online real data) can be implemented.

4.3 Examples of Linked Data Tools

Since 2011, the Mihajlo Pupin Institute (PUPIN) has been involved in two projects (LOD2 and GeoKnow) that, as a result, delivered the Linked Data Stack[17] [9]. In this period, the PUPIN team contributed open-source tools [27–29] and worked on several scenarios that directly support the EU strategies for scalable and interoperable Open Government Data ecosystem. Table 3 points to datasets, examples of potential use, as well as the expected benefits from using open data.

---

[17] http://stack.linkeddata.org/.

5 Conclusions

The goal of our research is to analyse the technical aspects related to the PSI Directive such as techniques for opening data, formats, platforms/tools, and quality issues and examine the innovativeness of approaches that are followed across Europe. The Directive envisions publishing of the public/private datasets in machine readable format, thus, making sharing, using and linking of information easy and efficient. In this process, metadata plays an important role as it provides a way to describe the actual contents of the dataset which can then be published on well-known portals and catalogues, thus allowing data consumers to easily discover datasets that satisfy their specific criteria (Fig. 3).

This paper introduces the latest open data and interoperability initiatives in the EU, including ISA recommendations, and points out to the Linked Data approach that could be used to publish open data on the Web in a machine readable format thus making the data easily accessible, and discoverable.

This study contributes to the state-of-the art in two ways. Firstly, in the period 2012–2015, we developed and integrated several tools for managing the statistical Linked Data lifecycle in the *Linked Data Stack*, as a state-of-the-art collection of Linked Data tools. Based on that experience we contributed to the SHARE-PSI Best Practices and recommendations (e.g. for innovative ways of managing Open Data) that were supposed to be wider adopted by national and local governments across Europe in future. Secondly, in addition to the analysis of technological aspects of PSI Directive implementation, we analysed also the actions needed at the organizational i.e. policy level and thus proposed a framework for implementing the PSI Directive. While technological solutions are fully re-usable, policy actions differ across countries and depend on the local context. The proposed actions in the last Section refer to a single country i.e. Serbia.

Acknowledgements. The research presented in this paper is partly financed by the European Union (CIP SHARE-PSI 2.0 project, Pr. No: 621012) and partly by the Ministry of Science and Technological Development of the Republic of Serbia (SOFIA project, Pr. No: TR-32010).

References

1. Directive 2013/37/EU of the European Parliament and of the Council of 26 June 2013 amending Directive 2003/98/EC on the re-use of public sector information (2003). http://eur-lex.europa.eu/LexUriServ/LexUriServ.do?uri=OJ:L:2013:175:0001:0008:EN:PDF
2. European Commission Notice – Guidelines on recommended standard licenses, datasets and charging for the reuse of documents of 24 July 2014, 2014/C 240/01 (2014). https://ec. europa.eu/digital-agenda/en/news/commission-notice-guidelines-recommended-standard-licences-datasets-and-charging-re-use. cf. European Commission, Press Release of 17 July 2014, IP/14/840. http://europa.eu/rapid/press-release_IP-14-840_en.htm
3. Van Herreweghe, N.: SHARE-PSI Elements of the Revised PSI Directive. https://www.w3. org/2013/share-psi/elements. Accessed 2015

4. Berners-Lee, T.: Design Issues: Linked Data. http://www.w3.org/DesignIssues/LinkedData. html. Accessed 2006
5. Bizer, C., Heath, T., Berners-Lee, T.: Linked Data - the story so far. Int. J. Semant. Web Inf. Syst. (IJSWIS) **5**(3), 1–22 (2009). doi:10.4018/jswis.2009081901. Heath, T., Hepp, M., Bizer, C. (eds.) Special Issue on Linked Data. http://linkeddata.org/docs/ijswis-special-issue
6. Hendler, J., Holm, J., Musialek, C., Thomas, G.: US Government Linked Open Data: Semantic.data.gov. IEEE Intell. Syst. **27**(3), 25–31 (2012). IEEE Computer Society
7. Loutas, N., De Keyzer, M., Tarabanis, K., Alvarez-Rodriguez, M., Burian, P.: Harmonising the public service models of the points of single contact using the core public service vocabulary application profile. In: Electronic Government and Electronic Participation: Joint Proceedings of Ongoing Research, Ph.D. Papers, Posters and Workshops of IFIP EGOV and EPart 2015, vol. 22, p. 224. IOS Press (2015)
8. Auer, S., et al.: Managing the life-cycle of Linked Data with the LOD2 stack. In: Cudré-Mauroux, P., et al. (eds.) ISWC 2012, Part II. LNCS, vol. 7650, pp. 1–16. Springer, Heidelberg (2012)
9. Van Nuffelen, B., et al.: Supporting the Linked Data life cycle using an integrated tool stack. In: Auer, S., Bryl, V., Tramp, S. (eds.) Linked Open Data – Creating Knowledge Out of Interlinked Data, vol. 8661, pp. 108–129. Springer, Heidelberg (2014). ISBN: 978-3-319-09846-3
10. Dekkers, M., Goedertier, S., Leipus, A., Lutas, N.: Metadata management requirements and existing solutions in EU institutions and member states, SC17DI06692 (2014). http://ec. europa.eu/isa/documents/metadata-management-requirements-and-existing-solutions-in-eu-institutions-and-member-states_en.pdf
11. Çağdaş, V., Stubkjær, E.: Supplementing INSPIRE through e-Government core vocabularies (2014). http://inspire.ec.europa.eu/events/conferences/inspire_2014/pdfs/20.06_4_09.00_ Volkan_%C3%87a%C4%9Fda%C5%9F.pdf
12. Ciasullo, G., Lodi, G., Rotundo, A.: Core Public Service Vocabulary: The Italian Application Profile. SHARE-PSI Workshop. http://www.w3.org/2013/share-psi/wiki/ images/7/73/AgID_BerlinWorkshop.pdf. Accessed 2015
13. Carera, W.: The Role of the European Data Portal (2015). http://www.w3.org/2013/share-psi/wiki/images/4/46/Share_PSI_2_0_EDP_paper_v1_1.pdf
14. Broomfield, H., Skagemo, S.: The potential within the Government for Innovation and Efficiency from Open Data – Examples from the Norwegian public Sector, Samos 2014 Summit on ICT-enabled Governance, June 30–July 5 2014, Samos, Greece (2014). https:// www.w3.org/2013/share-psi/wiki/images/d/d2/NorwegianPublicSectorSharePSISamos.pdf
15. Kotmel, B.: Identifying data sets for sharing. SHARE-PSI Workshop. https://www.w3.org/ 2013/share-psi/workshop/Timisoara/kotmel. Accessed 2015
16. Bargiotti, L., De Keyzer, M., Goedertier, S., Loutas, N.: Value-based prioritisation of Open Government Data Investments (2013). https://www.w3.org/2013/share-psi/wiki/images/c/ c0/Paper_Publishing_high-value_datasets_as_a_priority.pdf
17. Van Oorschot, N., Van Leeuwen, B.: Intelligent fire risk monitor based on Linked Open Data. http://www.w3.org/2013/share-psi/wiki/images/9/9b/Thesis_V1_Presentations_Paper_-_ Intelligent_fire_risk_monitor_based_on_Linked_Open_Data.pdf. Accessed 2015
18. Zylstra, T.: Open Data readiness assessment Republic of Serbia. World Bank. http://www. zylstra.org/blog/2015/12/open-data-readiness-in-serbia/. Accessed 2015
19. Directorate for Electronic Government of the Republic of Serbia: Serbian e-Government Strategy (2015–2018) and Action Plan for period 2015–2016 (2015). http://www.mduls.gov. rs/doc/Strategija%20razvoja%20eUprave%20sa%20AP%202015-2018.pdf, http://digitalnaa genda.gov.rs/en/

20. Fendler, M.: Development of the pan European Open Data portal and Related Services, Meeting with PSI Expert Group, 16 April 2015. http://ec.europa.eu/newsroom/dae/document.cfm?doc_id=9728
21. SHARE-PSI: Best Practices for Sharing Public Sector Information. https://www.w3.org/2013/share-psi/bp/. Accessed 2016
22. Heimstädt, M., Saunderson, F., Heath, T.: Conceptualizing Open Data ecosystems: a timeline analysis of Open Data development in the UK. In: Parycek, P., Edelmann, N. (eds.) CeDEM14: Conference for E-Democracy an Open Government (2014)
23. Ministry of Trade, Tourism and Telecommunications of the Republic of Serbia: The National interoperability framework was adopted, 10 January 2014 (2010). http://mtt.gov.rs/en/releases-and-announcements/the-national-interoperability-framework-was-adopted/
24. UNDP Serbia: Open Data: Open Opportunities, 12 January 2016. http://www.rs.undp.org/content/serbia/en/home/ourperspective/ourperspectivearticles/open-data–open-opportunities.html
25. Republic Geodetic Authority of the Republic of Serbia: Strategy for establishment of National Spatial Data Infrastructure (2010). http://www.rgz.gov.rs/web_preuzimanje_datotetka.asp?LanguageID=1&FileID=513
26. Janev, V., Mijović, V., Vraneš, S.: LOD2 tool for validating RDF data cube models. In: Web Proceedings of 5th ICT Innovations Conference 2013, Ohrid, Macedonia. Published on-line by Macedonian Society on Information and Communication Technologies (2013). http://ict-act.org/proceedings/2013/htmls/papers/icti2013_submission_01.pdf
27. Mijović, V., Janev, V., Paunović, D.: ESTA-LD: Enabling Spatio-Temporal Analysis of Linked Statistical Data. In: Zdravković, M., Trajanović, M., Konjović, Z. (eds.) Proceedings of the 5th International Conference on Information Society Technology, March 8–March 11 2015, Kopaonik, Serbia, Society for Information Systems and Computer Networks (2015). http://www.yuinfo.org/icist2015/Proceedings_ICIST_2015.pdf
28. Milošević, U., Stadler, C.: Mobile semantic geospatial visualization and exploration. In: Zdravković, M., Trajanović, M., Konjović, Z. (eds.) Proceedings of the 5th International Conference on Information Society Technology, March 8–March 11 2015, Kopaonik, Serbia, Society for Information Systems and Computer Networks (2015). http://www.yuinfo.org/icist2015/Proceedings_ICIST_2015.pdf
29. Mijović, V., et al.: Release of the Mobile Supply Chain Consolidated View and Application. GeoKnow Deliverable 5.6.1 (2015). http://svn.aksw.org/projects/GeoKnow/Public/D5.6.1_Mobile_SCD.pdf
30. Janev, V., Milošević, U., Spasić, M., Vraneš, S., Milojković, J., Jireček, B.: Integrating serbian public data into the LOD cloud. In: Budimac, Z., Ivanović, M., Radovanović, M. (eds.) Proceedings of the 5th Balkan Conference in Informatics, BCI 2012, ACM International Conference Proceeding Series, Novi Sad, Serbia, 16–20 September 2012, vol. 641, pp. 94–99. New York (2012). ISBN: 978-86-7031-265-4

E-Government Cases - Technical Issues

The Design of the Estonian Governmental Document Exchange Classification Framework

Dirk Draheim[1], Kaarel Koosapoeg[2], Mihkel Lauk[2], Ingrid Pappel[1(✉)],
Ingmar Pappel[3], and Jaak Tepandi[1]

[1] Tallinn University of Technology, Akadeemia tee 15a, 12618 Tallinn, Estonia
{dirk.draheim,ingrid.pappel,jaak.tepandi}@ttu.ee
[2] PricewaterhouseCoopers, Pärnu mnt 15, 10141 Tallinn, Estonia
{kaarel.koosapoeg,mihkel.lauk}@ttu.ee
[3] Interinx Ltd., Kadake tee 44, 12915 Tallinn, Estonia
ingmar@interinx.com

Abstract. The Digital Agenda 2020 for Estonia aims for a simpler state.
A crucial success factor in making the public sector more effective and
efficient is achieving a very high degree of paperless official communication. Therefore, in 2015, the Estonian government conducted an assessment of the document exchange between its authorities and institutions.
Given the large number of 400 assessed organizations and the complexity of the task, the assessment needed extensive and systematic preparation. Hence, a tailored assessment framework, the so-called document
exchange classification framework (DECF), has been developed for this
purpose. This article explains the rationales and problems in the design
of the DECF. The DECF enables the analysis of document exchanges
between different kinds of information systems, via different channels
and between different kinds of organizations. The feedback received with
the help of the DECF allows for counting the volume and kind of documents that an organisation produces whilst providing a service. It helps
to optimise the volume of produced documents and to optimise the service provision layer.

1 Introduction

Estonia is a successful state in the field of digital document and records management. One reason for this has been the implementation of electronic document management. This has allowed for digital procedure flows and reduced the
amount of paper documents due to electronic document management systems. In
addition, this has provided transparency to records management and facilitated
the involvement of citizens in the decision-making processes of organisations.
Several technical tools has been created such as the document exchange centre
(DEC) and the e-services located in the citizen portal eesti.ee environment that
enable the processing and management of a document life cycle in its digital
form from birth to death. Over the years, the volume of paper documents has
been decreased drastically, which in turn had a positive effect on the budget of
organisations.

© Springer International Publishing Switzerland 2016
A. Kő and E. Francesconi (Eds.): EGOVIS 2016, LNCS 9831, pp. 33–47, 2016.
DOI: 10.1007/978-3-319-44159-7_3

Since the long-term goal is a near 100 % paperless management [10], stable feedback on both electronic and paper documents in circulation is necessary. The aim of the document exchange classification framework (DECF) [17], that we present in this paper, is to provide organisations with tools that facilitate this. The DECF has been developed in a joint project of TTU Tallinn University of Technology and PricewaterhouseCoopers in service of the Estonian government. It has been developed for and formed the basis of the Estonian official assessment [9] of document exchange between governmental authorities and public institutions. A total of 400 organisations took part in this assessment, i.e., constitutional institutions, governmental authorities, city authorities, township authorities and public corporate bodies. The assessment was about a one-year period, i.e., the whole year of 2014. Figure 1 represents the outcome of the assessment. Overall, a total number of approx. 45 million documents have been exchanged in 2014. The level of information aggregation chosen in Fig. 1 is rather high but should still give the reader an impression of the accuracy of and value added by the DECF. As you can see, the DECF distinguishes between different kinds of document exchanges, e.g., whether a document has been exchanged via email, by a file transfer, whether it has been exchanged with or without the governmental value added network XROADS, whether document data emerged via web forms [3,5] or during a spoken conservation etc. Figure 1 gives an impression of the value added by DECF but also shows the need for clarification of many important issues: what should actually count as a document? What should count as a document exchange? Which different kinds of document exchanges exists and should be distinguishes? It is exactly the aim of this paper to delve into a discussion of question like this.

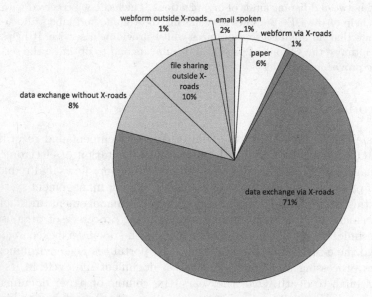

Fig. 1. Outcome of the 2014 Estonian document exchange classification project.

In Sect. 2 we delve into the purpose of the DECF and report on its key concepts. In Sect. 3 we carve out the problems discovered during the development of the DECF, which are different documents exchanges based on document management systems (DMS) and information systems different from document management systems. In Sect. 4 we come up with recommendations that solve the problems described in Sect. 3. We discuss related work and initiatives in Sect. 5. We finish the paper with a conclusion in Sect. 6.

2   Purpose and Key Concepts of the DECF

In order to measure document exchanges, it is necessary to determine the exact document exchange itself. Not all exchanges of information can be classified as document exchanges. As the concept of document can be very broad, this project based its concept of document on the Estonian Archive Act. In addition to defining a concept of document, it is important to have a clear understanding of what document exchange means. If official authorities exchange information in the course of their activities, such communication is not necessarily an official communication that results in a document in the legal sense. In light of this project, it became clear that it is important to have a clear understanding of official communication vs. so-called hidden official communication and to eliminate hidden official communication from the assessment.

A one-directional document displacement from one party to another constitutes a document exchange. In addition to a single concept of document exchange, we defined the concept of document exchange event, which has the purpose to fix an actual occurrence of a document exchange. A document exchange event is the smallest sequence of communication events that is necessary to displace a document. Here, communication events can be activities like sending, forwarding, or receiving. This unification of terminology was required for communication with other parties as the target group includes various parties – document exchange system developers, other information system developers, and end-users, i.e. representatives of official authorities. It was essential for all parties to have the same understanding of document exchange in order to adequately measure it later.

The eventual goal of the DECF is to measure all the official communication of the public sector and to elucidate the volume of documents exchanged with regards to the several possible document exchange methods. The outcome of a DECF-based assessment can in turn provide an input for analysing and predicting how to increase the digital information and document exchange rate. The developed classification should facilitate the measurement of document exchanges between information systems and offers suggestions to information system developers for developing the necessary queries. The document exchange classification describes how and by which means documents are exchanged.

Thus, the purpose of the DECF is to classify objects that are regarded as documents and that enable to count the number of times they have been exchanged in the context of specific document exchange methods. The classification must allow specifying the information located in information systems as a document and issue information such as what was the tool for the creation of the document, e.g., procedural flow or text field comment next to some information system form. It must be able to use the classification in the document management and other relevant information systems common in Estonia.

Classification entails classifying a document exchange events. Nevertheless, there are situations where a classification is not possible. Then, the situation is described in a way that allows it to be identified with a document exchange event. For this purpose, a classification equivalent table has been developed, which describes the use cases based on which the information system owners could specify the desired document exchange event.

The objective was that the addition of classification values to a document exchange event is as automatic as possible, which would ensure an adequate overview for measuring. If the information system does not enable proper automatization in getting statistics about the document exchange, the use of classification of the exchange types should facilitate measuring. DECF gives the opportunity to adjust to the information systems so that the objects contained therein, i.e. documents, could be classified as required.

3   Problems with Implementing Classification

In this study, the possibility of implementing classification in Estonian information systems was considered. In assessing the implementation chances of the document exchange method classification (DEMC), the focus was specifically on problems related to document management systems (DMS) and problems related to other information systems. With respect to other information systems, we mainly dealt with issues related to X-road. X-road is the data exchange layer used in Estonia that enables to mediate queries between different information systems.

It was necessary to have two separate focus areas in assessing the implementation, because the structure of document management systems allows counting document exchange events easily as the design of document management systems is document-centric – the most important objects are documents and the relevant metadata, including procedural flow. Other information systems are more focused on procedural acts and queries, which means that the single classification of a document could be complicated. Even an ordinary query may have the meaning of a document if it has all the important characteristics of a document.

3.1   Problems Related to DMS

The obstacles related to DMS can vary, ranging from the possible existence of inadequate metadata, to user work routines regarding filling in metadata, and also the level of automatization of the document registration process. In certain circumstances, not all forwarding events are traceable even if metadata exists. For instance, officials might not always fill in data properly, because recording such data is not considered important, or activities are carried out that do not allow uniquely determining the document exchange event. Document management systems have been built according to the logic of the paper world, wherein documents are forwarded along with a so-called cover letter and therefore the forwarding metadata is merely added to the letter. This means that the document itself is not fixed as a document exchange event and the fact of its forwarding remains outside the main statistics. Furthermore, a cover letter may not always be created in the electronic environment; if another document is forwarded, then corresponding information is not reflected in the metadata, which means that application of the DEMC can be difficult in that case. The metadata may not contain the required document exchange method data field, although this could be manually counted by analysing the logs of the document management systems.

Document exchange events are often used outside ones DMS where a document is forwarded to another party without using the document management systems functions. For instance, a contract is downloaded from the DMS and forwarded with an e-mail client. Then, DMS does not contain information about the fact that such a forwarding has taken place. The signed contract arrives to the e-mail account of the official, who saves the contract on her computer and then uploads into DMS. No information is available anywhere about the fact that communication took place via e-mail, however, at the same time the signature of the other party has appeared on the contract. Some processes related to document exchange can vary in nature depending on document exchange types. For instance, Fishery Information System (FIS-AGRI) in the Ministry of Agriculture provides different services for fishermen, see Fig. 2. The fishing-related data (logbooks, landing declarations, first sales and contracts) are submitted here. The data can be 1) submitted in a self-service environment by filling an e-form which goes directly into IS, or 2) as an alternative the fisherman has the opportunity to download the form, fill it in on his computer and send it by e-mail to an official. The third alternative is the option to download the form, print and fill it out, and send it to the official by regular mail. The official will then take the received paper and enter the information on paper into KIS-AGRI-i using an e-form. Data will be registered in KIS-AGRI-is, and then sent to the DMS. The approval process will take place within DMS and afterwards the decision will be sent back to the fisherman via e-mail or regular mail.

One issue with the usage of the DECF in case of DMS is the fact that a document may be forwarded several times. Information reflected in the document metadata does not provide a complete overview about forwardings through different communication methods. DMS usually describe forwardings as document-based, i.e., one document correspond to exactly one forwarding, an equation that does not work in real life, as one document can be sent back and forth many times.

In addition, an issue regarding the usage of DECF for document management systems is their level of automatization. Not all document management systems allow using simple tools to carry out statistics queries which would provide

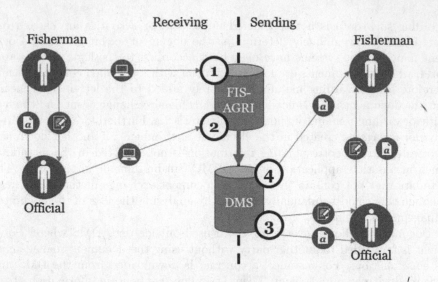

Fig. 2. The Fishery Information System (FIS-AGRI) communication channels

information about different methods of sending and receiving. The query should provide statistics that corresponds to the classification of DECF, which in turn would facilitate getting information about document exchange more automatically in the measuring process. The official does not have to conduct additional searches or calculate the results.

In conclusion, it can be stated that the usage of the DECF in case of document management systems is possible in a relatively simple manner. The aforementioned problems can easily be managed by the developers through improvements of the metadata. Implementing the classification requires certain changes which can be divided into organisational and information technology based. On the information technology level, the work of users should be made comfortable and whenever possible, implement the collection of information and the automatic recording of forwarding acts. A simple example could be recording an e-mail header either in system logs or near the document, which would easily determine the document exchange event. On an organisational level, activities are possible. If document exchange events cannot be identified automatically, awareness must be spread and the users taught how to correctly fill in the method of arrival of a document when it is forwarded from or registered in the DMS.

3.2 Problems Related to Other Information Systems

Information systems are very different, as is the development level of different information systems. Some databases have a document-based structure, where documents are clearly distinguished. In other databases with a more relational structure, it is difficult to identify information collections with the qualities of a document – the collection is formed out of a large amount of relational data. In Estonia, in the case of relational systems, information exchange with other systems is mainly carried out over x-road, but not always. Therefore, it is necessary to observe those situations where information exchange with outside systems is not done over X-road, in order to have adequate statistics about public sector document exchange. Even though X-road is the preferred communication channel, there are still information systems that communicate with one another, i.e., exchange documents by using some auxiliary interfaces.

A large part of digital communication and document exchange across an organisations borders occurs via the X-road. Observing document exchanges is complicated by several factors such as the complexity of classifying transactions. One document can be forwarded as a result of a large number of different transactions – the end result is an information collection with the qualities of a document for the recipient. However, it is difficult to differentiate which transactions were on the technical level and which on the business level. Moreover, in the classical document exchange context there are no senders and recipients in such communications, the communication parties can be distinguished as service providers and users. Thus, the substantive document moves from the user to the provider and/or from the provider to the user and to capture DEE, the aforementioned roles must be equalised. In communication carried out over X-road, from the DEMC perspective, the following transactions can be distinguished:

- Business-level transaction [11,12,15,16], results in an information collection with the qualities of a document in the service providing or using system, i.e. one of the parties receives an information collection comparable to a document. In the context of document management, this corresponds to the event of forwarding a document. One identification option is the fact that in the information system of one communication party, work with the received information will continue within the organisation – the procedural process occurs or continues, i.e. the information is permanent.
- Technical level transaction [14], during which the act of exchanging information occurs between the service provider and user, and which is part of the business-level transaction. If one technical level transaction creates such an amount of information (an information collection with the qualities of a document) that work can continue within the organisation, then this is the equivalent of a business-level transaction.

In the context of X-road communication, we can also discuss transactions that are required for the system to function, as a result of which activities no information with the qualities of a document is created but which are necessary for the system to function – forwarding classifications, status queries, data synchronisation. These transactions support the list above. For instance, it is possible to consume the services of ten different databases within one business-level transaction. It is difficult to identify the moment when information with the qualities of a document is created on the side of the recipient and to uniquely identify the document exchange event. For instance, the communication of the Prescription Center Information System (PCIS) is built on X-road queries and its objective is to enable giving medical prescriptions and electronic prescribing and/or digitization to the different stakeholders. Communication is carried out via X-road, see Fig. 3. In order to apply DECF, the service provider has to select the services which can be included in the classification. Based on that, the system automatically classifies the document exchange by determining the document exchange events. The identification of the document exchange events takes place on the side of the respondents request.

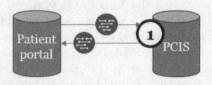

Fig. 3. PCIS is exchanging documents over the X-road

In addition, another potential risk could be the possible limitation of the systems for gathering the required information. Since not all information system statistics engines contain document exchange events (it is not possible to specify document forwarding method based on metadata and there is no forwarding log) and there is a lack of understanding of the classification equivalent guide, it is impossible to gather the required information in the given information system. If at all, it could only be done manually in a time-consuming manner. Therefore, it can be stated that implementing DEMC in different information systems can be divided into simple and difficult implementations, where different methods would have to be used for either option.

4   Implementation Activities and Recommendations

Consequently, it can be claimed that simple implementations constitute all information system instances, where activities related to forwarding documents can be easily identified and classified. For example, a citizen makes an application though an online form, which is automatically received in DMS or another information system.

Difficult implementations constitute such information system instances, where uniquely identifying the fact of document forwarding is complicated, yet the event(s) can be captured from several different locations. Classifying events may be easy in a specific information system, but the same DEE can occur in several different information systems. Technically, it is easy to identify DEEs from one or another system, but it is difficult to uniquely specify to which information system a specific DEE belongs.

4.1   Recommendations and Steps to DMS Owners

As mentioned above, implementing DEMC in DMS systems is relatively simple, although, additional improvements are required to increase the level of automatization. Mostly, application of the DEMC is possible with the necessary instructions, which would provide necessary knowledge how to apply DEMC. Analysis of the classification values which includes the DMS metadata evaluation will be required as well in order to prepare the list of missing classification values. Creation of the list for DMS improvements facilitates in automatization later on. It also gives an opportunity for mapping the attributing values automatically. Nevertheless, the analysis of composition of logged data should be thought out, and finally post-implementation analysis for future efficient application of the classification helps to apply DEMC principles more easily in future measurements.

4.2   Recommendations and Steps for Other Information Systems

If the implementation of DEMC is very difficult in the context of different information systems, an alternative to implementation could be analytics based on X-road services. This presupposes prior cost-benefit analysis in order to assess the required resources to attribute the principle of wider use of services to document exchange. If generalisations can be made about X-road document exchange based on queries, patterns will emerge, on the basis of which processes related to the organisations activities can be described which give an outline of the services provided by the organisation.

Implementing DEMC centrally would significantly improve the circumstances of information systems developers and owners. For this, the most used services would have to be elucidated based on general statistics and service owners contacted. Whether the service offered by the service providers adds value or not would have to be ascertained with them. Here, value is considered to be added where in the real world, a specific activity is done on paper. In the X-road environment, it is necessary to count the queries, which are related to analogous situations (solving an application), about specific information collections and to compartmentalise up to an information collection that can be equated to a document. In order to collect the necessary information from service owners, it is useful to conduct surveys that would allow identifying the level of a service and the queries made for carrying out activities. This would enable to classify queries as services (see different service levels above), which in turn makes the X-road query information more accurate. Today, it is possible to centrally measure the total amount of X-road queries but there is no option of defining the queries. Equally, comparison data about X-road queries sent by individual organisation is required in order to compare that to the total amount.

As regards information sent across the X-road, its content in the context of a service also needs to be assessed. If an organisation's services that move across the X-road are not clearly identifiable as different information collections, the basis must be the total amount of queries.

As mentioned above, the main issue regarding X-road queries is that they cannot be distinguished. In order to facilitate distinguishing business-level transactions and the moment of document creation, an alternative would be supplementing the existing X-road query WSDL. The WSDL would have to be altered so that technical level transactions and transactions required for the system to function can be distinguished. Supplementing the WSDL to distinguish technical level transactions and transactions required for the system to function is simple but it is difficult to identify which technical level transactions form a business-level transaction – this requires service analysis and description of process logic. The most important finding: if DEMC cannot be directly implemented, then equalise!

4.3   Findings and Main Limits of the System

Separate use of classifications does not provide a complete overview for assessing document exchange. In discussing the different versions of classification, it emerged that it is practical to present such a classification on a logical level as a compound classification, which would classify the events of sending and receipt. Such a compound classification is described as the compound classification of document exchange events (DEEC). As a compound classification is more complicated to administer than regular classification, sets of several different classifications are used on the level of realisation. If this is required from the perspective of readability, in future such components that are part of the DEEC composition will be termed, if necessary, as sectional classification.

DEEC contains both new and existing sectional classifications. The two main new DEEC sectional classifications are the document exchange automatization level classification (DEAC) and the document exchange method classification (DEMC). The top level categories of these classifications can be combined in various ways (e.g. automatically sent paper document). When discussing the measuring of DEE for a complete overview, it is necessary to apply composite classifications. The components of the Estonian composite classification are quite different which are used in different registries, for example, an Estonian-based location classification or Machine readability classification.

Although implementing DEMC provides an opportunity to assess and overview of document exchange by DEE, it is clear that DEE which are not directly classified as different forwarding methods are excluded from this selection. This mainly means queries related to X-road. A compound classification enables to more wholly include such information.

5   Related Work

In the case of the United States of America, two standards are relevant, one of which is the basis for modern document management systems and the other forms the basis for the exchange of electronic bills. Reducing paper and printing costs is emphasised but there is a lack of analysis of clear measuring methodology and cost calculation regarding the paperless system. Document exchange is only connected to security aspects [1]. The electronic records management software applications design criteria standard DoD 5015.02- STD used in the USA applies to the development and implementation of document management systems. The standard encompasses document exchange and is divided into three parts: transfer between document management systems, security, granting access rights. The standard focuses on describing the transferred document and less attention is paid to the means of transfer. A technical description of the document transfer method is less important compared to the existence of confirmation letters from the document transferor and recipient [2]. The standard has gained widespread use in the US national agencies. The standard was also used as a model for the creation of MoReq in Europe.

The EDI standard EDIFACT created by the United Nations describes the information being exchanged. EDIFACT contains a metadata field Communication address code qualifier that describes the method of information exchange. The used classification includes regular mail, electronic mail, walkie-talkies, Internet as well as the telegraph. The standard has undergone several renovations under the auspices of the UN and is now called UN/CEFACT. Since 2004, there have been few additions to the information exchange methods classification. The additions have been directed to reflecting documents being forwarded via e-mail, FTP and HTTP. In 2006, analysis of EDIFACT and standards derived from it was completed. It notes that this is a rather flexible standard which is independent of communication protocols and platforms. Therefore, if a message is forwarded using EDIFACT or UN/CEFACT, then using the communication channel classification has little importance.

In the EU, there exist standard that enable different member states and institutions to exchange documents and information. The EU does not have a central programme for measuring document exchange. Also, this is not a standard activity. However, the amount of documents exchanged has been measured in the case of certain document standards. These standards are related to a very limited number of information systems and may only be in use in one such system. Therefore, measuring is based on the document exchanges, queries or index entries in one information system. MoReq (Model Requirements for the Management of Electronic Documents and Records) used in Europe deals with document exchange. In the context of document exchange, their immutability, structural stability and formats were thoroughly examined. MoReq2 does not deal with document exchange channels [6]. The 2010 version of MoReq describes how data is forwarded, whether to the national archives or from an old system to a new one. Document links are also treated as document exchange, in which case there is no direct sending but rather a document link is sent and the user can view the sent document in the information system of the sender. Nevertheless, MoReq 2010 does not describe document exchange methods [4]. The European Interoperability Framework (EIF) for European public services describes the official communication channels [7]. These are face-to-face; e-mail; telephone; paper letters; text messages, etc. The aim is to offer services through several channels. However, the communication channels have not been described in detail or classified.

As regards Spain, the focus was on analysing the national initiative in developing the information society. The information society development strategy Plan Avenza 2 (continuation of the first 2005 Plan Avenza) which was adopted in 2011 established 10 goals, several of which are closely related to paperless management, chiefly the goal Implementing innovative ICT-reliant processes in public administration [13]. According to an OECD report, 90 % of public services were already in electronic format in 2013. According to the strategy, paperless public administration consists of mechanised and automatic administrative procedures; digitalised data, documents and services; wide use of e-services by citizens and businesses; and the development of infrastructure. In addition, 99 % of national administrative backroom processes were electronic. Nevertheless, this does not show the real amount of use. Spain measures the use of e-services by comparing the number of e-service use instances with the number of use instances of all services. According to Spains measuring methodology, the use of e-services by citizens is 51 % and by businesses it is 82 %. According to Eurostat, this was only 32 % for citizens and 67 % for businesses in 2010. Another established goal was digitalisation, wherein documents in paper form are transferred into electronic form. At the European Public Sector Awards in 2013 it was presented that since scanning had been implemented, approx. € 470 000 has been saved.

In order to exchange e-documents, twelve standard groups are common in the European Union, which are used to exchange information between states and public sector institutions. A message sending system is used for exchanging documents and the choice of channel depends partly on the standard and the security needs. For some standards, the document exchange channel is described in the metadata. The most common groups of e-documents [8] in the EU are the following: CEN/BII, e-CODEX, Electronic Exchange of Social Security Information (EESSI), European Criminal Records Information System (ECRIS), European Register of Road Transport Undertaking (ERRU), European Car and Driving Licence Information System (EUCARIS), Tachograph Network (TACHOnet), European Patients Smart open Services projects (epSOS), XBRL, Virtual Company Dossier (VCD), Omnifarious Container for e-Documents (OCD), International Commission on Civil Status (ICCS).

EUCARIS is a network for European Union member states for exchanging vehicle registration, driving licence and traffic fine information. The information system works in a closed network and the document exchange takes place directly between the systems of the member states. Before document exchange takes place, the query is verified in the EUCARIS system and is then sent to the recipient. If the query recipient authorises a reply, then the document is sent to the party who made the query. The central verification server is a place where queries and replies can be counted. A classification has not been applied. In 2013, 17 million queries were transmitted through this network.

ERRU, the information system created by the European Commission, supports information exchange between member states about road transport undertakings. Information is exchanged about road transport businesses and activity licences as well as about businesses who have committed serious infringements. The information system was created to link national registries. The system has a centralised structure, there is a central information exchange server and there are local client applications in the member states. Information queries are counted but a classification has not been applied. In 2013, more than 150,000 queries were made through the information system. It cannot be identified that a document was sent in response to each query.

ECRIS is used to exchange criminal records between EU member states. The documents are exchanged through a decentralised information system. By 2013, the information system had been introduced in five member states. In the future, there are plans for linking the information system with all EU member states. The number of records exchanged can be extracted from the logs of the information system. No classification has been applied to measure the number of records. In 2013, 862,643 criminal records were exchanged through the information system [8].

Tachograph Network (TACHOnet) is a European Union system that aims to provide safety, and equal competition between businesses, and to reduce the risks caused by exceeding the driving time. The system enables to exchange information about the issued tachographs and consists of two parts the central TACHOnet system and the client applications in member states. The central system is the intermediary between member state queries and the number of document exchanges is counted there. The system includes 26 EU member states and 11 non-member states. In 2013, over 1 million queries were made through the system.

XBRL is a file format that financial institutions use to send reports to the European Banking Authority and to the European Insurance and Occupational Pensions Authority. The reports include credit and operating risks, currency reserves, balance, income and insurance-related information. The system is decentralised and since there are two organisations that receive the documents, there is no overview of the exact amount of documents exchanged. Therefore, there is no precise overview of the number of sent reports.

The European Union uses surveys to measure document exchange. The surveys directed to businesses examine how much businesses communicate with the public sector using the Internet and/or e-bills. Many businesses send and receive e-bills when communicating with public and private sector institutions. How home pages and social networks are used was also studied, namely whether they are used for official communication (receiving complaints and answering questions). The surveys directed at private individuals inspect whether in the last year, the Internet has been used to communicate with the public sector and if not via the CIRCABC (Communication and Information Resource Centre for Administrations, Businesses and Citizens). According to the surveys, 95 % of Estonian businesses use the Internet to communicate with the public sector, while the European Union average is 88 % [19].

In 2011, businesses were asked for which activities e-forms were used the most to communicate with the public sector. In all categories, the EU average was exceeded. E-forms were used the most to declare taxes and the least for customs declarations [20]. 26 % of businesses used electronic procurement procedure in order to participate in public procurement, which is relatively close to the EU average [21]. It can be concluded from surveys directed at private individuals that 51 % of Estonian citizens use the Internet to communicate with the public sector, while the EU average is 47 % [18]. Using surveys gives an overview of the situation and allows comparing the states to a certain extent. Nevertheless, the questions do not further analyse different document exchange methods that can be used to communicate with the public sector. The surveys are confined to fixating the fact that during the surveyed period, there was communication with the public sector, while the number of times, with which intensity or through which means is left out of the survey.

6   Conclusion

Thanks to the X-road framework, today more than 90 % of the information exchanged in Estonia is digital. Document management forms a relatively small proportion, i.e., less than 10 %, of general information management. Today, a large part of information exchanges in document management is digital but not all of it. One solution would be to broaden the concept of document exchange so that all forwarding events within one specific service provision could be determined and to get rid of the idea of a document being created as such. Those forwarding points where the so-called classic document exchange does not occur, but information is forwarded that is important for providing a specific service instead, must also be fixed. In order to obtain sufficient information about the entire public sector information exchange, of which is document exchange is just a part, a more efficient of compound classification is required, which in turn presupposes a widening of the concept of document.

References

1. Artley, T., Blankenship, C., Dougan, M., Eathorne, R., Krantz, J.W., Richlie, G.: Action Learning Project Go Paperless! University of Michigan, Business & Finance Leadership Academy, Ann Arbor (2011)
2. Department of Defense: Electronic Records Managment Software Applications Design Criteria Standard. DoD 5015.02-STD. Department of Defense, United States of America, April 2007
3. Draheim, D., Weber, G.: Modeling submit/response style systems with form charts and dialogue constraints. In: Meersman, R. (ed.) OTM-WS 2003. LNCS, vol. 2889, pp. 267–278. Springer, Heidelberg (2003)
4. DLM-Forum Foundation. MoReq2010, Modular Requirements for Records Systems, vol. 1 - Core Services & Plug-in Modules. DLM Forum Foundation (2010)
5. Durno, J.: A web-based model for electronic document exchange. J. Libr. Trends 54(3), 346–358 (2006)

6. European Commission and DLM-Forum Foundation. MoReq2 - Model Requirements for the Management of Electronic Records. European Communities (2008)
7. Interoparability Solutions for European Public Administrations (isa). European Interoperability Framework (EIF) for European Public Services. European Commission (2010)
8. Interoparability Solutions for European Public Administrations (isa). Analysis of Structured e-Document Formats Used in Trans-European Systems - SC17DI06692 - D1.1 Survey on Standardized e-Document Formats. European Commission (2014)
9. Metsallik-Koppel, R.: Elektroonilise dokumendivahetuse osakaal 2014 (The Share of Electronic Document Exchange in 2014). Ministry of Economic Affairs and Communications, Information Society Services Development Department (2014)
10. Ministry of Economic Affairs and Communications. Digital Agenda 2020 for Estonia. Ministry of Economic Affairs and Communications (2013)
11. Norta, A., Grefen, P., Narendra, N.C.: A reference architecture for managing dynamic inter-organizational business processes. Data Knowl. Eng. **91**, 52–89 (2014)
12. Norta, A.: Creation of smart-contracting collaborations for decentralized autonomous organizations. In: Matulevičius, R., Dumas, M. (eds.) BIR 2015. LNBIP, vol. 229, pp. 3–17. Springer, Heidelberg (2015)
13. OECD. OECD e-Government Studies Reaping the Benefits of ICTs in Spain - Strategic Study on Communication Infrastructures and Paperless Communication. OECD (2012)
14. Pappel, I., Pappel, I.: Implementation of Service-based e-Government, establishment of state IT components interoperability at local authorities. In: Proceedings of ICACC 2011 - the 3rd IEEE International Conference on Advanced Computer Control. IEEE (2011)
15. Pappel, I., Pappel, I.: The service-oriented state, local authority - service orientation in public administration. In: Proceedings of the IADIS International Conference of Internet Applications and Research 2012. IADIS Press (2012)
16. Pappel, I., Pappel, I.: Integral and secure cloud architecture based system for backup and retention of public sector information. In: Proceedings of the IADIS International Conference on of Internet Applications and Research 2012, Lisbon, pp. 105–110. IADIS Press (2012)
17. Tepandi, J., Lauk, M., Pappel, I., Koosapoeg, K.: Dokumendivahetusviiside analüüs ja hindamise mudel - Lõpparuanne (Document Exchange Pathways Analysis and Assessment Model - Final Report). AS PricewaterhouseCoopers Advisors (2015)
18. http://appsso.eurostat.ec.europa.eu/nui/show.do?dataset=isoc_bde15ei
19. http://appsso.eurostat.ec.europa.eu/nui/show.do?dataset=isoc_bde15ee
20. http://ec.europa.eu/eurostat/web/products-datasets/-/isoc_cieg_map
21. http://appsso.eurostat.ec.europa.eu/nui/show.do?dataset=isoc_cieg_pep

How to Build Trust-Aware Voting Advice Applications?

Aigul Kaskina[1]([⊠]) and Nevena Radovanovic[2]

[1] University of Fribourg, Boulevard de Pérolles 90, 1700 Fribourg, Switzerland
aigul.kaskina@unifr.ch
[2] Swiss Federal Institute of Technology Lausanne, 1015 Lausanne, Switzerland
nevena.radovanovic@epfl.ch

Abstract. Voting advice applications (VAAs) are intelligent systems that provide personalized recommendations of political candidate/party to a voter with regard to her/his political attitudes. The existing gaps related to the improvements of the system design will be addressed in this paper. The paper presents a trust-aware Voting Advice Application which aims to improve the recommendation accuracy, in this way to facilitate voter's decision-making processes and enhance citizens' participation in eDemocracy. By establishing the candidates-to-voters communication via the forum channel, alternatively to traditional VAAs, the proposed system calculates the similarity of political profiles between voters and candidates including into the computation the candidates' reputation based on her/his behaviour within the forum. To test the proposed prototype, the evaluation framework has been designed, and a user study has been conducted. The results show that trust-aware VAAs give satisfactorily accurate and helpful recommendations. Furthermore, causal relationships of the evaluated constructs demonstrate that by participating in forum discussions, a user can improve the accuracy of her/his recommendation that is further helpful in her/his decision-making processes.

Keywords: Voting Advice Application · Recommender system · Reputation · Trust

1   Introduction

Recommender systems have become a crucial service in eCommerce. By recommending potentially interesting items according to the estimated personal interests and preferences, they generate a significant end-user value. In the past few years, recommender systems became an important research area, where various approaches have been suggested for providing more accurate recommendations. Most recommender systems use either one or the combination of both basic approaches: collaborative filtering or content-based filtering [8]. Many researchers proposed the extensions of basic approaches that tend to increase the interaction with the system and provide a richer user experience [5–7,21]. They claim that this

© Springer International Publishing Switzerland 2016
A. Kő and E. Francesconi (Eds.): EGOVIS 2016, LNCS 9831, pp. 48–61, 2016.
DOI: 10.1007/978-3-319-44159-7_4

could provide a system with additional information about the user and could lead to a more accurate recommendation. As an example, researchers have studied that systems that incorporate trust information have the ability to make more accurate predictions. Together with their robustness from shilling attacks they showed to be a better alternative than traditional recommender systems [16].

Along with eCommerce, in the field of eDemocracy the emerging tools called Voting Advice Applications (VAAs) are gaining great interest among researchers as well as among citizens who use the platform. Basically, VAAs are recommender-system oriented platforms that provide voters with recommendations of political candidates/parties that share their political attitudes. In recent years, these applications have been heavily used during the election period in the European countries [15].

Yet, the research of recommender systems in eDemocracy field is still in its infancy and less advanced, if to compare with recommender systems in eCommerce. Moreover, there is a minority of researchers [9,10,13,14] which is focused on the technical representation of VAAs, as those platforms has more interest from political sciences. Therefore, the aim of this work is to fulfil existing gaps in the technical approach of VAAs by applying existing advancements of the eCommerce recommender system technologies. Particularly the trust-aware recommender technique is used, to show that a trust adds an important end-user value and improves the accuracy in political recommender systems as well. Therefore, as features of the trust-aware technique, this paper proposes to extend the VAAs with the forum channel to establish a candidate-to-voters communication, through which the trust value will be inferred and used for the further computation of recommendations.

The rest of the paper is organised as follows: first, the Sect. 2 gives a review of the literature related to VAAs design methods, existing extensions, current issues, as well as advantages of trust-aware recommender systems. Then, the Sect. 3 highlights the architecture design of the proposed trust-aware VAA. The implementation details of the prototype are described in Sect. 4. Afterwards, the Sect. 5 describes the evaluation framework and gives a detailed explanation of the user study setup. Moreover, the analysis of the results and findings are discussed. Finally, concluding remarks and outlook for the future work are presented in Sect. 6.

2   Literature Review

Voting Advice Applications are online tools designed to help voters to choose a party or a candidate during political election campaigns. Voters are creating their political profiles, and by comparing them with profiles of nominated candidates/parties, using different statistical methods, the system decides (recommends) which candidate's/party's political view is the closest to the political view of the voter.

An example of widely used VAA is *smartvote* [25], an application used for the election processes in Switzerland since 2003, developed by Politools[1].

---
[1] Politools is a private, non-profit, politically neutral association in Bern.

Before the election start, candidates/parties are invited to answer all questions. In 2007 SmartVote questionnaire contained 70 questions. All questions are categorized either as a standard question (a question related to the approval or denial of a certain political issue) or as a budget question (user's opinion about how much should be spent for a certain domain). Possible answers to the standard questions are "Yes", "Rather yes", "Rather no" and "No", while for budget questions possible answers are "Clearly spend more", "Spend more", "Spend the same", "Spend less", "Spend significantly less". Candidates or parties are obliged to provide an answer to all available questions. Afterwards, the same smartvote questionnaire becomes accessible to voters. Contrary to candidates/parties, voters can choose between "deluxe" (or full) version and "rapid" version that contains 36 questions. Moreover, regardless of the choice of the questionnaire version, voters can leave any question unanswered. Voters can also express the level of importance of a certain question ("++" or important,"+" or somewhat important,"=" or normal weight, '–' or rather unimportant, "–" or unimportant). Additionally, for some questions a help is provided, by giving a voter more information about the subject of the question including pros and cons [13].

The impact of the VAAs on the voters' turnout vote is still subject of discussions. Some researchers claim the positive effect [15], others neutral [12], while some of them are more skeptical [11]. Nevertheless, all of them agree that such application has an effect on the turnout vote. As already mentioned, VAAs are entirely based on a number of statements used for matching between voter and candidates. This approach has multiple issues. First of all, profile similarity alone may not be enough to guarantee high-quality predictions and recommendations. Number of statements that are used to create political profiles are limited and relevant only to the elections in question. They do not take into account a general political position of peers involved. The greatest challenge of VAAs is considered to be the statement configuration. Walgrave et al. [11] show that depending on the statement configuration, VAAs can favor certain parties/candidates in contrast to others. Furthermore, VAAs are very limited in terms of taking advantage of the voter community in order to enable advanced features like collaborative vote suggestions or interactions between voters.

To overcome those weaknesses, Katakis et al. [9] propose to extend traditional VAAs by introducing a social network element. They developed a Social Voting Advice Application and deployed it during Greek elections in 2012. This application had the following features: *a collaborative filtering advice* that is a community-based recommendation, *a friend function* to enable the possibility of comparing political views with other users, and *a blog* to include the possibility to give comments and interact with the research group. According to their results, this application provided users with additional recommendations that are beyond issue-based recommendations and highlighted the importance of introducing the community-based approach in VAAs. Moreover, their approach outperformed traditional citizen-candidate similarity metrics and comparatively produced better recommendation results.

From the technical perspective, recommender techniques applied in VAAs usually use distance measure between candidate and voter profiles, or collaborative filtering, and in some applications model-based approach (fuzzy clustering) [18]. However, mentioned techniques are limited as the data can be inferred only from the policy-issues statements. The first attempts of VAA extensions with social elements proposed in [9], such as friend function, or blogs solely enable interactions between users, while the generated data from these functions remains unused. However, this data can improve the accuracy of the recommendation computation.

Looking from the political perspective, the core aim of VAAs is to facilitate decision-making processes of citizens and enhance the citizen's participation in eDemocracy. Research studies showed that the *trustworthiness*, namely reputation of a candidate has an influence on the voter's vote decision. In [19], Aragones et al. claim that voters predict that *"(a) candidates with a bad reputation will implement their ideal policy regardless of any promises, and (b) candidates with a good reputation will fulfil any promise that is not too costly to carry out, that is, for which the benefit of reneging is less than the decrease in their continuation payoffs if they renege"*. Thus, a voter will rather vote for a candidate with a better reputation.

In eCommerce recommender systems, a trust, which is also related to the reputation, is often a property improving the accuracy of the system. It has been studied that the trust value has an impact on the amount of recommendation [3,4], helps to avoid the interaction with undesirable participants [5], alleviates many issues from which traditional systems suffer such as data sparsity and cold start [2,3], protects from shilling attacks and most importantly has a positive impact on recommendation accuracy [16].

Yet, it is not the case with the political recommender systems, which is highly disadvantageous, as the trust is greatly valuable and important in such systems. Moreover, there is a high risk of appearing the situation with shilling attacks if the collaborative filtering approach [9] is applied in VAAs. To be clear, the shilling attack is when a malicious user creates a fake account by setting high rates to target items in such a way that they become similar to many profiles of regular users [1]. Thus, achieving a selling promotion (push attack) or discreditation (nuke attack) of the target item. Similarly, according to [14], while candidates are asked to answer to questions of political issues as explained in [13], this can allow candidates to manipulate the encoding by providing the answer that they presume is the most favorable answer by voters.

Kaskina et al. [20] proposed to adopt trust-aware techniques used in eCommerce recommender systems into a VAAs' design. The authors have developed a framework where trust network among users is integrated into the recommendation process of the VAA architecture. Based on this work, the system described in this paper aims to implement a trust-aware VAA part that uses a trust network inferred from the forum channel. In this work, trust is related to the reputation and considered as *"an expectation about an agent's behavior based on information about or its past behavior"*. This definition is given by Abdul-Rahman and Hailes [23], and is the closest to represent the online reputation of the candidate in the platform. Also, the reputation is highly connected to the trust. In recommender systems, the trust and the reputation have the same purpose: provide a score for a certain user to measure a level of her/his reliability. In [24], reputation is also considered as a *"collective measurement of trustworthiness"* that is based on ratings by one community. The difference lies in the number of users based on whose ratings this score is computed. While the trust reflects the opinion of one user, the reputation is based on the opinion of the entire community. The proposed VAA design is based on the opinion of the entire community of candidates and voters engaged within the platform. The next section describes in detail the architecture of the trust-aware VAA.

3   Trust-Aware VAA Architecture

The adapted from [20] VAA architecture (Fig. 1) includes three grey-boxes which represent the main computations of the system: *Global trust metric* calculates the community-based reputation of the candidate; *Issue-based similarity metric* measures the Euclidean distance between candidates' and voters' political profiles; and *Recommender engine* collects output of the two metrics' calculations and generates a final recommendation output. Each computation block is discussed in the detail below.

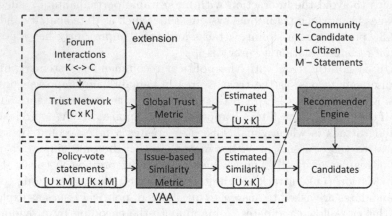

Fig. 1. Architecture of the trust-aware VAA

- **Global trust metric.** This block takes as an input a trust network matrix. According to [21], the trust network is a single, weighted, directed graph that represents all community's trust statements. The trust statements are inferred from the candidates-to-community (candidate's posts on forum) and community-to-candidate (votes, selected answers, etc.) interactions, while using the forum. Thus, a global trust metric [22], which predicts the global trust of the user (how the whole community sees him) is used to calculate the trust values between a candidate and voters. The estimated trust score predicted by the global trust metric is based on the users' activities in the political discussions within the forum channel. In fact, every forum activity gives a candidates a certain number of points called reputation points. We consider reputation points to be a measure of trust for the following reasons. First of all, voters are not limited to rewarding the answers that match their opinion. They are not limited to the one specific issue but they can observe the entire candidate's "campaign" within the forum. As a result, voters can have a general insight of candidates intentions and give their support to candidates that had consistent, most promising and realistic posts that do not necessarily match their convictions. Furthermore, the forum channel is considered to be a source of the information depending on which voters form their attitudes. The attribution of points and the detailed algorithm of the reputation calculation is described in the prototype Sect. 4.1.

- **Issue-based similarity metric.** This block is the core part of the VAA architecture. By collecting the policy-vote statements of voters and candidates the political profiles of both are constructed, as described in Sect. 2. After that the similarity of the candidate and the voter profiles are calculated by applying the issue-based similarity metric approach that is used in *smartvote* application. The computation of similarity metric itself is based on the weighted Euclidean distance which is in-depth described in the prototype Sect. 4.2.
- **Recommender Engine.** Having the output of the both, trust and similarity metrics, the recommender engine computes the final matching score between the voter and each candidate. In order to determine the proportion of trust and issue-based matching scores in the recommendation computation, a survey among 8006 *smartvote* users was conducted. The survey included three questions that were used to determine whether: (1) Users would appreciate the forum feature, (2) User's vote decision based on issue-based similarity is affected by his friends (local trust metric), (3) User's vote decision based on issue-based similarity is affected by the community (global trust metric). As a result, deduced from the survey analysis, the system combines the issue-based score and the global trust (reputation) score in a proportion of 60:40, with 60 % in preference to the issue-based similarity metric, and 40 % to the trust metric.

4 Prototype Implementation

The trust-aware VAA prototype extends traditional VAAs by implementing additional modules described below:

- *Forum channel* – a section that allows the interaction between voters and candidates. The goal of the forum channel is to offer the candidates possibility to promote their ideas and defend their attitudes, while voters could benefit from easily available information, opinion exchange, and the possibility to interact with candidates.

- *Vote advice* – a section used to create political profiles of the candidates and voters through the questionnaire subsection, and uses the collected data from the forum and political profiles of voters/candidates to generate and show final recommendations.

4.1   Forum Channel

The forum is a channel where voters and candidates can ask questions, provide answers and comments, vote on others' posts. The idea of structuring the interaction between voters and candidates in this way came from Stack Exchange platform[2], a network of question to answer communities including the community for people interested in politics (Political Stack Exchange). To participate in a forum discussion a voter is not obliged to register. When asking a question, s/he is asked to provide the title, content and categorize her/his question in one of the available categories. A voter who asked a question has the possibility of choosing the best answer and rewarding the candidate who gave that answer with reputation points. In essence, the more candidate participates, the more points s/he earns as s/he reveals extra information about herself/himself and her/his political intentions. Furthermore, a candidate gets additional points if her/his answer is up voted (negative points if it is down voted) by voters. The more good answers candidate gives, the better will be her/his reputation. Furthermore, rate limit (per IP/hour) for posting questions, answers, comments, voting, etc. can be set by the administrator. In this way, reputation spams are prevented. A total number of points reflects the user's reputation. The reputation points are calculated for the candidates as well as for voters. However, voter's reputation points do not affect the calculation of the recommendation.

4.2   Vote Advice

The vote advice section consists of two parts: a questionnaire and a voting advice. As described in Sect. 3, the questionnaire contains a list of categories with policy-issues related questions, which the voter and the candidate have to answer. The voting advice executes the computation of the candidate recommendation which consists of calculating the issue-based similarity amongst voters and candidates, and integration of the candidates' reputation into the computation.

The voting advice section is basically the recommendation process calculation that includes issue-based similarity and global trust (reputation) metrics (Sect. 3). The issue-based similarity metric is based on the computation of the Euclidean distance. Having the Euclidean distance calculated (Eq. 1), this value is normed using the value of maximal possible distance (Eq. 2), and converted to a percentage (Eq. 3).

$$dist_w(v,c) = \sqrt{\sum_{i=1}^{n}(w_{vi} * (v_i - c_i))^2} \tag{1}$$

---

[2] Stack Exchange - http://stackexchange.com.

$$maxdist_w(v) = \sqrt{\sum_{i=1}^{n}(w_{vi} * 100)^2} \tag{2}$$

$$match(v, c) = 100 - \frac{dist(v, c)}{maxdist(v)} \tag{3}$$

In turn, the trust value is computed using the global trust metric. The global trust metric calculates reputation points that reflect candidates' behavior in the forum. The number of reputation points of each candidate is divided by the number of reputation points of the best candidate and converted to the percentage. This gives each candidate a trust score in a range between 0 and 100. Having the matching score between the voter and each candidate, the system combines it with the trust score in a proportion of 60:40. Finally, a list of all candidates is displayed together with their recommendation scores, sorted in descending order.

5   System Evaluation

To evaluate the constructed prototype, we have built an evaluation framework to conduct a preliminary user study of a trust-aware VAA. The evaluation framework was built in two parts: the system's user study, and the evaluation survey of the participants.

5.1   User Study Setup

The user study was conducted among 20 students of the University of NIS in Serbia, coming from different study fields: computer science, medicine, laws, and philosophy. The elections for the member of Students Parliament of the University of NIS were setup. The questions (statements) used to create political profiles of voters and candidates were based on the goals and objectives of the Students Parliament. 4 participant (1 male, 3 female) were recruited as candidates while 16 of them (7 male, 9 female) were voters. Only 4 voters already used some VAA in the past. Before the experiment started all the participants were informed about the role and tasks of the member of the Students Parliament. Furthermore, candidates and voters were given different tasks.

Before the platform was available to voters, *candidates* were asked *(a)* to create a profile; *(b)* to answer all the question in the questionnaire part of the system, that is used to generate their political profiles; *(c)* to make an introductory post, which is suggested to be as a debatable question that will start a discussion and promote their ideas; *(d)* to participate in discussions on the forum within a period of 3 weeks. The main goal of the candidates was to earn as much reputation points as possible.

Once all the candidates profiles were created, the perspective *voters* were asked to *(a)* to create a profile; *(b)* to participate in discussions on the forum within a same period of time as candidates; *(c)* to answer at least one question (preferably more) in the questionnaire part; *(d)* to study the list of recommended candidates and their scores; *(e)* to assess the ordering of candidates list according to their political preferences, before they started answering the evaluation survey; *(f)* to answer the survey.

The candidates were already familiar or well-known to all participants. The candidate with the most reputation points was rewarded with 2500 rsd (25 chf), and 10 most active users were given 1000 rsd (10 chf) each.

5.2   Survey Setup

To construct a survey, a ResQue evaluation framework has been adopted [17]. ResQue framework is based on decision theory and trust issues. It tries to explore the evaluation issues from user perspective and is appropriate as it includes both an accuracy and an effort measurement model, as well as a trust-model.

The evaluation survey contained 13 questions related to user's background information and 23 questions related to the ResQue framework. All relevant questions from simplified ResQue model were included, together with full model questions that are related to the criteria that are the most relevant for this work (see Table 1).

5.3   Discussion of Results

The answers of 16 users were checked for their quality. We looked for users who gave conflicting answers, or same answers to all the questions. Unfortunately, one user in the already limited sample size who gave the same answers for all the questions has been detected and removed from a further analysis. Evaluated constructs are shown in the Table 1, and results are described in the detail below.

- **The quality of recommended items** refers to a measure of the system's success in predicting user's opinion. The qualities of recommended items that according to [6] influence user's intention to use the system are analyzed:
  - *Perceived Accuracy.* The results showed that users perceive the proposed system to be rather accurate in its recommendation. 66.7 % of participants answered that recommender gave them a (rather) good recommendation and that a recommended candidate has (rather) similar political views to theirs.
  - *Relative accuracy* was assessed by one positive and one negative question. The system seems to provide the recommendation accuracy proportional to the accuracy of the recommendation that a user might receive from a friend.
- **Perceived Ease of Use.** As already mentioned, the main goal of VAAs is to facilitate decision making of voters. Therefore, ease of decision-making was considered to be highly important criteria in this evaluation.
  - *Ease of Decision Making.* The results show that users found their decision-making facilitated by the system. Even though they were using the Forum for 3 weeks, they didn't consider the system to be too time consuming.

Table 1. Evaluation constructs

Criteria	Evaluated constructs	Items	Avg user response
Quality of recommended items	Perceived accuracy	The candidates recommended to me have similar political attitudes as me	3.73
		The recommender gave me good suggestions.	3.73
		My political attitudes oppose the attitudes of the candidates recommended to me. (reverse scale)	3.2
	Relative accuracy	The recommendation I received better fits my interests than what I may receive from a friend.	3.2
		A recommendation from my friends better suits my interests than the recommendation from this system. (reverse scale)	3
Perceived ease of use	Ease of decision making	Using the recommender to find the good candidate is easy.	3.15
		I was able to take advantage of the recommender very quickly.	3.46
		I quickly became productive with the recommender.	3.38
		Finding the candidate to vote for with the help of the recommender is easy.	3.76
		Finding the candidate to vote for, even with the help of the recommender consumes too much time	2.92
Perceived usefulness		The recommended items effectively helped me find the ideal candidate	3.42
		The recommendation influence my vote decision.	2.85
		I feel supported to find what I like with the help of the recommender	3.21
Attitudes	Overall satisfaction	Overall, I am satisfied with the recommender.	3.69
	Confidence & Trust	I am confident I will like the candidates recommended to me.	3.21
		The recommender made me more confident about my selection/decision.	3.5
		The recommender can be trusted	3.28
Behavioral intentions	Intention to use the system	If a recommender such as this exists, I will use it to decide who to vote for.	3.23
	Recommendation to friends	If a recommender such as this exists, i will tell my friends about it	3.84

- **Perceived Usefulness** is defined as *"the extent to which a user finds that using a recommender system would improve his/her performance, compared with their experiences without the help of a recommender"* [6]. The results showed that users found the system rather helpful. However, the recommender appears not to have the impact on user's vote decision. Given that VAAs are not designed to influence user's vote decision, it is not considered as a limitation of the prototype.
- **Attitudes** refer to user's overall opinion about the recommender. In general, the attitudes of users towards a proposed system are rather positive. 60 % of

participant were (rather) satisfied by the system, 40 % were (rather) confident that they will like system's recommendation, 53.3 % were more confident about their decision after using the recommender, while 40 % (rather) agreed that a recommender can be trusted.

- **Behavioral intentions** are highly important to stimulate users' future visits and participation within the system. In the study, behavioral intentions were assessed with two questions. One question was used to assess the intention of a user to use the system again while the other was used to assess the intention of a user to introduce this system to her/his friends. The results showed that users are likely to use the system in the future. Furthermore, 66.7 % or participants would introduce the system to their friends. Intention to introduce the system to other people is an important factor in enhancing the citizens' participation in eDemocracy.

- **Casual relationships among evaluated constructs.** To understand the influence of the candidates' forum participation on the recommendation accuracy, and relations between different system's properties at a more detailed level, this section indicates the investigated correlation among the measured constructs. Figure 2 shows correlation coefficients between evaluation constructs together with their coefficients of determination. Only the constructs with $R2 > 0.1$ are considered to be appropriate and informative to examine the significance of the path associated to them [17].

To determine whether a forum participation has an influence of recommendation accuracy, for each user, a value that reflects the intensity of her/his participation was computed. This value is based on the number of questions, answers and votes that a user gave. As the trust-aware approach aims to improve the recommendation accuracy by allowing users to interact and assess a general trustworthiness (reputation) of a candidate, the relation between the forum participation and the perceived accuracy is highly important. The correlation coefficient shows that the forum participation and the perceived accuracy are slightly correlated ($r = 0.41$, $p = 0.126$). Consequently, the more user participates more accurate recommendation will be generated. Furthermore, according to user's beliefs, perceived accuracy of a user is correlated with an ease of decision-making ($r = 0.62$, $p = 0.02$). Considering that a user can probably improve perceived accuracy by participating in the forum, it can be concluded that participation will also affect the ease of decision-making, since they are correlated). Consequently, the first conclusion is that *by establishing a candidate-to-voters communication through the forum channel, the perceived accuracy of recommendation will be improved, thus facilitating the decision-making processes of the voters.*

The perceived accuracy is also highly correlated with perceived usefulness ($r = 0.78$, $p = 0.005$) that shows significant impact on confidence and trust ($r = 0.63$, $p = 0.082$) and overall satisfaction ($r = 0.53$, $p = 0.056$). Finally, overall satisfaction seems to be significantly correlated with the user's intention to recommend the system to a friend ($r = 0.48$, $p = 0.09$). As already mentioned, this behavioural intention is highly important, as one of the goals of VAA systems is to enhance citizens participation in such systems. Therefore, the second conclusion states that *by improving the perceived accuracy, the VAA has potential to attract more citizens to participate in this system.*

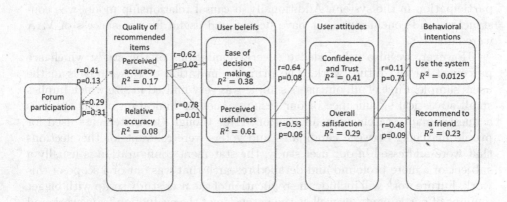

Fig. 2. Casual relationships among evaluated constructs

In general, the proposed trust-aware VAA design approach has advantage of not only improving the accuracy of the generated recommendations, but also of facilitating voters' decision-making processes and enhancing citizens' participation within this platform. Aforementioned conclusions incite to include the forum channel in the VAA design, thus enabling the candidate-to-voter communication, from where the trust values are inferred and further used for the recommendation calculation.

6   Conclusions

VAAs, as a type of recommender systems, face with problems of the recommendation accuracy as well as with privacy issues. Moreover, the risk of shilling attacks can jeopardise the citizens' participation. To tackle these problems, a trust-aware technique which is widely used in eCommerce has been applied in the VAA design. We have developed a prototype, that besides the traditional issue-based similarity metric between voters and candidates, also integrates the candidate's online reputation gained through her/his forum activities. This prototype tends to improve the accuracy of recommendations, thus facilitating citizen's decision-making processes and participation. After implementing the prototype, a preliminary user study and evaluation survey have been conducted, that gave a first insight into the impact of the social element (forum channel) and trust value on the overall success of VAAs.

The evaluation framework has been based on the user-centric approach used in recommender systems, allowing to assess several criteria of successful recommendations. Two parts of the evaluation have been conducted: the user study setup, and a survey analysis. The user study followed by the survey evaluation results showed that recommendations produced by the trust-aware VAA were positively assessed by users. Recommendations are considered to be sufficiently accurate, useful and helpful in decision-making processes and in enhancing users' participation in the system. Additionally, a causal relationship model was constructed, and conclusions that have been found useful for the success of VAA were stated.

However, we also acknowledge several limitations of the study which are perceived for the future work. The primary limitation of this study is in the users sample. First of all, our users sample was very limited in size which implies small statistical significance of our results. Another limitation of our study is a questionnaire statement configuration. Even though the statements used for profile matching between candidates and voters were relevant for the elections that were addressed in our user study, the statement configuration is usually a subject of a more profound and detailed research that was out of a scope of this work. Future work will include the replication of the user study setup with bigger amount of participants, as well as the extension of the evaluation framework and analysis methods.

Acknowledgments. The authors would like to thank Jan Fivaz and the members of smartvote project (smartvote.ch) for the cooperation in the survey with smartvote users. Also, Information System Research Group at the University of Fribourg (diuf.unifr.ch/is), together with Human Computer Interaction group of EPFL for contributing with valuable thoughts and comments.

References

1. Chirita, P.-A., Nejdl, W., Zamfir, C.: Preventing shilling attacks in online recommender systems. In: Proceedings of the Seventh ACM International Workshop on Web Information and Data Management - WIDM 2005, pp. 67–74 (2005)
2. Guo, G., Zhang, J., Thalmann, D., Basu, A., Yorke-Smith, N.: From ratings to trust. In: Proceedings of the 29th Annual ACM Symposium on Applied Computing - SAC 2014, pp. 248–253 (2014)
3. Massa, P., Bhattacharjee, B.: Using trust in recommender systems: an experimental analysis. In: Jensen, C., Poslad, S., Dimitrakos, T. (eds.) iTrust 2004. LNCS, vol. 2995, pp. 221–235. Springer, Heidelberg (2004)
4. Victor, P., Cornelis, C., Cock, M.D., Silva, P.P.D.: Gradual trust and distrust in recommender systems. Fuzzy Sets Syst. **160**, 1367–1382 (2009)
5. Knijnenburg, B.P., Willemsen, M.C., Gantner, Z., Soncu, H., Newell, C.: Explaining the user experience of recommender systems. User Model. User-Adap. Interact. **22**, 441–504 (2012)
6. Pu, P., Chen, L., Hu, R.: Evaluating recommender systems from the user's perspective: survey of the state of the art. User Model. User-Adap. Interact. **22**, 317–355 (2012)
7. Nunes, M., Cerri, S.A., Blanc, N.: Improving recommendations by using personality traits in user profiles. In: International Conferences on Knowledge Management and New Media Technology, pp. 92–100 (2008)

8. Park, D.H., Kim, H.K., Choi, I.Y., Kim, J.K.: A literature review and classification of recommender systems research. Expert Syst. Appl. **39**, 10059–10072 (2012)
9. Katakis, I., Tsapatsoulis, N., Mendez, F., Triga, V., Djouvas, C.: Social voting advice applications-definitions, challenges, datasets and evaluation. IEEE Trans. Cybern. **44**, 1039–1052 (2014)
10. Mendez, F.: What's behind a matching algorithm: a critical assessment of how VAAs produce voting recommendations. In: Matching Voters with Parties and Candidates Voting Advice Applications in Comparative Perspective, pp. 49–66 (2014)
11. Walgrave, S., Nuytemans, M., Pepermans, K.: Voting aid applications and the effect of statement selection. West Eur. Polit. **32**, 1161–1180 (2009)
12. Fivaz, J., Schwarz, D.: Nailing the pudding to the wall - e-Democracy as catalyst for transparency and accountability. In: Paper Presented at the International Conference on Direct Democracy in Latin America, Buenos Aires, Argentina (2007)
13. Teran, L., Ladner, A., Fivaz, J., Gerber, S.: Using a fuzzy-based cluster algorithm for recommending candidates in e-Elections. In: Applications and Classifications Fuzzy Methods for Customer Relationship Management and Marketing, pp. 115–138 (2012)
14. Djouvas, C., Tsapatsoulis, N.: A view behind the scene: data structures and software architecture of a VAA. In: 2014 9th International Workshop on Semantic and Social Media Adaptation and Personalization, pp. 136–141 (2014)
15. Garzia, D., Marschall, S.: Voting Advice Applications under review: the state of research. IJEG Int. J. Electron. Gov. **5**, 203–222 (2012)
16. Ray, S., Mahanti, A.: Improving prediction accuracy in trust-aware recommender systems. In: 2010 43rd Hawaii International Conference on System Sciences, pp. 1–9 (2010)
17. Pu, P., Chen, L., Hu, R.: A user-centric evaluation framework for recommender systems. In: Proceedings of the Fifth ACM conference on Recommender systems - RecSys 2011, pp. 157–164 (2011)
18. Luis, F.T.T.: SmartParticipation A Fuzzy-Based Recommender System for Political Community-Building. Springer, Cham (2014)
19. Aragones, E., Palfrey, T., Postlewaite, A.: Political reputations and campaign promises. J. Eur. Econ. Assoc. **5**, 846–884 (2007)
20. Kaskina, A., Meier, A.: Integrating privacy and trust in voting advice applications. In: 2016 Third International Conference on eDemocracy & eGovernment (ICEDEG) (2016)
21. Avesani, P., Massa, P., Tiella, R.: Moleskiing. it: a trust-aware recommender system for ski mountaineering. Int. J. Infonomics **20**(35), 1–10 (2005)
22. Victor, P., Cock, M.D., Cornelis, C.: Trust and recommendations. In: Ricci, F., Rokach, L., Shapira, B., Kantor, P.B. (eds.) Recommender Systems Handbook, pp. 645–675. Springer, New York (2010)
23. Abdul-Rahman, A., Hailes, S.: Supporting trust in virtual communities. In: Proceedings of the 33rd Annual Hawaii International Conference on System Sciences (2000)
24. Josang, A., Ismail, R., Boyd, C.: A survey of trust and reputation systems for online service provision. Decis. Support Syst. **43**, 618–644 (2007)
25. Smartvote.ch. https://smartvote.ch/

E-Government Services Migration to the Public Cloud: Experiments and Technical Findings

Taavi Kotka[1], Bruce Johnson[2], Tomaz Cebul[2], Luka Lovosevic[2], and Innar Liiv[1(✉)]

[1] Department of Informatics, Tallinn University of Technology, 12618 Tallinn, Estonia
taavi.kotka@gmail.com, innar.liiv@ttu.ee
[2] Microsoft Corporation, 1 Microsoft Way, Redmond, WA 98103, USA
{bjohnson,tomaz.cebul,luka.lovosevic}@microsoft.com

Abstract. E-government services migration to the public cloud presents novel policy and technical challenges. This paper explores possible technical obstacles one should anticipate when migrating e-government services to cloud. Technical experiment design is presented, implementation process and the steps taken are elaborated; performance experiments are presented together with findings that were considered significant in the process. Main findings of migration experiments are organized into six groups: security, identity and data architecture findings; operations architecture findings; application architecture findings; compute architecture findings; storage architecture findings; and network architecture findings.

1 Introduction

Current research project sought to understand how cloud based application packaging is able to help overcome the environmental dependencies that would have previously prevented the on-premises applications from being moved to either a different physical or online location.

Public cloud platforms provide the first real steps towards abstraction of the physical computing environment, which includes servers, networking equipment, and storage systems, through the use of different cloud application packaging types. Cloud-based application packaging can take the form of specialized installers, containers, virtual disks, or entire virtual machines. Virtual machine and virtual disks can be used as a type of cloud application packaging to virtualize physical host and hardware. They may also be used to capture system specific settings including device drivers, network interfaces and Internet Protocol (IP) addresses, routing paths, DNS settings for both hosts and subdomains, cryptographic keys, user and machine credentials as well as many other application specific settings. In the context of this project it was also proposed that the use of cloud application packaging would enable consolidation and portability of applications, as well as make the operations, maintenance, and application development simpler tasks by mitigating some of the more disruptive elements in application lifecycle management.

Furthermore, it was assumed a major benefit of a Virtual Data Embassy Solution [1] would be a consistent (seamless) online environment based on the latest versions of compatible hardware and software. The Solution is expected to eliminate the variability

© Springer International Publishing Switzerland 2016
A. Kő and E. Francesconi (Eds.): EGOVIS 2016, LNCS 9831, pp. 62–76, 2016.
DOI: 10.1007/978-3-319-44159-7_5

of stand-alone hardware and software environments, which have been developed (and upgraded) at different intervals over time. For example, when each application is free to dictate all layers of the software and hardware stack, there is a real risk that it can be extremely complex to move that application to a new physical, e.g. physical embassy, or cloud environment, e.g. Virtual Data Embassy. The research project looked at how, when using a public cloud platform, significant layers of the application stack could be consolidated, standardized, and scaled in ways that make it possible to move and operate all applications in a more standardized and repeatable fashion.

Finally, it was important to show how the use of a public cloud platform could help optimize for different sets of skill and operational models required by administrators of e-government services, building a critical mass of knowledge overall. To this end, the research project team sought to show how a basic IaaS platform could support two different applications using common operations up to the level of the specific application requirements. While it was assumed that the use of an IaaS platform would not completely eliminate the need for subject matter experts, it was found to reduce the amount of support needed. Moreover, software automation allows resources, previously allocated to support on premise applications, to be redeployed in other areas.

Following sections explore how the Virtual Data Embassy could be implemented within the context of the current Estonian government ICT architecture [1] (see [2] for discussion about policy and legal aspects). The implementation process and the steps taken are elaborated, followed by a section that compares and contrasts the results of the testing that was conducted, before ending with findings that were considered significant in the process.

2 Technical Experiment Design

At the onset of the research project a number of steps needed to be taken, from which a number of implications for the project as a whole, were derived. While not part of this document, the process of selecting from the different cloud options available and selecting the government services to be migrated was critical to the success of the research. To this end comprehensive risk assessments were conducted, which allowed the selection of the most appropriate services, as well as highlighting a number of opportunities for improvement overall.

Building on this, consideration was given to how to best migrate the services to the cloud. The challenges encountered in this process, as well as solutions used, are presented in the section below. The next section talks about how the different starting architectures across the two project workstreams were worked around in order to ensure that in the cloud operational efficiencies were achieved, e.g. common file storage, common backup procedures, and common load balancing technologies. Lastly, an overview of the testing conducted, once migration had been completed, is presented. Comparison of different cloud platforms was not in the focus of this project.

2.1 Migration to the Public Cloud

The migration of existing e-government services to a public cloud platform, and the feasibility of doing so has recently gained substantial interest and attention [3–5]. Related practical experiments represented a major part of the research project. If it had emerged that the migration process was too complex, costly, time consuming or that it required significant architectural changes, doubts would have been cast on the overall viability of the Virtual Data Embassy Solution. An assessment was therefore made at the beginning of the project to understand it would be feasible and whether any significant changes would be required.

Two main approaches were considered for migrating the selected government services, although it has to be pointed out that these cannot be seen as binary either/or options. It is expected that in other similar situations a combination of these two would be used, as one is a better fit for newer operating system migration and the other for more complex applications:

- **Virtualize the application and perform an "in-place" base operating system upgrade:** This approach consists of three distinct steps: (1) any physical servers are virtualized and any existing virtual servers cloned; (2) the operating system is upgraded to the latest version in-place; and, (3) all is uploaded onto the cloud platform. Typically, this approach is beneficial if there is a need to maintain a direct clone of the entire operating system environment on-premises. However, this approach requires significantly more time and bandwidth since the images to be uploaded can be large, e.g. over 50 GB.
- **Deploy directly onto the cloud platform:** This approach sees the base operating system provisioned directly by the cloud platform before any application components, such as databases or web servers, are deployed onto the operating system and the application content and data is synchronized. This approach has the benefit of requiring only the core application and its data to be uploaded to the cloud which frequently represents a much smaller data footprint.

For the migration to be possible, it had to be established whether the Microsoft cloud platform supported the operating systems currently used by the government services and their applications. As highlighted in the research project description, the two government services use FreeBSD and CentOS, which are not Microsoft products. Importantly, the cloud platform selected supports a number of non-Microsoft products, including UNIX & Linux operating systems, as well as FreeBSD and CentOS. However, it typically only supports the latest three versions of an operating system. This means that an operating system upgrade was required prior to migration, as the versions used by the selected applications were not supported. Furthermore, on-premises virtual machines can also be transferred onto the Microsoft's cloud platform directly, as it supports the open industry-standard virtual hard disk (VHD) format [6]. This is used by a number of on-premises hypervisors.

Given the base operating system upgrades required by both application workstreams, the second option, "deploy directly in the cloud", was selected as being quicker and less risky. One reason for this choice was that the software installation media for the application components was readily available, making it straightforward and fast to re-install them on the public cloud operating system. The second reason was that this option meant the content and data could be synchronized directly with the on-premises master, again with speed and ease. Finally, and most critically, the versions of FreeBSD and CentOS used originally did not natively support an in-place operating systems upgrade. As a result, the in-place upgrade, core to the first option, would have to be performed manually, introducing a higher level of risk.

2.2 Target Architecture for Public Cloud

While the two project workstreams had different starting architectures, the research project aimed to deploy the applications in a similar deployment architecture to help achieve operational efficiencies, such as common file storage, backup procedures, and load balancing technologies. Target deployment architectures were utilized as presented in following subsections.

2.2.1 Workstream #1 – Presidentee.cloudapp.net

Presidentee.cloudapp.net was a Microsoft cloud application version of www.president.ee site. The cloud service "presidentee.cloudapp.net" represented six virtual machine instances behind a load balancer configured in an availability set. The cloud service had been configured to use auto-scaling with minimum of two instances to a maximum of six instances. It is important to point out that two instances represent a minimum required to be able to achieve the level of availability needed. The overall design is depicted in Fig. 1 below.

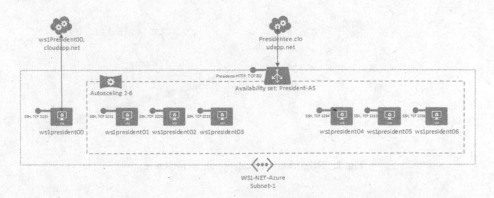

Fig. 1. Presidentee.cloudapp.net architecture

The cloud service had HTTP protocol on TCP port 80 published on the internet. The load balancer ensures that the network traffic is equally divided between all running virtual machine instances. Moreover, when a new virtual machine instance starts or stops, it is automatically included in the load balancer pool. As mentioned above, the cloud service was serviced by up to six virtual machines kept on geographically replicated storage and configured as an availability set.

All virtual machines used were sized Standard A1 (1 core, 1.75 GB memory), had a fixed IP reservation and a single disk sized 50 GB. The IP address was reserved in the WS1-NET-Azure Subnet 1 IP address segment. As a result, the cloud platform fabric always assigned the same IP address to the virtual machine. Finally, the content was synchronized from on-premises publishing servers using the custom rsync protocol over the Secure Shell (SSH) to ws1president00 server and, in the second stage, from ws1president00 to ws1president(01-06).

2.2.2   Workstream #1 – Riigiteataja.cloudapp.net

Riigiteataja.cloudapp.net was the portable version of www.riigiteataja.ee site running on the Microsoft cloud platform. The cloud service "riigiteataja.cloudapp.net" represented four virtual machine instances behind a load balancer configured in an availability set. The cloud service had been configured to use auto-scaling with minimum of two instances to a maximum of four instances. It is important to point out that two instances represent a minimum required to be able to achieve the level of availability needed. The overall design is depicted in Fig. 2 below:

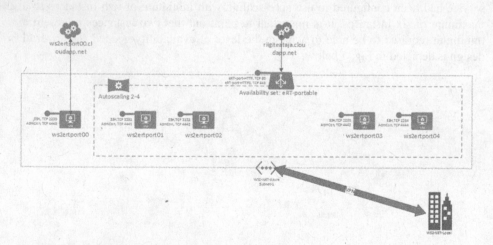

Fig. 2. Riigiteataja.cloudapp.net architecture

The cloud service had both HTTP and secure HTTPS protocol on TCP port 80 and 443 published on the Internet. The load balancer ensures that network traffic is equally divided between all running virtual machine instances. When a new virtual machine instance starts or stops, it is automatically included in the load balancer pool. As mentioned above, the cloud service was serviced by up to four virtual machines stored on geographically replicated storage and configured as an availability set.

All virtual machines used were sized Standard A5 (2 cores, 14 GB memory), had a fixed IP reservation and two disk drives (OS disk sized 30 GB, data disk sized 200 GB). The IP address was reserved in the WS2-NET-Azure Subnet 1 IP address segment. As a result, the cloud platform fabric always assigned the same IP address to the virtual machine. For synchronization purposes, a site to site Virtual Private Network (VPN) was also created between the WS2-NET-Azure virtual network and the network of the Ministry of Justice. Moreover, the cloud service riigiteataja.cloudapp.net was also assigned a reserved public IP address to make external DNS handling easier. Finally, the content was synchronized from on-premises publishing servers using custom *rsync* protocol over SSH to ws2ertport00 server and in the second stage from ws2ertport00 to ws2ertport(01-04).

2.3   Performance Testing Methodology

Once the migration of the two applications was completed, testing activities began across two dimensions: performance and demand. Two types of performance tests were used: load and stress testing. Load testing was used to understand the behavior of the system under a range of normal load conditions, and to compare the transactional response time with the on-premises solution. Stress testing, on the other hand, was used to determine the solution's robustness under peak load and to prove it would automatically scale-out elastically under sustained peak load situations.

Load testing involves simulated client and end user activity that could take place, if a large number of human end users were attempting to access the services at one time. The patterns and usage scenarios are designed to ensure that the correct activities are available to users. For example, if one million users were to go to the president's website due to an external event, this would be considered a load test scenario. The users are not trying to do unusual but their sheer numbers could impact performance. Conversely, the stress testing scenarios tend to simulate client and end user behavior designed to break or cause problems for the site, e.g. where multiple users try and overload it by playing videos to attempt to consume all the resources available, thus preventing the site from functioning. The load and stress testing were also repeated under two demand scenarios. The first was a normal demand scenario, which consisted of replicating the existing normal usage conditions whilst catering to organic expanded demand, as might occur if additional users were to utilize the e-government service. The second was a malicious demand scenario, which might occur if Estonian e-government services were under a cyber-attack intended to render the services incapacitated or unavailable. Section 3 covers the results of the testing.

2.3.1   Normal Demand Usage Scenario

The normal demand usage scenario was to demonstrate the cloud platform's ability to dynamically scale up the number of application servers, storage systems, and route traffic appropriate to the end user demand. For example, if a text based and media content update to the President.ee website were to occur, load testing should show that the cloud platform has supported increased demand for the media files and web server content. In an ideal situation, the cloud platform would dynamically scale up compute, storage, and network resources using the cloud platform load balancer to deliver the content to users via the closest Virtual Data Embassy, irrespective of where the data center is based.

Under normal load testing, it was expected that the cloud platform could demonstrate automatic scaling, eliminating the need for procurement, setup, or redeployment of applications by the administrator. The normal load testing scenario was also designed to show the reliability of the cloud platform under normal failure events, such as a (non-malicious) application crash due to a software bug in either the application or underlying guest operating system. If such an instance were to occur, the cloud platform should automatically use a replacement application instance with no staff involvement.

2.3.2   Malicious Demand Usage Scenario

The malicious load and stress testing was to demonstrate that the cloud platform is resilient to malicious attempts to consume compute, storage, or network resources, which would prevent a normal end user from accessing the application or monument websites within a reasonable response time. Under malicious load and stress testing, the cloud platform was expected to implement parameterized automatic scaling, which would eliminate the need for operator involvement or the procurement, setup, or redeployment of applications by the administrator.

The simulated malicious load testing scenario was designed to demonstrate the reliability of the cloud platform against malicious attacks that would attempt to exploit known (e.g. Heartbleed SSL) or unknown (e.g. zero day attacks) software bugs in either the application or underlying guest operating system. In a malicious failure scenario under load, the cloud platform should automatically use a replacement application instance with no operations staff involvement and begin to report malicious usage to key staff people for examination of possible mitigation techniques beyond simple load balancing.

3   Experiments and Performance

In this section, the performance results are outlined, comparing the applications' behavior in their original on-premises environments and the target cloud environment. All of the performance, load and stress test cases were built using Microsoft Visual Studio® 2013 and Visual Studio Online and run on the Azure™ cloud platform. The results were exported and analyzed by the testing team. Microsoft Azure™ was used to initialize a large number of distributed test agents that can successfully simulate a website load under different circumstances, such as different bandwidth, browser types, click pattern, etc. Figure 3 depicts the load testing approach and architecture.

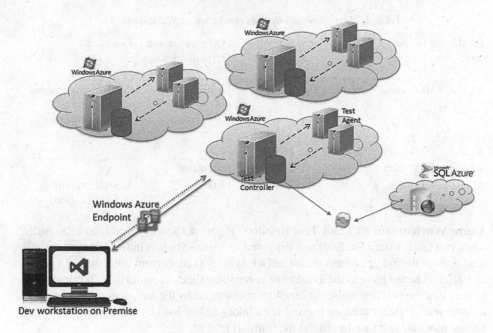

Fig. 3. Load testing architecture

3.1   Workstation #1 Load Test Results

The load tests were performed on both the on-premises and cloud versions of President.ee. Overall, the website performed as expected and the tests showed that the response time was in the proposed limit (goal) of 5 s. The tests we conducted that are particularly worth highlighting were:

- *#1.1 HomePageLoadTest:* Auto-scaling test, verifying that website scales up automatically under heavy load;
- *#1.2 SearchResultsLoadTest:* Basic performance test measuring load time of homepage and search results from the website;
- *#1.3 MediaImageLoadTest:* Media performance test measuring load time of random image and random video from the website;
- *#1.4 TestMixLoadTest:* Mixed performance test (also known as a mixed feature test), simulating a typical scenario in which the website is under heavy load in different areas: e.g. 70 % of the users on the home page, 16 % on the search page and 12 % on image content and 2 % on video content.

Table 1 represents average response times for different load test scenarios. Response times are listed for both cloud and on-premises version of President.ee.

Table 1. Overview of key tests conducted in Workstream #1

Load test	# of users	Duration of test	Azure avg. response time	On-premise avg. response time	Comments
#1.1	1000 users	30 min	3.14 s	3.38 s	Auto-scaling enabled, starting with 1 virtual machine instance
#1.2	1000 users	30 min	2.90 s	2.93 s	
#1.3	1000 users	30 min	0.20 s	*not tested*	
#1.4	500 users	30 min	3.19 s	4.08 s	Mixed tests will all features tested

Azure Workstream #1 Load Test Results: Figure 4 shows typical load test results, when run from Visual Studio® and deployed to Visual Studio Online. This is a sample load test for the image content (Load test #1.3) for 500 concurrent users during a period of 30 min. The test gave us the average page response time of around 0.2 s. It is important to note that the first few spikes in Fig. 4 were managed by the auto-scaling feature. This feature was demonstrated during the tests under heavy load by starting an additional virtual machine instance to offload the traffic (Fig. 5).

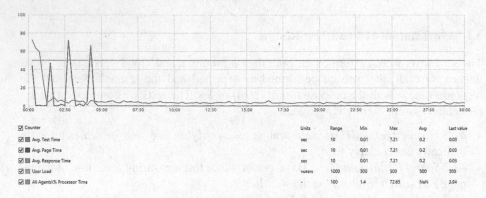

Fig. 4. Azure™ version of MediaImageLoad (#1.3) test results

On-Premises Workstream #1 Load Test Results: The on-premises version was running on the following hardware: CPU: Intel Xeon X3350 and RAM: 8 GB. The following diagram shows typical load test results when run from Visual Studio® (and deployed to Visual Studio Online). This is a sample load test for the image content (HomePageLoadTest, #1.1) for 500 concurrent users during 30 min. The first couple of spikes (Fig. 6) for the average page response time could be explained by "cold boot"; when the server/database is warmed-up, the page response time gets normalized.

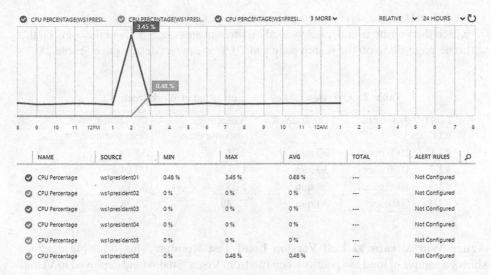

NAME	SOURCE	MIN	MAX	AVG	TOTAL	ALERT RULES
CPU Percentage	ws1president01	0.48 %	3.45 %	0.68 %	---	Not Configured
CPU Percentage	ws1president02	0 %	0 %	0 %	---	Not Configured
CPU Percentage	ws1president03	0 %	0 %	0 %	---	Not Configured
CPU Percentage	ws1president04	0 %	0 %	0 %	---	Not Configured
CPU Percentage	ws1president05	0 %	0 %	0 %	---	Not Configured
CPU Percentage	ws1president06	0 %	0.48 %	0.48 %	---	Not Configured

Fig. 5. Azure™ Monitoring Dashboard demonstrates auto-scaling features

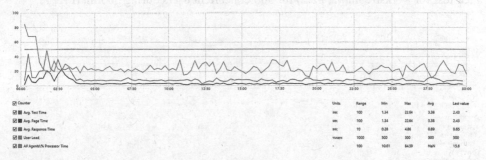

Fig. 6. Load test results on premises, Workstream #1

3.2 Workstation #2 Load Test Results

Tests were performed against a full version of the website, which had read, write, and modify functionalities enabled. The website ran both in the cloud and on-premises. As with the first workstream, the website performed as expected and the tests showed that the response time was in the proposed limit (goal) of 5 s. The tests conducted that are particularly worth highlighting were:

- #2.1 *HomePageLoadTest:* Basic performance test, measuring load time of home-page;
- #2.2 *SearchResultsLoadTest:* Measuring load time of search results from the website
- #2.3 *LawDetailsLoadTest:* Measuring load time of law/act details page

- #2.4 *TestMixLoadTest:* Mixed performance test, simulating a typical scenario in which the website is under heavy load in different areas, e.g. 50 % of the users on the home page, 30 % on the search page and 20 % on law/act details page (Table 2).

Table 2. Overview of key tests conducted in Workstream #2

Load test	# of users	Duration of test	Azure avg. response time	On-premise avg. response time
#2.1	1000 users	30 min	3.21 s	3.01 s
#2.2	1000 users	30 min	156.74 s	90.64 s
#2.3	1000 users	30 min	1.25 s	3.91 s
#2.4	500 users	30 min	72.49 s	25.28 s

Azure Workstream #2 Full Version Load Test Results: The following diagram shows a sample of load test results when run from Visual Studio (and deployed to Visual Studio Online). This is the load test for the search results page (part of the basic performance test for workstream #2, #2.2) for 500 concurrent users during 30 min (Fig. 7).

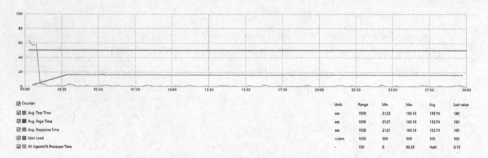

Fig. 7. Sample load test results, Azure™ workstream #2

It is worth noting that during the performance/load testing, the auto-scaling feature for the full version of workstream #2 government services on the cloud platform was not enabled. The following virtual machine sizes formed the basis of the solution: Application server (1 A5 virtual machine instance), Database server (1 A5 virtual machine instance).

On-Premises Workstream #2 Full Version Load Test Results: The following diagram (Fig. 8) shows a sample of load test results when run from Visual Studio (and deployed to Visual Studio Online). This is the load test for the search results page (part of the basic performance test for workstream #2, #2.2) for 500 concurrent users during 30 min. The following hardware was used for the on-premises solution: the application server: 4vCPU, 12 GB RAM and the database server: 4vCPU, 8 GB RAM.

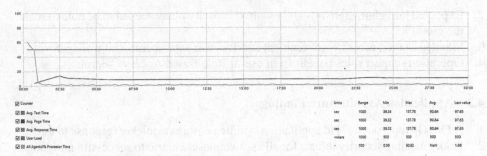

Counter	Units	Range	Min	Max	Avg	Last value
☑ ▮ Avg. Test Time	sec	1000	39.34	137.78	90.64	97.65
☑ ▮ Avg. Page Time	sec	1000	39.32	137.78	90.64	97.65
☑ ▮ Avg. Response Time	sec	1000	39.32	137.78	90.64	97.65
☑ ▮ User Load	vusers	1000	500	500	500	500
☑ ▮ All Agents\% Processor Time	-	100	0.59	60.82	NaN	1.69

Fig. 8. Sample load test results, on-premises, workstream #2

4   Findings

Why is this paper a unique contribution to e-Government scientific community? Is this (not) yet another service migration to cloud? What are those unique aspects to e-Government services? Estonia must be able to continue to function as a government, and as a people, even in the direst of scenarios, including the loss of its territory. Since Estonia docs not have paper backups of core registries, its demands for data protection, integrity, security, and privacy are unparalleled. Both experiments were conducted considering those worst scenarios, observations and findings were identified. This section presents main findings of migration experiments. They are organized into six main groups, where each group and finding would deserve a longer explanation and further discussion. However, authors see this as a guiding framework to spark academic discussion and comparisons between different migration projects. Technical reports, which describe each finding on a technical level in more detail are available to all researchers upon request.

4.1   Security, Identity and Data Architecture Findings

1. Data architecture and data security policies are essential for data integrity
2. A holistic data governance and security approach is required to facilitate migration to the cloud
3. Designing systems for 'separation of duties' and 'least privilege' is vital to maintaining security
4. Role Based Access Control (RBAC) and claims-based security increases overall security
5. Overall system control increases if operating system root credentials are restricted.
6. Isolation of user roles and accounts between environments prevents accidental changes
7. Isolating service accounts between application instances reduces security risk.

4.2   Operations Architecture Findings

1. Documented disaster recovery and cloud fail-over procedures ease pressure on teams

2. Expected load characteristics and required capacity plans needed to be able to scale the cloud
3. Standardization across e-government services can ease operational management
4. Operation support roles benefit from use of Role Based Access Control.

4.3 Application Architecture Findings

1. A DevOps approach [7] to application building ensures a quicker response to threats
2. Understanding security threats for all applications is central to successful mitigation
3. A modern design, which allows for portability, gives the government more choice
4. Public cloud can protect against DDoS attacks better than on-premises systems.

4.4 Compute Architecture Findings

1. Standardized sizing of physical servers and virtual machines helps migration
2. Master operating system images can drive standardization through virtual machine templates
3. Complexity reduced if distinct functions are separated onto different compute nodes
4. Isolated content roles minimize risk
5. Cloud design patterns using small scale-out units are preferable
6. Auto-scaling configuration requires further development
7. A server patch management strategy can help improve security.

4.5 Storage Architecture Findings

1. Standard file system disk structure for database, log, and application data improves performance
2. Any modification of the overall host, disk, and file system layout is dependent on boundaries
3. The primary operating system disks cannot be used for application or service storage needs
4. Data files can be shared between application servers
5. Data replication between on-premises and cloud systems is straightforward
6. Cloud storage architecture can enhance existing application storage
7. Regular updates of cloud virtual machine operating systems needed for wider use of Windows Azure Storage functionality.

4.6 Network Architecture Findings

1. Statically configured internal DNS naming conventions are required in the cloud environment
2. Ownership, configuration and maintenance of the DNS Start of Authority (SOA) is vital
3. Statically configured IP public and private addresses need to be carefully handled

4. Virtual network, IP address and name resolution function differently in the cloud
5. Applications need to be able to use the load balancer provided by the cloud platform.

5 Conclusions

The research project confirmed that both the Estonian President's website and the State Gazette website were able to successfully migrate to and operate in the public cloud for the duration of the project. Moreover, while certain issues were encountered, it also became clear that cloud computing can be leveraged to enhance the performance and resilience of the government services, given cloud capabilities, such as DDoS protection and auto-scaling. Indeed, virtual machines in the cloud environment can be hosted and stored in numerous locations, which may be situated in different countries, or even continents. This is necessary for Estonia's digital continuity [1] requirement – the functioning of the state in any situation or emergency.

It also emerged that while most applications, originally designed for on-premises use, can be moved to the cloud "as is", this might result in difficulties with scaling and achieving full functionality. For e-government applications to truly benefit from a migration to a cloud platform, they should be thoroughly evaluated, e.g. undergo a risk assessment, to ensure that the applications meet the current threat landscape and have a defined switching procedure and procedures for running services in cloud in place.

A critical challenge identified was that many existing information systems are poorly documented. Detailed documentation on information system architecture and functionality specifications, interfacing, or customizations is often missing and frequently only a small number of experts understand the workings of the system. This could lead to gaps in digital continuity, in particular when quick reactions are required and these experts are not available.

A very specific lesson that emerged was the need for the government to be able to request changes regarding the operation of DNS zones and records, which is critical to usage of the DNS by end users. The DNS system and certificate authority system will play a very significant role in establishing citizens' trust and their ability to get to the appropriate services during a crisis or cyber-attack. Presently, this is currently not the case, and the DNS and critical name resolution systems rely heavily on manual updates by a collection of civil servants and private companies.

Overall, the project demonstrated that from a technology perspective, the Virtual Data Embassy Solution is feasible, as only limited architectural changes would be required.

Acknowledgments. This paper is based on a section of an unpublished manuscript of a research project on "Public Cloud Usage for Government" and unpublished materials of doctoral dissertation of Taavi Kotka, authors did not receive payment for this publication. Authors wish to thank Mikk Lellsaar, Raivo Oravas, Rome Mitt, Ivo Vellend, Taavi Meos, Ardo Birk.

References

1. Kotka, T., Liiv, I.: Concept of Estonian Government cloud and data embassies. In: Kö, A., Francesconi, E. (eds.) EGOVIS 2015. LNCS, vol. 9265, pp. 149–162. Springer, Heidelberg (2015)
2. Kotka, T., Kask, L., Raudsepp, K., Storch, T., Radloff, R., Liiv, I.: Policy and legal environment analysis for e-Government services migration to the public cloud. In: Proceedings of the 9th International Conference ICEGOV 2016, Montevideo, Uruguay, 1–3 March 2016, pp. 103–108. ACM Press (2016)
3. Cellary, W., Strykowski, S.: e-Government based on cloud computing and service-oriented architecture. In: Proceedings of the 3rd International Conference ICEGOV 2009, Bogota, Colombia, 10–13 November 2009, pp. 5–10. ACM Press (2009)
4. Pokharel, M., Park, J.: Cloud computing: future solution for e-Governance. In: Proceedings of the 3rd International Conference ICEGOV 2009, Bogota, Colombia, 10–13 November 2009, pp. 409–410. ACM Press (2009)
5. Gongolidis, E., Kalloniatis, C., Kavakli, E.: Requirements identification for migrating eGovernment applications to the cloud. In: Linawati, Mahendra, M.S., Neuhold, E.J., Tjoa, A.M., You, I. (eds.) ICT-EurAsia 2014. LNCS, vol. 8407, pp. 150–158. Springer, Heidelberg (2014)
6. Microsoft: About VHD. https://msdn.microsoft.com/en-us/library/windows/desktop/dd323654(v=vs.85).aspx
7. Hüttermann, M.: DevOps for Developers: Integrate Development and Operations, the Agile Way. Apress, New York (2012)

Open Data and Transparency

Linked Open Data and e-Participation in the EU Law-Making Process

P. Schmitz[1], E. Francesconi[1,2(✉)], B. Batouche[3], B. Dombrovschi[4], D. Duy[3],
S.P. Landercy[4], and V. Parisse[5]

[1] Publications Office of the European Union, Luxembourg, Luxembourg
enrico.francesconi@publications.europa.eu
[2] ITTIG-CNR, Florence, Italy
francesconi@ittig.cnr.it
[3] infeurope S.A., Luxembourg, Luxembourg
[4] Trasys, Luxembourg, Luxembourg
[5] Aubay S.A., Luxembourg, Luxembourg

Abstract. In this paper a pilot project on Linked Open Data (LOD) and e-Participation, promoted by the European Parliament and developed by the Publications Office of the European Union (OP), is described. By exploiting the LOD service for pre-legislative documents available at OP, the project aims at allowing citizens to actively participate in public consultations within the EU decision-making process. In particular it gives citizens the possibility to participate in the preparation of standard-compliant and process-compatible documents throughout the law-making. In particular they can provide comments and amendments on each document fragment, as well express their sentiments on them. The data produced will be available as LOD; for this reason a specific semantic approach able to describe documents and users activities is implemented.

Keywords: Linked Open Data · e-Participation · e-Democracy

1 Introduction

Over the last few years the European Union institutions have intensively cooperated to define policies for developing a transparent decision and policy making framework, able to promote quality and accessibility for the EU legislation. The aim is to ensure that the Union regulatory environment is as simple and as clear as possible, so to avoid overregulation and administrative burdens for administrations, businesses and citizens, and especially for small and medium-sized enterprises.

In the *Better Regulation* initiative [1], the European Commission intends to foster such policies, in particular it aims to design a so-called *Smart Regulation* framework, able to approach the full policy cycle, from the drafting, implementation, enforcement, evaluation and revision of a piece of legislation. In this respect, with the REFIT [2] platform, the Commission aims to engage the Council and

A. Kő and E. Francesconi (Eds.): EGOVIS 2016, LNCS 9831, pp. 79–89, 2016.
DOI: 10.1007/978-3-319-44159-7_6

the Parliament in revising or repealing legislation where appropriate, to evaluate the EU regulatory measures, as well as to promote the consultation of citizens and stakeholders in the policy cycle.

Similarly the European Parliament has recently launched the pilot project "Promoting Linked Open Data, Free Software and Civil Society Participation in Law-Making throughout the EU". This pilot project aims to engage citizens all over Europe in the democratic game as developers of democratic values and working methods at all levels throughout the society. In this context the use of information and communication technologies is fostered, in particular Open Knowledge and Free Software solutions. The use of ICT in the context of civil society participation to the democratic processes represents a tremendous opportunity for the EU to reconnect citizens and the EU by opening up public institutions and by empowering citizens to play a more active role in public services and decision-making. With such pilot project the European Parliament is promoting an original synthesis between two of the main initiatives emerged over the last few years:

- the Linked Open Data approach to the Semantic Web implementation, which means following a set of guidelines to enable open data sharing and reuse on a massive scale according to the Semantic Web principles;
- the e-Participation initiative, originally promoted by the European Commission in the 2006 preparatory action and carried on within the ICT-PSP 2009 programme, aimed at improving the quality of the legislative process, enhancing accessibility and alignment of legislation at European level, as well as promoting awareness and democratic participation of citizens in the law-making.

By the pilot project on LOD and e-Participation, the European Parliament intends to give citizens the possibility to use and participate in the preparation of standard-compliant and process-compatible documents throughout the law-making. To achieve these objectives it is necessary to implement a set of standards and tools able to improve the quality of legislative documents so that they can be made publicly available as LOD datasets, as well as to provide citizens with a collaborative platform allowing them to play an active role in the decision making process. Essential for the project is the availability of EU-law related documents available in a standard format, so that they can be presented in a structured way to the stakeholders, allowing them to post their comments as well as proposing amendments on specific pieces of legislation.

As main provider of the EU law, as well as developer of multilingual technologies and localization processes, the Publications Office of the EU has been appointed to take the lead of such a project.

In this paper we present the main features of such LOD and e-Participation platform based on open source and semantic web technologies. In Sect. 2 similar e-Participation initiatives are reviewed with the aim to identify the system requirements for the project prototype. In Sects. 3 and 4 the approaches as regards documents and knowledge models, based on semantic web technologies, are respectively described. In Sect. 5 the main use-cases foreseen in the prototype are illustrated. In Sect. 6 the software architecture of the prototype is shown. Finally, in Sect. 7 some conclusions and future developments are briefly discussed.

2   Related Projects and Requirements for the Prototype

The different aspects of e-Participation have been analysed in several initiatives, either form the governance or the technical implementation point of view. The International Association for Public Participation (IAP[2]) identifies a spectrum of five point continuum of participatory processes: inform, consult, involve, collaborate, and empower. These five points are discussed in [3] in terms of different levels of citizen participation and shared decision-making authority. The main differences among such points is the level of public engagement they are pertaining, which tends to increase from one to the other according to the decision authority actually granted, as well as the instruments available to exercise it. In particular [3] distinguishes services which simply aim to provide the public with balanced and objective information, from others services which increase progressively the level of citizens' participation. Such services aim to obtain feedback on analyses, alternatives and decisions, to involve citizens ensuring that public concerns are consistently understood and considered, to collaborate with the public in the decision-making including the development of alternatives and the identification of the solutions, finally to place the actual decision-making in the hands of the public itself.

Several institutional or non-institutional services have been recently developed in this context at institutional levels, as well as in the research and open software communities. For example OpenCongress.org represents an open parliament platform developed as a service able to track the activity of the US Congress, as well as allowing citizens to participate in the legislative process. It includes social networks sharing of bills and blogs to involve other communities, as well as the possibility of subscribing RSS feeds to track news. Similarly, OpenParlamento.it, a platform managed by the OpenPolis association, is able to monitor the activity of the Italian Parliament, as well as providing participatory instruments. OpenParliament.ca and Theyworkforyou.com are other similar initiatives about monitoring the activities of Canadian and UK Parliaments respectively. Republique-numerique.fr, on the other hand, is the institutional service developed in France to allow open and interactive online consultation on government legislation before it is submitted to the Conseil d'Etat (French Supreme Administrative Court) and adopted by the Cabinet. On local basis an interesting example of e-Participation service is represented by Ars e-Democracy[1] promoted by the Sicily Region in Italy, involving citizens and stakeholders in the regional legislative process.

From the ICT point of view, environments of participatory democracy already exist like LiquidFeedback[2], Airesis[3], OpenDCN freE-Democracy[4] and

---

[1] http://www.ars.sicilia.it.

[2] http://liquidfeedback.org.

[3] http://www.airesis.eu.

[4] http://www.opendcn.org.

Open Active Democracy[5]. All all them provides a set of tools able to engage citizens in public consultations. More recently the D-Cent[6] European project has been launched with the aim of developing digital tools for direct democracy and economic empowerment. They will allow people to discuss and share content, engage in mass scale deliberation, collaborative policymaking, and voting.

The LOD and e-Participation pilot project aims to treasure these initiatives, as well as to develop a specific set of functionalities allowing people to participate in the EU decision making process, taking in consideration its multilingual nature.

In particular the prototype of the system under development is aiming to provide the following services:

- Fetch information (pre-legislative documents) from relevant authentic sources, in particular from CELLAR [4], the document and metadata repository of the OP, and make them accessible via semantic search facilities;
- Allow e-Participation services, including the formulation of comments and amendments to the bills under discussion at different granularity levels (entire document, paragraphs, and sentences), as well as rating and voting text fragments and comments;
- Management of citizens contributions and amendments in a dedicated semantic repository;
- Evaluate the input provided by e-Participation services (statistics);
- Visualize the proposals and the status of the discussion in an intuitive way.

An essential pre-condition to provide such services is the availability of documents in XML format, so that specific metadata, comments, amendments and statistics can be linked to the document fragments.

3   Pre-legislative Documents Organization

In the current EU legislative workflow, documents are drafted by the European Commission using the LegisWrite tool, a plugin of MS Word able to describe the structure of the documents using styles associated with specific semantics (ex: document title, articles, paragraphs, etc.). Then such documents are sent, in docx and pdf formats, to the OP which produces also the XHTML format for publishing pre-legislation in the related section of the EurLex website[7] The available XHTML format however is not useful for the aims of our project, since it is just a presentation-oriented format which does not follow the formal structure of a legislative document. Therefore, a preliminary phase has been needed to create a document dataset, able to describe the formal structure of legislative documents. For this reason we relied on the XML format available at

---

[5] http://p2pfoundation.net/Open_Active_Democracy.
[6] http://dcentproject.eu.
[7] http://eur-lex.europa.eu/collection/legislative-procedures.html.

the EU Parliament for pre-legislation, produced in the framework of the AT4AM[8] service for managing amendments.

From such format a transformation into AkomaNtoso[9] as pivot XML format and eventually in the Formex 5[10] XML format for the final publication is accomplished using XSLT technologies. Moreover, a specific extension of the European Legislation identifier (ELI) standard [5] is used in order to provide identification to the different fragments of pre-legislative documents. ELI [5] is a standard already adopted by the EU institutions able to identify legislative documents by a set of metadata at different levels of the FRBR model [6]. Such metadata are serialized into an http URI according to the following scheme: /eli/[doctype]/[year]/[natural_number]/[lang] where:

- doctype: indicates the type of the resource. Possible values are the authority codes published in the resource-type authority table at http://publications. europa.eu/mdr/authority/resource-type/index.html (examples are directive dir, regulation reg, decision dec);
- year: a 4-digit year;
- natural_number: number assigned to the document at the moment of the publication in the Official Journal (starting at 1 each year). The natural_number can, in some cases, be followed by a sequence number in parenthesis to disambiguate the cases where multiple documents have the same doctype+year+natural_number (typically 2 decisions from different authors published the same year with the same number);
- lang: a 3-letters language (ISO-6393), as published in the language authority table at http://publications.europa.eu/mdr/authority/language/index.html.

In the LOD and e-Participation pilot project we have extended the ELI identification scheme to the subdivisions of pre-legislative documents. In particular we have specified the metadata scheme for the various subdivisions: since document subdivisions of the same Work can be different in different languages and in different versions, for example generated by amendments, such metadata are assigned to the Expression level. In particular articles and paragraphs are identified by the prefix /eli/[doctype]/[year]/[natural_number]/, followed respectively by [article_number]/[lang] and /[article_number]/ [paragraph_number]/[lang]. The values of the [article_number] and [paragraph_number], as well as of the other subdivisions at deeper levels, follow the hierarchy and the IDs naming convention of the subdivisions in Formex documents: for example given the following ID "art.003.par.002" related to Art. 3 paragraph 2, the related URI fragment will be: [art_003/par_002]. The availability of such documents in XML format allows to visualize them properly structured, to qualify them with additional metadata, as well as to link them with users' activities (comments, amendments, ratings, expression of sentiments ("I agree", "I disagree") on legislative document fragments).

---

[8] https://blog.law.cornell.edu/voxpop/2013/08/15/at4am-the-xml-web-editor-used-by-members-of-european-parliament/.

[9] http://www.akomantoso.org.

[10] http://formex.publications.europa.eu.

4   The Semantic Approach

The LOD and e-Participation platform is based on a knowledge approach able
to describe documents, different types of users, their activities and relationships,
as well as providing LOD services by semantic web technologies. As described
in Sect. 3, legislative documents are made available in XML Formex 5, including
the metadata available in CELLAR. Such metadata are provided according to
the CDM[11] ontology [4] developed by the OP for bibliographic resources. In particular the Eurovoc thesaurus, available in SKOS[12], is used to qualify legislative
documents by subject, therefore a document browsing service, as well as search
and retrieval facilities, are provided based on the Eurovoc taxonomy.

A knowledge organization system is built on top of several ontologies typically
used for describing social activities, in particular SIOC[13] for information from
online communities and FOAF[14] for people and social groups characteristics, as
well as to link people and information.

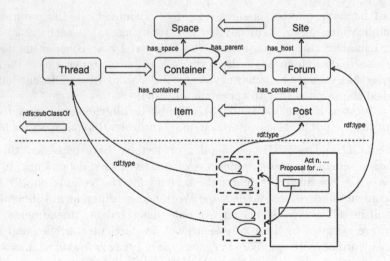

Fig. 1. SIOC instantiation

The basic social activities are implemented, in particular the possibility to
post comments on legislative text fragments, to amend them, to express sentiments associated to comments ("I agree", "I disagree"), as well as rating and
voting a specific text version or comment. Comments are identified by http URIs,
linked to legal text fragments identified by ELI-URIs. As represented in Fig. 1,
comments are classified as posts of the SIOC knowledge model, while a group

---

[11] Common Metadata Model.
[12] https://www.w3.org/2004/02/skos/.
[13] http://rdfs.org/sioc/spec/.
[14] http://www.foaf-project.org.

of posts are classified as threads. Moreover, an alignment is made between a legislative document and a forum as a container of posts, hosted by the LOD and e-Participation web site.

Users are described using the FOAF ontology able to specify several aspects of their profiles, including for example name, family name, nationality, language, the avatar, the group of interest they belong to, etc.

Statistics about users participation are also derived. In this respect specific properties are added to the different SIOC items and containers, so to consider the number of comments received by a document fragment or by the whole document, as well as the number of positive or negative comments a text fragment has received. Following user and document descriptions, statistics on the users activities are available, as described in Sect. 5.

5 Main Use-Cases

The system prototype focuses on the implementation of basic use-cases related to the possibility for the users to provide comments, replies, as well as to express their sentiments on document fragments or on the whole content.

A specific use-case includes the possibility for the users to provide amendments to legislative text fragments. In this respect the outcomes of the AT4AM project[15] of the EU Parliament, dealing with amendments management, as well as the results of the LEOS project[16] [7] of the EU Commission dealing with legislative document drafting, are considered. In particular, the CKEditor basic technology on which the LEOS editor has been developed, is used to provide the user the possibility to submit amendments to legislative text fragments through track-change facilities. Users will be able to provide change proposals (insertions, substitutions, repeals) to the original version of a text, and such changes will be described according to an ontology able to classify amendments [8]. A comment can be modified after it was published and the application stores and displays the history of the modifications.

A list of actions is displayed at the bottom of each comment. Such actions depend on the privileges of the user and allow to reply, score, tag, share and annotate a comment. The score action allows voting a comment up or down. The total score of a comment is the number of up votes minus the number of down votes. That score is displayed at the top right corner of the comment box. The reply action allows structuring the discussion with threads. The tag action allows classifying the comments and later select or regroup them. The share action allows sharing the comment on a social network (Twitter, Facebook, Google+, etc.). The annotate action allows to link comments with the subsumes relationship and to manage facts, rules and assertions.

A user can filter a set of comments based on their attributes and relationships (date, score, links, etc.).

---

[15] http://www.at4am.org.

[16] https://joinup.ec.europa.eu/software/leos/home.

On the other hand a user is able to display different graphical representations of the document to visualize its different characteristics: text length, positive/negative feedback, parts that received lots of comments and amendments, etc. Such graphical representations are organized either to respect the sequential order of the articles, or as graphs able to highlight the different activities on a document in terms of nodes representing document fragments and the number of comments/amendments submitted, as well as links between them.

The activities of the users are selectively registered and pave the way to the elaboration of statistics on the public consultation service. In particular statistics by nationality, by group of interest the users belong to, by language, as well as by document fragments and document topics are given. Such statistics are shown associated to each document and fragment as illustrated in Fig. 2. Users' activities and statistics are shown also using timeline or map views.

Finally, a use-case under analysis is the use of argument maps to graphically represent a summary of the debate. The comments are pieces of text that provide additional information, or try to confirm or invalidate the article they are attached to. A careful read of the comment will allow a user to extract the facts, the rules and the assertions used in its reasoning. A given fact, a given rules or a given assertion can be used by many different comments. Facts, rules and assertions are the building blocks of argument maps [9–11]. In an argument map, they are linked to make visible their relationships: deduction, confirmation, invalidation. Arguments maps are a powerful tool to summarize in a very synthetic graph the facts, rules and assertion extracted from a large set of comments.

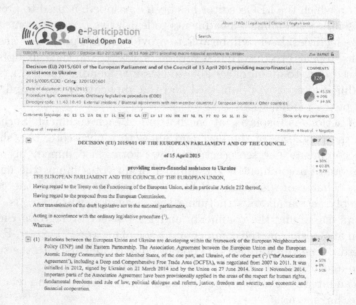

Fig. 2. The visualization of a document and the related statistics on users' activities

6 The LOD and e-Participation Platform Software Architecture

The software architecture of the LOD and e-Participation prototype platform is sketched in Fig. 3.

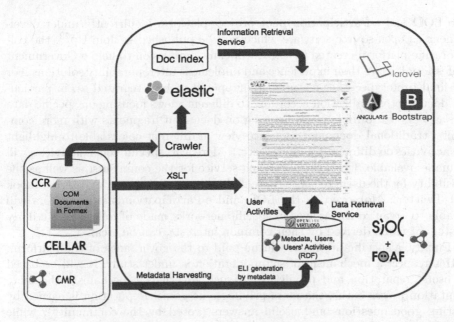

Fig. 3. e-Participation platform software architecture

The legislative resources are available through the CELLAR services, in particular document content is provided by the CELLAR Common Content Repository (CCR), while metadata are provided by the CELLAR Common Metadata Repository (CMR) as LOD. Documents from CCR are transformed using XSLT technologies from Formex format to XHTML format for visualization, as well as indexed using Elasticsearch[17] to provide Information Retrieval services. On the other hand document metadata, available in RDF format from CMR, are stored in a specific Virtuoso[18] database server for providing metadata retrieval services implemented by SPARQL queries. Similarly, users' profiles and their social activities are stored in RDF format in Virtuoso, which acts as SPARQL end-point of the Linked Open Data service of the project.

---

[17] https://www.elastic.co/products/elasticsearch.
[18] http://virtuoso.openlinksw.com.

The web interface is developed using the Laravel[19] php framework as server-side technology, as well as AngularJS[20] and Bootstrap[21] for managing client-side interactions and creating a responsive web interface, respectively.

7   Conclusions and Future Developments

The LOD and e-Participation pilot project platform is currently under development as open-source software which will be published in Join-Up[22], the collaborative platform created by the European Commission to help e-Government professionals share their experience and implement interoperability solutions. For the final prototype other features are supposed to be integrated as, in particular, document visualization according to different views focusing on specific data and aspects (ex: bubble views focusing on document fragments with more comments; traditional document sequence view in different colors able to highlight the activities on different fragments, etc.). Moreover, specific social activities will be made available, like a social tagging service for the comments, as well as the possibility for the users to share contents in other social networks (like Facebook and Twitter). Moreover, in the LOD and e-Participation platform users will be able to organize themselves in specific networks made of followers. Similarly clusters of users, derived by their common interests, can be created.

Finally, a specific attention will be paid to the governance of the platform: in this respect a mechanism of self-moderation is under study. It will be based on users' reputation and privileges. In such governance mechanism the more reputation a user earns, the more privileges he gains. Reputation is earned by posting good questions and useful answers (voted by the community), while specific privileges are granted according to the level of reputation earned, allowing selected users to manage accounts and comments (including privileges on filtering/summarizing comments, as well as amendments consolidation).

References

1. European Commission. Better regulation (2015). http://ec.europa.eu/smart-index_en.htm
2. European Commission. EU Regulatory Fitness. Technical Report COM(2012)746 final. European Commission (2010)
3. Nabachi, T.: A manager's guide to evaluate citizen participation. Technical report, Maxwell School of Citizenship and Public Affairs - Syracuse University (2012)
4. Francesconi, E., Küster, M.W., Gratz, P., Thelen, S.: The ontology-based approach of the publications office of the EU for document accessibility and open data services. In: Kö, A., Francesconi, E. (eds.) EGOVIS 2015. LNCS, vol. 9265, pp. 29–39. Springer, Heidelberg (2015)

---

[19] http://laravel.com/.
[20] https://angularjs.org.
[21] http://getbootstrap.com.
[22] https://joinup.ec.europa.eu.

5. Council of European Union. Council conclusions inviting the introduction of the European Legislation Identifier (ELI). Technical Report (2012/C 325/02) OJ C 325, Council of the European Union, October 2012
6. Study Group on IFLA. Functional requirements for bibliographic records. Technical report, International Federation of Library Associationsand Institutions (1998). http://www.ifla.org/VII/s13/frbr/frbr.pdf
7. Valayer, C.: ISA LEOS final results, May 2012. https://joinup.ec.europa.eu/elibrary/document/isa-leos-final-results
8. Francesconi, E.: Semantic model for legal resources: annotation and reasoning over normative provisions. Semant. Web J. Spec. Issue Semant. Web Leg. Domain **7**(3), 255–265 (2016)
9. Reed, C., Long, D., Fox, M.: Planning persuasive argument. In: Working Notes of the ECAI-96 Workshop on Gaps and Bridges, Budapest, Hungary, 11–16 August 1996, pp. 47–50 (1996)
10. Reed, C., Norman, T.J.: Argumentation Machines: New Frontiers in Argument and Computation. Kluwer Academic Publishers, Norwell (2004)
11. Reed, C.A., Walton, D.N.: Applications of argumentation schemes. In: Hansen, H.V., Tindale, C.W., Blair, J.A., Johnson, R.H. (eds.) Proceedings of the 4th Conference of the Ontario Society for the Study of Argument (OSSA2001) (2001)

A Strategy to Gradual Implementation
of Data Interoperability

João Baptista Gonçalves[1](✉) and Luisa Domingues[2](✉)

[1] Binomial, Lisbon, Portugal
joao.baptista.goncalves@gmail.com
[2] ISTAR, ISCTE-IUL, Lisbon, Portugal
luisa.domingues@iscte.pt

Abstract. Data interoperability is a major concern on e-government, both from the point of view of service offering and from the point of view of public administration efficiency. This paper purposes an incremental, pragmatic approach to data interoperability. It is argued that integration with minor required initial efforts from institutions is feasible, may provide useful solutions and is a solid ground basis for subsequent evolution. This paper presents general guidelines and model solutions to support this approach. Also, presents a demo implementation that proves feasibility of the purposed models and delivers useful solutions on a specific business e-government scenario. Although still limited in range and demonstrated on a quite specific business environment, it is expected that the analysis and the proposed strategies, solutions and models be of interest on a larger spectrum of data interoperability problems.

Keywords: Data interoperability · Taxonomy · Open data · E-government · DaaS · Data services catalogue

1 Introduction/Context

Access of citizens and enterprises to public administration services often involves the need to relate to various institutions or departments. This leads, frequently, to problems of redundancy, duplication of required data, etc. It is expected that electronic services contributes, quite significantly, to attenuate this problems. However, a lot of the traditional resilience of public administration services regarding coordination, normalization and integration of data and processes obstinately survives in electronic solutions.

Traditionally cooperation across public entities is an issue for (i) cultural reasons, i.e., lack of a Public Administration (PA) holistic view as a single entity which provides services to citizens. Instead each public entity performs a range of services in line with his mission acting as a stand-alone; (ii) organizational factors, i.e., bureaucratic organizations sometimes with highly politicized leaderships; and (iii) autonomous management.

Companies and citizens are, often, still forced to recurrently deliver the same information to different PA entities, and even in the same entity, to start different processes. The autonomous decision centers in each PA entity and the lack of a single ICT strategy for PA led to a technological landscape characterized by the existence of multiple and

© Springer International Publishing Switzerland 2016
A. Kő and E. Francesconi (Eds.): EGOVIS 2016, LNCS 9831, pp. 90–104, 2016.
DOI: 10.1007/978-3-319-44159-7_7

isolated information systems. Therefore, these information silos encumber data sharing between different public entities and even between organic units of the same entity. Moreover, the same concepts could have distinct meanings among different public entities, leading to different data.

This issue has been addressed over the last few years at policy and technical levels.

States and major public ICT institutions conduct efforts for that purpose. For instance, Europe encourages initiatives on data interoperability [1, 2] and prompt research projects in common taxonomy and ontologies, entitled as semantic web [3].

Data interoperability is major question on service integration. Services tend to define and treat data in their own terms. Therefore, often the same data appears differently across institutions, compromising exchange and reuse. Even only slightly differences in format, coding etc. are a major headache for data interoperability.

Besides meaning, data interoperability also traceability (who accesses to what information), data quality (validated by the competent authorities) and access profile. While in an internal circuit, the workflow allows to define which data the users can access, according to their working context. However it is hard to ensure this authentication when the access to the data is outside the boundaries of the workflow.

Whereas the intra-organizational data sharing has already taken significant steps with investments aiming IT integration [4], the lack of data sharing among public entities, raises a greater organizational, management and technology challenge. There are a widespread agreement that data sharing among public agencies would bring improvements in effectiveness (i.e., the level of service provided to economic agents and citizens) and efficiency (i.e., reducing the cost and time related with control and data validation).

The current state of technology offers several technical solutions to overcome data interoperability data (semantic web, XML, ...) [3]. Therefore the biggest challenge is not the technical view but the definition of cooperation and data management models.

This paper addresses the problem of data interoperability in PA. The main objective is to contribute to enforce cooperation between PA entities in order provide better service and improve efficiency.

PA entities often deal with limited resources. Projects oriented to data integration often require big effort and provide only long term results. This circumstances often discourage initiatives on this area.

This paper purposes a simple scalable model to data interoperability. It is argued that simple solutions, requiring minor initial effort might, in some circumstances, be a path to overcome this challenges.

A simple interoperability model is purposed for this matter.

Also, it is presented a system implementation targeted to specific actual business environment scenario where all the referred questions apply. The targeted scenario includes two main functionalities: (i) an enterprise that directs to a service (filling an application form, for example) might access and, if possible, reuse similar data available in the same public entity as well as in different public entities that relate themselves to provide this facility; and (ii) a public entity that is allowed to read information from another public entity about an enterprise.

Specific conditions that apply to this problem. The data involved is similar in concept, tough – not surprisingly - quite different in record organisation, fields, formats and codification.

The involved data is not public data, the problem of authorization must be considered. Every access must be authorized by the owner (i.e., the enterprise) and accesses must be tracked.

The paper is organized as follows: Sect. 2 describes the research methodology. The approach used is based on a lot or published work concerning the general problem of "data interoperability" and related areas and technological concepts, this is reviewed in Sect. 3. Section 4 presents strategic guidelines to deal with the problem and an architectural operational solution to implement those same guidelines. The Sect. 5 presents a developed demo, currently implemented for evaluation. Finally, Sect. 6 presents conclusions and proposes work evolution.

2 Research Methodology

The Design Science Research Methodology (DSRM) [5] was considered suitable in order to support this research. DSRM incorporates principles, practices, and procedures required to carry out research in information systems. This research methodology meets three objectives: it is consistent with prior literature, it provides a nominal process model for doing design science (DS) research, and it provides a mental model for presenting and evaluating DS research in information systems [5]. Selecting DSRM ensures the existence of a set of activities that underpin the coherence between the practical application and the principles and strategies defined for the proposal interoperability model. The DSRM includes six activities are: problem identification and motivation, definition of the objectives for a solution, design and development, demonstration, evaluation, and communication.

We define these activities in the context of our research as follows:

1. Problem identification and motivation. This research is driven by the need to overcoming of so-called eBarriers in the exchange of documents and information among public entities in order to deliver efficient and integrated electronic public services.
2. Objectives of the solution. The objectives of this research are:
   (a) To propose a model following a pragmatic approach which enables a smooth integration and semantic interconnection among public entities, without requiring a large initial effort or a disruption in the semantic data or technologies used; and
   (b) To demonstrate in a very restricted but real environment, the feasibility of the proposed model principles.

   The objectives will be realized through:
   (a) Identification of the strategies and principles to support an incremental model;
   (b) The definition of an interoperability model;
   (c) The definition of an ontology applied to a specific and narrow environment for demonstration purpose.

3. Design and development. We first analyze the existing initiatives to overcome the challenge of interoperability in general, and in the particular context of public administration (Sect. 3). In a second step we defined the strategy for the model implementation. Based on these strategy guidelines were specified the structure of business and usability metadata to achieve machine-readable representations of data contents (Sect. 4). Also were defined levels of service for each data component, in order to assure an incremental adherence.

4. Demonstration. We defined an ontology, named *"dip"* (data interoperability protocol) focused in a very narrow and specific usage context, i.e. the process to support co-financing projects submitted by enterprises, to demonstrate the model implementation.

5. Evaluation. The demo system was tested in the real context of a public entity, although in a test environment. The solution demonstrated versatility in terms of adaptation to different types of contents and does not represent a relevant change or efforts in the solution implementation.

6. Communication. We publish this paper to share our experience.

3 Conceptual Research Background - Issues and Approaches

In the last years, many efforts were directed towards enabling interoperable information systems through consistency and uniformity in the way that information is described, stored and retrieved, especially in complex organisations such as governments [6]. Therefore, many approaches, architectures, and protocols were proposed in order to make open data more machine-readable, and interoperable [7].

The Service Oriented Architectures (SOA) approach and the widespread use of Web Services, brought flexibility and interoperability to data integration through a class of web services, called Data Services [8], that access and query data sources. In a basic data service usage scenario, the owners of a data store enable web clients and other applications to access their, otherwise externally inaccessible, data by publishing a set of data services [8].

Defining the semantics of data services is a significant driver to enable data interoperability. An interesting approach to define the semantics of data services is by describing them as semantic views over a domain ontology [7].

A semantic interoperability asset is as a collection of reference metadata elements that sharing them among governments would contribute to increased interoperability across organizational and geographic boundaries [6]. Metadata, defined as information about data, identify the structure and meaning of data. According to Ralph Kimball [9] metadata elements can be classified into technical and business metadata. The technical metadata specifies how exactly the data is structured and stored in files or databases, in order to allow applications and tools access and manipulate it. The business data, expressed through business requirements, time-lines, business metrics, business process flows, and business terminology, help to understand the data and their usage requires extensive and in depth understanding of business entities, tasks, rules and the environment.

Many countries worldwide have defined metadata frameworks as part of their national e-Government strategies [4, 6]. Also, in Europe as part of the Digital Agenda for Europe, one of the seven flagship initiatives in the Europe 2020 Strategy for smart, sustainable and inclusive economic growth, the European Commission has adopted the Communication 'Towards interoperability for European public services', which aims to establish a common approach to effective interoperability among European public administrations [1]. In this context governments as well as the European Commission are sharing their metadata on the Web to encourage their reusability and consequently facilitate interoperability. This has led to a new kind of repositories focusing primarily on semantic interoperability assets, such as Digitaliser.dk in Denmark, the ESD toolkit standards lists in the UK and the European Union repository SEMIC.EU [6].

The SEMIC.EU platform promotes semantic interoperability among European Member states by collecting, evaluating, indexing and making available a large number of semantic assets from a single point of access. In this way, developers can easily discover and reuse assets like data models, taxonomies, codelists and vocabularies developed by others facing similar use case.

The Asset Description Metadata Schema (ADMS) is a standardized metadata vocabulary created by the EU's Interoperability Solutions for European Public Administrations (ISA) Programme of the European Commission to help publishers of standards document what their standards are about (their name, their status, theme, version, etc.) and where they can be found on the Web. ADMS descriptions can then be published on different websites while the standard itself remains on the website of its publisher (i.e. syndication of content). ADMS embraces the multi-publisher environment and, at the same time, it provides the means for the creation of aggregated catalogues of standards and single points of access to them based on ADMS descriptions.

Following a similar trend to vocabularies used as metadata on the web, definitions should first be agreed on fundamental concepts, where diverged and/or conflicting views can be handled. These concepts are defined as Core Concepts [10]. A Core Concept is a simplified data model that captures the minimal, global characteristics/attributes of an entity in a generic, country and domain neutral fashion. It can be represented as Core Vocabulary using different formalisms (e.g. XML, RDF, JSON). The Core Vocabularies are general semantic building blocks that can be extended into context-specific data models. Four Core Vocabularies were created: (i) Core Person which captures the fundamental characteristics of a person, e.g. the name, the gender, the date of birth, the location; (ii) Registered organisation, that captures the fundamental characteristics of a legal entity, e.g. its identifier, activities, which is created through a formal registration process, typically in a national or regional register; (iii) Core Location which captures the fundamental characteristics of a location, represented as an address, a geographic name or geometry; and (iv) Core Public service that captures the fundamental characteristics of a service offered by public administration.

A platform of e-Government Core Vocabularies hosted by European Commission are supported by W3C [11] promoting enormous visibility worldwide.

Nevertheless, all these efforts include only generic properties that are not sufficient for completely fulfilling the needs of the diverse audience of government semantic interoperability assets, e.g., developers interested in ontologies or codelists or project managers interested in UML diagrams or reference datasets. RDF-based models use the Resource Description Framework (RDF) as a data model. Semantic Web [3] and Linked Data technologies have been applied to many e-Government catalogues and repositories to achieve machine-readable representations of their content metadata using RDF. The adoption of such technologies has several benefits like decentralized publishing and Web accessibility.

4 Proposed Guidelines and Solutions – Incremental Model

4.1 Strategy

Interoperability requires common semantic and formats. An ideal approach to develop an interoperability solution is to promote some kind of consortium where one or more entities engaged themselves on a project to develop common models, adapt their data to these models and develop methods to data exchange.

However, this ideal approach may suffer a few drawbacks. It requires organisations commitment in the project, involving budget, resources and the willingness to change and adapt, which is often difficult to mobilize all together. It also requires a huge initial effort before results arise, which may be discouraging. In addition it closes the door to entities not engaged in the project, thus compromising the adhesion of new entities.

When these drawbacks prevails, a more gradually based approach can introduce some features in order to leverage an interoperable solution. The keynote of this approach is the principle that each entity contribution is fitted to its constraints and capabilities. Therefore, the data provider organisations offer data in the best possible way, regarding interoperability. As data client, organisations are willing to receive data in any available format. In such context each organisation defines its own pace depending on its know-how and available resources.

In order to support this pragmatic and incremental approach a set of guidelines are presented:

- Definition of interoperability service level. A low level indicates that the provider organisation is only able to provide data in hermetic formats. While a high level demonstrates the ability to provide structured data according to semantic annotations, enabling a large potential of interoperability.
- An evolutionary path background. The data may be provided at a low interoperability level in a first stage, and later, may evolve to higher levels of interoperability.

The higher levels of interoperability requires the usage of common semantics. A wide range of ontologies already exist, from those that apply to a generic scope (example Dublin Core [12]), to those which are focused into particular businesses or institutions requirements (example ISA – e-Government Core Vocabulary [10]). However, specialization of ontologies in particular business areas, is encouraged [13]. Therefore it is reasonable accept that in a near future will arise shelf-ready semantics with metadata definition to cover business specific requirements. Nevertheless, the use of the most widespread ontologies whenever possible should be appreciated even if mixed with more specific ontologies.

In the following sections a model is proposed to fulfill these guidelines.

The model defines a few rules to system interconnection and data exchange, starting from scratch and leaving a ground basis for evolution.

4.2   Interoperability Model

Consider two systems A and B. System B possesses data that might be useful to activity A. A and B operate in the same business area, therefore manipulating similar business data. However, they do not have previous effort on data integration or data standardization. Supposing A is a client which, for his activities, is interested to get data that B can supply in usable form. The model describes (i) the way B supply data and (ii) the way A acts in order to discover available data and retrieve it in usable forms.

For the sake of reasoning, we considered a targeted business scenario where queries concerns available data on a given entity.

In order to get data from system B, A issues a query identifying the entity, and system B responds presenting a catalog of available data on that entity. The catalogue of available data must include pertinent information for automatic data processing.

Information is organized in *chuncks* or *"records"*. Each record is a piece of information identified with a unique invariant *id*, issued by the server. The record can be retrieved using that identification. Despite the *id* be invariable, the information obtained based on it depends on the information available at the moment it is requested.

Concerning automatic processing purposes, each record should be enriched with business and technical metadata [9].

The business metadata includes: (i) basic information, such as description, classification type, and contents identification relevant to the business; and (ii) data management information, covering data life cycle features like retrieval date, origin/source, and validation status (assuring whether validated by public entities).

The technical metadata, referred as usability metadata, should include relevant information for automatic processing of retrieved data. For this purposes three service levels were defined:

- Level 1 – document;
- Level 2 – structured data;
- Level 3 – semantic data.

Level 1 applies if data is available as a document, a pdf for example.

The notation *"document"* in this context means access to data without possibility of content automatic treatment. This is a very low level interoperability stage, nevertheless, not absolutely useless. It allows download a document with a requested information. The same interoperability level can be reached if data is available in a manageable format retrieved by a third party application. This means that client, although not capable of access and manipulate data by itself, knows an application that may be used to that purpose. Associated metadata identifies the specific document format, allowing manipulation at application level.

Level 2 applies if data is retrieved *"as raw data"*, say as a XML file.

This allows a client application to reuse this data, if meaning is known, thus requesting specific development effort to cope with origin formats.

Associated metadata identifies formats, including data models if available. Typical scenario is a record formatted as XML, along with a XSD specification. This allows the client system to develop specific tools to handle data, say a HTML page to view data or a program to extract data into a database.

Level 3 applies if data is available along with pertinent semantic information.

For this purpose, the server system informs ontologies that apply to retrievable data. This may be proprietary, defined by a public entity, as well as standard, widely known ontologies. The key point is that no specific ontology is adopted. The data provider system just inform what ontologies it can apply to facilitate data reuse. This allows a client system to automatically extract data applying the used ontology. Whereas specific development effort to process non-standard data structures would be required if the data were provided according to the service level 2, in this level automatic processing is possible.

Naturally, the use of a standard and widely known ontologies is strongly advised. It seems consensual [1, 6] that using consolidated, independent and widespread ontologies may be a real step towards data interoperability.

The incremental approach proposed has as its ultimate goal, to achieve the provision of data using the existing and widespread ontologies aiming to increase the availability and usability of interoperable data.

5 System Description

5.1 Functional Description

A demo system, named DIP (data interoperability protocol) was developed to implement as proof of concept for the model.

The system is targeted to the following actual problem. The public administration implements several initiatives on co-financing of projects submitted by enterprises. The implementation of this mechanisms often involves the need for submission of forms by enterprises along the several stages of the process, carrying information like identification, contacts, enterprise activity data, and so on. Often, this same information is repeated on applications on different institutions, if not on different departments of the same institution. Support for data interoperability facilitates the implementation of data reuse mechanisms, minimizing duplication and redundancy.

On the other hand, institutions themselves are interested, and this right is granted by law, on accessing information that the enterprises provided to other public entity, for auditing and general information purposes.

Within this context, DIP targets two main application contexts. An institutional context that implements data access between public entities. In this context it is allowed that users from one institution, say A, accesses information that another institution B possesses about a given enterprise.

A second context implements a granted authorization by the enterprise user, to access own data in a public entity system. Thereby, on behalf of an enterprise user, is implemented the possibility of a public entity, owner of the system A, gather information from an external system B, for reuse in its own operation. For example filling an application form, on system A which requires information from external system B. It should be noted that this information is not public data. So each access must be supported on proper authorization. Institutional access is supported by law, however individual usage must be granted by the data owner.

The current versions of the system conveys the following record types:

- Entity description: name, address, activity, contacts, etc.;
- Balance sheet organized by year, both actual and predicted, in pdf file or structured data);
- Company history, in text format;
- Products and sales figures coded.

Although limited in extension, this set of record types include a wide range of data formats, including documents and structured data. Notice that similar data may occur in different formats, and therefore provided using different levels of service. For example to provide balance sheets, data may be available as pdf document or as XML data.

5.2   System Interconnection

System interconnection for entity crossover is straightforward. This type of interconnection requires previous setup at administrative level. Following this procedures, a specific cross connection is implemented between the systems.

On the other hand, individual reuse of data, should be possible with minor previous integration effort between organisations. It should be possible that a user at system A retrieves and reuses information at system B with no previous knowledge of the foreign system, taken that both convey to the basic DIP protocol. In this circumstances it should not only be possible to retrieve information in raw sense but also, if systems agree on common ontologies, process this information automatically.

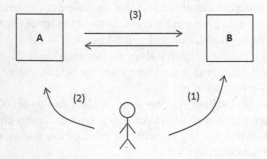

Fig. 1. System interconnection

For this purpose it is used a *"loosely coupled"* model for the system interconnection suggested in Fig. 1. Say a user in system A wants to access data in system B. The protocol goes like this:

(1) User issues a "credential" at system B.
(2) User registers this same "credential" at system A.
(3) System A issues a data request to system B, using the credential obtained in the step (2).

5.3 Query Model

An issued query takes the format of a URI: *http://(systemB)/dip/entity-list#id,* meaning "what information is available about entity Id".

The query access is certified by the credential, which was previously issued by system B. The data provider system responds with a catalog of available records on that entity. Each record is identified by a unique *id*. Retrieval for a specific record is available on an URI *http://(systemB)/dip/entity-record#rec-id.*

5.4 Business Metadata

Business metadata describes essential functional information. We developed a small utility business ontology and taxonomy to business domain, named *"dan"* from *"data annotation"*, including key aspects of business functionality.

The contents classification is carried out under the previously defined record types (Sect. 5.1). Each record is classified according to the following structure:

```
<dip:record-description about="id">
<dan:type>dan:Identification</dan:type>
```

Where *dip* tags the general name space of the interoperability proposed model and *dan* tags the business specific model. The *dan:type* tags record types value, which includes BalanceSheet, History and so on. In order to specify particular information, additional properties are defined depending of the record type. For instance if the record type is BalanceSheet the property year will be defined.

The *dan* namespace include fields for: origin identification, which describes how institution acquired data; date acquisition, representing when data was retrieved by organisation; and date validity, when data applies. Data origin is qualified as: "EntityInformation"- submitted by the entity as information; "EntityDeclaration" - submitted by the entity as formal declaration imposed by legal obligation; "PublicAdmin"- delivered from public administration services; or "ThirdPart". The data origin field has an additional property defining the "administrative quality" of data. The possible values for this property are: "Information" – the entity delivered data to public administration without commitment; "Declarative" – the entity delivered the information by legal imposition; or "Verified" – the data is endorsed by public administration.

This is an extension of record classification, intended only for demonstration purposes:

```
<dip:record-description about="id">
<dip:classification>dan</>
<dan:type>dan:Identification</dan:type>
<dan:origin>dan:EntitieDeclaration</dan:type>
<dan:date>2016-03-23</dan:date>
<dan:local-metadata>
  <dan:local-metadata-property>origin</>
  <dan:local-metadata-property-value>(application form on
call X)</>
  <dan:local-metadata-property-descritpion>(text descrip-
tion of property)</>
</dan:local-metadata>
<dan:local-metadata>
  <dan:local-metadata-property>contents</>
  <dan:local-metadata-property-value>partners </>
  <dan:local-metadata-property-descritpion>(includes en-
tities partners and group relationships)</>
</dan:local-metadata>
```

The use of *dip* ontology is required for protocol usage. Though the use of a specific business ontology is not required. Nevertheless, it is not expected that ontologies exists for every specific business environment and, on the other hand, it is difficult that general and abstract ontologies fulfil all the requirements of specific business areas.

However, public administration as a whole applies general rules of procedure and it might be possible that common vocabularies arise within consortiums of public entities, at national level or even at multinational levels [2]. If this happens, use of these ontologies is clearly preferable, as an alternative or complement.

The implemented system demonstrates the use of this business metadata. This is crucial mainly in the institutional context where users search for available information about a given entity. Metadata provides clues about each available records, and the user then proceeds, from that point, selecting the elements he finds of interest.

5.5 Level 1 Implementation

As indicated in Sect. 4, additionally to business metadata, each record is described in terms of interoperability, i.e. functional metadata. First item of this description is the "level of service" (described in Sect. 4.2).

Service level 1 indicates that the information is available as a document. Additional required information states if the document is provided by an application, allowing the client system to use it in the best possible way. The specification has a more functional intent than usual "myme type". At this point a simple taxonomy is used to qualify contents as "spreadsheet", "pdf", etc.

Actually, we considered this an area of future potential to work. It happens that in the context of the targeted specific business area there is a limited range of document formats. Although documents are generally closed to data extraction, they usually follow organizational standards. This might be exploited. There exists technological tools to deals with document contents: spread sheets, formatted text and even pdf. There is not, to our best knowledge, conceptual mechanisms to model internal contents. It seems possible to develop specific modeling of internal document contents thus depicting a way of extracting this information.

The implemented system uses level 1 services both at institutional and enterprise contexts.

At institutional level a general protocol for information viewing was implemented, using document classification type "html". This means the server provides an html file that might be "mounted" in a bowser or java application, for instance. This allows a client system to get a record in html and use it to directly show it in browser applications.

Actually, this constitutes a really useful functionality in the context of targeted business. Institutional access mainly deals with remote data consultation. It happens that institutions manipulates a lots of structured data, similar in concepts, but in different formats, codification, and so on. Although useful, it is a long process to proper classify all this different data structures in order to make them available according to a semantic classification. The simple possibility of having this information available, even only for viewing, in the local system with minor development effort is major breakthrough.

Enterprise interface uses this application level just for demonstration purposes, allowing the attachment a remote downloaded document when filling a local application form.

5.6 Level 2 Implementation

Level 2 implementation indicates that information is retrievable as structured data. The proposed *dip* classification indicates that further specification of data formats and data models are available. This earlier version of system implementation only uses XML and XSD files for that matter.

So, a record committed to services level 2 is enriched with the following properties:

```
<dip:record about=id>
<dip:service-level>2<>
<dip:service-level-description>stuctured-data<>
<dip:data-format>xml<>
<dip:data-model>xsd<>
```

This service level allows data to be processed in a model-dependent way. Client system must have previous knowledge of data semantics and develop specific procedures to benefit from data. Therefore, specific development effort is required.

System uses this model to implement a specific client/server interconnection between two systems, demonstrating import of remote data, available in XML, when filling a local application form. This requires specific development to convert and transfer data.

5.7   Level 3 Implementation

Level 3 implementation indicates that information is retrievable as structured data enriched with semantic information. The proposed *dip* classification indicates the specific ontologies applied.

System implementation on level 3 was developed just for record identification, which is the most general and structured record type handled by the system. In order to illustrate and demonstrate the proposed ideas, two different semantic models are used, one specially developed for this purpose and other using standard, well established and close-oriented to the target business environment.

A typical identification record includes fields like:

```
<id>….</id>
<name>…..</name>
<address>….</address>
```

Actually, there are several variations of these fields: different field list, field names, and so on. Implementation uses a specific business model, named *"eid"* and a wide-spread and well established ontology. The "E-Government Core Vocabulary" [10] was the ontology selected because it is closed to business environment – Core registered organisation.

A record deliverable in service level 3 is thus enriched with the information suggested by the following:

```
<dip:record about=id>
<dip:service-level>3</dip:service-level>
<dip:service-level-description>semantic-data</>
<dip:data-format>xml</>
<dip:data-model>xsd</>
<dip:semantic-annotation>(system)/eid</>
<dip:semantic-annotation>(core)</dip:semantic-annotation>
```

The data semantic is available in proprietary XML as well as in the named ontologies. Correspondent data is then noted as suggest d in the following:

```
<eid:id>….</edi:id>
<eid:name>…..</eid:name>
<eid:address>….</eid:address>
<core:LegalEntityIdentifier
>….</core:LegalEntityIdentifier>
<core:LegalEntityLegalName >….</core:
LegalEntityLegalName>
<core:LegalEntityRegisteredAddress >….</core:
LegalEntityRegisteredAddress >
```

This level of service is exploited in user interface. Within the process of filling a form application user may indicate an external system that is assumed to implement the *dip* protocol. The system is then queried for information available on a given entity. If data, specifically an identity record, is located with a recognized ontology classification, data is imported to the application form.

6 Conclusion

At time of paper writing the system described in Sect. 5 is implemented for evaluation purposes. The implementations makes clear that these ideas are feasible. Also demonstrates that it is possible to achieve useful results in data interoperability with minor development effort and with quite common, open source, technologies.

Furthermore, even mainly oriented to concept proof, the developed system is targeted in real environments and ready to be deployed in production environment after evaluation.

Meanwhile, the developed application is an earlier implementation and a lot of work is still do be done, both at conceptual, modeling and implementation level.

A few questions were pointed throughout the paper. The classification of contents at document level exchange, may be a major point of interest. For this purpose it requires minor effort on behalf of organisations to deliver documents and it may prove to be useful to data discovery and high level data manipulation.

The important question, however, is the further development of the purposed strategy for data interoperability and the associated models. The proposed model, being an earlier formulation, requires actual development and consolidation. It requires generalizations to cope with a more wide range of interoperability mechanisms. It requires additional operational skills, like service and data catalog discovery. Additionally it requires more elaborated models to cope with evolution from lower to higher level of interoperability and from specific to common and widespread ontologies.

References

1. Interoperability Solutions for European Public Administrations (ISA) - European Commission: European Interoperability Framework (EIF) - Towards Interoperability for European Public Services (2011). http://ec.europa.eu/isa
2. Interoperability Solutions for European Public Administrations (ISA) - European Commission: Federation of Semantic Assets Repositories - The SEMIC.EU approach, May 2011. http://ec.europa.eu/isa
3. W3C: Semantic Web (2016). https://www.w3.org/standards/semanticweb/. Accessed 2016
4. United Nations: United Nations e-Government Survey 2014 - E-Government for the future we want. United Nations Division for Public Administration and Development Management, New York (2014)
5. Peffers, K., Tuunanen, T., Rothenberger, M.A., Chatterjee, S.: A design science research methodology for information systems research. J. Manage. Inf. Syst. 24(3), 45–77 (2007-8)
6. Shukair, G., Loutas, N., Peristeras, V., Sklarß, S.: Towards semantically interoperable metadata repositories: the asset description metadata schema. Comput. Ind. 64(1), 10–18 (2013)
7. Malki, A., Barhamgi, M., Benslimane, S.-M., Benslimane, D., Malki, M.: Composing data services with uncertain semantics. IEEE Trans. Knowl. Data Eng. 27(4), 936–949 (2015)

8. Carey, M.J., Onose, N., Petropoulos, M.: Data services. Commun. ACM **55**(6), 86–97 (2012)
9. Kimball, R., Ross, M.: The Data Warehouse Toolkit: The Definitive Guide to Dimensional Modeling, 3rd edn. Wiley, New York (2013)
10. Interoperability Solutions for European Public Administrations (ISA) - European Commission: eGovernment Core Vocabularies, 5 May 2011. https://joinup.ec.europa.eu/sites/default/files/c1/23/4a/egovernment-core-vocabularies.pdf
11. W3C: Registered Organization Vocabulary. W3C Working Group, 1 August 2013. https://www.w3.org/TR/vocab-regorg/
12. European Union: e-Government Core Vocabularies handbook - Using horizontal data standards for promoting interoperability (2015). http://ec.europa.eu/social/publications

Italian Open and Big Data Strategy

Fernanda Faini[✉] and Monica Palmirani

CIRSFID - Interdepartmental Centre for Research in the History,
Philosophy and Sociology of Law and in Legal Informatics,
University of Bologna, Bologna, Italy
{fernanda.faini,monica.palmirani}@unibo.it

Abstract. In contemporary society, technology deeply changes our way of creating knowledge, making it active and dynamic. In light of that background, this contribution focuses on two key elements of knowledge creation, namely, *open data* and *big data*, highlighting their differences and their treatment under Italian law and discussing the projects and strategies developed in Italy. We will first look at *open government data*, whose ability to be reused enables them to act as tools for generating knowledge and offering new government services and products. We will then turn to *big data*, whose use carries complex legal and social consequences, and which also serve as a key tool for creating knowledge by making it possible to plot and forecast economic and social trends. We will finally consider the way *open data* and *big data* can be effectively used in combination to promote growth and forge an authentic *open government* in Italy.

Keywords: Big data · Open data · Public sector information · e-Government

1 Introduction

A distinguishing feature of the knowledge society lies in the central role played by the new technologies and by information and knowledge as key resources of economic, social, and cultural development. The Web of Data [3] is making an unprecedented amount of information available to us, and automated tools (e.g., the internet of things) has transformed our space into an *infosphere* where in humans are *hyperconnected* [12] and integrated in a way that was previously impossible. The growth of available information and the ease with which it can be accessed is profoundly changing our way of gaining and creating knowledge, transforming us in *prosumers* (at once producers and consumers) [26]. In this scenario, multichannel systems, the ability to access information using different sorts of devices, social media, cloud computing, and online applications collect *big data* defining our digital identity.

This *hyperhistory* [12] is having a profound effect on those who play a role in shaping digital society, especially where new actors, *inforgs*, are taking their place as new dominant agents next to government (thus, for example, according to the judgment the European Court of Justice rendered in *Google Spain*, C-131/12, EU:C:2014:317, Google is now an actor with the power to apply or not apply the right to be forgotten). The recent transition from *e-government* to *open government* makes government activity open to all and transparent, so as to make government itself more effective and accountable to

A. Kő and E. Francesconi (Eds.): EGOVIS 2016, LNCS 9831, pp. 105–120, 2016.
DOI: 10.1007/978-3-319-44159-7_8

the public. As suggested, *open government* relies on a wide and integrated use of the new technologies and recognizes a central role for citizens.[1] So, on the new open model framing government activity and the relation among government, citizens, and enterprises, a central role comes to be played by information and the knowledge it affords [19].

2   Open Data and Big Data

As noted in the previous Sect. 1, in the context just described a key role in shaping contemporary society is played by information, and specifically by *open data* and *big data*, making information active and dynamic, with the participation of public and private players alike. In this analysis we will therefore key in on the new information-and-knowledge configuration, looking in particular at *open data* and *big data*. We will discuss what they are and what they are used for, while analyzing their legal framework and the market implications of their use. The focus of the legal analysis will be on the Italian system, and we will accordingly discuss the projects and strategies the Italian government has developed in regard to *open data* and *big data*.

3   Open Data

3.1   What Is It and What Is It Used for

What is *open data*? According to the Open Knowledge Foundation,[2] content or data is open if anyone can use it, reuse it, and redistribute it, subject only to the condition that any further reuse or redistribution must take place on the same terms, and that the source may have to be acknowledged.

Open data can be created by private or public entities alike. Our focus here will be on the latter, whose data is specifically classified as *open government data* [5], but we will be using the more general term *open data*.

Open data are defined in Italian law under Article 68(3)(b) of Legislative Decree no. 82 of 7 March 2005, better known as CAD, short for Codice dell'Amministrazione Digitale (Digital Government Code), subsequently amended by (a) Law Decree no. 179 of 18 October 2012 (so-called Growth 2.0), amended and turned into Law no. 221 of 17 December 2012), and (b) Legislative Decree no. 102 of 18 May 2015. In this code, *open data* is described under three headings as a legal, a technological, and an economic concept:

- As a legal concept, it is data available under a license making it possible for anyone to use it, even for commercial purposes,
- As a technological concept, it is data that (*i*) can be accessed by information and communications technologies (ICT), including public and private networks, (*ii*) is

---

[1] *Open government* lays emphasis on horizontal participation, enabling a decision-making environment to emerge where the public and the private can collaboratively engage on an equal footing in a dialogue through which to govern with the contribution of all through the Internet.

[2] On the Web at http://okfn.org.

available in open formats, (*iii*) can automatically be used by software, and (*iv*) is equipped with metadata.

- As an economic concept, it is data made freely available by ICTs, including public and private networks, or it is made available at cost (the cost of reproduction and distribution). Exceptions are provided under Article 7 of Legislative Decree no. 36 of 24 January 2006, where the manner for setting fees is also described.

The reason why the law is interested in defining and regulating *open data* lies in the range of objectives that can be achieved by its use. In the first place, *open data* is a tool of government transparency and accountability, and in this way it makes for greater government efficiency, and it can also be used to fight corruption in government. This encourages citizens to place greater trust in government, while also participating in public affairs with a deeper sense of engagement.

In the second place, *open data* can be used to improve quality of life by enabling everyone to use, share, and compare it; at the same time, it can also be used to design better public policies, providing each jurisdiction with a competitive advantage.

Last but not least, *open data* can be used to support economic growth, considering that government data is highly valuable and can be reused to bring out new products and services. The value of the data increases with the increasing ability to use it to forge new knowledge and solutions for the benefit of the public. *Open data* can be made even more useful by designing apps and services developed by and for government, citizens, businesses, and the community, all of which can help drive economic development [23, 25, 28].

3.2   Legal Aspects and Market Implications

In recent years, *open government data* has been explicitly promoted by Italian lawmakers acting to implement EU directives.

The reuse of public sector documents was addressed in Italian law as early as with Legislative Decree 36/2006, transposing Directive 2003/98/EC (recently amended by Directive 2013/37/EU). Although public data was regarded in this decree as essential "raw material" for digital products and services, and as an economic and social asset, there was no provision in it requiring government agencies to make sure their data could be reused. Recently, Legislative Decree 102/2015 transposed Directive 2013/37/EU on *open data*. It did so amending Legislative Decree 36/2006 and introducing stronger *open data* obligations for government agencies, requiring them to ensure that government data can be reused for commercial or noncommercial purposes in keeping with the methods set out in the decree itself.

Articles 52 and 68 of Legislative Decree 82/2005 have been amended by the so-called Growth 2.0 Decree (Law Decree 179/2012, amended and converted into Law

221/2012) and recently also by Legislative Decree 102/2015. These provisions introduced the previously discussed definition of *open data*,[3] while setting out a general rule aimed at streamlining the process of turning public information into an asset. Specifically, Article 52 CAD provides that remote access to data, documents, and procedures, as well as the reuse of data and documents, be regulated by government agencies,[4] which are required to publish on their websites the catalogue of data and metadata and the relative databases in their possession, along with the rules governing their remote access and reuse, with the exception of data stored in fiscal registries (Art. 52(1) CAD).

The same code also introduces the significant principle of *open data* by default. This means that (a) all data a government agency releases in any way without any licence must be in an open format, with the single exception of personal data, and that (b), if any license is used, a reason for the decision must be provided in keeping with the national guidelines framed by the Agency for Digital Italy.[5]

Article 52(4) CAD seeks to ensure that the *open data* provisions can be meaningfully exercised. To this end it sets a managerial performance standard in light of which to judge the activities by which each government agency is to guarantee online access and reuse of its own public data, thus favouring *open data* in view of the objectives that can be achieved with this kind of data.

As far as governance is concerned, the provision seeks to leverage public information by attributing a key role the Agency for Digital Italy, an agency charged with ensuring compliance with *open data* legislation, while also guiding other government agencies through the process of making their data open (Art. 52(5–7) CAD).

In this body of law we also find Legislative Decree no. 33 of 14 March 2013,[6] which under Article 7, significantly titled "Open Data and Its Reuse," introduces the principle that all data, documents, and information subject to mandatory publication must be released in

---

[3] They also define open format data, meaning data available in a public, fully documented, and portable format (Art. 68(3)(a) of Legislative Decree 82/2005, replaced by Article 9 of Legislative Decree 179/2012, modified and enacted into Law 221/2012), and they also define the concept of reuse as the use of data pursuant to Article 2(1)(e) of Legislative Decree 36/2006: Reuse means that data held by a public body can in turn be used by natural or legal persons for commercial or noncommercial purposes other than its initial public purpose (Art. 1(1)(n-bis) of Legislative Decree 82/2005; the definition was inserted by way of Art. 9 of Law Decree 179/2012, amended and enacted into Law 221/2012).

[4] This obligation applies to all entities referred to in Article 2(2) of Legislative Decree 82/2005 (CAD).

[5] Art. 52(2) CAD. Further, Art. 52(3) CAD, provides that in drawing up public procurement contracts for products or services entailing the collection and management of public data, government authorities must include clauses enabling all natural and legal persons to remotely access and reuse that data, along with the relative metadata and databases.

[6] Legislative Decree 33/2013 absorbs provisions such as Art. 18 of Law Decree no. 83 of 22 June 2012, amended and enacted into Law no. 134 of 7 August 2012. The decree repeals Art. 18 (replacing it with its own Arts. 26 and 27), which singles out specific kinds of public information as particularly relevant (this applies to any kind of subsidy, payment, or financial aid provided to businesses, professionals, private organizations, or public bodies), requiring government agencies to make such data available in an open format subject to penalties for failure to do so.

an open format, and it must be possible to reuse them without further restrictions other than the requirement that they be sourced and their integrity be maintained [2, 10].

In making public information open, the government needs to also take into account legal exemptions and restrictions aimed at protecting interests such as secret of state, statistical confidentiality, copyright, and public security. Particularly difficult in this regard is the balance that needs to be struck between *open data* and the protection of personal data, especially in light of the Data Protection Guidelines of 15 May 2014 [13], under which data published online cannot be freely used by anyone for any purpose, and personal data can be reused in ways consistent with the purpose for which it was originally collected, and in keeping with data protection laws. Indeed, according to the Italian Data Protection Authority, the requirement that public government data be published in an open format does not mean that the same data is itself open: It is not data that can be used by anyone for any purpose, for otherwise the right to the protection of personal data would be undermined.[7] The Data Protection Authority also prohibits the reuse of sensitive and judicial data, and any personal data other than the kinds listed in Legislative Decree 33/2013 needs to be anonymized, in such a way that the person the data is referred to cannot later be identified, not even indirectly. Furthermore, under the Data Protection Guidelines, the obligation of all-purpose search engines (such as Google) to index data for a set term is limited to the data specified in the rules on transparency (and for no other purpose), and no sensitive or judicial data may be indexed (meaning that they won't turn up in any of these search engines).

Apart from these legal constraints, it also bears mentioning that *open government data* lacks any uniformity. This may be problematic from a market perspective, since not all data that might be available on the market is open—or it might be open in different formats or under different licenses, or the metadata might not be consistent—and this undermines the ability to reuse the data for commercial purposes.

3.3 Italian Strategies and Projects

Italy is particularly active in the push toward *open data*.

In 2011, the Italian government applied for membership in the international Open Government Partnership (OGP), which is aimed at promoting transparent government through the active participation of citizens, trade associations, and businesses. In the same year the government also launched a national *open data* portal (www.dati.gov.it). Then, in 2013, it adhered to the international G8 initiative called Open Data Charter, which is aimed at taking the data held and managed by national government agencies and making it available in an open format, so as to enable easy access to it by citizens and businesses. Under the Open Data Charter, open government data is to adhere to five strategic principles under the following headings: (1) *open data* by default; (2) quality and quantity; (3) usable by all; (4) releasing data for improved governance; and (5) releasing data for innovation.

---

[7] For this reason the National Data Protection guidelines require government agencies a notice to that effect under the "Administrative Transparency" section of their websites.

Even the regions in Italy are actively promoting strategies for open public data, and many of these regions have rules specifically devoted to *open data*. In 2010, Piedmont was the first region to release its public information by creating a regional *open data* portal (www.dati.piemonte.it). Furthermore, under Regional Law no. 24 of 23 December 2011, Piedmont enacted some provisions anticipating those passed by the national government, whose *open data* legislation did not get underway until 2012. The Piedmont example was followed in 2011 by Emilia-Romagna Region, which set up its own *open data* portal (http://dati.emilia-romagna.it). Subsequently, *open data* provisions and portals were introduced in Lombardy,[8] Lazio,[9] Apulia,[10] and the autonomous Province of Trento.[11] This happened in 2012, the same year in which the central government began to pass its own laws in this matter; in 2014, regional *open data* provisions and strategies were enacted in Friuli Venezia Giulia[12] and Umbria;[13] in 2015, the same happened in Marche,[14] Tuscany,[15] and Veneto.[16] Other Italian regions that have developed *open data* strategies and portals are Liguria,[17] Basilicata,[18] and Sardinia.[19]

In keeping with Article 14(2-bis) CAD, each regional law on *open data* entrusts the regional government with promoting an effort to digitize public data by cooperating with other regional and local governments toward a uniform *open data* standard across the national territory. For this reason, the regional laws lay emphasis on measures designed to enable governments to organize both among and within regions and to accordingly carry the *open data* plan into execution: This will not only support government agencies in achieving compliance and meeting their responsibility, but will also help consumers become digitally savvy and play an active role in maintaining a constant dialogue with government agencies. Since it is citizens and businesses that will be reusing the data, it is important to learn from them in figuring out which data needs to be made open and what products and services can be brought to life by relying on *open data*. As suggested, the regions also have an important role to play vis-à-vis local governments and other public bodies across the territory, by providing them with the tools and guidance needed to get *open data* strategies off the ground.

National and regional laws and strategies concerned with *open data*, and more broadly *open government*, integrate in a virtuous synergy enabling the national government to lay

---

[8] The portal is www.dati.lombardia.it, and the law is Regional Law no. 7 of 18 April 2012.

[9] The portal is https://dati.lazio.it/, and the law is Regional Law no. 7 of 18 June 2012.

[10] The portal is http://www.dati.puglia.it, and the law is Regional Law no. 20 of 24 July 2012.

[11] The portal is http://dati.trentino.it, and the law is Provincial Law no. 16 of 27 July 2012.

[12] The portal is www.dati.friuliveneziagiulia.it, and the law is Regional Law no. 7 of 17 April 2014.

[13] The portal is http://dati.umbria.it, and the law is Regional Law no. 9 of 29 April 2014.

[14] The portal is http://goodpa.regione.marche.it, and the law is Regional Law no. 9 of 29 April 2014.

[15] The portal is http://open.toscana.it (data section), and the law is Regional Law no. 19 of 18 February 2015.

[16] The portal is http://dati.veneto.it, and the law is Regional Law no. 2 of 24 February 2015.

[17] The portal is http://www.regione.liguria.it/opendata.html.

[18] The portal is http://dati.regione.basilicata.it.

[19] The portal is http://opendata.regione.sardegna.it.

out clear and homogeneous rules and regional governments to play a leading role in coordinating in digitizing administrative activity across the territories [11].

Even Italian users (meaning citizens, organizations, and private firms) are especially concerned with *open data*, and have accordingly developed some very useful projects. One example is Monithon (www.monithon.it), a bottom-up platform enabling communities to monitor projects funded under cohesion policies using the data stored on the Open Coesione portal.[20] Another example is the ConfiscatiBene platform,[21] a collaborative project designed to collect and analyze data on property confiscated from organized crime and to keep an eye on the same property.

4 Big Data

4.1 What Is It and What Is It Used for

In the March 2013 Opinion on Purpose Limitation, issued on 2 April 2013, Article 29 of the Data Protection Working Party defines *big data* as massive datasets that are held by large organizations (such as governments and multinational corporations), come from a variety of sources, and are analyzed using specific software algorithms and technologies. There are different types of *big data*: structured and nonstructured, user-generated and personal. The distinguishing features of *big data* can be described under five [9] main headings as follows:

- Volume: The data can be captured, memorized, and accessed in huge quantities.
- Speed: The data can be analyzed in real time or at high speed, so much so that it soon becomes obsolete.
- Variety: The data comes from a variety of sources, and different types of it exist (it can be structured or nonstructured, for example).
- Veracity: The quality and accuracy of *big data*.
- Value: How much *big data* is worth as an asset.

In *big data* we may therefore find voluntarily offered data (as on Facebook, Twitter, or LinkedIn), data that is "traded" for a return (as in the case of trading stamps, coupons, loyalty cards, and various discounts), data that users give up more or less consciously (banking transactions, GPS data sent out by mobile devices, biometric readers), and data requested by public authorities.

Unlike what is the case with *open data*, *big data* has no definition in Italian law.

The interest in *big data* lies in its potentially huge economic value [1], which can be appreciated from its description and the multiple uses it can be put to. But an important caveat is in order here: *Big data* strategies do not as yet make it possible to know in advance what the data will or may be used for once it is collected [20, 27].

If there is one overarching objective that *big data* supports, that would have to consist in the additional information and knowledge it makes it possible to generate. Within that broad range, and precisely on account of the distinguishing features of *big data*, this

---

[20] On the Web at http://www.opencoesione.gov.it.
[21] On the Web at http://www.confiscatibene.it/it.

data can be used to predict needs, profile users, monitor consumers, and support organizations in their decision-making. Particularly interesting in that regard, and the reason why *big data* attracts so much attention, is the predictive capacity that can be extracted from this data once it is appropriately analyzed. So it can be used to predict political outcomes or market trends, or indeed whatever the object of analysis is. As can be appreciated, this aspect of *big data* makes it a socially, politically, and strategically crucial resource, promising to deliver great competitive advantage to firms and governments that make use of it [4, 20, 30]. The qualifier *big* therefore describes not only the data itself but also the objectives that can be pursued with it, and these objectives attract the interest of both the public and the private sector [21, 22].

4.2   Legal Aspects and Market Implications

Just as *big* describes the volumes that *big data* comes in and the aims it makes possible, so the adjective can also describe the legal issues and market implications of its use. And as is the case with *open data*, so with *big data* the biggest legal issues come up in relation to data protection. The legal framework hasn't quite caught up with the technology: Even the proposed EU regulation neglects to explicitly address *big data*.[22]

4.2.1   Privacy Dilemma

In Italy in particular, the use of *big data* comes up against the principle governing the *purpose* for which data may be collected and processed under data protection law,[23] considering that *big data* strategies often do not make it possible to know in advance what the expected result of its use might be, and this is also a problem when it comes to the privacy notice and the informed consent the law requires in connection with the use of personal data. These difficulties threaten to undermine the legitimacy of practices through which personal data is processed. A promising tool in dealing with that difficulty is that of privacy by design, along with the so-called data protection impact assessment—both contained in the EU regulation proposal, and both aimed at dealing with data protection risk *ex ante*, that is, before the risk can even materialize. If we are going to use *big data* as a matter of course, we will need to set out the legitimate objectives of that use, coupled with policy guidelines, an obligation to post a privacy notice, and indeed an entire regulatory framework. We will also have to guarantee that the information extracted from the processing of *big data* meets certain quality and security standards: This can be done by regulating the technology, requiring compliance with specific protocols designed to avert the risk of human exposure [18, 29]. In this endeavour, however, we need to take into

---

[22]   COM (2012) 11: Proposal for a Regulation of the European Parliament and of the Council on the Protection of individuals with regard to the processing of personal data and on the free movement of such data (General Data Protection Regulation).

[23]   Under Article 11(1)(b) of Legislative Decree no. 196 of 30 June 2003, personal data may be collected and stored only for explicit, determinate, and legitimate purposes, and any other processing of the same data needs to me consistent with such purposes.

account the geopolitical situation involving the different ways in which different countries address data protection in the law, a case in point being the different approaches taken in the United States and Europe.[24]

4.2.2   Accuracy and Anonymization for Big Data Value

The quality of *big data* depends on the ability it affords to trace out unexpected relationships among data and thus profile the future behaviour of people (e.g., mobility in the city) or to predict events in society (e.g., epidemics). These correlations reveal more than the holder of the data can expect to find on the basis of the originally provided single isolated dataset. *"Big data applications may find spurious correlations in data even in cases where there is no direct cause and effect between two phenomena that show a close correlation"* [8]. The technical analysis is an approximation process, and there is the risk of drawing inaccurate and discriminatory conclusions. As far as the market is concerned, we have the problem of how accurate and reliable *big data* is in its predictive capacity. The information overload that comes with such high volumes of data does not necessarily translate into knowledge: In order to turn the noise into a signal we have to make sure that we are appropriately contextualizing, analyzing, and interpreting the massive data at our disposal.[25]

The UK government [16] claims that *big data* combined with personal data are a minor portion of the large volume of data, and this does not bode well for innovation. However, it is also true that *big data* analysis could achieve a de-identification of anonymized data through the "mosaic effect" [9] (e.g., neutral data like traffic), making it possible to disclose a person's identity and the connected behaviour (such as the person's daily movement).

In this scenario data mining, predictive algorithms, and data analysis techniques do not give us foreknowledge of which new information can be detected or inferred and which conclusions can be drawn; therefore, any prior information consent under the current legislative framework will prove inadequate. The recent European General Data Protection Regulation (GDPR) does not provide specific principles for managing the *big data* conundrum of bringing benefits to society and the market, while protecting the privacy of individuals [8].

At the current state of the art, some technical mechanisms could make it possible to at least guarantee that personal data is anonymized[26] (e.g., K-anonymity and differential privacy); however, those best practices are not transparent and cannot easily be audited by neutral third parties. Secondly, the anonymization process in any case requires complete for a given timeframe, and the temporary processing of the data is a vulnerable and critical step in the anonymization chain. It is also clear that in this context the *right to be forgotten* is difficult and costly to achieve [8].

---

[24] See the broader discussion in A. Mantelero [20].

[25] See in that regard A. Mantelero [20] pointing out that information overload may even *impair* knowledge, considering the risk of confusing our sources and failing to judge their reliability.

[26] On the Web at https://www.enisa.europa.eu/publications/big-data-protection.

4.2.3   Ownership of Big Data and Antitrust Strategy

Another legal issue is that of ownership, meaning Who "owns" the data contained in the massive volumes of *big data*? Under copyright law, digital content always belongs to someone, even if we may not be able to determine or agree on who that is (as in the example of platforms such as Facebook), and this, too, may be a problem, depending on the kind of data being collected. Nor should we forget, in that regard, the protection the law provides for "noncreative" databases, in which we can include the datasets making up collections of *big data*. And equally important is the correlative protection of the *sui generis* database right, where we also have to address the discrepancy between EU and US law.[27]

Another problem is the ownership of the new data produced by combining different sets of *big data* originally collected from individuals or from third parties. If we have to work out the intellectual propriety rights of the original resources, the problem is how to ascribe ownership of the new data emerging from the mash-up of those datasets. Companies often claim the property of those new data as their own business asset, but a competition law and data report put out on 10 May 2016 by the German Bundeskartellamt (Federal Cartel Office, or FCO) and the French Autorité de la Concurrence (French Competition Authority) underlines the risk of violating antitrust rules. The *big data* picked up by large companies under the "network effect" [15] can become a prized element for dominant players on the market, and this creates a high risk of discrimination in the use of data, with barriers of access of those data. An alliance between the private and public sectors could make it possible to avoid the privatization of "data sovereignty" locked in proprietary databases, and in the meantime this could guarantee fair access and free market competition.

4.2.4   Information Asymmetry

Another issue where the market is concerned lies in the information asymmetry [24] that *big data* may engender by giving data processors an undue information power over consumers and small to medium enterprises. This is because it is only a handful of large corporations that collect and process *big data*, creating a class of "data overlords"[28] in possession of information that everyone else lacks.

On top of that comes the issue of social control. Public authorities can use private databases to support the decision-making and political forecasting, and even though they do not engage in direct monitoring, they could even use Google, Facebook, and the like, whose information is held on a contractual basis. This amounts to indirect control, in which data is sourced from large gatherers of private data, leading to a form of social control that may drive a wedge between the governing and the governed—precisely the opposite of what *open government* is trying to achieve.

---

[27] Cf. M. Bogni, A. Defant [1] pointing out that the use of *big data* may also give rise to IP protection and confidentiality issues.

[28] The term is used in A. Mantelero [20].

4.3   Italian Strategies and Projects

A few particularly interesting *big data* projects are underway in Italy. Here we will look at some of the most recent and significant ones.

In 2013, recognizing that *big data* gathered from different sources and structured in different ways can have a considerable bearing on official statistics, the Italian National Institute of Statistics (ISTAT) set up an investigative panel charged with advising ISTAT itself on the question of *big data* [17], so as to enable the agency to set medium- and long-term goals on the effective use of *big data* in putting out official statistics. The panel accordingly laid out a roadmap supporting the production of official statistics. The Italian Data Protection Authority has also issued specific guidelines in that regard, authorizing ISTAT to analyze *big data* gathered from mobile devices for the purpose of compiling national statistics [14].

Another Italian project that holds great promise is Km4city,[29] developed by the Information Engineering Department of the University of Florence. This is a platform that aggregates open, private, static, and dynamic data, some of it updated in real time, pertaining to Tuscany and the areas in and around cities like Florence and Empoli. The platform collects data from various portals in Tuscany and the *open data* held by various municipalities in the region, first among them Florence, interconnecting all this data so as to enable users to query it in ways that would not otherwise be possible. Km4City is an innovative platform—being interoperable, enabling "smart" querying of the data, and supporting applications for private and public use alike—and as such it provides a unified system on which basis to develop a "knowledge-making model" for the city of Florence and its environs, guide decision-making, optimize services, support the growth of the local economy, improve the life of the community, and develop further applications. The data the project aggregates includes the regional roadway network, weather data from LAMMA,[30] the *open data* held by the City of Florence, traffic management data (geolocalization of public transit vehicles, parking, traffic flow), events across the city, digital locations in Florence, and regional online services.[31] An application has been developed using Km4City services and APIs: It is called "Km4city: Firenze dove, cosa" (Km4City Florence: Where and When), enabling users to see all services available near their current location and move about in the city in search of establishments, bathrooms, Wi-Fi access points, bike paths, parks, digital locations, ATMs, parking spaces, and pharmacies, among other things, while also checking for arrival times on selected bus lines. The positioning services available through the application also cover historic sites, hospitals, the weather, and power lines, among many other resources, providing images, audio, and textual information. The full list of accessible data is available on the Web:[32] It comprises some 100,000 services in Florence, Pisa, Prato, Pistoia, Arezzo, and Empoli; these services span across the entire Tuscany Region, with a focus on the province of Florence.

---

[29] On the Web at http://www.disit.org/km4city.

[30] LAMMA is a consortium between Tuscany Region and Italy's National Research Centre (CNR), and its focus is on meteorology, climate science, geographic information systems, and geology. On the Web at www.lamma.rete.toscana.it.

[31] Accessible through the Website http://servicemap.disit.org.

[32] At http://www.disit.org/6726.

Another strategic project is Sii-Mobility, supporting integrated interoperability for citizen services and government agencies.[33] This is a national smart-city project cofinanced by MIUR (the Italian Ministry of Research and Higher Education), jointly developed and coordinated by various research centres and firms with the support of several government agencies, so as to conduct tests on the ground in Tuscany and other Italian regions. It relies in part on *big data* and was launched on 1 January 2016. Sii-Mobility uses new technologies and social media platforms so as to improve urban mobility and optimize citizen services. The project will develop solutions for managing transport and mobility systems and offering information and services to citizens, businesses, and government agencies.

Still another project is RESOLUTE H2020 (RESilience management guidelines and Operationalization appLied to Urban Transport Environment).[34] Its purpose is to improve urban transport in European cities facing emergency situations, drawing up guidelines to that end and testing them in Florence and Athens. The project will assess the state of the art in the matter of urban resilience, and on this basis it will develop models and simulations with which to improve emergency preparedness. Km4City can be used to that end to develop flexible models that take into account factors such as whether the emergency strikes during the day or the night, whether large public gatherings are underway, and whether schools are open or closed. The project is spearheaded by the Engineering Information Department of the University of Florence. It was started in June 2015 and is financed under the European programme Horizon 2020.

Finally, Italy is at the helm of the European project SoBigData,[35] which got underway in 2015 and "proposes to create the *Social Mining & Big Data Ecosystem*: a research infrastructure (RI) for ethic-sensitive scientific discoveries and advanced applications of social data mining to the various dimensions of social life, as recorded by '*big data*.' Building on several established national infrastructures, SoBigData will open up new research avenues in multiple research fields, including mathematics, ICT, and human, social and economic sciences, by enabling easy comparison, re-use and integration of state-of-the-art big social data, methods, and services, into new research. It will not only strengthen the existing clusters of excellence in social data mining research, but also create a pan-European, inter-disciplinary community of social data scientists, fostered by extensive training, networking, and innovation activities. In addition, as an open research infrastructure, SoBigData promotes repeatable and open science. Although SoBigData is primarily aimed at serving the needs of researchers, the openly available datasets and open source methods and services provided by the new research infrastructure will also impact industrial and other stakeholders (e.g. government bodies, non-profit organisations, funders, policy makers). [...] The mission of the European Laboratory on *Big Data* Analytics and Social Mining is to perform advanced research and analyses on the emerging challenges posed by *big data*, namely the digital breadcrumbs of human activities continually sensed by the ICT systems that people use. The extreme detail of these data is surprising and, ultimately, they are at the heart of the very

---

[33] On the Web at www.sii-mobility.org.

[34] On the Web at http://www.resolute-eu.org.

[35] On the Web at http://www.sobigdata.eu.

idea of a knowledge society." The SoBigData consortium joins twelve partners from six EU member states: Italy, the UK, Germany, Estonia, Finland, the Netherlands, and Switzerland.[36] The project is headed by the Pisa CNR and is financed under a four-year, 6-million-euro grant from the Horizon programme.

Also worthy of mention is the European project BYTE,[37] with the participation of the Rome CNR and the Institute of Atmospheric Pollution Research.[38] The project investigates the benefits and barriers of *big data* in six vertical domains: healthcare, environment, oil and gas, cultural heritage, crisis informatics, and smart cities. Two years into the project, the analysis has shown the environmental and oil-and-gas domains to be the most advanced by judging by volume, speed, and value. No privacy issues have emerged, even though a harmonized national regulation in the sector could go a long way toward facilitating data sharing. The healthcare, crisis informatics, and smart cities domains are very promising but held back by privacy and unresolved legal issues. The cultural heritage sector could in principle be free of privacy issues if the effort to further harmonize it under a common framework regulation (such as PSI) were carried forward, but it is not mature enough from the technical and organization point of view.

In the education sector, MIUR is promoting a *big data* group through a decree[39] aimed at mapping all existing *big data* collections in universities and research centres so as to work out a strategy for improving the education and research system in Italy.

4.4   Private-Public Partnerships on Big Data

When open government data meets the *data*, we need a Private-Public Partnership (or PPP) strategy. In Italy, Telecom[40] and ENEL[41] are releasing a big dataset using the *open data* method, and so is Gestore Servizi Energetici (GES)[42] in public utility companies. Analysis in the internet-of-things sector underlines the fact that *big data* plays a major role, especially in *domotic* (e.g., *Energy@Home* coalition),[43] where the public-private partnership is strong, as well as in smart cities. Emilia-Romagna Region has set up an excellence centre on *big data* including several players in the private and public sectors. This means that PPP in *big data* could be the right solution for serving society while creating a sustainable ecosystem for a responsible business model based on human dignity.

---

[36] The full description of the project is available at www.sobigdata.eu.

[37] On the Web at http://byte-project.eu/.

[38] On the Web at http://www.iia.cnr.it/?lang=en.

[39] On the Web at http://blog.debiase.com/wp-content/blogs.dir/8328/files/2012/05/Decreto-GdL-Big-Data.pdf.

[40] On the Web at http://www.telecomitalia.com/tit/it/bigdatachallenge.html.

[41] On the Web at http://data.enel.com/blog/open-data-and-big-data?language=en.

[42] On the Web at http://opendata.gse.it/opendata/.

[43] On the Web at http://www.energy-home.it/SitePages/Home.aspx.

4.5 New Digital Ethics and Big Data

In this scenario, where the normative framework proves limited in its ability to keep abreast of technology, the PPP ecosystem can mitigate risks on a mutual monitoring model where (i) government agencies monitor businesses to make sure they are complying with privacy rules designed to protect citizens in the effort to use *big data* to improve the quality of life and services, and (ii) businesses push government to develop a coherent antitrust strategy for guaranteeing fair competition. The entire process has to be supervised by neutral parties (e.g., Data Protection Officer) applying regulations, and it should also balance the interest of society in promoting knowledge against the individual right to privacy. The Data Protection Office role may not be enough. The European Data Protection Supervisor has launched a new initiative called "New Digital Ethics" [7]: It is based on an interdisciplinary and "more holistic approach to enforcement" [6], and it could ensure a proper balance among economic growth, privacy, and innovation. Like the European Data Protection Supervisor, so also other European and non-European countries are working out *big data* strategies (e.g., UK Big Data Dilemma [16], Australian Big Data Strategy)[44] by introducing the Council of Data Ethics. Italy is not yet working on any similar strategy, and it risks being a latecomer in providing a proper framework for this asset of great importance to citizens' quality of life and to the economy.

5 Conclusions

From the foregoing analysis of *open data* and *big data*—the two main tools that are driving change in the contemporary information society—we can arrive at the conclusion of a misalignment between law and technology, meaning what technology allows us to do as a matter of fact is not always allowed as a matter of law. This suggests a need to design a new *ad hoc* system of rules superseding the traditional paradigms, no longer adequate to the task of dealing with the implications of the new technology. Moreover, a new holistic approach based on "new digital ethic" is necessary.

In light of public sector move toward *open government*, we can envision a synergistic use of *open data* and *big data* so as to foster growth and establish a new relationship between government and the private sector (PPP), thus protecting the freedoms of citizens and the *sovereignty of data* for future generations.

To this end, and in order to even out the information asymmetry, we would propose a "free pass" at the time data is collected, after which point data is to be released in an open format, in such a way as to move away from the "closed data" management we are all too accustomed to [20]. We could, in other words, work toward the idea of "*open big data*." This would open countless possibilities, making

---

[44] On the Web at http://www.finance.gov.au/archive/big-data/.

it possible to level the information asymmetries we are currently subject to, even if that inevitably means taking power away from governments and large corporations.[45]

References

1. Bogni, M., Defant, A.: Big data: diritti IP e problemi della privacy. Il Diritto industriale, Ipsoa, vol. 2, pp. 117–126 (2015)
2. Carloni, E. (ed.): L'amministrazione aperta. Regole strumenti e limiti dell'open government. Orizzonti di diritto pubblico. Maggioli, Rimini (2014)
3. Castells, M.: The Rise of the Network Society. Oxford University Press, Oxford (2000)
4. De Pasquale, D.: La linea sottile tra manipolazione della rete e pubblicità. Il Diritto industriale, Ipsoa, vol. 6, p. 552ff (2012)
5. Di Donato, F.: Lo stato trasparente Linked open data e cittadinanza attiva. Edizioni ETS, Pisa (2011)
6. European Data Protection Supervisor: Privacy and competitiveness in the age of big data, preliminary opinion (2014)
7. European Data Protection Supervisor: Opinion 4/2015, Towards a new digital ethics, 11 September 2015
8. European Data Protection Supervisor: Opinion 7/2015, Meeting the challenges of big data, 19 November 2015
9. European Union Agency for Network and Information Security (ENISA): Privacy by design in big data, December 2015
10. Faini, F.: Trasparenza, apertura e controllo democratico dell'amministrazione pubblica. Ciberspazio e Diritto, Mucchi editore, Modena, vol. 1, pp. 39–70 (2014)
11. Faini, F.: Italian open government strategy in national and regional regulation. In: Kö, A., Francesconi, E. (eds.) EGOVIS 2015. LNCS, vol. 9265, pp. 271–286. Springer, Heidelberg (2015)
12. Floridi, L.: The Fourth Revolution – How the Infosphere is Reshaping Human Reality. Oxford University Press, Oxford (2014)
13. Garante per la protezione dei dati personali (Italian Data Protection Authority): Linee guida in materia di trattamento di dati personali, contenuti anche in atti e documenti amministrativi, effettuato per finalità di pubblicità e trasparenza sul web da soggetti pubblici e da altri enti obbligati, Rule No. 243, 15 May 2014 (Official Gazette No. 134, 12 June 2014), doc. web 3134436 (2014)
14. Garante per la protezione dei dati personali (Italian Data Protection Authority): Opinion no. 411, 18 September 2014 on the 2014–16 PSN, 2015–16 update, doc. web 3458502 (2014)
15. German Bundeskartellamt (Federal Cartel Office or FCO) and the French Autorité de la concurrence (French Competition Authority): Competition Law and Data (Report), 10th May 2016
16. House of Commons, Science and Technology Committee: The Big Data Dilemma: Government Response to the Committee's Fourth Report of Session 2015–16

---

[45] In that regard, A. Mantelero [20] suggests some tools that may be useful in reining in the information power wielded by the coterie of "data overlords." These tools include the ability to freely access and share information, empowering a plurality of players, and supra-national oversight bodies. A. Mantelero himself stresses the key role that *open data* can play in making information accessible.

17. Istituto Nazionale di Statistica (ISTAT - Italian National Institute of Statistics): Resolution no. 20/PRES, 14 February 2013
18. Kemp, R.: Legal aspects of managing big data. Comput. Law Secur. Rev. **30**(5), 482–491 (2014)
19. Lathrop, D., Ruma, L.: Open Government: Collaboration, Transparency, and Participation in Practice. O'Reilly Media Inc., Sebastopol (2010)
20. Mantelero, A.: Big data: i rischi della concentrazione del potere informativo digitale e gli strumenti di controllo. In: Il Diritto dell'informazione e dell'informatica, vol. 1, pp. 135–144. Giuffrè, Milano (2012)
21. Marr, B.: Big Data: Using Smart Big Data Analytics and Metrics To Make Better Decisions and Improve Performance. Wiley, New York (2015)
22. Mayer-Schonberger, V., Cukier, K.: Big Data: A Revolution that Will Transform How We Live, Work, and Think. Houghton Mifflin Harcourt, New York (2013)
23. Mockus, M., Palmirani, M.: Open government data licensing framework. In: Kö, A., Francesconi, E. (eds.) EGOVIS 2015. LNCS, vol. 9265, pp. 287–301. Springer, Heidelberg (2015)
24. Organisation for Economic Cooperation and Development (OECD): Data-Driven Innovation: Big Data for Growth and Well-Being, OECD Publishing, Paris (2015)
25. Palmirani, M., Martoni, M., Girardi, D.: Open government data beyond transparency. In: Kö, A., Francesconi, E. (eds.) EGOVIS 2014. LNCS, vol. 8650, pp. 275–291. Springer, Heidelberg (2014)
26. Rifkin, J.: La società a costo marginale zero. Mondadori, Milano (2015)
27. Sartor, G., De Azevedo Cunha, M.V.: Il caso Google e i rapporti regolatori USA/EU. Il Diritto dell'informazione e dell'informatica, vol. 4–5, p. 657ff (2014)
28. Tiscornia, D. (ed.): Open data e riuso dei dati pubblici. Informatica e diritto, nos. 1–2 (2011)
29. Williamson, A.: Big data and the implications for government. Legal Inf. Manage. **14**(4), 253–257 (2014)
30. Yiu, C.: The Big Data Opportunity: Making Government Faster, Smarter and More Personal. Policy Exchange, London (2012)

Knowledge Representation
and Modeling in E-Government

Using a Citizen Language in Public Process Models: The Case Study of a Brazilian University

Luiz Paulo Carvalho, Flávia Santoro, and Claudia Cappelli[✉]

Departamento de Informática Aplicada,
Universidade Federal do Estado do Rio de Janeiro - UNIRIO, Rio de Janeiro, Brazil
{luiz.paulo.silva,flavia.santoro,claudia.cappelli}@uniriotec.br

Abstract. Increasingly information transparency becomes necessary in public organizations. Either due to the imposition of laws and decrees, or to the yearning for the society. In addition to information, business processes are equally important, responsible for all the treatment and processing of information in the organization. It is important not only know the information, but the way it was generated. Providing transparency of business processes requires presenting their operating models in which are explicit the actors involved, the activities carried out and the rules that support them, among other types of information. Currently the notations used to represent process models are extremely technical, consequently difficult to understand by ordinary citizens. It seems not sufficient to provide transparency. This paper presents a case study of using a transformation method that aims to make the process easier to understand for citizens and the result shows that laypeople understand most the citizen language than technical notations. In addition, experiences, collected during the execution of a case study, illustrate the method.

Keywords: Transparency · Process understandability · Process modeling

1 Introduction

A number of laws have been signed to guarantee the transparency within organizations. Sarbanes-Oxley [1], BASEL - Basel Committee on Banking Supervision [2], EITI – Extractive Industries Transparency Initiative [3] and the Open Government Partnership - OGP [4] are some examples. In Brazil, the Transparency Law [5] and the Access Law [6] guide public organizations toward publishing information. But, besides giving information access, to be transparent, organizations have to guarantee among other things citizens understanding about what is happening inside the organization and how information is generated and used [7].

Business process models can be artifacts to be used in this case. They can help with this because they comprise important information about organizational processes (ex: actors, sequence of activities, rules, inputs and outputs) [8]. To represent business process models, organizations in general use a methodology [9] and a language (ex: BPMN, EPC, Petri net). However, it is not inherent to citizens, knowledge about these technical notations and diagrams interpretation suggested by processes modeling

© Springer International Publishing Switzerland 2016
A. Kő and E. Francesconi (Eds.): EGOVIS 2016, LNCS 9831, pp. 123–134, 2016.
DOI: 10.1007/978-3-319-44159-7_9

methodologies, hindering the transparency, clarity and ease of interpretation of the organization's procedures. This prevents not only the understanding of the process, but also service use and, ultimately, an opinion about the service. Business process models can be used to increase understandability about public service processes. However, the simple presentation of a technical model may result ineffective.

Engiel et al. [10] discussed this issue and proposed a way to address this problem, defining, organizing and detailing characteristics that can be applied in designing public service process models to allow more understandability to process models. This proposed solution relies on the concept of organizational transparency defined by [7] as a set of five aspects: access, use, presentation, understandability and auditability. So achieving transparency means it is necessary to achieve understandability before.

This paper presents a practical experience of applying Engiel et al. [10] work in processes models of a public university in Brazil with the objective of:

i.   Illustrate a practical use of mechanisms and operationalization contained in the catalogue of understandability characteristics for the design of process models;
ii. Suggest new mechanisms to the catalogue of understandability characteristics for the design of process models.

The original contribution of this paper is the citizen language, generated from an instrumentalization instance of Engiel work. The case study verifies if indeed the operationalization proposals here and adapted from Engiel lead us in fact a citizen language.

The paper is organized as follows. Section 2 describes the concept of organizational transparency and more detailed concept of understandability. Section 3 presents the case study. Section 4 details a research made to verify the real process understand among some users and Sect. 5 concludes the paper.

2   Business Process Models as a Tool for Understanding

Business process models seem difficult to be understood by citizens, due to their language. In general they are construct as internal documents in the organizations where the people knows technical details about process. Citizens may be not interested in technical details, but rather in understanding how it works, who does each activity, its objectives, rules and about information transformation. So how to translate these kind of models to a citizen language?

2.1   Process Models

Process models area set of interrelated activities, performed in response to an event, aiming at achieving a specific result for one or more clients [9]. The process shows how information is transformed and the decisions taken during its execution. Activities consume/generate work products (data, documents etc.) are executed by actors and have to follow a set of rules [11]. These models help the organization better to understand how it works, so can be used as an instrument to communicate how organization operates [8]. Figure 1 depicts one example of a business process model.

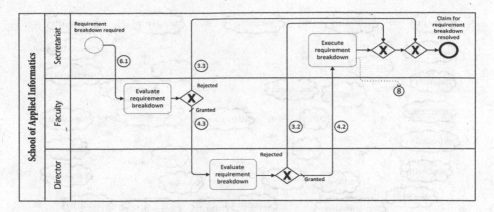

Fig. 1. Process model example

2.2 Process Model Understandability

Transparency on process service provision turns citizens well informed. Knowing the process, citizens can be more knowledgeable and can use better information. Leite and Cappelli [7] defined the Catalogue of Transparency. It proposes a SIG [12] to define the concept of transparency.

Five groups of characteristics compose it:

i.   Accessibility: information about the organization is available to the external environment;
ii. Usability: available information can be easily obtained and used;
iii. Informative: information is made available with expected quality;
iv. Understandability: external users can understand the available information;
v.   Auditability: external users can manipulate, criticize and generate new data with the available information.

Figure 2 shows each one of these groups indicating others characteristics that must be deployed in order to implement full transparency.

As can be seen one of five main transparency characteristic is understandability. Converting a process model into a model to promote public understanding does not seem so easy. To do this many characteristics need to be inserted in the process models and it leads us to a design task. The design for better understandability comprises the specification and construction of a new process model, based on the exiting business process model.

Engiel et al. [10] specialized understandability characteristic from Transparency Catalog. They used understanding concept as a human ability to consciously reproduce previously obtained information [13]. Understanding a process model is assuring that someone can read a process model and be able to reproduce the information it contains. They considered some transparency characteristics as adaptability, clarity, concision, intuitiveness, simplicity and uniformity, the most important to public process models. Figure 3 shows the SIG of catalogue of public service process models understandability attributes.

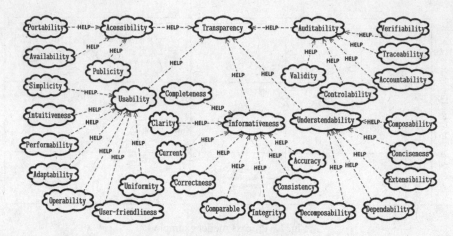

Fig. 2. Transparency SIG [7]

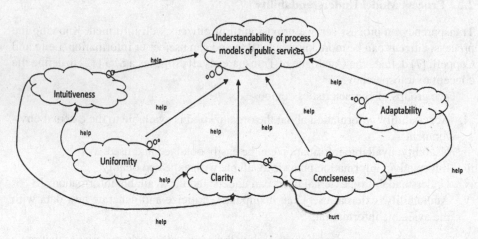

Fig. 3. SIG of public service process models understandability attributes [10]

Engiel et al. [10] defined a set of operationalization and implementation mechanisms for each characteristic in this SIG. "For instance, *Adaptability* can be implemented through 'defining different views of the process model representation according to the target audience'". This implementation is suggested to be performed by:

i.   Identifying the target audience – which actor takes part in the process; who in the external environment is interested in information about the process; describing the profile of each representative of the audience group;
ii. Associating which process elements should be presented in the model for each profile in the audience group;
iii. Defining the way each element will be contrasted (color, size) in the model, considering each profile.

Another operationalization for the *Adaptability* attribute is describing the process model, which means providing a textual description of the model".

To use the catalogue, it is necessary to have a previous process modeled, described using workflow representations as can be seen in Fig. 1. Another requirement is to know the audience's needs about the public service/product. These two things can guide the designer to choose the operacionalizations and mechanisms in the catalogue.

3   Brazilian University Case Study

The applied case study scenario was in some processes of the Secretariat of the Information Systems Course of Federal University of the State of Rio de Janeiro. This Secretariat has as, input of many of its processes, a request form in which the student describes the type of service he/she needs. The student signs this form after completing his personal information. Each of the request types that are present in the form follows a different process. None of these processes were documented and for the requesting student to know about his/her request, he/she should go to the Secretariat from time to time to ask about the response. Likewise, when the student request has some sort of inconsistency or error, the process stays stopped without him to know what happened.

All knowledge about the processes belongs to the Secretariat employees and older employees who participated at some point of the process. The teachers were aware only of parts of the processes that touch them, as well as the direction, the applicant, the secretariat and others involved. None of the actors had a complete view of the processes. In addition, it had no knowledge of the terms or limits prescribed by the Secretary, also many of the items in the request form no longer used. Applications have no confirmation that were required or were duly delivered. After the brief analysis it was noticed that the students requesting services could not meet, let alone understand the workings of the processes making evident the need to give transparency to them.

Therefore, it was necessary first to build the process models and then make them available for all students (citizens) interested. To this end the following activities were planned:

i.   Review the application and the processes contained therein excluding the not necessary ones and organizing existing redundancies;
ii. Modeling and redesign when necessary processes that remained;
iii. Transforming the process models using a citizen language for better understanding and presentation to students;
iv. Evaluating the models with current users and potential users of real understanding of the processes.

The analysis was performed (i) Then the processes that remained were modeled (ii) The model of the "Break Requirements" process can be seen in Figs. 4 in technical language, here in BPMN [14].

As well as those ones, all other processes that remained in the application form were also modeled, thus fulfilling the first requirement for the application of Engiel et al. [10] methods. Following the steps outlined in the case study, it was necessary to transform

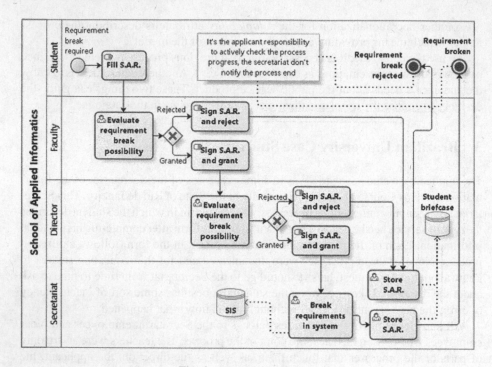

Fig. 4. Break Requirements

the models in a citizen language. Therefore, it was used Engiel et al. [10] Catalog which already provides a number of mechanisms that could be introduced into the process models to make them better understandable to the common citizen. To perform this method it is necessary to define the target audience characteristics in order to make better choices of implementation mechanisms.

3.1   The Use of the Catalog of Understanding Public Service Delivery Process Models

Engiel et al. [10] built a Catalog that is applicable in service delivery processes to improve understandability and its Implementation Guide says that, it must be adapted to the needs of the organization and the target audience. Thus, the basis of the characteristics necessary for a better understanding of the processes of the School of Informatics Department, some operationalization of the catalog were selected and others were created. They are:

   i. Use no lanes within the models;
   ii. Use for each activity the same color of its actor;
  iii. Include big arrows among activities (*new*);
   iv. Remove administrative activities that are not of interest of the citizen and have no influence in the process of understanding (*new*);
   v. List the activities (*new*);

vi.   Write the text more explanatory and less technical (*new*);
vii. Insert comment boxes for essential information related to activities (*new*);
viii. Do not use logical connectors (*new*).

From this operationalization, new flows of each process were drawn. Figure 5 show the processes "Break Requirements" in the proposed "citizen language".

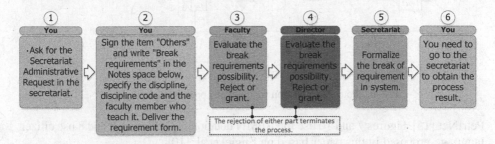

Fig. 5. Break Requirements - represented in citizen language

4   Evaluating the Effectiveness of Model

After the transformation of models into citizen language, we sought to identify if indeed the changes made processes more understandable by students (citizens). The goal was to identify among the models written in technical and non-technical language, which one: (i) allows greater understanding; (ii) better understand; (iii) have greater difficulty in understanding; (iv) is more complete; (v) is more easily understood by laymen and ordinary citizens. In this study, beyond the technical language BPMN [14], Petri Net [15] language was also included, in order to work more technical language as the technical standard notations adopted by organizations is variable. The process transformation from technical notation into citizen language, used in this work, can be seen fully in Carvalho et al. [16]. It was used a sample of the population made up of students with incomplete higher education in computer science courses in higher education or not, in various institutions in Brazil, public or private. In the sample there were seventeen individuals to sixty years since some with computer knowledge minimum to subject matter experts in various areas of training (e.g. Information Systems, Education, Engineering, Agronomy, systems analysis, etc.).

4.1   Data Collection

An online survey that reached one hundred and twenty-six individuals was prepared. The questionnaire exhibited six business process models. Each model was represented by an image using the same scenario. Figures 6, 7 and 8 have only the syntax without text elements in order to evaluate the understanding of the syntax of graphical notation; Figs. 5, 9 and 10 have syntax and text in the elements aiming to raise understanding of interpreting diagrams and semantics. Figures 6 and 9 represent the process notation

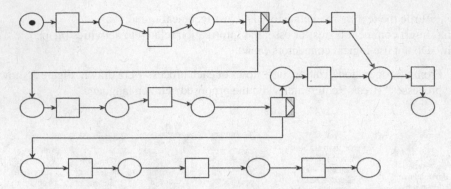

Fig. 6. Petri Net notation representing process model syntax

PetriNet [15]. Figures 7 and 10 use the BPMN notation [14]. Figures 5 and 8 use citizen language proposed in this paper based on Engiel et al. [10].

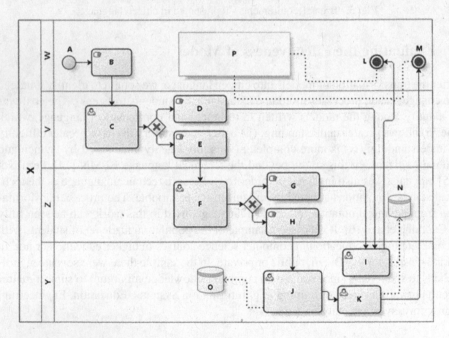

Fig. 7. BPMN notation representing process model syntax

4.2 Analyses and Results

The analysis was based on the understanding of the following groups: (1) all individuals in the sample; (2) the individuals of the sample from non-computer science courses; (3) individuals of the sample from computer science courses. Groups 2 and 3 are contained in 1. The questions intended to capture: (i) if the model allows greater under-standing; (ii) which model is better understood; (iii) which model presents greater

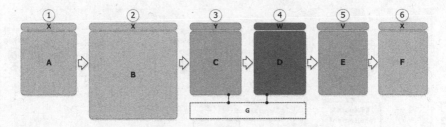

Fig. 8. Citizen language notation representing process model syntax

difficulty of understanding; (iv) which model is more complete and (v) which model is more easily understood by lay people. For each of these issues the results obtained are described below.

(A) Question 1: Which notation allows greater understanding
In this issue Figs. 5, 6, 7, 8, 9 and 10 were used. The responses have shown that:
  i.   Individuals from computer area understand diagrams built using BPMN [14] or Petri Net [15] as much as the one adapted to understanding;
  ii. Individuals from other areas do not understand diagrams adapted to understanding better than the other or using BPMN [14] or Petri Net [15];
  iii. The behavior of individuals in all areas is normalized by the behavior of individuals of not informatics areas, so for all areas of the diagram adapted for citizen language appears as the most understandable.

(B) Question 2: Which diagram has better understanding
To analyze the individual understanding of the models, Figs. 5, 9 and 10 were exposed. Looking at the responses it could be noted that the computer area people had better understand the BPMN [14] notation or Petri Net [15], while other people understand better citizen language. The twenty-five percent who best understood the adaptation for citizen language, instead of the models in BPMN [14] notation or Petri Net [15],

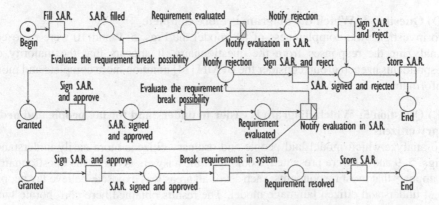

Fig. 9. Petri Net representing process model

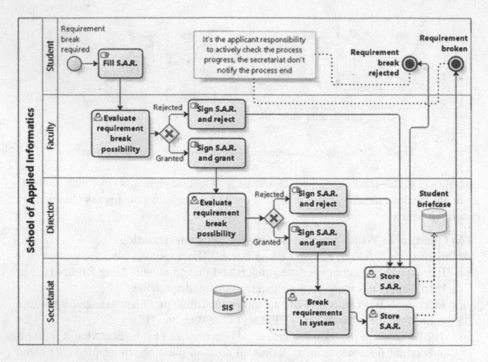

Fig. 10. BPMN representing process model

lead us to assume that they are beginners in the courses and have not yet been exposed to the skilled knowledge of notation and interpretation diagrams.

(C) Question 3: Which diagram had greater difficulty in understanding

To analyze the difficulty of understanding of process models the Figs. 5, 9 and 10 were exposed. Analyzing the responses obtained in the survey it was found that, regardless of area, the notation less suited to the understanding of a model a process is the Petri Net [15].

(D) Question 4: Which the diagram is more complete

To investigate the completeness of the model the Figs. 5, 9 and 10 were exposed. Analyzing the responses from the questionnaire, it appears that the majority of respondents in each group consider the BPMN [14] notation more complete and more informative.

(E) Question 5: Which diagram is easier to understand for lay people and ordinary citizens

To analyze which model laid people and ordinary citizens more easily understand, Figs. 5, 9 and 10 were presented. Looking at the answers given in the questionnaire, it appears that most respondents, each set of all areas was exposed, believe lay people best understand citizen language model. The results obtained here corroborate with [18–20] in the sense that technical notations are hard to understand for lay people.

From the application of this questionnaire, we concluded that for a scenario with individuals from computer science courses, it is more efficient and effective to understand business process models using BPMN [14], while for individuals from non-computer science courses, it is better to use a citizen language. The work about data collection, measurement and statistics can be seen fully in Carvalho et al. [17].

5   Conclusion

This paper described how to implement understandability in public service process model. The main contribution of this research is application of a Catalogue of Understandability Attributes for Public Service Process Models. The catalogue was used to convert business process models described in a technical language into process models in a citizen language [16]. Furthermore, this research suggests the use of business process models to improve organizational transparency.

The citizen language is easier to understand, however it obviously lacks expressiveness. We argue that the absence of other elements would not be an issue due to the purpose of this language. Anyway, future work includes a deep analysis of other forms of representing some missing elements such as gateways.

This work brings some contributions such as:

i.   Application of the Catalogue of Understandability for Public Service Process Models in a real scenario;
ii.   Creation of new implementation mechanisms adapted to the specific context;
iii. Comparison among technical and citizen languages for process models understanding.

The practical perspective of this research is related to the immediate usage of the language proposed in public institutions that must be adherent to the existent laws, as well as private organizations that aims to provide clear information for its clients and collaborators. In this sense, the paper described in an easy manner the steps to generate such models.

As future work, we propose an automatic performing of the model transformation. This automatic transformation will facilitate business process model manutenability. It is also important to perform more case studies and experiments in different scenarios to obtain more evidences about the application of the citizen language. Semiotic engineering methods can also be great allies to assess the communicability of this language.

References

1. SOX - Sarbanes-Oxley Act of 2002, Pub. L. No. 107–204, 116 Stat. 745 (codified amended in scattered sections of 15 U.S.C.) (2002)
2. BASEL - Basel Committee on Banking Supervision, 2 March 2016. http://www.bis.org/
3. EITI – Extractive Industries Transparency Initiative, 2 March 2016. http://eitransparency.org
4. OGP – Open Government Partnership, 2 March 2016. http://www.opengovpartnership.org/
5. Law 131 Transparency Law, 2 March 2016. https://www.planalto.gov.br/ccivil_03/Leis/LCP/Lcp131.htm

6. Law 12.527 Information Access Law - Regulation of access to information, 2 March 2016. http://www.planalto.gov.br/ccivil_03/_Ato2011-2014/2011/Lei/L12527.htm
7. Leite, J.C.S.P., Cappelli, C.: Software transparency. Bus. Inf. Syst. Eng. **2**(3), 127–139 (2010). Springer, Heidelberg
8. Ferreira, J.S.J., Araujo, R.M., Baião, F.A.: Identifying ruptures in business-IT communication through business models. In: 12th International Conference on Enterprise Information Systems, Funchal-Madeira-Portugal (2010)
9. Sharp, A., Mcdermott, P.: Workflow Modeling: Tools For Process Improvement and Application Development. Artech House, Norwood (2010)
10. Engiel, P., Araujo, R., Cappelli, C.: Designing public service process models for understandability. Electron. J. e-Government **12**(1), 95–111 (2014)
11. Eriksson, H., Penker, M.: Business Modeling with UML: Business Patterns at Work. Wiley, New York (2000)
12. Chung, L., Nixon, B., Yu, E., Mylopoulos, J.: Non-Functional Requirements in Software Engineering. Kluwer Academic Publishers, Massachusetts (2000)
13. Recker, J., Dreiling, A.: Does it matter which process modeling language we teach or use? an experimental study on understanding process modeling languages without formal education. In: 18th Australasian Conference on Information Systems, Toowoomba, Australia, pp. 356–366 (2007)
14. OMG - Object Management Group - Business Process Model and Notation (BPMN) v2.0 (2011)
15. Petri, C.: Kommunikation mit Automaten. Ph.D. thesis (1962) (in Deutchen)
16. Carvalho, L.P., Santoro, F., Cappelli, C.: Transparência e entendimento de processos em uma universidade pública. WTRANS' **15**, 2015 (2015). (in Portuguese)
17. Carvalho, L.P., Santoro, F., Cappelli, C.: Um estudo sobre o entendimento de processos através de modelos com base no público alvo. ERSI' **15**, 2015 (2015). (in Portuguese)
18. Dumas, M., La Rosa, M., Mendling, J., Reijers, H.A.: Fundamentals of Business Process Management. Springer, Heidelberg (2013)
19. Davies, I., Greenb, P., Rosemann, M., Indulska, M., Gallo, S.: How do practitioners use conceptual modeling in practice? Data Knowl. Eng. **58**(3), 358–380 (2006)
20. Ottensooser, A., Fekete, A., Reijers, H.A., Mendling, J.: Making sense of business process descriptions: an experimental comparison of graphical and textual notations. J. Syst. Softw. **85**(3), 596–606 (2012)

Application of Legal Ontologies Based Approaches for Procedural Side of Public Administration

A Case Study in Hungary

Bálint Molnár[1]([✉]), András Béleczki[2], and András Benczúr[2]

[1] Information Technology Foundation of Hungarian Academy of Sciences,
Konkoly-Thege út 29-33, Budapest 1121, Hungary
molnarba@inf.elte.hu

[2] Information Systems Department, Eötvös Loránd University of Budapest,
Pázmány Péter Sétány 1/C, Budapest 1117, Hungary
{bearaai, abenczur}@inf.elte.hu

Abstract. A case study is described about a "Knowledge Warehouse" that stored originally a vast amount of texts about laws and other legal rules in spreadsheet-like structure; it permitted a full-text search to support public officers to give helping hand in various Life Events of citizens. The requirements for efficiency and effectiveness enforced a redesign and re-planning of the whole system. A preliminary conceptual design and a proof of concept prototype are developed that exploits the most recent database technologies with combination of ontologies and Description Logic.

Keywords: Public administration · Legal ontology · Life events · Procedural rules · Modern databases · Document centric

1 Introduction

The state of the art produced several ontologies that aimed at supporting the domain of the law. Within this domain, there exists a specialized area, namely the procedural rules of public administration. Within public administration a public service that helps the citizens/customers to navigate and to solve their own problems related to life events is an essential user-friendly function. As the rules representing the procedural legal side of public administration are codified at some level within the legal environment. Assistance for both the citizens and public officers/servants can be provided by some approach of IT as "Knowledge Warehouse". The Citizen Relationship Management (a kind of Customer Relationship Management, CRM) as the organization of Public Administration has a usual office system and underlying data handling facilities. However, very wide selections of technologies are available to yield state of the art support at a high service level. However, for several reasons, typically some basic technologies are used that are readily available. As the calculation tables in the office automation packages provides more structured solutions as plain documents the spreadsheets approach has been chosen. Basically, the calculation tables offer the opportunities for creating fairly

© Springer International Publishing Switzerland 2016
A. Kő and E. Francesconi (Eds.): EGOVIS 2016, LNCS 9831, pp. 135–149, 2016.
DOI: 10.1007/978-3-319-44159-7_10

flexible table structure although it is not structured in the terms of relational databases. A set of calculation tables are enable to store legal and procedural information in textual format and the stored data can be retrieved through some searching mechanism. Moreover, a Web interface can be created that can ensure that the stored content of legal procedures can be accessed. The combination of spreadsheet and Web accessibility provides a comfortable enough function for both citizens and public officers.

The characteristic of the above outlined approach is that it facilitates full text search that is very helpful in several situation but is not perfect solution to assist in complex circumstances. The legal rules compose a complex network through the concepts and their relationships. An intelligent searching and retrieving environment should provide responses that contain semantically related elements besides the syntactically matching ones. Hence, we should concentrate on an integrated approach that combine intelligent systems' services with more traditional searching and retrieval facilities. To buttress the idea a prototype system is under development as proof of concept. There is a full text search based system that helps the public officers in the call center of Citizen Relationship Management and a Web page for citizens. To raise the service level, the readily available technologies should be put together to support a much more intelligent approach. The specific domain is the various procedural rules that are codified at different levels of legal hierarchies and contain prescriptions for specific life events of citizens.

2   Literature Overview

MacCarty advocated [1] to use a conceptual model to support intelligent systems within the legal domain. An intelligent system on the legal domain may consist of two parts an *analysis* and an *advisory*. The analysis part can be regarded as a traditional legal system in which the client specifies the state of the facts about the legal situation then gets a response in the form of guidance or decision. The advisory part is a conceptual retrieval system that can generate answers more intelligent way that a key-word, full text search system. Such an integrated, intelligent system demands that the various technologies should be put into a framework that is grounded in a uniform and unified platform.

Life-events consist of a set of actions that may contain at least one occasion to use a public service. This public service when executed in a duly manner should fulfill a specific demand of a citizen that may have arisen from a new life situation. In the literature, two approaches can be found to interpret life events: (1) life-events can be considered as something that triggers a workflow of related services of public administration [2]; (2) or life-events can be modeled through making use of ontologies [3]. Ontology can be perceived as a complex network of concepts and their relationships that describe a specific domain. The ontologies can be represented by very precise formal, mathematical tools as description logic [4] and lattices [5, 6].

In the domain of public administration, there were several attempts to create ontologies and architectures. The *Governance Enterprise Architecture* (GEA) and its high level, conceptual model is a good starting point to create ontology for representing life-events. OntoGov project [8] is another example for proposing a meta-ontology for e-Government. The *Legal Knowledge Format* (*LKIF*) and the Core Ontology of Basic Legal

Concepts that was a European Framework project [9] and the aim of the project was to enable the translation and mutual mapping between legal knowledge-bases that were created by various descriptive methods of knowledge representation, additionally it attempted to define a common knowledge representation on the legal domain that may serve as a hub among the different approaches of knowledge representation. The advances on text mining techniques enabled several applications related to ontologies that can be used in a document-centric electronic public administration environment [10, 11].

3   The Necessity to Integrate Various Technological Approaches

The proposed models that may come into play can contain ontologies, a coherent document model, moreover formalized business and transformation rules that assure the mutual mapping between the different representations (Fig. 1). The document-centric approach has a significant role to put into a uniform framework of the different aspects emerging within a public administration environment [12, 13].

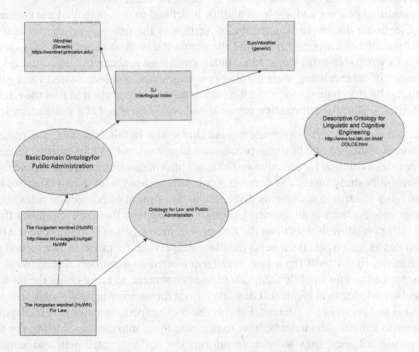

Fig. 1. High level conceptual structure for ontologies within public administration

In our case, there was an intensive and extensive transformation work previously whereby the paper-based and basically unstructured office documents (as e.g. .pdf, .doc etc.) was transformed into tables and represented in spreadsheet. These documents contained the laws and the related procedural rules that regulate the activities when citizens are involved in life-events.

To find a suitable solution for comprehensive treatment of e-documents, information management for the help-desk of public administration, and ontology engineering several approaches were investigated in terms of

- How can the ontological aspects of the specific legal domain be dealt with?
- Whether can integrating the document-centric and ontology-based methods provide an appropriate solution for organizing, presenting and retrieving e-documents?
- What the preconditions are to implement a sound technical solution that fits to the requirements of the public administration?
- What kind of ontology-based method is appropriate for a document-centric approach and e-document management in public administration?

However, there were previous efforts when the paper-based and heterogeneous format of electronic documents were made over to calculation sheets and tabulated forms, a number of problems emerged:

- Despite efforts, the electronic records are neither complete nor up-to-data.
- An auditing process and a role of auditor is defined to designate that the content of an electronic document is authentic, nevertheless the process and the authenticity attribute of e-documents lag behind the actual status. A stock of files in a specific directory requires extra works to maintain consistency, accuracy and actuality.
- The set of spreadsheets, their naming convention and semi-structured form give a helping hand to public officers in the citizen relationship section to find the relevant information but the information retrieval and provision is not at a satisfactory level.

The first stage of project is to create a feasibility study. In this first stage, the project's objective is to analyze the business processes and to work out an implementable design that provides a solution for effective and efficient information retrieval and maintenance. The feasibility study intends to develop recommendations for an overarching solution to managing electronic documents dedicated to description of procedural rules related to life-events. As there is an operating solution that supports the work of public officers in the citizen relationship sections the first goal of investigation is to improve the business processes, electronic documents handling and services for citizens. The second goal is to discover the state-of-the-art on *intelligent electronic* document management that can be applied within a public administration environment, to make better the information and knowledge management. The study aims at the *improving public administration processes* and *services* for citizens. For this reason, the focus of analysis is on the question how to structure documents, how to organize them into databases using the most modern technologies, how to retrieve information utilizing intelligent and semantic based techniques. The ontology-based, intelligent e-document management requires common domain terminologies [14]; as the ontologies can serve as an integration tool between several enterprise/organization *architecture building blocks* as e.g. business processes, Web interfaces, services based on semantic technologies and knowledge management. The outstanding issue is concerned with the successful communication among the stakeholders, and the orchestration and choreography among IT services

(Web services, REST/RESTful etc.) that permeates the dimensions that are manifested in the form of people, organization, collection of data, information, and knowledge, moreover technology architecture. The ontologies lay the foundation for communication among the disparate stakeholders that exist in partly in the real world and partly in the cyberspace. The ontologies provide support for those roles who know and who want to know, furthermore they aid processing, retrieving and storing information. In the field of Enterprise Architecture and Integration of Enterprise Architecture several methodologies are developed for this problem area. These methodologies and techniques can be customized to be applied on the field of e-government and public administration, and the use of IT. The ontology-based approaches allow contributing to the following goals within the processes of public administration:

- Efficient and effective management of electronic documents and other electronic resources grounded in standards (local and general ones);
- Underpinning business processes that flow through the borderlines between public administration and citizens;
- Efficiently and effectively reacting on demands of actors for retrieving information and pieces of knowledge.

4 Vocabularies, Taxonomies and Ontologies

WordNet is a lexical database of words and a reference knowledge base that can be accessed on-line; it was created primarily for English words, but later on, versions came into existence for other languages as e.g. Hungarian [15, 16]. One of the roles of ontologies is to organize and structure information within a specific domain of expertise. Ontologies serve as suitable tools for describing the concepts, phenomena and properties of the domain of interests. The ontology can be utilized as a lexicon of terms and a standard that defines the allowed statement or sentences in terms of semantics. Thereby, the ontologies can be used as sources of professional terms and logical inferences, e.g. finding the reasons of some legal actions then triggering some automated transactions in a semantic Web environment through Web services. In public administration, the ontologies may appear as the source of definitions for legal vocabulary. Nonetheless, the ontologies in the domain of law steps beyond a simple vocabulary, a legal ontology embodies the universe of discourse for a world that is the subject of law or legal rules. The scope of the law may be in force on taxing, crime, immigration, transportation etc.

In a public administration environment, the fundamental function of ontologies is to represent knowledge of the procedural legal rules so that a reasoning engine can interpret the formalized and codified knowledge then can carry out inferences to create recommendations how to solve the given problem. Ontologies can be specified using description logic and OWL (Ontology Web Language, [17]) that makes possible operationalization of the declarative knowledge. The business or administrative rules can be specified in a different partition of the knowledge base and forward and/or backward chaining rules engines can execute the reasoning. The description logic (OWL-DL) can formulate the assertions about the problems to be solved.

The ontologies can be used to provide a framework for interpretation of documents as e.g. spreadsheets. The ontologies may comprise a hierarchy, the lowest level; the domain specific layer should refer to the facts that should be stored in some kind of database (document, XML database etc.). The ontologies may operate as systems of semantic index that allows the semantic searching for the content of electronic documents. The procedural rules related to life events are collected into electronic documents, especially spreadsheets. A full text search and indexing is a partial solution, nevertheless an intelligent retrieval system requires a semantic based searching mechanism that goes beyond word and keywords. In the legal environment handling life events is fairly typical that multiple meaning may exist even for a specific technical/legal terms. The domain ontologies and WordNet like approaches can help cope with these problems. Besides the extensional handling of information stored in documents there is an opportunity for intensional way, i.e. the terms within ontologies can be extended by annotations, it means a marking scheme that permits an expert to semantically mark content of documents so it can be retrieved by an intelligent search later on. The combination of intentional and extensional approach – fact base and annotations – can be the principal use for managing and accessing information in public administration. Furthermore, these ontological approaches permit to transform the information retrieval mechanism that is currently yielded by search engines into *legal information consultancy services*. A Web interface exists that allow full text search for the life event related legal rules, but an advanced service can make possible for users to negotiate their requirements and will obtain responses that fit to their specific demands, moreover generates adequate answers for the specific issues instead of generating vast amount chunk of legal texts that are contained in the potentially relevant electronic documents.

In addition to the above-mentioned roles that ontologies can fulfill, the ontologies can give a comprehensive view about the domain of interests whereby the ontologies can assist to design specialized representations; these types of ontologies can be considered as core ontologies that serve as a basis for creating various layers of ontology hierarchy.

Ontology for electronic documents management should maintain a vocabulary. The list of keywords can be a starting point to allow referencing descriptions and content related to keywords. In our case, there are several spreadsheets files that contain detailed descriptions and wording of procedural rules. The combination of these files and the Hungarian Legal WordNet [16] can be used to create an initial set of keywords. The set of keywords can serve as an informal ontology, a thesaurus; the WordNet give a helping hand to treat the *synonyms*, subcategories, *homonyms*, *hyponyms* and *hypernyms* whereby the domain specific ontologies can be formalized. The foundation of formal description is based on XML (eXtensible Markup Language) and RDF (Resource Description Framework). The logical formalization to describe relationships and hierarchies requires OWL [17] and description logic [4]. The hierarchical ontology approach permits a logical separation of information architecture between document management and various formats of knowledge representations. The different knowledge representations can interlink ontologies with document management and complex, semantic queries to enable automatic answering.

5   A Proposed Model for Combination of Ontologies and Document Management

There already exist vast amount electronic documents in the form of spreadsheet and they can be considered as a semi-structured data collection. Implicitly the electronic documents contain metadata as well as structuring principle; the texts stored in the documents and the WordNet dedicated to the legal field can be perceived as the basis of the vocabulary. The legal concepts and their relationships represented in a complex, semantic network the reconciliation between the hierarchy of ontologies and the initial network of the vocabulary carried out by step by step.

The objectives of the project were clearly formulated that helped define the model. The responsible section of the public administration declared that the electronic documents will be used across departments to propose modifications, to perform audit, to check and to retrieve them. A central unit will be responsible for verification and validity of documents. The actors and roles belong to a complex hierarchy of access rights thereby a Role Based Access and an Attribute-based Control system was created. The model of processes in public administration answered the questions as follows:

- What roles and actors in terms of public administration should take part in the related processes?
- What are their access rights?
- What kind of *ad-hoc* access right should be defined through temporary attributes?
- What are the activities, acts and processes of public administration that relates to the subject domain and should be supported?
- What kind of technology can be selected that may serves as a compromise between the ability and capability of public administration and sophistication level of available technologies.

Investigating the above mentioned questions from the viewpoint of document and information management within public administration, the use of ontology-based approach seems to be appropriate, especially in the long term. Legal documents present a well-defined structure; there is a meta-rule set that describes the patterns for a "normative" specification of rules codified by laws or other legal format (orders, resolutions etc.). The general pattern is that there is *hypothesis* or *pre-condition*, then a prescription and/or *order*, then *sanction*, remedy or reward. Recently, the documents are represented by XML [18]; this representation can be perceived as a hierarchy that can be mapped onto tree structures, i.e. acyclic graphs. However, the electronic word processor tools permit complex data structure too as follows: annotations, footnotes, sidebars and cross-references. The hypergraph [19, 20] as a fairly general data structure is apt to depict complex structures of documents. This document model [12, 13] is attractive since it allows relationships between parts or sections of documents that can be characterized by logical statements and the representation – at the same time – simple, elegant and direct. The content of the documents can be mapped into a hypergraph structure; however it requires a meticulous work to map the "fields", the "name of fields" onto a conceptual model. (Figs. 2 and 3)

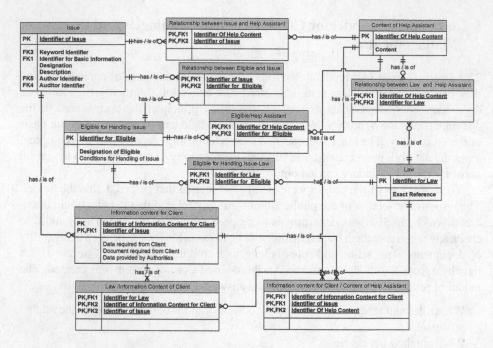

Fig. 2. A conceptual model of a document type dedicated to a generic type of official issues

The reason is that the human editors rewrote and re-structured the original legal texts that contained the legal, procedural rules for a life event of citizens into spreadsheets. The spreadsheet-like tools allows some structuring although it does not enforce a strict, table structure in spite of this it permits a flexible data structure. The collection of spreadsheets contains more than two thousand pieces of files; each of them covers a specific issue, and the related legal text is arranged by some structuring principle. A higher level structure was found that helped define roughly seven areas of official issues. The conceptual model and the structure of the related generic type of documents on specific areas can be considered uniform; the differences emerge in the specific textual and data content.

The first idea is that the underlying structural organizing principle of most recent spreadsheets follows XML structures and thereby the existing documents can be converted or represented into a tree structure and table format that can be handled by either document or e.g. relational database management system. However, structure of the existing spreadsheets can be perceived as slightly structured, i.e. the structure pursues a logic of the authors with a law background. For that reason, the transformation is not self-evident and straightforward. Although, at both theoretical and practical level, we follow the service options that are available in the XML as XPath, XQuery, XSL and XSLT that yield chances for automated and programmatic handling the raw data.

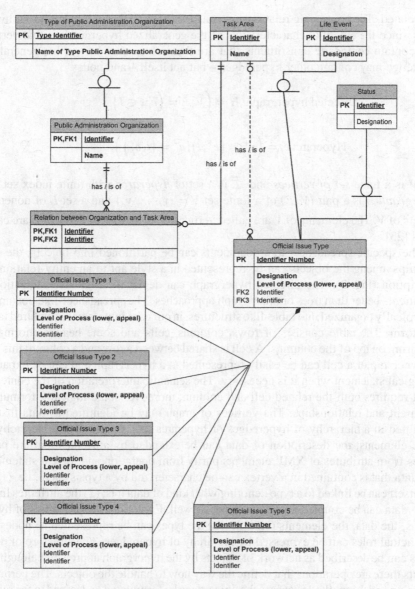

Fig. 3. The relationships of official issues

5.1 A Document Model Based on Hypergraph Approach

As the general document model is described in [13], we represent a document as a directed *hypergraph*. The *nodes* of hypergraphs can designate "*objects*" that can be any components of documents in the sense of DOM (Document Object Model, [22]) and XML. A hyperedge denotes that the nodes that belong to the hyperarc are logically interrelated. The containing relationship can be expressed through hierarchy of hyper-edges since the essential characteristics of the generalized hypergraph is that vertices may contain composite constituents that are themselves may be graphs; generalized hyperedge may contain other hyperedges – but not itself – and nodes.

$$\text{Directed hypergraph: } \vec{H} = \left(V; \vec{E} = \left\{ \vec{e_i} : i \in I \right\} \right) \qquad (1)$$

$$\text{Hyperarc: } \vec{e_i} = \left(\vec{e_i^+} = (e_i^+, i); \vec{e_i^-} = (i, e_i^-) \right) \qquad (2)$$

The V is a finite *set of vertices* end $\vec{E}$ is a set of *hyperarcs* with finite index set I. A *hypergraph H* is a pair *(V, E)* of a finite set $V = \{v_1, ..., v_n\}$ and a set E of nonempty subsets of V. The elements of V are called vertices (nodes), the elements of E are called edges [23]

The specific spreadsheet-like documents can be partitioned into objects; the relationships among the objects can be represented in a style apt to an entity-relationship description (Fig. 2). The directed hypergraph can depict the logical organization of documents better than trees or other graph approaches. The spreadsheet-like documents are typically organized into table-like structures, in our case into a semi-structured table-like form. The table consists of rows, columns, cells and some header information appearing on top of the columns. A cell is shared between a row and a column; this type of ownership of a cell can be easily represented in a hypergraph and can be expanded by logical statement when it is necessary. The semantic interpretation of the content in a cell requires both the related cell and column; moreover some logically formulated statement and relationships. The vertices of graph may be identified as data that are contained in a hierarchy of hyperedges or hyperarcs that represent of a hierarchy for XML elements; the description of data can be extended by attributes that are partly comes from attributes of XML elements partly from operation and logical statements. The data that is contained in a vertex can be characterized by a type system, i.e. (1) the data itself can be linked to a type denoting what kind of data it is; (2) the attributes linked to the data can be coupled to specific types as well. Exploiting the properties of hyper-graphs, the data, the elements (XML), and the types can be represented as nodes and their actual roles can be expressed by hierarchy of hyperedges. The structure of documents can be described as network of objects by the hypergraph approach; belonging to objects there are operations that define the way how to handle the objects. The permitted operation and the method to access the objects can be formulated and joined to the related objects. The objects can be represented by hyperedges and hyperarcs as they are being complex structures containing data, attributes and related operations. The applicability of specific operations to objects can be linked to specific elements within the hierarchies of hyperedges. The hierarchies of hyperedges can be perceived as a kind of inheritance and subtype relationships.

5.2   Application of Ontologies and Description Logic

There are several precursors that can be used to outline ontology for Public Administration and Life Events [21]. A customized version of Life Event ontologies can be seen
in Fig. 4. The ontologies can complement the relevant operations and constraints that
can be deduced from the documents and their transformation into a hypergraph structure.
The hierarchy of ontologies (core ontology, domain specific etc.) may assist in the
semantic interpretation and in the decision what operation can be applied to data and to
the related concepts. The hyperedges – as they describe the data and schema of the
documents that can be reconstructed from the networks of relationships – can be used
to map onto the concept of *role* in Description Logic [4].

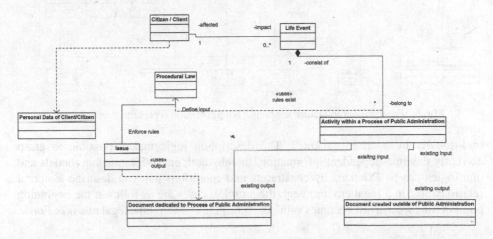

Fig. 4. Ontology for handling life events in public administration

The generalization hierarchies, composition and aggregation that formulate the situation
that an entity/notion is disjoint union of the *extensions* of other entities/notion can be
expressed by entity-relationship and object-oriented modeling method for databases through
the logical *Is-A* relationship that can be easily transformed into logical statement in Description Logic. Several examples can be seen in Figs. 4 and 5. The relationships represented in
a database may contain a structure that granularity should be expressed with help of ontology
and Description Logic (I), i.e. specific instances of an entity should be linked to a more
specialized entity that may be obvious the relationship between the entities and the role
described in DL. Such constraints can be formalized easily in DL through universal quanti-
fication over the specified role between entities/concepts. The conditions for instances that
an instance is a *member* in a particular entity/notion can be formulated in necessary and
sufficient conditions (in terms of mathematics); and they can be enforced through the schema
of the database and ontology.

The unambiguous identifiers of entities/notion can be grasped through the concept
of *keys* that implement the relationships among the entities. The *DL* allows describing
the constraints in terms of *roles* (DL) that distinguish uniquely entities, instances of
notion. The time is an important element in a legal environment that is handled

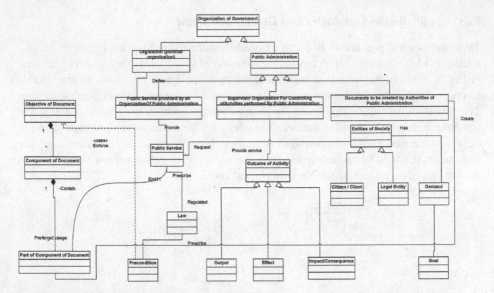

Fig. 5. Enterprise architecture for public administration represented as ontology

traditionally by a *"time-machine"*. The description logic makes possible to grasp correctly the time-dependent information, thereby both entity-relationship models and ontologies can be extended by constraints and conditions that can describe temporal relationships. In a legal environment, the simplest cases are as follows: the beginning point in time when a law becomes valid, the time period when some legal rule is *In Force*.

5.3   Reconciliation of Document Models and Ontologies

The *DL* and *ontology* can provide a representation for concepts and their relationships. The description of relationships in logical formalism makes allowance for *reasoning*. The database representation coupled to ontologies permits consistency checking of database schema, detection of redundancy, inferring stricter constraints on *roles* exhibiting relationships, moreover entity/notion *subsumption*, i.e. whether the instances of the extension of a concept is a subset of the instances of the extension for another concept; furthermore whether relationship *subsumption* exists.

As it was outlined above, the loosely, semi-structured documents were transformed into semi-structured XML documents, and document *objects* in the sense of Document Object Model that can be mapped into an appropriate hypergraph structure. The objects contain the data, or tuples of data. The hypergraph structure and the graph database provide a flexible data structure and maintain the rigor of a database management system. The hierarchy of elements in XML is reflected and at the same time they can be handled in an object-centered way. The set of ontologies fits to the levels of hierarchies of components within the generic document type that conceptualize the major classes of *official issues* that have similarities in syntactic and semantic terms. The ontologies can be considered as categorized information. The taxonomies of concepts together the logical statement within ontologies can be used for reasoning. The formalized knowledge can be used for semantic interpretation of stored facts and for enforcing the various rules codified into document structure and ontologies. One of the critical problems is how to keep up-to-date the data stored in the documents and graph database in time. The selected approach, the hypergraph database provides basic operations for modification and retrieval. Exploiting the hypergraph structure that is defined for document objects, operations for document updating can be formulated. The modification of certain objects within graph should be in concert with the underlying specific and/or generic document in order to mirror the changes. In a rule base attached to the structure of the hypergraph, the rules define how to update the graph in the case of modifications of the related documents when a section is added, deleted or updated, moreover how to actualize the logical links that expresses the relationships within document and inter documents and they are represented by hyperedges and hyperarcs in the graph. The elements of the rule base can be formulated as production rules, i.e. it consists of a logical predicate, an input sub-graph SHG_1, an output sub-graph SHG_2. For a given SHG_i the predicate is valid and SHG_i contain a sub-graph SHG_1 or an isomorphic sub-graph then it should be replaced by SHG_2.

The ontology and DL approach provides two levels of logical axioms, namely a terminological/concept level ($TBOX$) and extensional and assertion level ($ABOX$). The extension of concepts is identified with the instances of objects represented as nodes and objects in the hypergraph. The graph manipulation rules are collected in a rule base. The rules can be applied to individual elements appearing in $ABOX$ or instances. The documents and legal concepts contained in the documents are represented in the hypergraph. The combination of terminological, assertion level axioms and production rules yield a tool set for management and manipulation of the Knowledge Warehouse. The above described approach makes possible the operation of a knowledge base. The ontologies provide the categorization of concepts. The actual facts stored in the hypergraph as data, nodes, hyperedges and hyperarcs. The rules are encoded in three different types (TBOX, ABOX, production) that can carry out the required reasoning process. As it is obvious, the factual knowledge and the logical statement are strongly coupled, the application rules are accurately defined on facts, data, and component of documents exhibiting the strict link between them. The hypergraphs allows the representation the logical connections among disparate collections of data and information in the factual database, the interdependencies among the logical statement and rules can be expressed by the reasoning tool as DL and production rules.

5.4 Knowledge Warehouse for Public Administration

The typical encounter between Public Administration and citizens happens when some events in life of the citizen come about. An ontology for Life Events was developed [23]. This ontology is employed as guidance to structure the available textual document and factual knowledge (Fig. 4). The primary service of Knowledge Warehouse is to give help to the public servants; however a Web interface was created as well to assist the average citizen for searching solution for a certain issue.

The trade-off between the elapsed time of full-scale implementation of all rules of procedures in the form of tasks within workflows and quality of service that is provided for citizens and public officers was created by balance between textual information and programmatic forms. In the solution, some governing rules for legal procedures are realized in search and workflow engines. However, the detailed, codified set of rules is stored in textual forms. The semantic searching utilizes the factual, textual knowledge in the hypergraph database, the concepts within ontologies and the logical axioms. The tasks described by process structures in workflows and logical inferences in engines for rule interpretation. These combination provides a reasonable compromise between an intelligent support and usability that can be implemented in finite time.

6   Conclusion

To exploit the ontology-based approach requests a complex IT infrastructure. Beyond a prototype implementation in an academic environment, an ontology-based comprehensive project is associated with high risks; the public administration prefers risk-avoidance and the required resources are generally higher than a government may bear except there is some external fund as EU financing. The trade-off between the elapsed time of full-scale implementation and quality of system should be balanced.

A prototype system is created in an academic environment whereby the feasibility of the proposed approach is validated using open source tools. That opens the way for an implementation for a full-scale semantic searching and integration of e-documents and ontologies. However, there are open questions and chances for further research. There is a requirement for automation of processes as workflows. The more than two thousand, detailed rules described in the text of the electronic documents, several hundred diverse processes makes practically impossible a comprehensive automation in the sense of the required time and other resources. The research question is that whether an appropriate meta-level of business processes can be found that provides opportunities for reasonable workflows, the maintenance efforts can be kept under control but the factual knowledge base and the underlying set of rules can be exploited for efficient and effective support for public officers.

References

1. McCarty, L.T.: Intelligent legal information systems: problems and prospects. Rutgers Comput. Technol. Law J. **9**, 265–287 (1982)
2. Trochidis, I., Tambouris, E., Tarabanis, K.: Identifying common workflow patterns in life-events and business episodes. In: The Second International Conference on e-Government, pp. 234–243 (2006)
3. Sanati, F., Jie, L.: Life-event modelling framework for e-Government integration. Electron. Gov. Int. J. **7**(2), 183–202 (2010)
4. Baader, F.: The Description Logic Handbook: Theory Implementation and Applications. Cambridge University Press, Cambridge (2003)
5. Stumme, G., Maedche, A.: FCA-Merge: bottom-up merging of ontologies. In: IJCAI, vol. 1, pp. 225–230 (2001)

6. Formica, A.: Ontology-based concept similarity in formal concept analysis. Inf. Sci. **176**(18), 2624–2641 (2006)
7. Peristeras, V., Tarabanis, K.: Advancing the government enterprise architecture–GEA: the service execution object model. In: Traunmüller, R. (ed.) EGOV 2004. LNCS, vol. 3183. Springer, Heidelberg (2004)
8. Apostolou, D., Stojanovic, L., Lobo, T.P., Thoenssen, B.: Towards a semantically-driven software engineering environment for e-Government. In: Böhlen, M.H., Gamper, J., Polasek, W., Wimmer, M.A. (eds.) TCGOV 2005. LNCS (LNAI), vol. 3416, pp. 157–168. Springer, Heidelberg (2005)
9. Breuker, J., Boer, A., Hoekstra, R., van den Berg, K.: Developing content for LKIF: ontologies and frameworks for legal reasoning. In: The Nineteenth Annual Conference on Legal Knowledge and Information Systems, JURIX 2006, vol. 152, p. 169. IOS Press (2006)
10. Gillani, S., Ko, A.: Incremental ontology population and enrichment through semantic-based text mining: an application for it audit domain. Int. J. Semant. Web Inf. Syst. (IJSWIS) **11**(3), 44–66 (2015)
11. Husaini, M., Ko, A., Tapucu, D., Saygın, Y.: Ontology supported policy modeling in opinion mining process. In: Herrero, P., Panetto, H., Meersman, R., Dillon, T. (eds.) OTM-WS 2012. LNCS, vol. 7567, pp. 252–261. Springer, Heidelberg (2012)
12. Molnár, B., Benczúr, A.: Modeling information systems from the viewpoint of active documents. Vietnam J. Comput. Sci. **2**(4), 229–241 (2015)
13. Molnár, B., Benczúr, A.: Facet of modeling web information systems from a document-centric view. Int. J. Web Portals (IJWP) **5**(4), 57–70 (2013)
14. Casellas, N.: Legal Ontology Engineering: Methodologies, Modelling Trends, and the Ontology of Professional Judicial Knowledge. Law, Governance and Technology Series, vol. 3. Springer, Netherlands (2011)
15. Princeton University "About WordNet." WordNet. Princeton University (2010). http://wordnet.princeton.edu
16. University of Szeged, Department of Informatics, The Hungarian wordnet (HuWN) (2011). http://rgai.inf.u-szeged.hu/project/nlp/download/HuWN/HuWN.pdf, http://rgai.inf.u-szeged.hu/index.php?lang=en&page=HuWN
17. W3C, OWL Web Ontology Language Use Cases and Requirements Recommendation (2004). https://www.w3.org/TR/2004/REC-webont-req-20040210/
18. W3C, Extensible Markup Language (XML) (2015). https://www.w3.org/XML/
19. Bretto, A.: Hypergraph Theory: An Introduction. Mathematical Engineering. Springer, Switzerland (2013)
20. Iordanov, B.: HyperGraphDB: a generalized graph database. In: Shen, H.T., et al. (eds.) WAIM 2010. LNCS, vol. 6185, pp. 25–36. Springer, Heidelberg (2010)
21. Peristeras, V., Tarabanis, K.: The governance enterprise architecture (GEA) high-level object model. In: Wimmer, M.A. (ed.) KMGov 2004. LNCS (LNAI), vol. 3035, pp. 101–110. Springer, Heidelberg (2004)
22. Marini, J.: The Document Object Model: Processing Structured Documents. McGraw-Hill, New York (2002)
23. Bretto, A.: Hypergraph Theory: An Introduction. Springer, Switzerland (2013)
24. Trochidis, I., Tambouris, E., Tarabanis, K.: An ontology for modeling life-events. In: 2007 IEEE International Conference on Services Computing, SCC 2007, pp. 719–720 (2007)

Modeling Relevant Legal Information for Consumer Disputes

Cristiana Santos[1,4(✉)], Víctor Rodriguez-Doncel[2],
Pompeu Casanovas[1,3], and Leon van der Torre[4]

[1] IDT-UAB, Barcelona, Spain
cristiana.teixeirasantos@gmail.com
[2] Ontology Engineering Group, Universidad Politécnica de Madrid,
Madrid, Spain
vrodriguez@fi.upm.es
[3] Centre for Applied Social Sciences, Royal Melbourne Institute of Technology,
Melbourne, Australia
pompeucasanovas@gmail.com
[4] University of Luxembourg, Luxembourg, Luxembourg
leon.vandertorre@uni.lu

Abstract. Accessing relevant legal information found in text excerpts from heterogeneous sources is essential to the decision making process in consumer disputes. The Ontology of Relevant Legal Information in Consumer Disputes (ric) is the domain-independent ontology modeling this relevant legal information comprising rights, their requisites, exceptions, constraints, enforcement procedures, legal sources. Its use is exemplified with one extension thereof, the Air Transport Passenger Incidents Ontology (ric-atpi), representing both the possible incidents triggered by a complaint in the air transport passenger domain and the related legal information that might be applicable. The Ontology models the key provisions found in hard law, and those in soft law, comprising heterogeneous sources in a structured manner. An ontology-based system provides the knowledge embedded in the legal sources and their relation to the specific scenario.

Keywords: Relevance · Legal ontology · Access to legal information

1 Introduction

The exponential growth of legal information online (case-law, legislation, etc.) is making evident the need for better mechanisms to retrieve the legal information that is most relevant for each situation, mitigating the current information overload suffered by the legal community and laymen end-users in general.

Relevance is a fundamental concept in information systems. The general meaning of 'relevance' is bound to a context in relation to which a problem is addressed. The ability to have a formal conceptual model of the multifaceted aspects of the relevant sources compounding relevant legal knowledge is a key factor for the development and deployment of applications that benefit from the real usage of the legal-document

© Springer International Publishing Switzerland 2016
A. Kő and E. Francesconi (Eds.): EGOVIS 2016, LNCS 9831, pp. 150–165, 2016.
DOI: 10.1007/978-3-319-44159-7_11

knowledge in favor of citizens, public administrations, and businesses. Hereby we contextualize relevance within our case-study of consumer disputes and enable its representation through an ontology-based system, backing a web application providing relevant legal information, in particular, in the air transport passenger domain (ATP).

For this regard, two ontologies are presented: the Relevant Legal Information in Consumer Disputes Ontology (RIC) and its specialization the Air Transport Passenger Incidents Ontology (RIC-ATPI). It is asserted that lack of commoditized information is a root-cause of disputes [6] and we assume that enabling the modeling and disclosure of relevant legal information enhances the decision-making of disputants. Consumers and citizens should be given with new tools and affordances for self-government, self-monitoring, and market and political participation.

Ontologies, as a formal representation of domain knowledge, may fundamentally affect the way in which systems/applications are constructed and shall interoperate via specific shared domain knowledge. The competency questions the ontologies (RIC and RIC-ATPI) give answer to are of interest in multiple scenarios. They have been formulated so that the ontologies can support the provision of relevant legal information in actual information systems. Still might be useful for:

- establishing a shared conceptual framework that favors understanding between the interested parties (which are of heterogeneous nature);
- providing a terminology with valuable definitions in specific domains (e.g. ATP) declaring a categorization of incidents (RIC-ATPI) which might be used by additional information systems (e.g. automatic classification of complaints).

In this paper we outline how work carried out in the past [2] is revisited within the relevance perspective applied as a knowledge engineering requirement.

Our research questions are the following: What is relevant legal information? How could relevant legal information be acquired and represented through an ontology-based system?

The remainder of the paper is structured as follows. Section 2 presents the related work. Section 3 provides the ontological artifacts and its engineering process. Section 4 describes the evaluation of both the ontologies and the ontology-based system. The paper ends with set-up ideas for future research.

2 Related Work

This paper proposes an ontology-based system to access relevant legal information. This knowledge engineering (KE) approach can be confronted with traditional information retrieval (IR) approaches, including those using NLP techniques. This section briefly describes the state of the art for these approaches, with special emphasis in the consumer law domain and with a short overview of commercial solutions.

If we consider that relevant legal information can determine the success in court, it is no surprise that as early as computers had a minimal processing power in the sixties they were used to aid obtaining legal information [11]. The early systems implemented a Boolean model of IR which is still in use nowadays: both the user query and the documents are regarded as a set of terms; the system simply returns documents including the terms in the query. The recall of this approach is modest [12]. The limitations of this simple strategy lie in dealing with ambiguity, synonymy and complex expressions [16]; and the biggest hurdle is that Law is about ideas and these ideas may not be directly related to a single word. These difficulties were soon alleviated by taking advantage of the structure of documents (permitting queries per field, where each field has a meaning) or simple linguistic approximation dealing with the problems of homonyms/synonyms appeared [18].

An alternative is representing legal documents in a vector space model and ranking them with similarity metrics [19]. With these IR techniques, documents can be high ranked if they are relevant even if they lack some of the words in the query.

The selection of features to compose the vector representing a document started being only the keywords (as in the FLEXICON system [20]) but nowadays is made up of all the words in the document (or in general n-grams), possibly after having made *part of speech* tagging and being weighted via inference network analysis [21]. These systems yield much better results both in terms of precision and recall [16].

The latest efforts towards populating the feature vector with more discriminative elements have been in the area of topic models [22, 23], which are a type of statistical models for discovering the latent topics that occur in a collection of documents.

As an alternatively to IR techniques, ontology-based knowledge engineering techniques have been used to improve the retrieval of the most relevant documents, reporting better results [9]. However, the cost of manually developing ontologies is high and not many ontologies have been specifically used to drive information systems.

With the purpose of facilitating knowledge representation, consumer ontologies have been designed, such as the Customer Complaint Ontology (CCO) and the Consumer Protection Ontology. CCO [10] has been developed in the EU CCFORM project with the aim of studying the foundation of a central European customer complaint form and to underpin an online complaint platform.

Also within the KE paradigm, the cognitive computing paradigm proposed by IBM, deals with uncertainty in a probabilistic manner using reasoned arguments. It has started to be applied in the legal domain in different industrial scenarios, like the RossIntelligence system or the IBM partnership with Thomson Reuters[1], but no technical details have been reported.

Within the ATP realm, fee-charging claim websites incorporate a B2C consumer-related business model dedicated to getting passengers compensation from flight companies when their flights are delayed, denied or cancelled. The procedure of operation of these companies follows: calculation of the potential compensation that a passenger might be entitled to in case of cancellation, denied boarding or long flight delay, based solely on article 7 of the Regulation from the compensation calculator (software module based on an automatic logic). Overall, these existing companies do not manage baggage nor service incidents which unleashes disputes and legitimate grounds of redress. The contextualized information regarding the procedures to claim and involved institutional entities are out of the spectrum of the provision of these

---

[1] http://thomsonreuters.com/en/press-releases/2015/october/thomson-reuters-ibm-collaborate-to-deliver-watson-cognitive-computing-technology.html.

services, information which we assume a priori welfare-enhancing self-litigation and empowering of the decision-making process. They do not comprehend overall legal framework, case law, best practices nor links to official sources.

Other information systems provide access to legal documents, as the openlaws.eu platform which grant an alternative access to legal documents found in Eur-Lex with enhanced functionalities (metadata explicitly shown, comments by the community are possible). The European project eucases.eu also harvested case law from Eur-Lex to offer it in a better form. Metadata is offered as RDF and most notably there is a public SPARQL endpoint to make complex queries. These portals are increasingly using better methods to obtain the relevant documents to a particular user query.

3 Modeling Relevant Legal Information for Consumer Disputes

We aim to represent relevant knowledge in a domain of reference. To build and tailor relevance to a legal ontology, producing actionable information, we used the conceptual framework developed by Saracevic, as elaborated below. Saracevic defined 'relevance' as: *'pertaining to the matter at hand'* [4], or, more extended: *'As a cognitive notion relevance involves an interactive, dynamic establishment of a relation by inference, with intentions toward a context.'* Ontologies provide a model or view of the world with respect to a domain - a shared vocabulary (i.e., subject to queries and assertions) in a coherent and consistent manner [5]. The relevance of the queries to be answered is established by the knowledge engineer: he will know which facts are relevant to be modelled. The facts which are considered to be relevant by the end-user cannot be taken into consideration if not modelled in advance. Accordingly, we adapt the manifestations [6] of relevance to our domain:

1. *Systemic or algorithmic.* A *"relation between a query and information objects in the file of a system as retrieved by a given procedure or algorithm. Each system has ways and means by which given objects are represented, organized, and matched to a query. They encompass an assumption of relevance, in that the intent is to retrieve a set of objects that the system inferred (constructed) as being relevant to a query'. Comparative effectiveness in inferring relevance is the criterion for system relevance"*. Our system represents the information objects through ontologies, in a specific ontology language, querying the knowledge base. The intent is to retrieve the information objects the system deemed relevant to a query.

2. *Topical or subject relevance* (topicality match). A *"relation between the subject or topic expressed in a query and topic or subject covered by information objects (retrieved or in the systems file, or even in existence). Aboutness is the criterion by which topicality is inferred."* The definition entails the existence of a taxonomy classifying the documents/information objects, and the information needs correspond to this taxonomy. In our case, the topics were computed in the ontology; they correspond to the ATP domain and the taxonomy defines the relevant incidents of this domain. Therefore, the topicality match relates the incident queried by the consumer - and the retrieved information objects from the ontology-based system.

The user is limited to formulate his request to align it with the available classification system. *"Manual indexing is only as good as the ability of the indexer to anticipate questions to which the indexed document might be found relevant. It is limited by the quality of its thesaurus. It is necessarily precoordinated and is thus also limited in its depth. Finally, like any human enterprise, it is not always done as well as it might be"* [7].

3. *Cognitive relevance or pertinence.* The *"relation between the cognitive state of knowledge of a user and information objects (retrieved or in the systems file, or even in existence). Cognitive correspondence, informativeness, novelty, information quality, and the like are criteria by which cognitive relevance is inferred"*. Cognitive relevance is user-dependent: the features of the system should take into account the user's background knowledge, should be tailored to his search experience, and should be able to explicitly or implicitly understand the information needs of each individual user, and hence, knowledgeable of these questions: which are the users? What information needs the users have? Is the document or information recovered really related to the underlying information need of the user? In our case, supported by, e.g. the Report from the European Consumer Centre Network on Air Passenger Rights (2015) described in Table 3, and in studies on information-seeking behaviour of legal professionals, and on theory of behavioral economics embedded in consumer policy [8] has been demonstrating the information needs among consumers.

4. *Situational relevance or utility.* The *"relation between the situation, task, or problem at hand and information objects (retrieved or in the systems file, or even in existence). Usefulness in decision-making, appropriateness of information in resolution of a problem, reduction of uncertainty, and the like are criteria by which situational relevance is inferred"*. Accordingly, the information objects retrieved in the system should be deemed appropriate to solve the consumer's legal problem or useful in decision-making. Questions may arise: does the document/information found really help the user to solve his (legal) problem? Discovering the actual problem of the users derive from problem-oriented research, or disputes (in our case). The context of legal decision-making requires access to facts derived from empirical observation analysed in our research (through complaints, sectorial reports, case-law, etc.). The ontologies provide the most important and legally disputed problems in the ATP domain and the correspective rights, amenable to a better decision-making. The user formulating a query will attempt to find the norms encompassing the *rights, conditions, exceptions, constraints, interpretations,* requisites that matches the facts of the case/task/problem at hand, e.g. what are the rights of a passenger in case of a cancelation of a flight? What are the exception to the right of compensation?

5. *Domain relevance or legal importance.* Marc Van Opijnen delineates this manifestation of relevance as domain relevance, 'legal authority', 'legal importance' - defined as the general opinion of the legal community on the significance of a case for legal theory and practice [26]. It is two- folded, requesting the most important domain documents within the specific legal domain. Adapted to our case, the ontology should present the most the most important legal documents (even at the level of subdocument, the specific content) within the ATP domain, such as: case law

from the CJEU, Regulations, EU Communications and Official Reports - the most authoritative sources which the 'legal crowd' [26] considers relevant (Table 3).

The interplay and adaption of the various intertwined relevance manifestations (*"system of relevancies"* [4]) is considered in our ontologies, e.g. what are the most authorative documents within the ATP domain (domain)? What does the user need to know to solve a dispute (cognitive)? What is the legal problem of the user (situational)?

For eliciting and engineering the legal relevant information, relevance was considered to inform our knowledge base. Ontology Engineering refers to the set of activities concerning the development process, life cycle, methodologies, tools, etc. [14]. Herein, we use the legacy guiding methodologies: MeLon (Methodology for legal ontologies) and Neon specification tasks [13] to ensure sustainable modeling.

3.1   Ontology Requirements Specification

The Ontology Requirement Specification Documents (ORSD) [15] described below refers to the activity of collecting the requirements that the ontologies should fulfill: (a) purpose, intended scenarios of use, end-users, etc.; (b) level of formality; (c) scope. Tables 1 and 2 present the ORSD for the RIC and RIC-ATPI ontologies.

Table 1. Ontology requirements document of RIC

RIC ontology requirements	
Purpose	This ontology supports the representation of relevant, legal information in consumer disputes, regardless the sub-domain within consumer law, able for reuse in other domains (telecommunications, banking, utilities, etc.) within consumer law
Scope	The Ontology uses a general granularity at the level of legal terms, identifying rights, obligations, prohibitions, exceptions, constraints, enforcement procedures
Implementation	Implemented in OWL 2 language using Protégé as the ontology development environment
	Documentation in http://ricontology.com/ontoric.html
End-users	Legal professionals, decision makers and drafters
Uses	Allows to index and retrieve normative documents from a semantic point of view. Legal professionals may query a Legal Information System (LIS) where documents are indexed on the basis of these analytical metadata, searching for relevant information, obtaining a selective retrieval
	Can be used in the drafting phase, giving the drafter the possibility to annotate metadata and drawing up new documents starting from their structure
	Allows diagnosis on normative texts to analyse the coherency of the legal system
	Ontology-driven systems

Table 2. Ontology requirements document of ATPI

RIC-ATPI ontology requirements	
Purpose	The ontology models the relevant legal information in the ATP domain
Scope	Expresses the relevant legal information according to each ATP incident: the concrete exceptions, constraints, further interpretations and enforcement procedures
	Uses the specific content refracted in the elicited sources, thus, at the level of normative provisions, recitals from legislation, paragraphs from a specific case-law or from the documents of the European Commission
	Declares as class the *AirTransportPassengerIncident* that is a subclass of *RIC:Incident*; it also includes the relevant legal information as class-instances of RIC classes
	Describes as use-case the ATP incidents, within the EU geographical delimitation
	Even though ATPI is consumer-based (related to business-to-consumer (B2C) transactions), our approach is broader, as a passenger might be considered a consumer or a professional
	It is out of the scope of the ATPI accidents, death or any other bodily injury suffered by a passenger, incidents related to package tours and contractual problems between online bookings, rights for disabled passengers, and persons with reduced mobility
Functional requirements	Requirements are represented through informal competency questions (CQs) [36]. The answerability of CQs hence becomes a functional requirement. CQs from were extracted from expert generated content sources
	The ontology should articulate the manifestations of relevance
	The CQs are: (1) What are the Air Transport Passenger incidents? (2) For any given incident, which enforcement procedures should be followed? (3) Which are the exceptions in case of a cancelation, delay, denied boarding? (4) Which are the constraints in case of cancelation, delay, denied boarding? (5) Which are the passenger's rights in case of a cancelled flight? (6) What is the further interpretation of extraordinary circumstances? (7) Which are the requisites for the entitlement of rights? (8) What are the legal sources that support the right to accommodation and transportation?
Implementation	Implemented in OWL 2 language using Protégé as the ontology development environment
	Documentation in http://ricontology.com/ontoricatpi.html
End-users	Air carriers, Passengers, Regulators, National Enforcement Bodies (NEBS), ECC-Networks, Consumer Agencies and Ombudsmen, Alternative Dispute Resolution Bodies, Courts, Legal Assistance Consultancies, Enterprise Europe Network, Travel Agencies, Intermediate Booking Platforms or Price Comparison Websites, and collaborative economy
Uses	Ontology driven system

3.2 Knowledge Acquisition

The user-context of our ontologies confines both the *elicitation* and the *knowledge acquisition tasks* both for RIC and RIC-ATPI ontologies. The types of expert-consultant documents identified below as elicited sources for the knowledge acquisition gather a correspondence and a "semantic deepness"[2] between the use of the terminology in current practice, and an ecologically valid ontology. We assumed a broad approach towards the law, considering more than explicit legal knowledge [25], codified in specific and standardized ways by the legal community. We followed a pluralistic perspective of legal sources, fitting into a pragmatic approach [39, 40]. We captured the following the bulk legal material:

(i)   Secondary sources of law: EU Regulations and Directives;
(ii) Supplementary law: CJEU case law;
(iii) Soft law instruments[3] - fluidizing the soft law/hard law[4] divide.
(iv) *'Practical legal professional knowledge'* [42] (PLK), such as public policies (ECC Reports, NEB's decisions), complaints, a.s.o. that provide good descriptions and raw data concerning everyday problems. It consists in knowledge *"that goes beyond codified legal knowledge in the aforementioned forms and consists in the know-how that tells how to apply codified knowledge in concrete situation (...) this knowledge is acquired through experience rather than by formal training, it is unequally distributed among the members of the community and it is difficult to elicit."* [1]. Nevertheless, is part of the multilevel structure of legal knowledge.

In our research, we resort both to Hard and Soft law. Soft law are "[r]*ules of conduct that are laid down in instruments which have not been attributed legally binding force as such, but nevertheless may have certain – indirect – legal effects, and that are aimed at and may produce practical effects*" [27], which have been used historically to alleviate a lack of formal law-making capacity and/or means of enforcement, European Parliament Resolution (2007/2028(INI)). We assume means that soft law norms: (i) can be used by courts and by decision makers to interpret and complement another rule hard law, by giving interpretations or additional information, and exert influence on actors, without resorting to judicial coercion; (ii) may have a practical impact as a hard law norm [27]. In practice, we may derive from soft law instruments legal and practical effects which are considered by the CJEU and national courts, in particular, rights, obligations, constraints, even with soft or no enforcement, echoing from them.

It is our assumption that there is a *continuum* line from non-binding legal positions to legally binding [27] ones. We base our understanding of soft law as comprising both legally binding and non-legally binding norms. The fact that norms have 'legal relevance' is sufficient to place them on the 'legal' side of the norms continuum, albeit their

---

[2] http://www.estrellaproject.org/doc/D1.4-OWL-Ontology-of-Basic-Legal-Concepts.pdf.

[3] http://europa.eu/eu-law/decision-making/legal-acts/index_en.htm.

[4] Hard law corresponds to the situation where hard obligation and hard enforcement are connected [29].

non-binding character. Less formal sources of law still needs to be referenced to provide a more complete traceability [41]. Some examples are referred (Fig. 1).

Decision of the CJEU[5]: held that national courts are *bound* to take EU Recommendations from the Commission into consideration in order to decide disputes submitted to them, in particular, where they cast light on the interpretation of national measures adopted in order to implement them or where they are designed to supplement binding Community provisions.

Recitals 14 and 15 of the EC Regulation: enunciate events which are regarded as extraordinary circumstances. These cases have been used by the CJEU to determine to which extent the air carrier is exempted from paying compensation.

NEB's Draft list of Extraordinary Circumstances[6]: purports to provide guidance on which circumstances should be considered extraordinary; this list is considered in national courts.

Table 3. Relevant sources in the ATP domain evoked by consumer-based organizations or airline industry

Type of norms	Binding nature	Sources
Norms: Hard law	Binding	**Legislation:** Regulation 261/2004/EC, Montreal Convention 1999
		Case Law
		Contractual terms
Norms: Soft law	Binding norms with a soft dimension	EU Commission Communications, Recommendations, Public Consultations, Working Documents
		Policies: IATA Glossary, IATA Reports, IATA General Conditions of Carriage (Passenger and Baggage)
	Non-binding norms	**Doctrine:** BEUC positions; European Consumer Centres Network (ECC-Net) Reports, NEB's Draft list of Extraordinary Circumstances
		EU complaint-form
Non legal norms (documents)	Non-binding (generally evoked)	**Reports, Surveys, Statistics, Datasets** Eurocontrol Reports Eurobarometer Surveys European Low Fares Airline Association (ELFAA) statistics Database consumer complaints from the CCA

---

[5] Case C-322/88 *Grimaldi* [1989] ECR 4407, paragraph 18. In Community law, a *Recommendation* is a legal instrument that enables the Commission to establish non-binding rules for the Member States or, in certain cases, Union citizens. Article 211 of the EC Treaty provides that "[i]n order to ensure the proper functioning and development of the common market, the Commission shall formulate recommendations (...)".

[6] http://ec.europa.eu/transport/themes/passengers/air/doc/neb-extraordinary-circumstances-list.pdf.

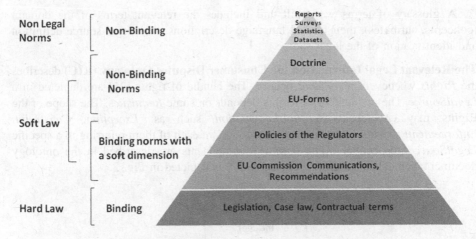

Fig. 1. Hierarchy of the information resources.

An advocated property when representing legislation is that its executable representation, within legal knowledge based systems, should be isomorphic to their sources [28–31]. This principle evokes a one-to-one correspondence between the concepts in the knowledge base system to the source texts, as a basic principle of system construction in the legal domain [32]. It is thereby argued that keeping the structure of the formalisation as close as possible to the original sources, assures and benefits, among other things, verification, validation and maintenance as the legislation is amended. Complete isomorphism challenges the peculiar structural features of legal texts [33]. AI&Law tools [34] usually are focused on the task of applying a logic formalism to achieve isomorphism (e.g. often using plain text, paraphrase techniques or simplified English text—ACE[7]), relying their attention only on the norm modeling and on the foundational logical theory. Representing legislation, far from a mechanical process, requires interpretation against the context of applicable legal conventions, and the way in which the legislation is applied in practice. In our KB one source unit is formalized in more source unit, and one single KB unit conflates material from several source items (contiguous source units are mixed in one KB). Nonetheless we aim to make visible in the text the "evidence" that there is a minimal, but reasonable interconnection of a textual legal link, within a formal representation. Legal experts and policy-makers are interested in verifying the results of the legal formal representation and its applications and in finding evidence in the legally binding text that more and more, nowadays, is available on the web in digital format.

3.3   Ontology Conceptualization

The ontologies' conceptualization activity implied the organization and conversion of the informally perceived sight of our domain into formal components specification.

---

[7] ACE—Attempto Controlled English: http://attempto.ifi.uzh.ch/site/.

A glossary of terms was built and includes the relevant terms of the domain (concepts, attributes), their natural language descriptions, their legal source definition and identification of the legal source.

The Relevant Legal Information for Consumer Disputes Ontology (RIC) describes the *Rights* whenever an *Incident* occurs. The bundle of rights [35] are depicted in a *LegalSource*. The entitlement of Rights depends on some *Requisites*. The scope of the Rights may encompass *RelevantInformation*, such as: *Exception*, *Constraint*, *EnforcementProcedure* and *Further Interpretation*, each of them referring to a specific *LegalSource*, respectively. The ontology components are described in the ontology documentation. Their graphical representation is depicted in Fig. 2.

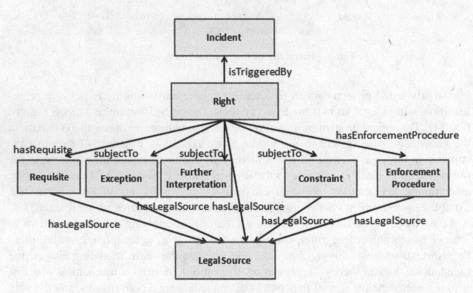

Fig. 2. RIC ontology. Arrows denote object properties, domain and range.

The Air Transport Passenger (RIC-ATPI) Ontology extends the RIC ontology representing the objects in one specific domain of discourse: the main clustered flight disruptions that frame the ATP dispute market. The taxonomy of incidents is aligned with the Recommendation of the EU Commission on the use of a harmonised methodology for classifying consumer complaints SEC (2010)572 and the expert knowledge has been modeled accordingly to this common framework, shaping it after the analysis of incidents in actual complaints. *Air-Transport-PassengerIncident* is the main class and compounds three types of sub-incidents *FlightIncident*, *BaggageIncident* and *ServiceIncident* as described below in Fig. 3. An *AirTransportPassengerIncident* can be subsumed to atomic or composite incidents (combining an interplay of more than one incident detected in the same complaint), which means it is conceivable to ascertain in one dispute a combination of incidents, e.g. a *DelayedFlight* and a *DelayedBaggage*.

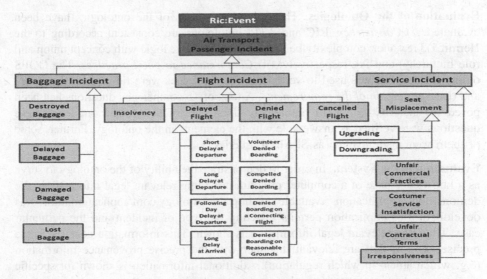

Fig. 3. Class diagram of the ATPI ontology.

The relevant information is represented as class-instances of the RIC-ATPI ontology. We illustrate an example of the relevant information regarding the right to meals and refreshments that applies when a flight is cancelled. It includes requisites, constraints and enforcement procedures modeled as class individuals (Fig. 4).

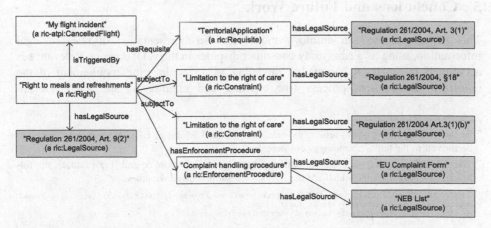

Fig. 4. RIC-ATPI: boxes denote classes, arrows denote object properties, with the arrow meaning domain and range.

4   Evaluation

The proposed ontologies can be used to drive an ontology-based system providing relevant information for each of the previously foreseen cases. This section provides an evaluation of both the ontologies and the system.

Evaluation of the Ontologies. The following aspects of the ontologies have been evaluated. (i) *Consistency*. RIC and ATPI ontologies are consistent according to the Hermit 1.3 reasoner; complexity being ALUH (attributive logic with concept union and role hierarchy) and AL respectively; (ii) *Conformance to good practices*. The OOPS online service [38] was used to verify that the ontologies were rid of critical pitfalls[8] and (iii) *Satisfaction of the requirements*. A total of 15 competency questions had been posed for the RIC and ATPI ontologies. Upon construction of the ontology, these questions were verified as answerable with the elements in the ontology. Further, some of them were made explicit as SPARQL queries[9].

Evaluation of the System. In order to demonstrate the ability of the ontology to serve as a knowledge base of a computer program providing relevant legal information, the demonstrative application available at http://ricontology.com/application.html was developed. This application permits selecting the type of incident and the particular case. Then, the relevant legal information is shown. This information consists of the precise excerpts that are relevant, together with the precise provenance information (e.g. which article in which regulation). Additional information is shown for specific circumstances or interpretations when moving the mouse over the general description. The demonstrative application proves the feasibility of the idea, but in the future an extended evaluation will be made. Equivalent efforts have been extrinsically evaluated in the past, namely, comparing the obtained results with those obtained from other procedures and estimating the precision and recall of the system.

5 Conclusions and Future Work

This paper presented an ontology model for the representation of relevant legal information, using as a case study consumer disputes in the ATP domain. Relevance is accounted in the legal knowledge modeling as an engineering requirement of the ontology development process (for eliciting and engineering the legal relevant

---

[8] At the time of writing of this article, the ontologies had as URI the git URL, but they it is planned to be moved to the http://ricontology.com domain.

[9] The SPARQL queries are available online as http://ricontology.com/cq.hml. For example, the following query determines which are the rights for a short delayed departure

```
    ? SELECT  (str(?lab)  as  ?label)  (str(?com)  as  ?comment)  (str(?sour)  as  ?sourcelabel)
(str(?sc) as ?sourcecomment) (?r as ?uri) ?tipo{
       ?r ric:isTriggeredBy ric-atpi:shortdelayedatdeparture .
       ?r rdfs:label ?lab .
       ?r rdf:type ?tipo .
       OPTIONAL {
         ?r rdfs:comment ?com .
       }
       OPTIONAL {
         ?r ric:hasLegalSource ?ls .
         ?ls rdfs:label ?sour .
         OPTIONAL {
           ?ls rdfs:comment ?sc .
         }
       }
     FILTER (?tipo != owl:NamedIndividual) .
   } ORDER BY ?label LIMIT 50
```

information). Accessing hard law, but also relevant soft legal sources of information plays a role in the decision-making process of the parties, *maxime*, in legal information systems. Soft governance and the use of soft law might be viewed as a new form of soft governance in the *continuum* line of soft law hardening. It can be argued that soft law is helping to reduce the democratic deficit by the emphasis it puts on deliberation and participation of the stakeholders.

As future work, RIC ontology will cumulate other modalities, such as obligation, permission, sanction. A web-based application is being construed backing up the present ontology-based system. While the ontology has been evaluated in this paper, no proper evaluation has been given for the ontology-based system. The evaluation of this system necessarily has to be compared in terms of precision, recall and access time with other means of accessing the same information: Google search, queries in Lexis and Westlaw systems or the intermediating companies. This remains as future work.

Acknowledgements. Research presented in this paper is conducted as a PhD research at the Universities of Barcelona and Luxembourg, within the Erasmus Mundus Joint International Doctoral (Ph.D.) programme in Law, Science and Technology.

References

1. Fernández-Barrera, M., Sartor, G.: The legal theory perspective: doctrinal conceptual systems vs. computational ontologies. In: Sartor, G., Casanovas, P., Biasiotti, M., Fernández-Barrera, M. (eds.) Approaches to Legal Ontologies, Theories, Domains, Methodologies. LGT Series, pp. 15–47. Springer, Amsterdam (2011)
2. Rodríguez-Doncel, V., et al.: A model of air transport passenger incidents and rights. In: Hoekstra, R. (ed.) Proceedings of the 27th JURIX, pp. 55–69. IOS Press (2014)
3. Cortés, P.: ODR for Consumers, ODR Methods for Settling B2C Conflicts, Online Dispute Resolution: Theory and Practice: A Treatise on Technology and Dispute Resolution, p. 164. Eleven Law Publishing, Utrecht (2012)
4. Saracevic, T.: Relevance reconsidered, information science: integration in perspectives. In: Second Conference on Conceptions of Library and Information Science, pp. 201–218 (1996)
5. Gruber, T.R.: Toward principles for the design of ontologies used for knowledge sharing. Int. J. Hum. Comput. Stud. **43**, 907–928 (1995)
6. Saracevic, T.: Relevance: a review of the literature and a framework for thinking on the notion in information science. Part II: nature and manifestations of relevance. ASIS&T **58**(3), 1915–1933 (2007)
7. Dabney, D.P.: The curse of Thamus: an analysis of full-text legal document retrieval. Law Libr. J. **78**, 5–40 (1986)
8. Micklitz, H.-W., et al.: An introduction to the special issue on behavioural economics, consumer policy, and consumer law. JCP **34**, 271–276 (2011)
9. Saravanan, M., et al.: Improving legal information retrieval using an ontological framework. Artif. Intell. Law **17**, 101–124 (2009)
10. Jarrar, M.: Towards effectiveness and transparency in e-business transactions, an ontology for customer complaint management. In: Semantic Web Methodologies for E-Business Applications, pp. 127–149 (2007)
11. Bing, J.: Let there be LITE: a brief history of legal information retrieval. EJLT **1**(1) (2010)

12. Blair, D., Maron, M.: An evaluation of retrieval effectiveness for a full-text document-retrieval system. Commun. ACM **28**(3), 289–299 (1985)

13. Suárez-Figueroa, M.C., Gómez-Pérez, A., Motta, E., Gangemi, A. (eds.): Ontology Engineering in a Networked World. Springer, Heidelberg (2012)

14. Gómez-Pérez, A., Fernandez-Lopez, M., Corcho, O.: Ontological Engineering: with Examples from the Areas of Knowledge Management, e-Commerce and the Semantic Web. Springer, New York (2003)

15. Suárez-Figueroa, M.C., Gómez-Pérez, A., Villazón-Terrazas, B.: How to write and use the ontology requirements specification document. In: Meersman, R., Dillon, T., Herrero, P. (eds.) OTM 2009, Part II. LNCS, vol. 5871, pp. 966–982. Springer, Heidelberg (2009)

16. Dabney, D.P.: The curse of Thames: an analysis of full-text legal document retrieval. Law Libr. J. **78**(5), 5–40 (1986)

17. Alvite, M.L.: Tendencias a la investigación sobre la recuperación de Información Jurídica. Revista española de Documentación Científica, vol. 26, no. 2 (2003)

18. Schweighofer, E.: The revolution in legal information retrieval or: the empire strikes back. J. Law Inf. Technol. **1** (1999)

19. Moens, M.F.: XML retrieval models for legislation. In: Legal Knowledge Systems JURIX, pp. 1–10 (2004)

20. Gelbart, D., Smith, J.C.: Toward a comprehensive legal information retrieval system. In: DEXA 1990, pp. 121–125 (1990)

21. Turtle, H.: Inference networks for document retrieval. Ph.D. thesis, Computer Science Department Univ. Massachusetts, MA 01003, COINS Technical Report 90-92 (1990)

22. George, C.P., et al.: SMART Electronic Legal Discovery via Topic Modeling [URL]. FLAIRS-27, Pensacola, Florida, USA (2014)

23. Blei, D.M., Ng, A.Y., Jordan, M.I.: Latent Dirichlet allocation. J. Mach. Learn. Res. **3**, 993–1022 (2003)

24. Uschold, M., Gruninger, M., et al.: Ontologies: principles, methods and applications. Knowl. Eng. Rev. **11**(2), 93–136 (1996)

25. Casanovas, P., Casellas, N., Vallbé, J.-J.: Empirically grounded developments of legal ontologies: a socio-legal perspective. In: Sartor, G., Casanovas, P., Biasiotti, M., Fernández-Barrera, M. (eds.) Approaches to Legal Ontologies. LGT Series, vol. 1, pp. 49–67. Springer, Amsterdam (2011)

26. Opijnen, M.V.: A model for automated rating of case law. In: ICAIL, pp. 140–149 (2013)

27. Terpan, F.: Soft law in the European union the changing nature of EU law. Eur. Law **21**, 68–96 (2014). Wiley

28. Bench-Capon, T., Coenen, F.: Isomorphism and legal knowledge based systems. Artif. Intell. Law **1**(1), 65–86 (1992)

29. Routen, T.: Hierarchically organised formalisations. In: Proceedings of the Second ICAIL. ACM Press, Vancouver, pp. 242–250 (1989)

30. Karpf, J.: Quality Assurance of Legal Expert Systems. Jurimatics, no. 2, Copenhagen Business School, Denmark (1989)

31. Prakken, H., Schrickx, J.: Isomorphic models for rules and exceptions in legislation. In: Breuker, J.A.P.J., et al. (eds.) JURIX 91: Model-Based Legal Reasoning. Koninklijke Vermande, Lelystad, pp. 17–27 (1991)

32. Palmirani, M., Contissa, G., Rubino, R.: Fill the gap in the legal knowledge modelling. In: Governatori, G., Hall, J., Paschke, A. (eds.) RuleML 2009. LNCS, vol. 5858, pp. 305–314. Springer, Heidelberg (2009)

33. Sergot, M.J.: The representation of law in computer programs. In: Bench-Capon, T.J.M. (ed.) Knowledge Based Systems and Legal Applications, pp. 3–68. Academic Press (1991)

34. Gordon, T.F.: The Carneades web service. In: Verheij, B. (eds.) Proceedings of Computational Models of Argument, COMMA 2012. IOS Press, pp. 517–518 (2012)
35. McCarthy, L.T.: Onwnership: a case study in the representation of legal concepts. AI&Law J. **10**, 135–161 (2002)
36. Gruninger, M., Fox, M.S.: The role of competency questions in enterprise engineering. In: Rolstadås, A. (ed.) WG5.7 Workshop on Benchmarking - Theory and Practice. IFIP, pp. 22–31. Springer, New York (1994)
37. Uschold, M., King, M.: Towards a methodology for building ontologies. In: Workshop on Basic Ontological Issues in Knowledge Sharing (1995)
38. Poveda, M., et al.: Oops! (ontology pitfall scanner!): an on-line tool for ontology evaluation. Int. J. Semant. Web Inf. Syst. **10**(2), 4–14 (2014)
39. Casanovas, P., et al.: The role of pragmatics in the web of data. In: Poggi, F., Capone, A. (eds.) Pragmatics and Law. Practical and Theoretical Approaches. Springer Verlag, Heidelberg (2016)
40. Gaines, B.R.: Knowledge acquisition: past, present and future. Int. J. Hum. Comput. Stud. **71**, 135–156 (2013)
41. Boella, G., et al.: A critical analysis of legal requirements engineering from the perspective of legal practice. In: IEEE 7th International Workshop RELAW, pp. 14–21 (2014)
42. Benjamins, V.R., et al.: The SEKT legal use case components: ontology and architecture. In: Gordon, T. (ed.) Legal Knowledge and Information Systems, JURIX 2004, pp. 69–77. IOS Press, Amsterdam (2004)

Intelligent Systems in E-Government

Design of Public Sector Websites: Findings from an Eye Tracking Study Emphasizing Visual Attention and Usability Metrics

Hanne Sørum[✉]

Westerdals Oslo School of Arts, Communication and Technology, Oslo, Norway
hanne.sorum@westerdals.no

Abstract. This explorative eye tracking study investigates visual attention and perceptions of usability within eGovernment environments. We argue that such insights help in understanding users for better design of user Web experiences. In an initial test to identify areas of interest (AOI) on public sector websites, subjects (n = 8) were exposed to the start page of ten different websites with slightly different designs. Two websites (old versus new design) were then selected to investigate attention to different visual elements (n = 16). The System Usability Scale (SUS) was used to investigate performance on usability metrics. The results indicate differences in viewing behavior and visual attention across different designs, in terms of both eye tracking metrics and usability scores. The concluding remarks include suggestions for further research.

Keywords: Public sector websites · eGovernment · Human-computer interaction · Eye tracking · Visual attention · Usability · SUS (System Usability Scale)

1 Introduction

In many countries, almost every public organization has its own website. However, there are huge differences in the information and services provided online, and in the resources invested in website development and quality improvement. Differences in the design of public websites can affect website quality and usability performance. In recent years, the design of websites has changed in relation to layout, content, online services and integration with other systems (e.g. search engines, blogs, chat functions), as new and innovative technologies enable organizations to create great user experiences. In this context, "Innovations in ICT offer rich opportunities for governments to significantly improve the delivery of their services and to interact more openly with their constituents." [1, p. 103]. Today, it is also easier to arrange for two-way dialogues and digital interactions between government bodies and citizens. In consequence, users tend to expect great user experiences, raising the pressure of expectation for individual organizations. For this reason, organizations need to know their users, the expectations among different target groups, and their individual requirements for information search and task performance. In short, it has become essential to adopt a user-centric approach to development and quality issues.

A. Kő and E. Francesconi (Eds.): EGOVIS 2016, LNCS 9831, pp. 169–181, 2016.
DOI: 10.1007/978-3-319-44159-7_12

The increasing use of digital channels for communication and interaction within the public sector [e.g. 2], makes it all the more vital to understand website viewing behavior and task performance. Given that central governments in many countries are ambitious with regard to digitalization, increasing attention is devoted to website quality improvement, and goals and strategies focus on citizens' interests and needs from a customer perspective [3]. The extent to which such thinking is implemented in a given organization is likely to vary widely according to the organization's size, available resources, target groups, stakeholders and other interests. We have observed that most public sector websites serve a large and heterogeneous group of users, making usability issues, accessibility requirements and information quality especially important. In our digital society, everyone (that is, all citizens) should have equal access to digital information and online services [4], especially as access to eGovernment resources through the Web may be the only viable option for some users [5].

Knowledge of how users allocate visual attention is important for interaction designers, advertisers and others [6] in understanding how users acquire and search for information and services on the Web. Citizens visit public sector websites for many and varied reasons, but in most cases, they are looking for specific information, unlike when browsing online newspapers and magazines. Not surprisingly, then, "Paying attention to how users look for information on websites is becoming increasingly important in designing positive user experiences. Users are no longer impressed with the basic utility of a website and are now more demanding for websites that have superb user experiences." [7, p. 27]. Although there are many great examples of eGovernment initiatives (e.g. www.gov.uk), many public websites lack quality and are in need of significant improvement from a user perspective.

Because online interactions and dialogues have largely replaced many traditional face-to-face interactions, examination of viewing behavior (eye movements) and task performance provides unique knowledge of how users interact with websites. This knowledge includes deeper insights into how the placement and appearance of visual elements and text influence user experiences and perceptions. Eye tracking is one technique that is now widely used to investigate user behavior within various disciplines involving human-computer interaction (HCI) [8], especially for usability research [e.g. 9]. Prior studies have established that eye tracking is a highly effective method for studying interface design and other issues relating to user behavior and satisfaction: "With the help of an Eye tracker the users pupils and their position on a screen are tracked and thus provide detailed data about the users visual attention on user interface elements. It can be used as a valuable source of information about users behavior." [10, p. 141]. With high precision is the eye movements recorded and can then be subject to detailed and thorough analysis on various levels.

The general research objective of the present paper is to assess how the design of public websites influences visual attention and performance on usability metrics. We have chosen to focus on the websites of municipalities in Norway because of their huge differences in design and content provision, ranging from old-fashioned traditional designs to the modern and minimalistic. Consequently, the following research questions are addressed in this paper: (1) *Which elements and areas of public sector websites attract attention from users?* and (2) *How does the visual appearance and design of public sector websites influence performance on usability metrics?*

To answer these questions, we conducted a usability eye tracking study on websites with slightly differing designs and administered a post-test questionnaire on perceptions of usability. The overall contribution of this study is twofold: (1) the use of eye tracking as a method for assessing public sector website designs, and (2) how design influences viewing behavior and usability metrics in an eGovernment context.

The rest of the paper is organized as follows. Section 2 reviews the relevant literature. Section 3 describes the methodology of the present study. Findings are described in Sect. 4 and discussed in Sect. 5. The concluding remarks in Sect. 6 include suggestions for further research.

2 Literature Review

The present study draws on literature from the fields of eGovernment and human-computer interaction (HCI). "Human-computer interaction is a discipline concerned with the design, evaluation and implementation of interactive computing systems for human use and with the study of major phenomena surrounding them." [11]. One of the main developments in HCI during the past fifteen years is the emergence of usability inspection techniques [12]. The International Organization for Standardization (ISO) defines usability as "The extent to which a product can be used by specified users to achieve specified goals with effectiveness, efficiency, and satisfaction in a specific context of use." [13]. In recent years, usability metrics have received increased attention within the public sector, along with provision of new technologies, apps, and digital channels for interaction to ensure great interactions and user satisfaction. Users who easily can switch to another website do not tolerate bad usability.

Eye tracking is a commonly used technique in usability analysis [14]: "Eye tracking is sometimes able to detect usability problems even when conventional usability testing methods such as behavior observation and participant feedback elicitation don't indicate that there is a problem." [15, p. 27]. We can imagine that a user makes all the actions correctly and perform a given task with success. Despite this, it may prove that the user has been interrupted, which can reflect itself in the eyes movement pattern. Designers need to adopt a user-centric approach and have in-depth user knowledge, rather than placing technology at the center of the development process. However, there are many examples to show that this is not always the case - that is, programmers often design systems without any clear knowledge of users' interests and needs [16].

We are witnessing a growing degree of digitalization, which also gives us unique and great opportunities. In this regard, "Since the commercial inception of the Internet, the ability of Web sites to track the behavior of their visitors has been considered one of the most promising facts of the new medium. The detailed records of Web behavior (click stream data) provide researchers and practitioners with the opportunity to study how users browse and navigate Web sites and to assess site performance in various ways." [17, p. 249]. Another feature of Web behavior is that users tend to scan through text rather than read it all [18]. There is also evidence that Web users often focus on the left side of the webpage when they read, paying less attention to information on the right side of the screen [19]. Shrestha and Lenz [20] discussed visual scan paths during activities such as browsing and searching for websites containing text and/or pictures. Their findings indicate that users follow a uniform scan path when browsing through pictures and a more random path when searching more specifically. Additionally, users appeared to follow Jakob Nielsen's "F-pattern" [19] when both browsing and searching text-based sites.

Regarding this, Nielsen [21] suggested that because it is an effort for users to read on-screen text, they tend to scan, reading only those parts they find interesting. Studies investigating where and when users fixate on images have identified three factors that influence fixation positions: salience of image area, memory and expectations about where to find information, and task and information requirements [6]. Buscher, Cutrell and Morris [6] noted that authors and designers of websites could usefully employ models of visual attention to improve design by ensuring that users pay attention to the website design elements (including text) considered most important. "Visual perception is an essential part of users' interaction with interfaces. Modern eye tracking equipment makes it possible to record and analyze parts of this process. Which elements are actually seen? Where do users look first? What do users look at the most? Did modifications of the graphic design lead to a wanted change in user gaze patterns?" [22, p. 923]. Every little detail could be important to create a good user experience on the Web and sometimes we need to go *behind the scene* to acquire such knowledge. Eye tracking may be one method for digging into details and explore what we cannot observe in traditional usability testing.

On different websites, Roth et al. [23] investigated the effects of location (object placement) on efficiency in finding the target. The results demonstrated that location matters; web objects that are placed according to users' expectation are easier and faster to find, and fewer fixations are needed. Sutcliffe and Namoune [24] investigated visual attention to website elements (e.g. text, animations and images), as well as aesthetic design and user recollection. Based on their findings, they proposed design guidelines for directing users' attention. According to Djamasbi, Siegel and Tullis [25], users most often favor the top and left side of webpages and may therefore overlook information that is not placed in those areas. They also found that inclusion of images on webpages had an impact on the users' viewing pattern. The increasing use of Web technologies during the last decade includes actions at national level such as yearly quality assessment of public websites and web awards highlighting great examples of best practice within eGovernment environments. "Many government agencies now face challenges of trying to process huge amounts of information quickly enough to regulate corporations and perform other critical missions. Likewise, government agencies must serve citizens whose expectations have been redefined by their experiences with e-commerce. The design of e-government information systems (both hardware networks and software) is more than instrumental plumbing. Design decisions are not merely technical or even merely administrative." [26, p. 473]. In many cases, private and public sector websites are not dissimilar, and for that reason, quality aspects developed for private websites might be useful for the public sector as well. Therefore, indicators evaluating usability issues and general design principles will, most likely, be applicable in both sectors [27] and must be taken into consideration in development and quality improvement.

In contrast to this, we also find quality aspects that are particularly relevant for the public sector. The emergence of eGovernment services raises important issues and expectations related to trust in digital information and services provision [28] and accessibility requirements. A study by Fath-Allah et al. [29] emphasized e-government portal best practices and noted that the success of any such portal will depend on design, implementation and the services provided to users (citizens and businesses). Albayrak and Çağıltay [5] examined the usability of five Turkish e-government websites and identified problems in using public services, leading to specific recommendations for dealing with such issues. In many countries (e.g. Norway and Denmark), the government also provide some guidelines that public organizations can relate to and must strive to fulfil. The aim is to guide the public sector in the right direction and focus on important quality aspects perceived from a user's point of view.

3   Methodology

3.1   Study Design

To understand how users interact with public sector websites, we first (Phase 1) performed a test (n = 8) to establish a basic knowledge of visual attention across websites with slightly differing designs. The participants in this test were aged 20–44; four were male and four were female. Each subjects was exposed to each of ten websites (home page) for 25 s each. The subjects were told to look at the website and to familiarize themselves with the information provided on the home page (visual elements and text) during the time available. In Phase 2, we performed a usability test, in which subjects (n = 16) were each exposed to two websites. Subjects first spent two minutes (120 s) browsing each website to become familiar with the information and services provided, with no task assigned at that time. Subsequently, subjects were assigned five tasks for each of the two websites. The subjects were told to look for specific information typical of such sites (answering the questions asked), e.g.: # Imagine that you have a meeting with one person within the organization, please find the address; # Imagine that you want to apply for a job in the municipality, please find the job opportunities available on the website. Along with eye tracking measures, the System Usability Scale (SUS) was used to assess how each of the two websites performed on usability metrics. The whole test (including the SUS questionnaire) was implemented by using software from iMotions (2016). In total, the test (Phase 2) lasted between 13 and 17 min, depending on the subject's efficiency.

3.2   Stimulus

For the usability test, we chose to use two websites that could be viewed as extremes in terms of design: a typical "old" design (Website A), containing lots of visual elements throughout the website; and Website B, a typical "new" design with a minimalistic layout and aesthetic. For the purposes of this paper, we have chosen to withhold the names of the organizations concerned. In total, subjects were exposed to 33 stimuli from beginning to end of the test. The stimulus set contained various types of information, including tasks to be conducted, questionnaires for the usability test (SUS), and instructions for subjects.

3.3 Subjects and Procedures

The sample for the usability test included 16 subjects (eight males, aged 20–42 years and eight females aged 21–45 years). The average male age was 31.8 years (median age 32 years), and the average age for females was 28.2 (median age 23.5 years). As users of public sector websites come from all age groups, we chose to recruit students and staff from an educational institution in Norway. After subjects entered the usability lab, they were informed about the purpose of the study, and participants then signed a consent form concerning handling of data, voluntary participation and ethics. At that point, they were also encouraged to ask questions, if any.

3.4 Apparatus

iMotions 6.0 software was used to design and present stimuli, and Tobii X2-30 Compact was used to collect data. The tests were conducted in a usability lab, using a computer with Intel Core i7 1.8 GHz processor. Monitor resolution was 1920×1080 pixels, and a standard mouse was used to navigate the website during the test.

3.5 Data Analysis

Both qualitative and quantitative analyses were performed, adopting eye tracking measures suggested by Bergstrom and Schall [7]. Heat maps were created in iMotions 6.0 for qualitative analysis of reading patterns, along with standard eye tracking measures represented by numbers (statistical data) generated by the software. The System Usability Scale (SUS) was used to capture subjects' perceptions of usability for Website A and Website B. The SUS scale is widely cited in research [30] and seen as an effective method of assessing the usability of websites [31]. The questionnaire contains of ten statements (five negative and five positive), measured on a five-point scale ranging from *Strongly disagree* to *Strongly agree*.

4 Findings

The first set of findings presented here (Sect. 4.1) are from the initial test (Phase 1), involving ten websites with slightly different designs. We then present the findings from the usability test (Phase 2) in Sects. 4.2 and 4.3, as conducted on two municipality websites (Website A and Website B).

4.1 Phase 1: Viewing Behavior (Visual Attention) and Areas of Interest (AOI)

To understand how the design of public sector websites influences viewing behavior and reading patterns among users, we conducted an initial test on ten websites. Patterns of fixation (represented as heat maps) reveal the distribution of visual attention among subjects. Qualitative analysis of the resulting heat maps can be summarized as follows. (1) Great attention is paid to the menu(s), whether placed at the top or on the left side. (2) Users scan the webpage by first looking at the upper left part. (3) If no information is provided in the upper part, users tend to start scanning in middle-center. (4) The left side of the webpage receives more attention than the right side. (5) The upper part of the webpage is given more attention than the lower area. (6) Visual elements that are likely to require actions attract more attention than those that do not.

In all ten designs, visual elements included logo/name of the organization, a main menu (links to information and services) and a search field (where it is possible to enter text). Measures used to investigate how the placement of these three elements influenced user attention included time to first fixation (TTFF) and the number of subjects attending to each (ratio). TTFF is the median time to first fixation across all subjects, who were exposed to each of the ten websites for 25 s (see Table 1).

Table 1. Eye tracking metrics: AOI for all ten websites.

#	Logo/name	Main menu	Search field
1	TTFF: 2.5 s; Ratio: 8/8	TTFF: 2.4 s; Ratio: 8/8	TTFF: 24.7 s; Ratio: 1/8
2	TTFF: 2.8 s; Ratio: 8/8	TTFF: 1.3 s; Ratio: 8/8	TTFF: 18.0 s; Ratio: 3/8
3	TTFF: 3.9 s; Ratio: 8/8	TTFF: 6.4 s; Ratio: 7/8	TTFF: 16.4 s; Ratio: 4/8
4	TTFF: 2.3 s; Ratio: 8/8	TTFF: 2.3 s; Ratio: 8/8	TTFF: 14.7 s; Ratio: 8/8
5	TTFF: 2.6 s; Ratio: 8/8	TTFF: 0.3 s; Ratio: 8/8	TTFF: 18.7 s; Ratio: 3/8
6	TTFF: 2.4 s; Ratio: 8/8	TTFF: 8.2 s; Ratio: 8/8	TTFF: 17.5 s; Ratio: 5/8
7	TTFF: 2.7 s; Ratio: 8/8	TTFF: 5.6 s; Ratio: 8/8	TTFF: 9.3 s; Ratio: 8/8
8	TTFF: 4.1 s; Ratio: 7/8	TTFF: 5.4 s; Ratio: 8/8	TTFF: 25 s; Ratio: 0/8
9	TTFF: 0.7 s; Ratio: 8/8	TTFF: 2.2 s; Ratio: 8/8	TTFF: 11.9 s; Ratio: 7/8
10	TTFF: 4.2 s; Ratio: 8/8	TTFF: 8.2 s; Ratio: 8/8	TTFF: 10.3 s; Ratio: 8/8

We found that 6 of the 10 websites placed the logo top left, which is currently the most common placement of organization logos. Two of the ten websites placed the logo at the top of the page (centered), one placed the logo in the middle center, and one placed it top right. Independent of placement, the logo received relatively quickly attention from most subjects (ranging from 0.7–4.2 s). There were no obvious differences in TTFF, which can be explained by the logo's size, layout, and placement on the webpage. The findings also indicate that placing the logo top right, in the middle, or on the right had no significant impact. With regard to the main menu, Table 1 shows differences in TTFF (ranging from 0.3–8.2 s), which can possibly be explained in terms of how the menu is integrated into the design, and by size, location, and visibility. Regarding the search field, there were huge differences in both placement and attention from users (TTFF). The results range from 9.3–25 s (i.e., not seen at all). Here again, we found no significant difference with regard to size and placement.

4.2   Phase 2: Metrics on Eye Tracking Data from the Usability Test

Based on the initial test (Phase 1), we chose to perform a more in-depth test on two of the websites in relation to usability metrics. As stated earlier, we performed this test on two municipality websites (Website A and Website B), representing differences in design and content provision on the home page. Subjects were first asked to explore the website for 120 s (2 min) before being asked to perform a number of tasks. On completion of all the given tasks, they were asked to complete a questionnaire (the System Usability Scale) focusing on usability metrics. Given that public websites are slightly different in design, emphasis was placed on AOI identified in Phase 1: the organization's logo/name, the search field, and the main menu. We report first on TTFF, ratio, number of revisits (among subjects), fixations (duration of looking at a specific element) and time spent on each AOI (see Table 2).

Table 2. Eye tracking metrics: AOI for Websites A and B.

	AOI 1: Main menu	AOI 2: Logo/name	AOI 3: Search field
Website A	TTFF: 8.1 s	TTFF: 11.2 s	TTFF: 30.4 s
	Ratio: 16/16	Ratio: 15/16	Ratio: 11/16
	Revisit: 15/16	Revisit: 12/15	Revisit: 5/11
	Fixations: 104	Fixations: 59	Fixations: 30
	Time spent: 1.2 s	Time spent: 0.8 s	Time spent: 0.4 s
Website B	TTFF: 2.5 s	TTFF: 10.4 s	TTFF: 34.6 s
	Ratio: 16/16	Ratio: 14/16	Ratio: 12/16
	Revisit: 16/16	Revisit: 14/14	Revisit: 6/12
	Fixations: 1148	Fixations: 142	Fixations: 48
	Time spent: 8.1 s	Time spent: 1.8 s	Time spent: 0.7 s

Website A contained significantly more information and visual elements on the start page than Website B. This is reflected in the findings in Table 2, which shows that TTFF on the menu is longer (in seconds) for Website A than for Website B. This may be influenced by the placement and size of the menu. The menu on Website B is more visible than on Website A because the design for Website B is minimalist and the menu therefore differs clearly from other elements of the site. Regarding the logo/name of the organization, TTFF values are more or less the same for both websites (11.2 s vs. 10.4 s). The same applies to TTFF values for the search field (30.4 s vs. 34.6 s). However, in both cases, more attention (fixation counts) is given to the menus than to the logo or the search field. This is consistent with our assumptions, as subjects were looking for elements that could provide required information and those requiring further actions and/or additional information. The results show that the menus received high numbers of revisits, which is not the case for search fields. The times spent on each of the AOI are significant in terms of the fixations results; again, the menus receive more attention than logos and search fields. Regarding mouse clicks on the start page during the 120 s when subjects were first asked to explore the website (at the beginning of the test), Website A returned 28 mouse clicks and Website B returned 113 mouse clicks in total. This huge difference can mostly likely be explained by the website design, as Website A contains significantly more elements and text on the start page than Website B.

4.3   Perception of Usability (System Usability Scale)

After the subjects had completed the usability test tasks, they were asked to complete a questionnaire. This ensured that they were qualified to answer the questions (statements) related to usability metrics for each of the two websites (A and B). Table 3 shows the distribution of answers on a scale ranging from 1 (*Strongly disagree*) to 5 (*Strongly agree*).

Table 3. Results from the System Usability Scale questionnaire (n = 16).

Website A vs. Website B					
Statements	1	2	3	4	5
I think that I would like to use this website frequently	3 (0)	1 (0)	9 (8)	1 (8)	2 (0)
I found the website unnecessarily complex	5 (4)	6 (10)	2 (1)	2 (1)	1 (0)
I thought the website was easy to use	0 (0)	2 (1)	2 (3)	7 (9)	5 (3)
I think that I would need the support of a technical person to be able to use this website	15 (15)	1 (1)	0 (0)	0 (0)	0 (0)
I found the various functions in this website were well integrated	0 (0)	1 (1)	9 (2)	4 (9)	2 (4)
I thought there was too much inconsistency in this website	8 (6)	3 (6)	4 (1)	1 (3)	0 (0)
I would imagine that most people would learn to use this website very quickly	0 (0)	2 (2)	4 (1)	7 (7)	3 (6)
I found the website very cumbersome to use	10 (11)	4 (3)	1 (2)	1 (0)	0 (0)
I felt very confident using the website	1 (1)	1 (1)	3 (3)	5 (7)	6 (4)
I needed to learn a lot of things before I could get going with this website	12 (11)	4 (4)	0 (1)	0 (0)	0 (0)

Table 3 shows that subjects were more positive about Website B, which had a clean and minimalist design, than Website A. The main differences related to frequent use of the site, the extent to which different functions were well integrated on the website, and consistency in the design. To calculate the SUS score (as mainly emphasized here), we created an Excel spreadsheet of important raw data from iMotions. Figure 1 shows the scores at subject level (minimum score is 0 and maximum score is 100).

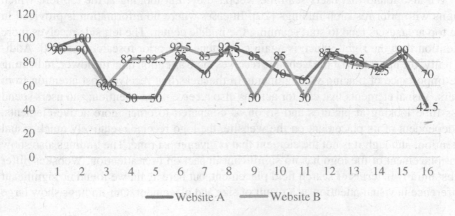

Fig. 1. SUS score calculated for each subject (n = 16).

For Website A, the average score is 74.53, median is 77.5, and standard deviation is 17. For Website B, the average score is 78.28, median is 83.75 and standard deviation is 13.87. The results shows that the SUS score for Website A is lower than for Website B. The same results apply to the median score. The standard deviation is higher for Website A than for Website B. In summary, Website B performed generally better than Website A. Although a SUS score above 70 is acceptable [5], we identified potential for improvements, as the maximum possible score is 100.

5   Discussion

The use of IT and innovative technologies offers new opportunities for public sector provision of information and services [1] whose goals and requirements are largely user-focused [3]. The present paper reports on an eye tracking study investigating visual attention and perceived usability of public sector websites in Norway. We argue that such insights help to understand users in designing better user experiences on the Web. The present paper addresses two research questions: (1) *Which elements and areas of public sector websites attract attention from users?* and (2) *How does the visual appearance and design of public sector websites influence performance on usability metrics?*

Findings from the testing of ten websites (Phase 1) show that public sector sites (i.e., municipalities) differ slightly in their design in terms of placement of visual elements (including text and pictures), services provided, and content provision. We found no standards for how public websites should or actually appear on screen; on the contrary, there is a wide range of website designs and ways of structuring information. From a user perspective, usability is important for successfully finding required information and performing tasks [21], and so, by the same token, are usability inspection techniques [12]. We argue that this issue is of particular importance within an eGovernment context, given the increasing public sector use of digital channels for communication and inter-action with citizens [2], making it essential to ensure that everyone is included in our digital society [4]. When designing websites, we need to adopt a user-centric approach, and knowledge about visual attention is an important element in this regard [6].

We also found that users scan the webpage by first looking at the top left, which aligns with prior research findings [20]. In cases where no information is provided in the top area, users tend to start scanning the middle center. The left side receives more attention than the right, which is again consistent with prior research [e.g. 19]. Additionally, the upper part of the webpage receives more attention than the lower, indicating the importance of placing vital elements in the areas that receive most attention from users. Visual elements that call for actions also receive more attention, and users spend less time looking at pictures and so on as compared to other more active elements. Independent of its placement on the website, the logo receives relatively quick visual attention, although it is not the element that is given most time. The findings also show that placement of the logo has no significant impact on user attention. Websites differ substantially in terms of search field placement, but here again we found no significant difference in visual attention as a result of size and placement. Our findings show large differences in the number of fixations in a comparison of two websites; a large number of fixations may indicate a complex or poor website user interface [5].

The usability test conducted in Phase 2 investigated two municipality websites with quite different designs. While both were representative of public sector websites, one was a typical old design that included many visual elements throughout the website (start page) while the other was typical of a newer minimalistic, clean design. There are many examples of such websites within eGovernment environments, along with many examples midway between. We can assume that users are likely to act differently depending on a website's appearance, and among municipality websites, there is potential for improvement. One factor that must be taken into account in development and quality improvement is that it can be hard to read text on the screen [21]. Therefore, we must avoid information overload and ensure a great design, that meet the users requirements and needs.

With regard to visual attention and fixations, prior research referred to three factors influencing the placement of fixations: images, user memory and expectations, and task and information requirements [6]. This is, to some extent, confirmed in the present study, as the findings indicate that menus receive high numbers of revisits, which is not the case for search fields. As stated earlier, users tend to pay attention to elements that provide information and/or call for action. When subjects were told to explore the website, there was a large variance between websites in terms of number of clicks; the site containing many visual elements on the start page (Website A) had noticeably fewer clicks than the website with a minimalistic design, possibly because users could access a lot of information without returning as many times to the start page (compared to Website B).

To assess performance on usability metrics, we used the SUS, which is a widely used and effective method for quality assessment of websites [20, 31]. The observed scores clearly differ, in that the website containing fewer visual elements scored highest overall. However, the findings also shows variance and disagreement among subjects linked to frequent use of the website, the extent to which functions were found to be well integrated, and consistency in design. Safety and security is clearly important in an eGovernment context [28], and both websites scored relatively well in this regard. With regard to ease of use, both websites performed generally well, although this may be influenced by factors other than aesthetics and placement of design elements.

6   Conclusions

In this eye tracking study investigating visual attention and perception of usability within public sector websites, we argue that such insights help to understand the needs of users (citizens) in designing public sector websites, which can be expected to contribute to the creation of great user experiences on the Web. We have demonstrated that eye tracking, in combination with a post-test usability questionnaire, is an effective means of gaining insights into user behavior, visual attention and user satisfaction. Users pay great attention to visual elements (including text) that they expect to require action and/or provide information. Users scan the webpage by first looking at the upper left; in cases where no information is provided in the upper area, users proceed to scan the middle center. The left side receives more attention than the right, and the upper area receives more attention than the lower. The present findings also confirm that the website containing fewer visual elements scores higher overall on usability metrics. These results indicate differences in viewing behavior and visual attention across different designs, in terms of both eye tracking metrics and usability performance scores. Differences were also found in number of mouse clicks and attention to visual elements, regardless of placement.

It seems clear that eye tracking and usability studies of this kind should be conducted with larger samples. However, the present study provides some initial explorative results on which to ground further research. Based on these findings, future research can usefully focus on (1) how website design influences information seeking and task performance within an eGovernment context; (2) how different website designs impact on various target groups (e.g., in terms of age, gender, user background and experience); and (3) how to optimize public sector websites on the basis of eye tracking and usability data.

References

1. Irani, Z., Love, P.E.D., Montazemi, A.: e-Government: past, present and future. Eur. J. Inf. Syst. **16**, 103–105 (2007)
2. Asgarkhani, M.: The effectiveness of e-Service in local government: a case study. Electron. J. e-Government **3**(4), 157–166 (2005)
3. Axelsson, K., Melin, U., Lindgren, I.: Exploring the importance of citizen participation and involvement in e-government projects: practice, incentives, and organization. Transforming Gov. People, Process Policy **4**(4), 299–321 (2010)
4. Ministry of Modernisation (2009). www.regjeringen.no/globalassets/upload/fad/vedlegg/ikt-politikk/enorway_2009.pdf. Accessed 11 Mar 2016
5. Albayrak, D., Çağıltay, K.: Analyzing Turkish E-government websites by eye tracking. In: Proceedings of 2013 Joint Conference of the 23nd International Workshop on Software Measurement (IWSM) and the Eighth International Conference on Software Process and Product Measurement Mensura, pp. 225–230 (2013)
6. Buscher, G., Cutrell, E., Morris, M.R.: What do you see when you're surfing? Using eye tracking to predict salient regions of web pages. In: Proceedings of CHI 2009, Boston, USA (2009)
7. Bergstrom, J.R., Schall, A.J.: Eye Tracking in User Experience Design. Elsevier Inc., Amsterdam (2004). ISBN 978-0-12-408138-3
8. Blascheck, T., Kurzhals, K., Raschke, M., Burch, M., Weiskopf, D., Ertl, T.: State-of-the-art of visualization for eye tracking data. In: Eurographics Conference on Visualization (Euro Vis) (2014). http://www.visus.uni-stuttgart.de/fileadmin/vis/pdf_s_fuer_Publikationen/State-of-the-Art_of_Visualization_for_Eye_Tracking_Data.pdf
9. Jacob, J.K., Karn, K.S.: Eye tracking in human-computer interaction and usability research: ready to deliver the promises. In: The Mind's Eye: Cognitive and Applies Aspects of Eye Movement Research (2003). ISBN 978-0-444-51020-4
10. Manhartsberger, M., Zellhofer, N.: Eye tracking in usability research: what users really see. In: Empowering Software Quality: How Can Usability Engineering Reach These Goals? Usability Symposium 2005, vol. 198, pp. 141–152. OCG Publication (2005)
11. ACM SIGCHI: The Association for Computing Machinery Special Interest Group on Computer-Human Interaction (1992). www.sigchi.org. Accessed 14 Mar 2016

12. Frøkjær, E., Hornbæk, K.: Metaphors of human thinking for usability inspection and design. ACM Trans. Comput. Hum. Interact. **14**(4), 1–20 (2008)
13. International Organization for Standardization (ISO) 9241-11: Ergonomic Requirements for Office Work with Visual Display Terminals (VDTs) – Part 11: Guidance on Usability (1998)
14. Ehmke, C., Wilson, S.: Identifying web usability problems from eye-tracking data. In: Proceedings of the 21st British HCI Group Annual Conference on People and Computers: HCI…but not as we know it, vol. 1, pp. 119–128 (2007)
15. Bojko, A.: Eye Tracking the User Experience: A Practical Guide to Research. Rosenfeld Media, LLC, New York (2013). ISBN 1-933820-10-1
16. Benyon, D.: Designing Interactive Systems: A Comprehensive Guide to HCI, UX and Interaction Design, 3rd edn. Pearson Education Limited, Harlow (2014). ISBN 978-4479-2011-3
17. Bucklin, R.E., Sismeiro, C.: A model of web site browsing behavior estimated on clickstream data. J. Mark. Res. **XL**, 249–267 (2003)
18. Duggan, G.B., Payne, S.J.: Skim reading by satisficing: evidence from eye tracking. In: Proceedings of CHI 2011, Vancouver, Canada, 7–12 May (2011)
19. Nielsen, J.: F-Shaped Pattern for Reading Web Content (2006). www.useit.com/alertbox/reading_pattern.html. Accessed 01 Mar 2016
20. Shrestha, S., Lenz, K.: Eye Gaze Patterns while Searching vs. Browsing a Website (2007). http://usabilitynews.org/eye-gaze-patterns-while-searching-vs-browsing-a-website. Accessed 15 Mar 2016
21. Nielsen, J.: Designing Web Usability. New Riders Publishing, Indianapolis (2000). ISBN 1-56205-810-X
22. Johansen, S.A., Hansen, J.P.: Do we need eye trackers to tell where people look? In: Proceedings of CHI, Canada, 21–27 April 2006, pp. 923–928 (2006)
23. Roth, S.P., Tuch, A.N., Mekler, E.D., Bargas-Avila, J.A., Opwis, K.: Location matters, especially for non-salient features – a eye-tracking study on the effects of web object placement on different types of websites. Int. J. Hum. Comput. Stud. **71**, 228–235 (2013)
24. Sutcliffe, A., Namoune, A.: Getting the message across: visual attention, aesthetic design and what users remember. In: Proceedings of DIS, Cape Town, South Africa (2008)
25. Djamasbi, S., Siegel, M., Tullis, T.: Visual Hierarchy and Viewing Behavior: An Eye Tracking Study, pp. 331–340 (2011). http://digitalcommons.wpi.edu/uxdmrl-pubs/19
26. Brewer, G.A., Neubauer, B.J., Geiselhart, K.: Designing and implementing e-Government Systems: critical implications for public administration and democracy. Admin. Soc. **30**(4), 472–499 (2006)
27. Flak, L.S., Olsen, D.H., Wolcott, P.: Local e-Government in Norway: current status and emerging issues. Scand. J. Inf. Syst. **17**(2), 41–84 (2005)
28. Tan, C.-W., Benbasat, I., Cenfetelli, R.: Building citizen trust towards e-Government services: do high quality websites matter? In: Proceedings of the 41st Hawaii International Conference on Systems Sciences (2008)
29. Fath-Allah, A., Cheikhi, L., Al-Qutaish, R.E., Idri, A.: E-government portals best practices: a comprehensive survey. Electron. Gov. Int. J. **11**(1/2), 101–132 (2014)
30. Brooke, J.: SUS: a retrospective. J. Usability Stud. **8**(2), 29–40 (2013)
31. Bangor, A., Kortum, P., Miller, J.: Determining what individual SUS scores mean: adding an adjective rating scale. J. Usability Stud. **4**(3), 114–123 (2009)

Research Challenges of ICT for Governance and Policy Modelling Domain – A Text Mining-Based Approach

Andrea Kő[1(✉)] and Saira Gillani[2]

[1] Corvinus University of Budapest, Budapest, Hungary
andrea.ko@uni-corvinus.hu
[2] Department of Computer Science, COMSATS Institute of Information Technology,
Islamabad, Pakistan
Saira.a.gillani@ieee.org

Abstract. This paper investigates the main emerging (current and new) research challenges and areas of ICT for Governance and Policy Modelling field and its taxonomy. Several articles are dealing with future trends and challenges of eGovernment and its areas, like policy making, policy modelling and governance. These papers apply various research methods, but in the majority of the articles identification of future research issues rely only on human expertise, which is a valid, but time and human resource consuming option. Another drawback of these methods is related to the limited volume and variety of data source. We suggest a different semi-automatic solution for this investigation, which is based on our semi-automatic text mining method to identify and describe the main new research areas of ICT for Governance and Policy Modelling field, and its taxonomy. Our text mining solution combines four modules; linguistic analysis module, information extraction, information filtration and information categorization module. The main contribution of this work is to present a semi-automatic method to identify and describe the main new research areas.

Keywords: ICT for Governance and Policy Modelling · Text analytics · Information extraction · Information categorization

1 Introduction

Societies in EU have to face with several challenges, like financial crisis, unpredictability and migrant crisis. At the same time the amount of data and online content available is increasing exponentially, provided through sensors (such as Radio-frequency identification-RFID), mobile and smart devices and social media. Policy making in traditional sense is performed by experts, stakeholders' involvement is limited. In general policy-making cycle can be described using the stages agenda setting, policy creation, policy implementation and monitoring [1–5]. New technologies provide new approaches in policy making through new methods of citizens' engagement, so traditional boundaries between governments and the public are also changing [6, 7]. eGovernment field is becoming more important and decisive nowadays than before, because citizens, administrations, companies are interacting more through online services. Additionally, these

© Springer International Publishing Switzerland 2016
A. Kő and E. Francesconi (Eds.): EGOVIS 2016, LNCS 9831, pp. 182–193, 2016.
DOI: 10.1007/978-3-319-44159-7_13

services can save cost and reduce administrative burden. A new eGovernment Action Plan 2016–2020 is formulated by EU, which completes the Digital Single Market (DSM) and aims to modernize public administrations, achieve cross-border interoperability and facilitates easy interaction with citizens. The application of "Once Only" principle is estimated to generate an annual net saving at the EU level of around 5 billion per year by 2017 [8]. ICT for Governance and Policy Modelling domain include technologies that can be applied for public decision-making improvement.

Several articles are dealing with future trends and challenges of eGovernment and its areas, like policy making, policy modelling and governance [8–10]. Lampathaki and her colleagues prepared a taxonomy classifying the research themes, the research areas and the research sub-areas that challenge this domain [11].

These papers apply various research methods, mainly qualitative ones, amongst other scenario design, experts' workshops, trend analysis, panel discussion and question-naires. In the majority of the articles identification of future research issues rely on human expertise, which is a valid, but time and human resource consuming approach. These investigations didn't apply those intelligent techniques (text analytics, data and web mining), which makes possible to analyse the huge amount of open and available eGovernment related content (eGovernment reports, articles, project documentation).

Our approach completes the previously mentioned methods; we aim to provide a grounded analysis of ICT for Governance and Policy Modelling domain applying content analysis and text mining. The paper tackles the following research questions:

RQ1: What are the main emerging (current and new) research challenges and areas of ICT for Governance and Policy Modelling field?

RQ2: How these research issues can be categorized and used to build taxonomies?

To answer for these questions, we developed a text mining solution, which combines four modules; linguistic analysis module, information extraction, information filtration and information categorization module. Our main contribution is to present a semi-automatic approach to identify and describe the main new research areas, and their taxonomy applying a new text mining solution.

This paper will be structured as follows:

First, eGovernment related challenges are outlined; then, related works and theoret-ical background are discussed. Research method is presented afterwards, followed by the text mining solution overview. Next section is detailing results and evaluation. Finally, conclusion and future work is presented.

2   Theoretical Background – Related Work

Several research aimed to identify the main research challenges and areas of eGovern-ment, with various methods. Consultation report on ICT for Governance and Policy Modelling of FP7 Work Programme investigated ICT-enabled policy modelling methods and governance models that can be effectively utilized in policy making and involve citizens in decision making [12]. Charalabidis applied roadmapping method-ology in the investigation of the new ICT-enabled governance models and methods of monitoring, interaction, collaboration for policy making and enforcement [9]. The main goal of CROSSROAD[1] was to identify and characterize the key research challenges in the domain and prepare a roadmap for future research. CROSSROAD involved researchers and practitioners from across Europe and applied a consensus-driven approach based on collaboration [27]. Results were validated by a large number of experts in online workshops and face-to-face events. Phases of roadmapping methodology were the following [9]:

- State of Play ("providing an overview of the state of the art in ICT for Governance and Policy Modelling in terms of research, practice/application, market and policy"). Outcome of this phase was a taxonomy of research areas. The method of the phase: taxonomy has been discussed and validated by a large set of experts as well as by relevant EU-funded projects in this domain.
- Visionary Scenarios "Digital Europe 2030". During this phase they outlined a set of extreme visionary scenarios on how governance and policy modelling could develop at the horizon 2030. Scenario design was built on two axes: openness and transparency, and integration in policy intelligence).
- Gap Analysis assessed developments in ICT for Governance and Policy Modelling and identified the need for research and technology development (RTD) which was not yet in place.
- Research Roadmap composition defined a set of Grand Challenges which are addressable by 2020, containing specific Research Challenges. It was a collaborative effort of academia, business, civil society and government on new research directions in the domain of governance and policy modelling. The applied method was online and offline brainstorming and validation workshops.

Charalabidis and his colleagues identified three trends: the explosion in the quantity of data available; the proactive role assumed by citizens in contributing to the policy making process, by authoring and elaborating the data increasingly made available; and the advanced capabilities, affordability and accuracy of simulation and modelling techniques.

Brooks and his colleagues analysed how ICT can bring innovation into the policy making process [6]. The applied method was panel discussion, experts discussed with the audience the research questions. Before and during the panel discussion more broad views was collected by and excerpts was made available on social media, primarily via LinkedIn. The objective of their panel was to advance understanding of how research in various disciplines can contribute to new ways of policy making, in particular the role of information systems. The panelists represented various academic backgrounds and cultures and the audience was invited to share their experiences and contribute to the debate. They identified three main areas, which influence the traditional policy-making: crowdsourcing, public engagement and open data.

Gianluca Misuraca, David Broster and Clara Centeno investigated visionary scenarios of Digital Europe 2030 [10]. They analysed what ICT tools will be needed for future governance and policy making, assuming that the possible future scenarios may

---

[1] A Participative Roadmap for ICT Research in Electronic Governance and Policy Modelling, Contract No: FP7-ICT-248484.

be radically different, then nowadays. Their method was scenarios design, which resulted four different scenarios how governance and policy making could develop by 2030. Their two dimensional framework applied "openness and transparency" and "integrated policy intelligence" axis. The four scenarios, which they identified are determined by these dimensions:

- Open Governance: characterized by High Openness and Transparency and High Integration in Policy Intelligence.
- Leviathan Governance: characterized by Low Openness and Transparency and High Integration in Policy Intelligence.
- Privatized Governance: characterized by Low Openness and Transparency and Low Integration in Policy Intelligence.
- Self-Service Governance: characterized by High Openness and Transparency and Low Integration in Policy Intelligence.

They analyzed key policy challenges by scenarios and directions for future ICT research.

Rony Medaglia and Lei Zheng performed a grounded analysis of social media research in the public sector [13]. Their main research questions were the following:

- RQ1: What are the current foci and gaps of government social media research?
- RQ2: How can we frame relationships between constructs focused on in government social media research?

They applied literature review-based method. They selected the relevant sources to be searched, and defined the search strategy in terms of time frame, search terms, and search fields. Their source was eight top IS journals indicated by the Senior Scholar's Basket of Journals of the Association for Information Systems (AIS), in line with Baskerville and Myers [14] and Sidorova et al. [15], using the EBSCO database. 37 articles have been analysed and discussed by the research team in their entirety, in order to identify common themes. They followed a grounded content approach; content analysis in terms of observing repeating themes and categorizing them using a coding system. Common repeating themes in the full text of the 37 selected papers were identified and grouped to provide a two-tier classification scheme that was recorded in a tabular form, and used the classification scheme to build a model of the literature. The research output is a research agenda for future government social media studies.

Lampathaki and her colleagues developed a taxonomy for research areas on ICT for Governance and Policy Modelling. ICT for Governance and Policy Modelling (FP7 2009–2010 Objective 7.3) was defined as the Research Domain. The first level of the taxonomy is called Research Theme; the second level is named as core Research Area; and the third level of the taxonomy includes Research Sub-Areas. They defined baseline rules for the design of the taxonomy, like "number of papers with at least 10 citations" [11].

All the methods which are discussed here are applying mainly manual processes, which can be subjective. Another drawback of the methods above is related to the volume and variety of data source, which is limited and don't apply the huge eGovernment-related open data sources.

3   Research Method

The first step of our method is the review of the relevant content and corpus building. A thorough investigation of a research field requires amongst other a systematic and structured literature review [16, 17]. This literature review was performed aiming a corpus building. Relevant steps of corpus building are selecting relevant publication outlets, content sources, identifying relevant topics and keywords, and a relevant period of time. Our domain of interest is of eGovernment - special attention for the field of ICT in policy making, modelling and governance. Corpus was extended with the related conference proceedings and project deliverables. One corpus was built in 2012 to analyse the content related to ICT in policy making, modelling and governance [18]. That corpus was updated and extended for this research. This version of the corpus will be further extended in the following phase of the research with decisive conference proceedings, and journals. We selected Government Information Quarterly and the Electronic Journal of eGovernment as sources, because these journals are leading and high-quality journals of eGovernment field according to the journal rankings.

Corpus contains the following materials:

- Journals
  - Journal of Electronic Governance (2014)
  - Government Information Quarterly (2014–2015)
- Conference proceedings and workshop materials
  - Electronic Government and Electronic Participation proceedings (2013–2015) [19–21]
  - EGOVIS proceedings (2014–2015) [22–24]
  - ICEGOV proceedings 2011 [25]
  - 7th International EGOV Conference proceedings, EGOV 2008 (DEXA cluster) [26]
  - International Eastern Europe e|Gov Days, 2007
  - 3rd International Conference on eParticipation - ePart 2011 and Workshop on Modelling Policy-making (MPM 2011)
  - ICT for Governance and Policy Modelling Constituency building Workshop, Brussels, 2010
  - ICT 2010: Digitally Driven conference, Brussels 2010
  - Transforming Government Workshop (tGOV 2010), 2010 London, and tGOV 2011
- Project deliverables
  - ICT-2009.7.3 ICT for Governance and Policy Modelling (source: projects' web sites): Cockpit, Impact, OCOPOMO, ProgEast, Spaces, Ubipol, Wegov deliverables (downloaded in 2011)
  - CROSSROAD project (A Participative Roadmap for ICT Research in Electronic Governance and Policy Modelling), Contract No: FP7-ICT-248484.

Our text mining solution needs seed ontology as input, so initial taxonomy was built to describe the investigated field (ICT in policy making, modelling and governance). This seed ontology was prepared in [18] for ICT in policy making, modelling and governance domain with text analytics (see Fig. 1). The main categories/research fields identified were the following:

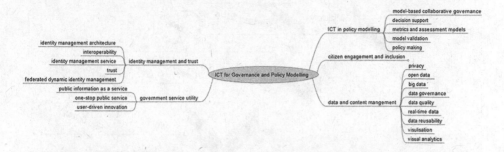

Fig. 1. Initial taxonomy for ICT in policy making, modelling and governance

- Identity management and trust
  Identity management domain has a key role in eGovernment services, because these services require identification of citizens or other entities, who use the service. There are several architecture approaches applied in identity management, like government gateway or federated architectures. Trust is important aspect of this field, it determines citizens' openness for service utilization.
- Government service utility
  Service creation and delivery are key elements of public sector effectiveness. Future internet provides additional catalyst for stakeholders to shape government services.
- ICT in policy modelling
  Several ICT solutions can be applied in policy modelling, like decision support systems and simulation. These models and solutions can simplify and enhance decision makers work in various ways, like they help to manage decisions' context, show decisions' consequences.
- Citizen engagement and inclusion
  This category includes those ICT solutions, which are supporting citizens' inclusion to decision making. Web 2.0 solutions, social media applications are good examples for this category.
- Data and content management
  Data produced by the government is very valuable, but the methods and solutions for exploitation of this resource are complex; usage of data mining, text analytics and web mining are typical.

Figure 1 presents the above listed categories and their subcategories.

Next step of our method was to apply our text mining solution to update and extend eGovernment seed ontology (Fig. 1) according to the text mining process described in the next section (Fig. 2).

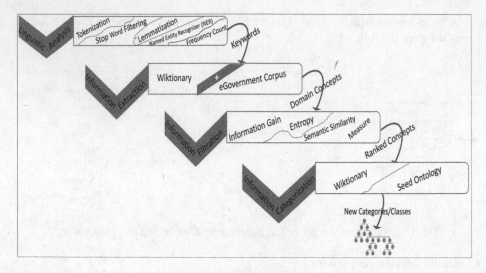

Fig. 2. Text mining solution

4   Text Mining Process for Identification of EGovernment Research Challenges

As it is mentioned earlier the majority of the proposed identification methods for research challenges are manual, therefore they have many drawbacks such as its time and resource consuming. This complex task requires professional experience involving a lot of expert discussions and efforts. Another limitation of the other methods is related to the volume and variety of data sources. Subjectivity is an additional problem of manual methods and it is very hard to manage and update knowledge of prospective eGovernment challenges. Therefore, we applied an automatic process (with a limited human exert) to discover future research challenges in eGovernment field. We developed a text mining process and solution that will extract new concepts/trends for eGovernment field and will also categorize these new extracted knowledge elements to enrich the initial taxonomy of eGovernment.

This text mining process can be further divided in four modules; linguistic analysis module, information extraction, information filtration and information categorization module. The process starts with linguistic analysis module in which small sized input files are given to the system. These input files can be in the form of xml file or any text file or some semantic lexicon that consists of words that identify a domain uniquely. In our case, we are using semantic lexicon of eGovernment that is prepared by domain expert. Linguistic analysis module performs tokenization, parts-of-speech tagging, stop word filtration and lemmatization on the given input text using Stanford NLP package. At the end of this process, our input data is in such form that we can apply machine learning or text mining algorithms on it. This text mining solution extracts all keywords by using the frequency count method and list of keyword set is populated.

In the second module of concept extraction, the extracted keyword list is used as an input and a set of synonyms is taken against each keyword from the WordNet.

We are taking this set of synonyms to enrich our concept list and these synonyms are providing the semantic variants of a given word. However, it is not necessary that each synonym belongs to our selected domain. To remove such ambiguity, this text mining solution prepares a domain corpus and each word from this potential set of words including the keyword is compared with the domain corpus. This comparison is necessary, because WordNet is not a domain dependent lexical database so there are chances that many irrelevant words may also be in this set of words. We need to eliminate such words from this synonym list. For this purpose, our text mining process apply some algorithms to filter out the above mentioned ambiguities. This module also performs one more important function that is the automatic extraction of domain-specific key-concepts in the form of compound words from the domain corpus. WordNet database does not provide all compound words/multiword terms. Concepts can be more informative in compound or multiword terms as compared to single words. In this process, we are considering that each concept is a noun that occurs in the domain corpus [28]. After removing such concept ambiguities, this text mining solution apply statistical and semantical similarity measures to filter out more keyword related words [29]. As a result of this module, a new refined rich list of concepts against each key word will be generated.

In the last module of the defined text mining process, automatic concept categorization process is performed on the refined list of extracted concepts that are semantically relevant to the keyword. For this purpose, an algorithm is defined that uses the knowledge of existing concept categories (initial taxonomy abut ICT in policy making, modelling and governance) with the help of external knowledge resources such as Wiktionary. The proposed approach tries to find a semantic relationship between extracted concepts and already defined ontology/taxonomy's categories by using some fragments of the ontology that describe a certain category. The outline of this approach is presented in [28]. Each extracted concept is passed through this module for categorization. At the end of this module, every extracted concept is categorized into defined class by using our proposed semantic algorithm of categorization. According to this algorithm, if any new extracted concept can't fit in any category then it is put in miscellaneous category.

5 Result and Evaluation

At the end of this text mining process, a validation process starts for results verification. This evaluation process is iterative in nature. As it is mentioned above that the concept extraction process starts with the selection of a keyword. For example, we have selected a word "innovation". A list of concepts against this keyword (that contains words such as innovation capability, governance innovation policy, governance innovation program, innovation management standardization, technology policy innovation, innovation strategy and innovation policy, etc.) is generated and the last module of the text mining process categorizes this list of words according to already defined categories/classes as in our case it is the initial taxonomy abut ICT in policy making, modelling and governance. This categorization module not only categorize new concepts in their corresponding category rather put all remaining concepts which cannot fit in any category according to our system put in miscellaneous category. Above mentioned words are not fit into any defined category so our text mining solution put such words into miscellaneous category. Now for the evaluation, domain experts manually evaluate the results, they check each category and all words that are linked to this category. In this way they point out the words that are wrongly categorized or even they also assign categories to concepts of miscellaneous category. Here interesting point of our text mining process is that if the expert identifies such concepts which cannot be fit into any category but they are meaningful then the expert can define a new category in the ontology. Here, the first cycle of our text mining process is completed and the second cycle will start with the selection of a new keyword. And this text mining process will also consider this newly defined category in the very next cycle.

For example, when we have selected a keyword "innovation", the text mining process generated a list of concepts that are related to this keyword and during concept categorization, in miscellaneous category we got these concepts (amongst others) as result: innovation capability, governance innovation policy, governance innovation program, innovation management standardization, technology policy innovation, innovation agency, innovation agenda, innovation process and etc. The domain expert observed these concepts of miscellaneous category and have decided that these concepts can formulate a new category in the existing taxonomy as new class/category label "eGovernment and innovation". The beauty of this text mining process is its adaptability. After the completion of the process including results validation, when new cycle will start with the selection of next keyword, it will generate again a new concepts list related to this new selected keyword. However, when concept categorization process will start again it will also consider the newly defined category "eGovernment and innovation" and enrich the taxonomy (seed ontology) with new concepts.

We have performed seven cycles for evaluate our results and outcome is positive. This process can continue until no more information can be extracted from the corpus or until a human satisfied taxonomy/ontology is built. Actually, it is a user's decision to continue modifying the ontology/taxonomy and teaching the system to learn or stop. The accuracy in the result will improve gradually. When we have started our evaluation process for categorization process the existing seed ontology (taxonomy) has five major categories/classes and all five categories have total 51 concepts (Fig. 1). But at the seventh cycle, our text mining process resulted two new top categories "eGovernment and innovation" and "Governance" in the existing taxonomy and 294 new concepts are added in these seven categories. Additionally, the previous nodes in the taxonomy were more precisely defined (named according to the decisive concepts), as follows:

- Citizen engagement/eParticipation - modified category
- Data and content management (open government data) - modified category
- eGovernment service
- ICT in policy modelling - modified category
- Identity management/architecture - modified category

- this category was extended with architecture-related topics; not only identity management related concepts were highlighted, but other architecture-related ones as well (46 new concepts in after 7 cycles)
- eGovernment and innovation - new category
  - we got huge number of concepts (n-grams) related to innovation (51 new concepts in after 7 cycles) in the investigated content, so we separated it to a new category. It means that in the latest research-related content innovation is highly emphasized.
- Governance - new category
  - governance area was also extensively discussed (127 new concepts in after 7 cycles) in the research related content, so we decided to have a new category for this topic.

These results show that we can easily and automatically find new research directions in any domain by using our text mining process and solution. Our text mining process also have been applied in different domains, e.g. in IT audit domain the experiment provided 89 % precision rate and 86 % recall [28, 29]. In this paper focus was slightly different, then categorization, we aimed to identify main research areas of the investigated field.

Appearance of these new categories (governance; eGovernment and innovation) are not really surprising. Governance reform, "good" governance principles are discussed recently by several researchers [30–32]. Innovation take place in various ways in public sector, they can be technological, supporting the redesign of all kinds of processes; organizational and conceptual innovations [33] (Table 1).

Table 1. Evaluation of the text mining process for future research directions

	At the start	After 7 cycles
No. of categories/classes	5	7
No. of concepts	51	345

6 Conclusion

This paper aimed to analyze the main emerging (current and new) research challenges of ICT for Governance and Policy Modelling domain applying our text mining process and solution. In the related work section, we discussed similar initiatives; methods to identify the main research challenges and areas of eGovernment. The drawback of these approaches are, that the majority of them apply manual processes, which can be subjective, time and resource consuming. Another disadvantage is related to the limited volume and variety of data source. Our approach offers an extension of these ones through semantically enriched text mining. We dealt with the following research questions in this paper:

RQ1: What are the main emerging (current and new) research challenges and areas of ICT for Governance and Policy Modelling field?

RQ2: How these research issues can be categorized and used to build taxonomies?

Our main contribution is to present a semi-automatic approach to identify the main new research areas, and their taxonomy applying a new text mining process and solution. Our text mining solution combines various text analytics functions in four modules; linguistic analysis module, information extraction, information filtration and information categorization module. After seven cycles of application of our text mining process we could enrich the initial taxonomy with two new top categories. One is innovation related, which is not a surprise because e.g. of the rise of "open innovation" and its link to social media. Another top category is related to governance, which is also an emphasized field nowadays (e.g. in some decisive standards, like in COBIT 5, governance became a separate category). Number of concepts in the taxonomy were enriched significantly from 51 to 345. Future work include further investigation of this domain through corpus extension and applying our text mining process again for the new corpus. Another possible extension of this work is to apply our text mining process for new domains.

References

1. Birkland, T.A.: An Introduction to the Policy Process: Theories, Concepts, and Models of Public, 2nd edn. M.E. Sharpe, Armonk (2005)
2. Hill, M.: The Policy Process in the Modern State. Prentice-Hall, London (1997)
3. Parsons, W.: Public Policy. Edward Elgar, Cheltenham (1995)
4. Hofferbert, R.: The Study of Public Policy. Bobbs-Merrill, Indianapolis (1974)
5. Macintosh, A., Renton, A.: Argument visualisation to support democratic decision-making. In: Proceedings of the eChallenges e-2004 Conference, Vienna, Austria (2004)
6. Brooks, L., Zinner Henriksen, H., Janssen, M., Papazafeiropoulou, A., Trutnev, D.: Public sector information systems (PSIS): how ICT can bring innovation into the policymaking process. In The 22nd European Conference on Information Systems (ECIS) (2014)
7. Kő, A., Gábor, A., Szabó, Z.: Policy making improvement through social learning. In: Kő, A., Leitner, C., Leitold, H., Prosser, A. (eds.) EDEM/EGOVIS 2013. LNCS, vol. 8061, pp. 226–240. Springer, Heidelberg (2013)
8. eGovernment Action Plan 2016–2020. https://ec.europa.eu/digital-single-market/en/news/egovernment-action-plan-2016-2020-public-consultation-faq
9. Charalabidis, Y., Lampathaki, F., Misuraca, G., Osimo, D: ICT for governance and policy modelling: research challenges and future prospects in Europe. In: 2012 45th Hawaii International Conference on System Science (HICSS), pp. 2472–2481. IEEE (2012)
10. Misuraca, G., Broster, D., Centeno, C.: Digital Europe 2030: designing scenarios for ICT in future governance and policy making. Gov. Inf. Q. **29**, S121–S131 (2012)
11. Lampathaki, F., Charalabidis, Y., Passas, S., Osimo, D., Bicking, M., Wimmer, M.A., Askounis, D.: Defining a taxonomy for research areas on ICT for governance and policy modelling. In: Wimmer, M.A., Chappelet, J.-L., Janssen, M., Scholl, H.J. (eds.) EGOV 2010. LNCS, vol. 6228, pp. 61–72. Springer, Heidelberg (2010)
12. Consultation report on ICT for Governance and Policy Modelling. FP7 Work Programme 2011–2012, February 2010. http://ec.europa.eu/information_society/activities/egovernment/research/fp7/docs/consultation_report_feb2010.pdf
13. Medaglia, R., Zheng, L.: Characterizing government social media research: towards a grounded overview model. In: The 49th Hawaii International Conference on System Sciences, HICSS 2016, pp. 2991–2999 (2016)
14. Baskerville, R.L., Myers, M.D.: Information systems as a reference discipline. MIS Q. **26**(1), 1–14 (2002)

15. Sidorova, A., Evangelopoulos, N., Valacich, J., Ramakrishnan, T.: Uncovering the intellectual core of the information systems discipline. Manag. Inf. Syst. Q. **32**(3), 467–482 (2008)

16. Bandara, W., Miskon, S., and Fielt, E. A systematic, tool-supported method for conducting literature reviews in information systems. In: Proceedings of the 19th European Conference on Information Systems (ECIS 2011) (2011)

17. Webster, J., Watson, R.T.: Analyzing the past to prepare for the future: writing a literature review. MIS Q. **26**(2), xiii–xxiii (2002)

18. Kő, A.: Innovative ICT solutions in eGovernment - research challenges and possible solutions, habilitation dissertation, Corvinus University of Budapest (2012)

19. Wimmer, M.A., Janssen, M., Macintosh, A., Scholl, H.J., Tambouris, E.: Electronic government and electronic participation. In: Joint Proceedings of Ongoing Research of IFIP EGOV and IFIP ePart 2013, Koblenz, Germany, 16–19 September 2013. LNI 221, GI 2013 (2013). ISBN 978-3-88579-615-2

20. Janssen, M. F. W. H. A., Bannister, F., Glassey, O.: Electronic government and electronic participation. In: Joint Proceedings of Ongoing Research, Posters, Workshop and Projects of IFIP EGOV 2014 and EPart 2014, vol. 21. IOS Press (2014)

21. Tambouris, E., Scholl, H. J., Janssen, M. F. W. H. A., Wimmer, M. A., Tarabanis, K., Gascó, M., Pardo, T.A.: Electronic government and electronic participation (2015)

22. Kő, A., Leitner, C., Leitold, H., Prosser, A. (eds.): EDEM/EGOVIS 2013. LNCS, vol. 8061. Springer, Heidelberg (2013)

23. Francesconi, E., Kő, A. (eds.): EGOVIS 2014. LNCS, vol. 8650. Springer, Heidelberg (2014)

24. Kő, A., Francesconi, E. (eds.): EGOVIS 2015. LNCS, vol. 9265. Springer, Heidelberg (2015). doi:10.1007/978-3-319-22389-6

25. Estevez, E., Janssen, M.: Proceedings of the 5th International Conference on Theory and Practice of Electronic Governance, ICEGOV 2011, Tallinn, Estonia, 26–28 September 2011. ACM (2011). ISBN 978-1-4503-0746-8

26. Ferro, E., Scholl, H.J., Wimmer, M.A. (eds.): EGOV 2008. LNCS, vol. 5184. Springer, Heidelberg (2008)

27. A Participative Roadmap for ICT Research in Electronic Governance and Policy Modelling, Contract No: FP7-ICT-248484, CROSSROAD Project (2011). http://www.crossroadeu.net

28. Gillani, S., Ko, A.: Incremental ontology population and enrichment through semantic-based text mining: an application for IT audit domain. Int. J. Semant. Web Inf. Syst. (IJSWIS) **11**(3), 44–66 (2015)

29. Gillani, S., Kő, A.: ProMine: a text mining solution for concept extraction and filtering. In: Gábor, A., Kő, A. (eds.) Corporate Knowledge Discovery and Organizational Learning. Knowledge Management and Organizational Learning, vol. 2, pp. 59–82. Springer, Cham (2016). ISBN 978-3-319-28915-1

30. Bicking, M., Wimmer, M.A.: A scenario-based approach towards open collaboration for policy modelling. In: Janssen, M., Scholl, H.J., Wimmer, M.A., Tan, Y.-h. (eds.) EGOV 2011. LNCS, vol. 6846, pp. 223–234. Springer, Heidelberg (2011)

31. EC: European governance - a white paper, COM/2001/0428 final (2011). http://eur-lex.europa.eu/legal-content/EN/TXT/?uri=CELEX%3A52001DC0428

32. Shore, C.: 'European governance' or governmentality? the European commission and the future of democratic government. Eur. Law J. **17**(3), 287–303 (2011)

33. Jansen, A.: Innovation in eGovernment information infrastructures. In: Electronic Government and Electronic Participation: Joint Proceedings of Ongoing Research, Ph.D. Papers, Posters and Workshops of IFIP EGOV and EPart 2015, vol. 22, p. 232. IOS Press (2015)

Semantic Application for the Internationalization Audit of Higher Education Institutions

Katalin Ternai[✉] and Ildikó Szabó

Department of Information Systems, Corvinus University of Budapest,
Fővám tér 13-15, Budapest 1093, Hungary
katalin.ternai@uni-corvinus.hu,
iszabo@informatika.uni-corvinus.hu

Abstract. Institutions are getting increasingly motivated to participate in an internationalization audit because the competitiveness of higher education institutions resides not only in the number of qualified students employed by organizations within a given period, but the Internationalization is also a crucial point in the evaluation. The aim of an audit is to help institutions with detailed recommendations to increase efficiency and quality of their internationalization activities.

The present paper aims to provide and elaborate a semi-automatic application, which can be used to perform the internationalization audit of higher education institutions. The guidelines must be adapted by institutions are articulated in unstructured texts shaped into Erasmus+ Programme Guide, but business processes are formalized into business process models.

This paper presents an information system that is capable of extracting business process elements from unstructured texts. Process ontologies store these extracted elements and actual business process elements as well for providing a unified base to execute compliance checking investigation between actual and reference business processes.

Keywords: Higher education · Internationalization · Erasmus mobility · Semantic business process management · Ontology matching · Compliance check

1 Introduction

In the globalized world internationalization became increasingly important in the strategy of higher education institutions. Reputation of higher education institutions is measured with their position in global rankings. Competitiveness of higher education institutions resides not only in the number of qualified students employed by organizations within a given period, but the Internationalization is also a crucial point in the evaluation. The international orientation, mobility activities, changing students and teaching and research products play significant roles in the mission of higher education institutions.

Mobility is an efficient tool for distributing knowledge, innovative results among students, researchers, teachers and administrative staff. It enhances collaboration and communication between higher education institutions. A mobility strategy was interpreted on the EHEA Ministerial Conference held in Bucharest in 2012 for promoting

© Springer International Publishing Switzerland 2016
A. Kő and E. Francesconi (Eds.): EGOVIS 2016, LNCS 9831, pp. 194–205, 2016.
DOI: 10.1007/978-3-319-44159-7_14

high quality mobility. Ten measures were determined for facilitating better implementation of the mobility aims. Internationalism, mobility targets, open higher education system, balanced mobility dismantled existing obstacles, usage of quality assurance, transparency tools and improved communication were emphasized among others [1].

Internationalization is part of the quality culture of an institution, as well. Hungarian higher education institutions are required to operate quality assurance systems.

Some of the Hungarian institutions take part in international accreditation. The objective of our work is to assist the institutions in producing well-based descriptions on their international activities and to increase the chance of their international accreditation.

The institutions are getting increasingly motivated to participate in an internationalization audit.

The basis of the qualification procedure is the internal evaluation the self assessment report. The most important product of this phase is a development plan and to give support to the institution in further development of the internationalization activities.

The present paper aims to provide and elaborate a semi-automatic application, which can be used to perform the internationalization audit of higher education institutions. The main goal is to investigate the alignment of process ontologies, based on ontologies derived from process models and regulations, guidelines. The applicability of our solution is presented through the Erasmus student mobility programme use case. The guidelines must adapted by institutions are articulated in unstructured texts shaped into Erasmus+ Programme Guide [2], but institution processes are formalized in business process models. This papers present an information system that is capable of extracting business process elements from unstructured documents. Process ontologies store these elements for providing a unified base to execute compliance checking investigation between actual and required business processes.

2 Theoretical Background

2.1 Semantic Business Process Management

Business process management (BPM) is now getting adopted by many organizations. BPM provides many possibilities to improve business processes. Modern BPM suites are evolving to automate the modeling, monitoring and redesign of complex, collaborative processes [3]. Conceptual model captures the semantics of an application through the use of a formal notation, but the descriptions resulting from conceptual model are intended to be used by humans and not machines. The semantics contained in these models are in a large extent implicit and cannot be processed. With the web-based semantic schema such as Web Ontology Language (OWL), the creation and the use of the conceptual models can be improved, furthermore the implicit semantics being contained in the models can be partly articulated and used for processing [4].

The usage of Semantic Web technologies like reasoners, ontologies, and mediators promises raising business process management to a completely new level of possibilities. This approach is known as semantic business process management (SBPM) [5].

When a new regulation is established the business process have to comply with this regulation. This means to start digging into the business processes to find all business functions handling this occurence. If the business processes have been documented in a BPM repository, this task is supported by visual navigation and search functionalities. It is the business expert performing this analysis.

In semantic business process management, the above mentioned scenario is simplified, because the business processes as well as the new regulation are defined in a way that a machine is able to understand them. Therefore, no manual work is needed to verify that the business processes comply with the new regulation.

The core paradigm of SPBM is to represent the business requirements view on the process area and the actual process area using ontology languages and to employ machine reasoning for automated or semi-automated translation. The basic idea of Semantic Business Process Management is to combine Semantic Web Services frameworks ontology representation, and Business Process Management methodologies and tools [6].

The SUPER project has been a big public research project which has been supported by the EU Commission. In the SUPER project, well known companies like SAP, IBM, and IDS Scheer have been working together with leading research institutes from all over Europe to achieve the vision of semantic business process management. A semantic application for compliance management has been elaborated. They presented five perspectives on compliance checking: design-time/run-time; forward/backward; active/passive; task checking/process checking or engine-based/query-based perspective [7].

2.2 Ontology Matching

The discrepancies between ontologies can be derived from different perspectives possessed by experts, granularity of expressiveness and related descriptive language used during the formalization process. Subfields of ontology methodology domain work with discovering, registering and handling these discrepancies. Ontology mapping defined by Su [8] means that "for each concept (node) in ontology A, try to find a corresponding concept (node), which has same or similar semantics, in ontology B and vice verse."

This definition was extended with additional parameters – an input alignment of A for future extension, matching parameters (threshold, weights etc.), external resources (common knowledge, domain specific thesauri) by Euzenat and Shvaiko [9] (Fig. 1).

Matching techniques can be distinguished by their focus points. Some techniques work at element level, focusing on matching entities and its instances without any information about their relationships with other entities and instances. It investigates these entities as strings, words or through the elements of their definitions with using external sources e.g. linguistic resources. Other ones – so called structure-level matching techniques - scrutinize not only matching entities but their relations with other entities and instances as well. These use different representation techniques e.g. graphs etc. to run matching procedures.

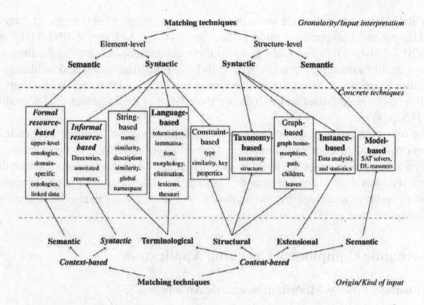

Fig. 1. Matching techniques classification by Euzenat and Shvaiko [10]

3 The 'Erasmus Student Mobility' Use Case

Our aim is to perform the internationalization audit of higher education institutions. The main goal is to scrutinize the matching of process ontologies, based on ontologies derived from process models and regulations, guidelines. We use the 'Erasmus student mobility' as a use case to demonstrate our approach. The guidelines must adapted by institutions are articulated in unstructured texts shaped into Erasmus+ Programme Guide, but institution processes are formalized in business process models.

The Erasmus+ Programme
Erasmus+ is the new EU programme for boosting skills, employability and modernization activities on Education, Training, Youth and Sport field. This programme supports transnational partnerships among institutions and organisations to enhance cooperation, knowledge sharing. It handling skill gaps by providing a bridge the worlds of Education and work [2]

Student mobility for studies, the centrepiece of the Erasmus+ programme, is an efficient tool for distributing knowledge, innovative results among students, researchers, teachers and administrative staff.

The objectives of student mobility for studies:

- "To enable students to benefit educationally, linguistically and culturally from the experience of learning in other European countries;
- To promote co-operation between institutions and to enrich the educational environment of host institutions;
- To contribute to the development of a pool of well-qualified, open-minded and internationally experienced young people as future professionals" [15, p. 1].

In 2013, Internationalization audit processes were conducted in the case of some of the Hungarian universities under the aegis of TÁMOP-4.2.4B/1-11/1 and TÁMOP-4.2.4B/2-11/1. The main goals of these audit processes are "to facilitate the external quality assessment process with elaborating the dimensions and indicators of internationalization" to assist the institutions in producing well-based descriptions on their international activities and to increase the chance of their international accreditation" [16, p. 4].

The following semantic compliance checking application can facilitate these endeavours by processing reference documents and providing reports related to these indicators based on actual processes of higher education institutions. The Erasmus student mobility process serves as a use case to present this system, but this system can be used for other processes on the internationalization domain as well, because it can also be customized for other processes.

4   Semantic Compliance Checking Application

4.1   Business Process Modeling; Semantic Annotation

Business Process Modeling is the first phase of the Business Process Management lifecycle. The 'Erasmus student mobility' process of a Hungarian university was selected as use case, the business process models were implemented by using BOC ADONIS modeling platform [11].

There are several parameters that can be set or defined when modeling a business process. The vertical level in details of a business process model gives the focus point of the model: we can specify operational areas only, or process areas, process models, sub processes, activities, or even deeper; the algorithms. The horizontal level in details of a business process model gives the level of extra information modeled within the business process: organizational information can be specified in an organogram; the roles can be referred in the RACI matrix of the process model, the input and the output documents in the document model and the applied IT system elements can be added to the IT system model as well.

In our case, the business process models are used for their compliance checking with regulations and guidelines. To achieve this goal, during the modeling of business processes the following parameters have to be set:

- the logical shell of the business process model with the core objects (e.g. task);
- the organizational structure needed for the business process model, in working environment model;
- the inputs and outputs needed for the business process model, in document model;
- the IT elements needed for the business process model, in IT system model;
- name of activities in the business process models;
- description of activities in the business process models;
- the Responsible role for all the activities in the business process models;
- input, output, IT system information for all the activities in the business process models, where available.

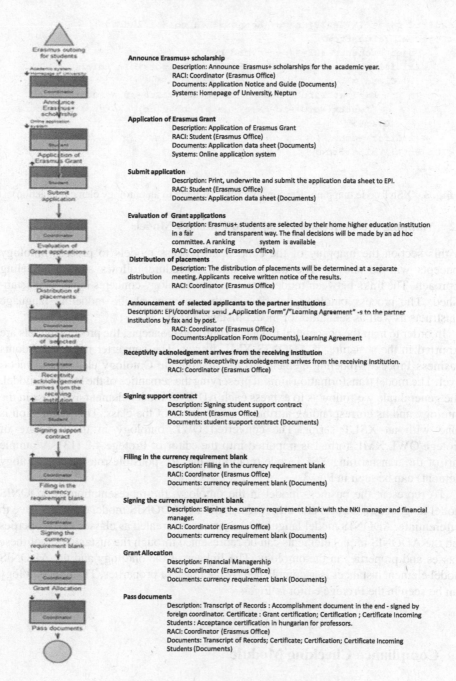

Announce Erasmus+ scholarship
>Description: Announce Erasmus+ scholarships for the academic year.
>RACI: Coordinator (Erasmus Office)
>Documents: Application Notice and Guide (Documents)
>Systems: Homepage of University, Neptun

Application of Erasmus Grant
>Description: Application of Erasmus Grant
>RACI: Student (Erasmus Office)
>Documents: Application data sheet (Documents)
>Systems: Online application system

Submit application
>Description: Print, underwrite and submit the application data sheet to EPI.
>RACI: Student (Erasmus Office)
>Documents: Application data sheet (Documents)

Evaluation of Grant applications
>Description: Erasmus+ students are selected by their home higher education institution
>in a fair   and transparent way. The final decisions will be made by an ad hoc
>committee. A ranking   system is available
>RACI: Coordinator (Erasmus Office)

Distribution of placements
>Description: The distribution of placements will be determined at a separate
>distribution   meeting. Applicants receive written notice of the results.
>RACI: Coordinator (Erasmus Office)

Announcement of selected applicants to the partner institutions
Description: EPI/coordinator send „Application Form"/"Learning Agreement" -s to the partner
institutions by fax and by post.
>RACI: Coordinator (Erasmus Office)
>Documents:Application Form (Documents), Learning Agreement

Receptivity acknoledgement arrives from the receiving institution
>Description: Receptivity acknoledgement arrives from the receiving institution.
>RACI: Coordinator (Erasmus Office)

Signing support contract
>Description: Signing student support contract
>RACI: Student (Erasmus Office)
>Documents: student support contract (Documents)

Filling in the currency requirement blank
>Description: Filling in the currency requirement blank
>RACI: Coordinator (Erasmus Office)
>Documents: currency requirement blank (Documents)

Signing the currency requirement blank
>Description: Signing the currency requirement blank with the NKI manager and financial
>manager.
>RACI: Coordinator (Erasmus Office)
>Documents: currency requirement blank (Documents)

Grant Allocation
>Description: Financial Managership
>RACI: Coordinator (Erasmus Office)
>Documents: currency requirement blank (Documents)

Pass documents
>Description: Transcript of Records : Accomplishment document in the end - signed by
>foreign coordinator. Certificate : Grant certification; Certification ; Certificate Incoming
>Students : Acceptance certification in hungarian for professors.
>RACI: Coordinator (Erasmus Office)
>Documents: Transcript of Records; Certificate; Certification; Certificate Incoming
>Students (Documents)

Fig. 2. The 'Erasmus student mobility' process

The 'Erasmus student mobility' business process model and the main activities and parameters of the process can be seen in Fig. 2.

```
<xsl:if test="INTERREF[@name='Responsible role']/IREF">
<ObjectAllValuesFrom>
    <ObjectProperty IRI="#performed_by"/>
    <xsl:for-each select="INTERREF[@name='Responsible role']/IREF">
        <Class >
            <xsl:attribute name="IRI">#<xsl:value-of select=
            "functx:words-to-camel-case(@tobjname)" /></xsl:attribute>
        </Class>
    </xsl:for-each>
</ObjectAllValuesFrom>
</xsl:if>
```

Fig. 3. XSLT code mapping 'Responsible role' attribute to an ontology element (fraction)

4.2   Mapping the Conceptual Models to Ontology Models

In this section the mapping of the conceptual process models to process ontology concepts will be shown. The transformation procedure follows a meta-modeling approach. The links between model elements and ontology concepts have been established. The process ontology describes both semantics of the modeling language constructs as well as semantics of model instances [12].

In order to map the conceptual models to ontology concepts, the process models are exported in the structure of ADONIS XML format. The converter maps the Adonis Business Process Modeling elements to the appropriate Ontology elements in meta-level. The model transformation aims at preserving the semantics of the business model. The general rule we follow is to express each ADONIS model element as a class in the ontology and its corresponding attributes as attributes of the class. This conversion is done with an XSLT script. The converted OWL ontology in the structure of Protege/OWL XML format is imported into the editor of Protege 4.2 [13]. A sample part of the transforming XSLT code (mapping the 'Responsible role' to an ontology element) can be seen in Fig. 3.

To represent the business model in the ontology, the representation of ADONIS model language constructs and the representation of ADONIS model elements have to differentiate. ADONIS model language constructs are created as classes and properties and the ADONIS model elements can be represented through the instantiation of these classes and properties in the ontology. The linkage of the ontology and the ADONIS model element instances is accomplished by the usage of properties. The final ontology can be seen in the Protégé editor in Fig. 4.

5   Compliance Checking Module

This module consists of three main parts: process ontology building and matching engine and report generator

The **process ontology building engine** contains grammatical and semantic processing tools. It uses the actual process ontology converted from the actual business process

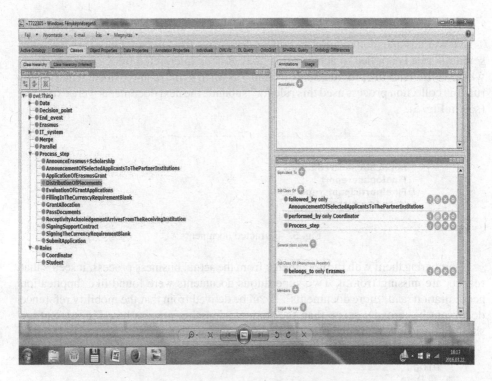

Fig. 4. The process ontology in Protege 4.2

model by using XSLT transformation for identifying process steps within the reference document. Grammatical processing tool was built in Rapidminer and is integrated into this engine. This is capable of collecting part-of-speech tags from texts. It picks every process steps from the actual process ontology in order to build a reference process ontology from documents. It splits these expressions into terms. It seeks them through texts and measure the frequency of their occurrence within a given sentence. The sentence providing the higher value will validate this process step. Semantic rules are used to search other process elements (like IT resources, roles, input/output documents). Having identified these elements, they are connected to a process step discovered nearby (namely within a given radius). The process ontology building engine creates the reference process ontology containing process elements from the reference document.

The ontology matching engine compares the actual reference ontology with the reference process ontology and collects similarities and differentiations between them into a technical report [14]. This report is processed by **a report generator** that is responsible for creating a transparent, user-friendly report required by the stakeholders in the respect of its content.

5.1   Audit Questions

This section will present how the system is capable of answering three audit questions [16].

What kind of documents are changing between the various levels managing the activities?

To answer this question requires to collect documents from the reference text. The next semantic rule is applied to achieve this goal. Rule is interpreted by X "verb" Y, form where verb ∈ {submit, provide, send…} and Y is equal to the required document. Having run this collection process used this rule for "submit", the next documents were extracted (see in Fig. 5).

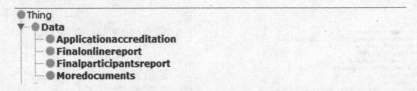

Fig. 5. Extracted documents

Comparing them with the documents from the actual business process, it seems that reports are missing from it. Two superfluous documents were found like 'application accreditation' and 'more documents'. It can be derived from that the mobility reference document has broader scope than the student admission process has (Fig. 6). But we should consider to make the rules more punctual as well.

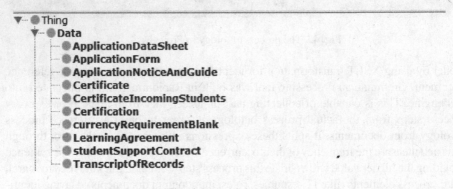

Fig. 6. Actual documents

These statements are derived from manual comparison. The next questions can be answered with generating a report by this system.

Are foreign students responsible for which activities? Which are missing from the actual admission process?

To get an answer we need collect roles and process steps similar to the actual process steps from the reference texts. The collection process uses X 'by the' Y semantic rule to get roles. Later it picks a process step and splits it into terms, searches these terms within the texts and choose them that provide maximum value of the occurrence of these terms. It puts the accepted actual business process steps into the reference ontology with texts validated it as comments. Connects these steps with the roles reside nearby (e.g.

Fig. 7. Extracted process steps and roles

within a given radius). Accepted process steps without roles are put into the reference ontology as well. It may be considered as additional information not mentioned in the actual business process (Fig. 7).

Draft version of the Semantic Compliance Checking Report

created by Corvinno Technology Transfer Center

Actual business process	Reference business process
HEI	Erasmus Mobility Handbook
Report generated at 23-3-2016	

Process steps from the reference document are not in the actual business process

Process step
eirSendingOrganisationandBeforeSigningTheirLearningAgreement-allLearners exceptNativeSpeakerS BenefitingFromTheOnlineServiceWillC arryOutAnOnlineTesTToAssessTheir CompetenCesInTheLanguageTheyWil lUseForTheirTraineeship

Process steps that are not in the reference document

Process step	
AnnounceErasmus+Scholarship	DistributionOfPlacements
FillingInTheCurrencyRequirementBlan k	GrantAllocation
PassDocuments	
	SigningTheCurrencyRequirementBlan k

Same process steps, but performed by different roles

Process step

ApplicationOfErasmusGrant	EvaluationOfGrantApplications
ReceptivityAcknoledgementArrivesFro mTheReceivingInstitution	SigningSupportContract

Fig. 8. Semantic compliance checking report

The extracted process steps and roles will be reviewed in future in order to refine the algorithm. Having used this process ontology, the system is capable of creating a report that contains information about the discrepancies between the actual and reference process steps (Fig. 8).

Having used DL Queries the reference ontology can be filtered by only one specific role like Students (see in Fig. 7). In this case, this report will be provided for only tasks performed by students within the actual and the reference business process. This report shows that four process steps were adapted by the Hungarian university and six process steps were not mentioned in the Erasmus Programme Guide. The auditor get information about that which documents should be processed in order to get insight into the reasons of missing and surplus process steps.

6   Conclusion and Future Work

The internalization is an important activity for making competitive higher education institutions. The internalization process is regulated by the Erasmus Programme Guide within the European Union. The audit of the internalization of a given institution can be achieved an easier way if required information are collected easily by an information system. This paper presented a solution that can provide information for answering three audit questions. Its development is ongoing. Its algorithm will be reviewed after scrutinizing the actual results and it will be extended with new ones to collect new process elements for trying to answer other audit questions. This system was developed in Java and reused OWL API functions, DLQueryExample.java and SVN repository of Protégé 4 OWL Diff ontology matcher.

Acknowledgements. The authors wish to express their gratitude to Dr. András Gabor, associate professor of the Corvinus University of Budapest, for the great topic and the powerful help provided during the development process.

References

1. MobStrat - Mobility_strategy_for adoption - 2012 EHEA mobility strategy.pdf. http://www.ehea.info/uploads/(1)/2012%20ehea%20mobility%20strategy.pdf
2. Lifelong Learning Programme - European Commission (2016). http://ec.europa.eu/education/tools/llp_en.htm
3. Gábor, A., Kő, A., Szabó, Z., Fehér, P.: Corporate knowledge discovery and organizational learning: the role, importance, and application of semantic business process management—the ProKEX case. In: Gábor, A., Kő, A. (eds.) Corporate Knowledge Discovery and Organizational Learning, pp. 1–31. Springer, Cham (2016)
4. Cardoso, J., Hepp, M., Lytras, M.D.: The Semantic Web: Real-World Applications from Industry. Springer, New York (2007). ISBN 0387485309
5. Koschmider, A., Oberweis, A.: Ontology based business process description. In: Proceedings of the CAiSE 2005 Workshops, pp. 321–333. Springer (2005)

6. Hepp, M., Roman, D.: An ontology framework for semantic business process management. In: Proceedings of Wirtschaftsinformatik 2007, 28 February–2 March 2007, Karlsruhe (2007)
7. El Kharbili, M., et al.: Towards a framework for semantic business process compliance management. In: Proceedings of the Workshop on Governance, Risk and Compliance for Information Systems, pp. 1–15 (2008)
8. Su, X.: A text categorization perspective for ontology mapping. Department of Computer and Information Science, Norwegian University of Science and Technology, Norway (2002)
9. Shvaiko, P., Euzenat, J.: Ontology matching: state of the art and future challenges. IEEE Trans. Knowl. Data Eng. **25**(1), 158–176 (2013)
10. Otero-Cerdeira, L., et al.: Ontology matching: a literature review. Expert Syst. Appl. **42**(2), 949–971 (2015)
11. BOC Group: Business Process Management with Adonis (2013). http://www.boc-group.com/products/adonis/
12. Kramler, G., Murzek, M.: Business Process Model Transformation Issues (2006)
13. Protégé Community. http://protege.stanford.edu/community.php. Accessed 2 Aug 2014
14. Ternai, K.: Semi-automatic methodology for compliance checking on business processes. In: Kö, A., Francesconi, E. (eds.) EGOVIS 2015. LNCS, vol. 9265, pp. 243–256. Springer, Heidelberg (2015)
15. StudMob: ERASMUS Student Mobility for Studies (2015). http://www.esci-paris.eu/wp-content/uploads/2015/05/3-erasmus-student-mobility-studies.pdf
16. Temesi, J.: Internationalization in the Hungarian higher education. Audit materials, Tempus Public Foundation (2013)

Using Collaborative Filtering Algorithms for Predicting Student Performance

Juan Manuel Adán-Coello$^{(\boxtimes)}$ and Carlos Miguel Tobar

Pontifícia Universidade Católica de Campinas, Campinas, Brazil
{juan, tobar}@puc-campinas.edu.br

Abstract. Models that accurately predict student performance can be useful tools for planning educational interventions aimed at improving the results of the teaching-learning process, contributing to saving government resources and educators' and students' time and effort. In this paper it is studied the performance of collaborative filtering (CF) algorithms when applied to the task of student performance prediction. CF algorithms have been extensively and successfully used in recommender systems, but not in the considered educational scenario. The performances of two baseline methods and six state-of-the-art CF are compared when predicting if students would hit or miss multiple-choice questions, using two large educational datasets, created from the interaction between students and educational software. It was verified that CF algorithms account for consistently higher performance than the baselines for most metrics. Among the CF algorithms, memory based methods presented an overall better accuracy, precision, and recall. Nevertheless, all CF algorithms presented relatively low recall in identifying incorrect answers.

1 Introduction

Educational information systems can store large amounts of data from several sources with different formats. Educational data mining (EDM) is an interdisciplinary emergent research field that uses these data to try to understand how students learn and to identify the environment and conditions under which they effectively learn. The EDM objective can be to explain educational phenomena or to improve their results [1].

One of the main tasks of EDM is to predict students' performance, estimated, for example, by a score. An improved model for predicting student performance can save government resources and millions of hours of teachers' and students' time that they could devote to other activities, including leisure [2]. Furthermore, it is common that teaching and non-teaching staff spend significant time preparing and applying standardized tests. A good model that accurately predicts the performance of students can replace some of these tests and allow applying personalized and adaptive tests, which can contribute to increase students' deep learning [3].

Student performance prediction can also be used in planning educational interventions to improve the results of the teaching-learning process. It allows early detection of

---

This work was partially supported by CNPq and Fapesp.

A. Kő and E. Francesconi (Eds.): EGOVIS 2016, LNCS 9831, pp. 206–218, 2016.
DOI: 10.1007/978-3-319-44159-7_15

students with difficulties, as well as detection of which students can be exposed to more challenging educational situations, without the need for an excessive number of assessments that require time and effort from teachers and students [4, 5].

The ability to predict the grade a student will get in new activities allows implementing systems to guide him through the teaching-learning process, suggesting materials to study and tasks to accomplish. If the predicted score for a given task is high, it can be inferred that the student masters the knowledge and skills needed to perform it, and there is no gain in assigning that task to the student. On the other hand, if the predicted score is low, it is unlikely that the student is able to perform it at this point. In both cases, the system can recommend personalized tasks and educational objects that can help the student to enhance his knowledge and skills.

The search for models to predict the performance of students has been the subject of much research. Most of them focus on data mining and machine learning methods, including neural networks, Bayesian networks, rule based systems, decision trees, regression and SVM [4, 6–8]. In the work described in this paper the problem was approached using collaborative filtering (CF) algorithms, which are still not much explored in this context, but have been successfully used in recommender systems.

Recommender systems are intended to simplify the identification of information and resources that are of interest to the user in environments where the number of available items[1] is very large and potentially dynamic, such as the Internet. These systems proactively scan the space of options and identify items not yet accessed that may be of interest to the user. The recommendation problem can be reduced to the problem of predicting the rating a user would give to items he has not accessed yet and to recommend to him the items with the highest predicted ratings.

Recommender systems are usually constructed using CF or content-based filtering (CBF) methods, or a combination of both approaches. CF is the process of filtering or evaluating items using the opinions of other people [9]. CBF systems recommend items based on the descriptions of items and on a profile of users' interests [10]. CBF has its roots in the information retrieval field and has been successfully implemented in domains where items are associated with textual information. A content-based recommendation system can, for example, recommend to the user a Web page based on the similarity between the content of that page to the content of a page the user accessed before. One of the limitations of CBF methods is their dependence on the characteristics ascribed to the items (e.g. the words that make up a page). CBF systems are also characterized by being able to only recommend items that are similar to items accessed by the user in the past (overspecialization). For example, if the user accessed and enjoyed a page about football, the system may recommend other similar pages to the user, i.e., about football, possibly about sports, but it is very unlikely that it will suggest a page dealing with international politics.

Recommender systems based on CF do not depend on the characteristics associated with the items and so do not suffer from overspecialization. Their recommendations are social; they are based on the ratings on items of a community of users. Because of that,

---

[1] An item can be virtually any resource, including a Web page, a blog, a movie, a book, a user to follow on Twitter, an educational object, or a Web service.

CF-based systems can recommend any type of item, even items different from those accessed by the user in the past, as long as they are of interest to users with similar profiles.

In CF-based systems, the ratings given by the community of users are stored in a user-item matrix, each row of which contains the ratings of a particular user to the items considered; and each column of the matrix contains the ratings received by a particular item from the users. Positions of the matrix corresponding to unrated items are kept empty.

If students are mapped to users and questions (or exercises or problems) to items, the problem of predicting the performance of a student on questions that he has not yet solved can be treated as the problem of predicting the rating that the user would give to items he has not yet accessed.

Despite the great popularity of recommender systems, the use of CF methods for the problem of predicting student performance is still not much explored. In this context, the main objective of this paper is to analyze and compare the performances of state-of-the-art CF algorithms when applied to the problem of student performance prediction. To this end, Sect. 2 presents the CF algorithms that will be considered, Sect. 3 presents the educational datasets used in this study and describes the setting for the experiments conducted to evaluate the algorithms and, finally, Sect. 4 summarizes the main results and provides some concluding remarks.

2   Collaborative Filtering Algorithms

Six algorithms were compared: Two baseline methods (random and global average), two memory based algorithms (user-kNN and item-kNN), two matrix factorization algorithms (Matrix Factorization and Biased Matrix Factorization), and two Slope One algorithms (Slope One and Bipolar Slope One). These algorithms are presented in the following paragraphs and sections.

The baseline algorithms are very simple: The random method predicts ratings randomly and the global average method always predicts the average of all ratings in the dataset.

Memory-based CF algorithms make predictions directly from the available data, while model-based CF algorithms employ the available data to build a model that will then be used to make predictions. The literature points out that model-based algorithms can be more accurate and faster to make predictions (after the model is built) but, on the other hand, memory-based algorithms can provide a concise and intuitive rationale for the predictions made.

2.1   The kNN-i and kNN-u Algorithms

The kNN-i and the kNN-u algorithms make predictions using the weighted average of the ratings of a neighborhood of users or of items, respectively.

A neighborhood is formed based on the degree of similarity between a target user (or item) and other users (or items). The most common methods to calculate the similarity between users (or items) are the Pearson correlation coefficient and the cosine similarity, widely used in the field of information retrieval. The work described in this article uses the cosine similarity.

If R is the user-item matrix with dimensions $m \times n$ (for m users and n items), the similarity between items i and j, if both items have been evaluated by all users, is defined as the cosine between the m dimensional vectors corresponding to columns i and j of matrix R, as shown in Eq. (1).

$$sim(i,j) = \cos(\boldsymbol{i},\boldsymbol{j}) = \frac{\boldsymbol{i} \cdot \boldsymbol{j}}{\| \boldsymbol{i} \| \| \boldsymbol{j} \|} \tag{1}$$

If not all users necessarily rated both items, the cosine similarity between items i and j is given by Eq. (2), where U is the set of users who rated both i and j and $r_{u,i}$ denotes the rating of user u to item i.

$$sim(i,j) = \frac{\sum_{u \in U} r_{u,i} r_{u,j}}{\sqrt{\sum_{u \in U} r_{u,i}^2} \sqrt{\sum_{u \in U} r_{u,j}^2}} \tag{2}$$

After computing the similarity among items, the predicted rating of user u to item i, $\hat{r}_{u,i}$, is given by Eq. (3), where $S^k(i;u)$ denotes the set of k nearest (most similar) items to item i that were evaluated by user u.

$$\hat{r}_{u,i} = \frac{\sum_{j \in S^k(i;u)} sim(i,j) r_{u,j}}{\sum_{j \in S^k(i;u)} sim(i,j)} \tag{3}$$

Analogously to what was done to determine the similarity among items, the similarity between two users u and v is given by the cosine of the vectors defined by rows u and v of matrix R, if all items were evaluated by both users, or by the Eq. (4), when not necessarily all items were evaluated. where I is the set of items that both users, u and v, have evaluated.

$$sim(u,v) = \frac{\sum_{i \in I} r_{u,i} r_{v,i}}{\sqrt{\sum_{i \in I} r_{u,i}^2} \sqrt{\sum_{i \in I} r_{v,i}^2}} \tag{4}$$

The prediction of the rating of user u to item i, $\hat{r}_{u,i}$, takes into account the average of all ratings done by u, the difference between the average ratings of neighbor users, the ratings that these users gave to the target item, and the similarity between the target user and his neighbors, as shown by Eq. (5), where $\bar{r}_u$ is the average of all ratings made by u and $S^k(u)$ is the set of the k nearest neighbors to u that have rated item i.

$$\hat{r}_{u,i} = \bar{r}_u + \frac{\sum_{v \in S^k(u)} sim(u,v)(r_{v,i} - \bar{r}_v)}{\sum_{v \in S^k(u)} sim(u,v)} \tag{5}$$

As previously mentioned, the methods based on neighborhoods are widely used in recommender systems because they are intuitive and simple to implement, and also because they have two very useful properties: (1) their predictions and subsequent recommendations can be explained; and (2) new users' ratings can be used as they become available. The ability to explain how a given prediction was made is very important because, in general, users want to know the reasons that led to a prediction instead of receiving black box recommendations. The neighborhood concept, defined using the similarity among users, allows the ability to adequately explain the recommendations from the past actions and preferences of similar users. New ratings allow to deal with new users as soon as they perform some evaluation, without having to train a new model and make new estimations of parameters, as is the case with model-based approaches.

2.2   The Slope One and Bipolar Slope One Algorithms

Slope One algorithms are based on the intuitive principle of the popularity differential among items for users. According to [11], these algorithms allow easy implementation of CF models with accuracy comparable to more expensive memory-based CF schemes, as the neighborhood based ones presented above.

In the Slope One algorithm, the average deviation of item i with respect to item j, $d_{i,j}$, is given by Eq. (6), where U is the set of users that rated both i and j.

$$d_{i,j} = \frac{1}{|U|} \sum_{u \in U} r_{u,i} - r_{u,j} \qquad (6)$$

Using the average deviation among items, the Slope One scheme (SO) formula for rate predicting is as shown in Eq. (7), where $|R_u - \{i\}|$ is the set of all items rated by user u, except item i.

$$\hat{r}_{u,i} = \bar{r} + \frac{1}{|R_u - \{i\}|} \sum_{j \in |R_u - \{i\}|} d_{i,j} \qquad (7)$$

The experiments described in the next section also used a variant of SO named Bipolar Slope One (BSO) that splits the prediction into two parts; one prediction is derived from items users liked and another prediction from items users disliked. By splitting likes and dislikes, it effectively doubles the number of users; however (1) only deviations between two liked items or deviations from two disliked items are taken into account, and (2) only deviations from pairs of users who rated items i and j and share a like or dislike of item i are used to predict the rating for item j [11].

2.3   The Matrix Factorization and Biased Matrix Factorization Algorithms

The construction of CF models based on matrix factorization have become very popular recently, in part due to the success of these approaches in the Netflix Prize [12]. Matrix factorization can be understood as the task of approximating an array of partially observed data, $R \in \mathbb{R}^{|U||I|}$, by the product of two smaller matrices W and H. Each line u of W is a vector containing the K latent factors that describe user u, and H is a matrix where each row i is a vector containing the K latent factors that describe item i. Once matrices W and H are determined, the rating of user u to item i is estimated by Eq. (8), where w_{uk} and h_{ik} are elements of W and H, respectively.

$$\hat{r}_{u,i} = \sum_{k=1}^{K} w_{uk} h_{ik} = (WH^T)_{ui} \tag{8}$$

Latent factor matrices W and H can be determined by the minimization of the regularized quadratic error of the known rating set, as shown by Eq. (9).

$$\min_{W,H} \sum_{(u,i) \in L} (r_{u,i} - \hat{r}_{u,i})^2 + \lambda (\|W\|^2 + \|H\|^2) \tag{9}$$

In Eq. (9), L is the set of pairs (u,i) for which $r_{u,i}$ is known (the training set), λ is the regularization term used to prevent overfitting. In the implementation used it this work, the optimization of the above equation is done using as criterion the Root Mean Square Error (RMSE).

The prediction scheme using matrix factorization seeks to represent ratings as the results of the interaction among latent factors of users and items, but the variations in ratings may be due to user and item biases, which are independent of any interaction. For example, some users may have a tendency to give high ratings while others low ratings.

The Biased Matrix Factorization Algorithm (BMF) is the result of incorporating these biases into the above Matrix Factorization (MF) algorithm [13]. In BMF, predictions are done using Eq. (10), where b_u and b_i represent the user and item bias respectively.

$$\hat{r}_{u,i} = b_u + b_i + \sum_{k=1}^{K} w_{uk} h_{ik} \tag{10}$$

3 Comparing the Performances of CF Algorithms for Educational Datasets

This section presents the setting of experiments conducted to compare the performance of the algorithms described in the previous section and discusses their results. The experiments were performed using the Recommender Extension [14] for the Rapidminer tool[2].

---

[2] https://rapidminer.com/.

3.1   The Educational Datasets

The experiments described in this section used the assistments_2009_2010[3] and álgebra_2005_2006[4] datasets created from the interaction between students and educational software.

The assistments_2009_2010 dataset was produced by the ASSISTment system, an online tutoring system created in 2004 using 8th grade MCAS[5] test items from 1998 to 2007. These test items have been turned into ASSISTments by adding tutoring. If students working on ASSISTments answer an item correctly, they are given a new one. If they get it wrong, they receive a small tutoring session where they must answer a few questions that break down the problem into steps. Each ASSISTment consists of an original question and a list of scaffolding questions. The original question generally has the same text as the MCAS test while the scaffolding questions were created by content experts to coach students [3].

The algebra_2005_2006 dataset is stored in The Pittsburgh Science of Learning Center (PSLC) DataShop[6], a large repository of data on the interactions between students and educational software and a suite of tools to analyze that data.

For both datasets, training and test data were obtained from a chronological partitioning of data. A data split with the first 80 % records of the dataset was used for the training/learning phase of the models, and a split with the remaining 20 % of records was used to evaluate the models produced by the algorithms. For memory-based algorithms, which do not produce explicit models, the training phase involves computing values that are then used in the prediction phase, e.g. the similarity between users and items for the kNN-u and kNN-i algorithms.

The adopted chronological partitioning strategy aims at a more realistic assessment than other methods used in the areas of data mining and machine learning, such as k-fold cross-validation, because real systems can only use past data to make predictions for future events. A second reason to use this partition scheme is that this was the method used by the Netflix Prize, which made it a very popular evaluation method in the field [15].

The assistments_2009_2010 dataset contains 1,011,079 records with responses from 8,519 students to 35,978 math problems gathered in the school year 2009-2010. From the 20 attributes available for each record the experiments used only the attributes that identified the student (the user), the problem and the result of the student answer (correct/incorrect). When a question was answered more than once, it was considered only the first attempt. This involved the removal of 54,294 records of the original set, leaving 956,786 responses. In a further filtering step, only the answers to original multiple choice questions answered by at least 30 students were retained (scaffolding

---

[3] http://teacherwiki.assistment.org/wiki/Assistments_2009-2010_Full_Dataset.

[4] https://pslcdatashop.web.cmu.edu/.

[5] Massachusetts Comprehensive Assessment System (MCAS) is the graduation requirement in which all students in the state educated with public funds are required to participate. Students must pass the 10th grade tests in English Language Arts (ELA), Mathematics and one of the four high school Science and Technology Engineering tests as one condition of eligibility for a high school diploma.

[6] http://pslcdatashop.org/.

questions were removed), resulting in a collection of 175,179 responses. As previously explained, this dataset was divided into a training set with 80 % of the data and an evaluation set with 20 % of the data. In the training partition, 71.3 % of the records correspond to questions answered correctly, while this percentage is 78.9 % in the evaluation subset.

The algebra_2005_2006 dataset contains 809,694 responses of 575 students to 214,547 questions of algebra, gathered in the school year 2005-2006. Similarly to what was done for the assistements_2009_2010 dataset, from the 20 available attributes per record, the experiments used only three: student identification problem identification, and the result of the student first attempt to solve the problem. In the training partition, 77.1 % of the records are of correct answers while in the evaluation partition there are 78.1 % correct answers.

3.2 Performance Metrics

The algorithms were evaluated from three perspectives: the normalized mean absolute error (NMAE), the classification performance, and the time involved in learning and applying the CF models.

The NMAE is the result of normalizing the MAE (Mean Absolute Error), as indicated by Eqs. (11) and (12).

$$MAE = \frac{\sum_{u,i} |r_{u,i} - \hat{r}_{u,i}|}{N} \tag{11}$$

$$NMAE = \frac{MAE}{\sum_{u,i} r_{u,i}/N} \tag{12}$$

In the Eqs. (11) and (12), N is the number of predicted ratings, $r_{u,i}$ is the rating of user u for item i, and $\hat{r}_{u,i}$ is the predicted rating for that user-item pair. The lower the NMAE the better.

The classification performance seeks to assess whether the predicted ratings correctly classifies a question not yet answered by a student as correct or incorrect.

For each question in the datasets, a 0 indicates a missed question and a 1 a hit. The evaluated CF algorithms predict ratings as real values between 0 and 1, so the NMAE metrics measures the average error between the predicted and actual ratings.

In educational settings, performance predictions will typically be used to infer if a student will hit or miss a question not yet carried out in order to implement an educational strategy. Therefore, besides knowing the average numerical prediction error of the algorithms, it is perhaps more important to know their classificatory performance. For this purpose, each predicted numerical rating has to be mapped to a label denoting that the prediction is a correct (a hit) or of an incorrect answer (a miss) to the corresponding question. In the experiments described in this section, this was done by attaching the label Correct to questions with predicted values greater or equal to 0.5 and otherwise label Incorrect.

The classificatory performance of the algorithms was measured using the accuracy, precision, and recall metrics expressed as percentages. These metrics are computed using the number of true positives (tp), true negatives (tn), false positives (fp), and false negatives (fn) for each class, easily visualized in a confusion matrix, as the one shown in Table 1, for a problem with two classes (Positive/Negative).

The accuracy indicates the percentage of correct predictions. For a two-class problem, it is given by Eq. (13).

$$accuracy = \frac{tp + tn}{tp + fp + tn + fn} \tag{13}$$

Table 1. Confusion matrix for a two-class problem

Predicted class	Actual class	
	Positive	Negative
Positive	tp	fp
Negative	fn	tn

The accuracy gives an overall estimation of the performance of a classifier, but it can be misleading for unbalanced datasets where a classifier may never predict correctly one of the classes and still obtain high-accuracy values. This is the case in the datasets used in this work, where the number of examples of the class Correct is much higher than class Incorrect. For this reason, it is also important to consider the metrics precision and recall for each class.

In a two-class classification problem, precision and recall for the class Positive are computed as defined by Eqs. (14) and (15), respectively. For the class Negative, precision and recall are computed in an analogous way.

$$precision = \frac{tp}{tp + fp} \tag{14}$$

$$recall = \frac{tp}{tp + fn} \tag{15}$$

3.3   Experimental Results

Tables 2 and 3 show the performances of the evaluated algorithms when applied to the assistments_2009_2010 and algebra_2005_2006 datasets. The first eight rows of the tables show the results for the considered algorithms, respectively: Randon (R), Global Average (GA), User-based kNN (kNN-u), Item-based kNN (kNN-i), Matrix Factorization (MF), Biased-Matrix Factorization (BMF), Slope One (SO) and Bipolar Slope One (BSO). The diff_all line indicates the performance difference between the algorithms lowest and highest performance values for the metric of the respective column. The diff_CF line does the same, but just considers CF algorithms, i.e. Random (R) and Global Average (GA) algorithms were excluded. In both tables, best result for each metrics is written in bold and the worst result is underlined.

It is possible to notice in Tables 2 and 3 that the performances of the CF based algorithms are significantly higher than those of the R and GA baselines for most metrics.

Table 2. Performance for the assistments dataset

	NMAE	Accuracy	Precision (Correct)	Recall (Correct)	Precision (Incorrect)	Recall (Incorrect)	Training time (ms)	Testing time (ms)
R	0.500	50.05 %	78.92 %	50.15 %	21.18 %	**50.00 %**	94	**94**
GA	0.377	78.87 %	78.87 %	**100.00 %**	0.00 %	0.00 %	47	**94**
kNN-u	0.368679	79.02 %	**79.57 %**	98.77 %	53.55 %	5.30 %	281	484
kNN-i	**0.367211**	78.91 %	**79.57 %**	98.57 %	50.81 %	5.50 %	218	156
MF	0.374772	78.98 %	79.11 %	99.67 %	**59.01 %**	1.77 %	1139	**94**
BMF	0.375496	**79.06 %**	79.28 %	99.41 %	57.59 %	2.97 %	1716	**94**
SO	0.371066	79.02 %	79.33 %	99.26 %	55.43 %	3.45 %	1451	172
BSO	0.367788	78.96 %	79.19 %	99.46 %	54.60 %	2.40 %	2106	218
diff_all	36.22 %	57.96 %	0.89 %	99.40 %			4400 %	416.67 %
diff_CF	2.26 %	0.19 %	0.58 %	1.12 %	16.14 %	210.73 %	864.29 %	416.67 %

Table 3. Performance for the algebra dataset

	NMAE	Accuracy	Precision (Correct)	Recall (Correct)	Precison (Incorrect)	Recall (Incorrect)	Training time (ms)	Testing time (ms)
R	0.499259	50.15 %	78.34 %	50.08 %	22.01 %	**50.43 %**	281	**109**
GA	0.34697	78.16 %	78.16 %	**100.00 %**	0.00 %	0.00 %	203	125
kNN-u	**0.28074**	**81.93 %**	**84.17 %**	94.67 %	65.57 %	36.30 %	1342	156
kNN-i	0.294992	80.87 %	82.32 %	96.18 %	65.60 %	26.06 %	16099	2980
MF	0.346727	78.19 %	78.20 %	99.98 %	77.78 %	0.22 %	6209	**109**
BMF	0.346916	78.19 %	78.19 %	99.98 %	72.97 %	0.21 %	7176	156
SO	0.347013	78.18 %	78.19 %	99.98 %	71.43 %	0.18 %	104302	250
BSO	0.346969	78.17 %	78.17 %	**100.00 %**	**88.24 %**	0.06 %	141041	172
diff_all	77.84 %	63.37 %	7.69 %	99.68 %			69446.15 %	2628.57 %
diff_CF	23.61 %	4.81 %	7.68 %	5.63 %	34.57 %	60400.00 %	10412.79 %	2628.57 %

The R method has a NMAE unmistakably higher than those of the CF algorithms (the higher the NMAE, the higher the average error and thus the worse the performance). The NMAE of the GA method is not significantly higher than those of most CF algorithms. This happens because the training and testing partitions have a high percentage of correct responses, which is reflected in the overall average used to make predictions. This method presents, however, accuracy and recall equal to zero for the incorrect class. For both datasets, neighborhood-based algorithms have the lowest predictive errors: kNN-i for the assistments dataset (closely followed by kNN-u) and kNN-u for the algebra dataset (closely followed by kNN-i).

For the assistments dataset, the highest overall accuracy (percentage of correct classifications for both classes - Correct/Incorrect) is obtained by the BMF algorithm, closely followed by kNN-u and SO. Overall, the performances of the CF algorithms were very alike. For the algebra dataset, kNN-u presents the highest accuracy, closely followed by kNN-i. For this dataset, there is a meaningful difference of 4.81 % between the CF algorithms with the best and worst accuracy, kNN-u and R respectively.

The precision in classifying answers of the class Correct varies slightly between the algorithms for the assistments dataset, with a slight advantage for the algorithms based on neighborhood. For the algebra dataset, the precision in classifying answers of the class Correct of most CF algorithms and baseline methods is similar. The exceptions are the kNN-u and kNN-i algorithms, with performances that are 7.69 % and 5.3 %, respectively, higher than the method with the worst performance, GA.

The recall of all algorithms, except R, for answers of the class Correct is high, for both datasets. GA has the highest recall for both datasets (100 %) for the class Correct at the expense of recall zero for the class Incorrect. For the assistments dataset, among the CF algorithms, MF has the highest recall. The difference between the recall of this algorithm and that of the CF algorithm with the worst performance, kNN-i, is of 1.12 %. For the algebra dataset, BSO is the CF algorithm with the highest recall, which is 5.63 % higher than that of the algorithm with the lowest recall, kNN-u.

For the Incorrect class, regarding both datasets, especially assistments, the precision and recall of the algorithms are considerably lower than those that were observed for the Correct class. GA has precision and recall zero for both datasets. This is easy to explain: this method makes predictions using the average rating of the entire base, which in both datasets is greater than 0.7, so it will predict that all answers belong to the Correct class. The precision of R is quite low for both datasets, around 20 %, when compared to the CF algorithms that range from 50 % to 88 %. For both datasets, the neighborhood algorithms exhibit a somewhat lower precision than the other algorithms, but a much higher recall. For the assistments dataset, MF has the highest precision and the kNN-i the smallest, with a difference of 16.14 % between them. However, the recall of kNN-i is 210.73 % higher than that of MF; even so, the recall of kNN-i does not exceed 5.5 %. For the algebra dataset, the precision of BSO (88.24 %) is significantly higher than that of kNN-u (65.57 %), but the recall of the former is negligible (0.06 %) as compared to the latter (36.30 %). Similar behavior is observed when comparing the algorithms based on neighborhood with SO and with the algorithms based on matrix factorization.

When comparing the algorithms through the perspectives of training and testing times, it is possible to notice that the algorithms that require the highest computational times to produce models tend to be the fastest to make predictions. This trend is evident for the model-based algorithms (SO, BSO, MF, BMF). The R and GA methods require low and similar computational times in both steps. Noteworthy is the high computational time required at training time by kNN-i for the algebra dataset, compared with the timing requirements of this algorithm for the assistments dataset. This is an expected result as the algebra dataset is much larger than the assistments dataset, and the computational complexity of kNN-i at training time is known to be $O(mn^2)$, for m users and u items [16].

4 Related Work

Using CF algorithms to predict the performance of students is a relatively unexplored approach. Among the few works that use these methods it is noteworthy to mention [17] where the authors compare matrix factorization methods with The Knowledge Tracing using Brute Force method (KT-BF) [18], a state of the art method in student modeling, and with the baseline method's global average, student average, and user-item-baseline [19]. The authors also propose the Weighted Multi-Relational Matrix Factorization (WMRMF) method, based on the Multi-Relational Matrix Factorization Method (MRMF) [20]. The Tree datasets, including assistments_2009_2010, were used to evaluate these methods. For assistments_2009_2010, WMRMF outperformed the remaining methods with a root mean squared error (RMSE) of 0.460. Although that result cannot be directly compared with the results of the work described in this paper, because the evaluation protocol used in [17] is not sufficiently described, it is interesting to mention that in the experiments described in this paper the kNN-u method gives an RMSE of 0.413. The authors of [17] also did not evaluate the classification performance of the algorithms they studied.

5 Final Remarks

The experiments described in this paper have shown that the evaluated CF algorithms (kNN-u, kNN-I, MF, BMF, SO and BSO) present better performance than the baseline methods (R and GA). The main performance differences observed among the CF algorithms are related to classifying incorrect answers, where the neighborhood algorithms, especially kNN-u, had higher recall than the other algorithms. Though, the precision and recall of all algorithms for identifying incorrect answers is significantly low when compared to the results for correct answers, particularly for the assistments_2009_2010 dataset. In future work this limitation should be addressed. One possibility is to construct hybrid algorithms that combine collaborative filtering with content based filtering, using more of the available attributes. For instance, in the described experiments, only three (user_id, question_id, and correct) of the 20 attributes available on the assistments_2009_2010 dataset were used. The construction of ensembles of CF algorithms and classifiers is also a planned strategy to deal with the diversity observed in the datasets.

References

1. Romero, C., Ventura, S.: Educational data mining: a review of the state of the art. IEEE Trans. Syst. Man Cybern. Part C Appl. Rev. **40**, 601–618 (2010)
2. Cen, H., Koedinger, K., Junker, B.: Learning factors analysis – a general method for cognitive model evaluation and improvement. In: Ikeda, M., Ashley, K.D., Chan, T.-W. (eds.) ITS 2006. LNCS, vol. 4053, pp. 164–175. Springer, Heidelberg (2006)

3. Feng, M., Heffernan, N., Koedinger, K.: Addressing the assessment challenge with an online system that tutors as it assesses. User Model. User-Adap. Inter. **19**, 243–266 (2009)
4. Márquez-Vera, C., Cano, A., Romero, C., Ventura, S.: Predicting student failure at school using genetic programming and different data mining approaches with high dimensional and imbalanced data. Appl. Intell. **38**(3), 1–16 (2013)
5. Peña-Ayala, A.: Educational data mining: a survey and a data mining-based analysis of recent works. Expert Syst. Appl. **41**, 1432–1462 (2014)
6. Minaei-Bidgoli, B., Kashy, D.A., Kortmeyer, G., Punch, W.F.: Predicting student performance: an application of data mining methods with an educational web-based system. In: 33rd Annual Frontiers in Education (FIE 2003), pp. T2A–13. IEEE (2003)
7. Koutina, M., Kermanidis, K.L.: Predicting postgraduate students' performance using machine learning techniques. In: Iliadis, Lazaros, Maglogiannis, Ilias, Papadopoulos, Harris (eds.) EANN/AIAI 2011, Part II. IFIP AICT, vol. 364, pp. 159–168. Springer, Heidelberg (2011)
8. Pardos, Z.A., Gowda, S.M., Baker, R.S., Heffernan, N.T.: The sum is greater than the parts: ensembling models of student knowledge in educational software. ACM SIGKDD Explor. Newslett. **13**(2), 37–44 (2012)
9. Schafer, J.B., Frankowski, D., Herlocker, J., Sen, S.: Collaborative filtering recommender systems. In: Brusilovsky, P., Kobsa, A., Nejdl, W. (eds.) Adaptive Web 2007. LNCS, vol. 4321, pp. 291–324. Springer, Heidelberg (2007)
10. Pazzani, M.J., Billsus, D.: Content-based recommendation systems. In: Brusilovsky, P., Kobsa, A., Nejdl, W. (eds.) Adaptive Web 2007. LNCS, vol. 4321, pp. 325–341. Springer, Heidelberg (2007)
11. Lemire, D., Maclachlan, A.: Slope one predictors for online rating-based collaborative filtering. Soc. Ind. Math. **5**, 471–480 (2005)
12. Koren, Y.: The bellkor solution to the netflix grand prize. Netflix Prize Documentation **81**, 1–10 (2009)
13. Koren, Y., Bell, R., Volinsky, C.: Matrix factorization techniques for recommender systems. Computer **42**, 30–37 (2009)
14. Mihelčić, M., Antulov-Fantulin, N., Bošnjak, M., Šmuc, T.: Extending RapidMiner with recommender systems algorithms. In: RapidMiner Community Meeting and Conference (RCOMM 2012) (2012)
15. Gantner, Z.: Supervised Machine Learning Methods for Item Recommendation (2012). http://opus.bsz-bw.de/hsof/volltexte/2012/167/
16. Cacheda, F., Carneiro, V., Fernández, D., Formoso, V.: Comparison of collaborative filtering algorithms: limitations of current techniques and proposals for scalable, high-performance recommender systems. ACM Trans. Web (TWEB) **5**(1), 2 (2011)
17. Thai-Nghe, N., Drumond, L., Horváth, T., Schmidt-Thieme, L.: Multi-relational factorization models for predicting student performance. In: KDD 2011 Workshop on Knowledge Discovery in Educational Data, KDDinED (2011)
18. Baker, R.S.J.D., Corbett, A.T., Aleven, V.: More accurate student modeling through contextual estimation of slip and guess probabilities in bayesian knowledge tracing. In: Woolf, B.P., Aïmeur, E., Nkambou, R., Lajoie, S. (eds.) ITS 2008. LNCS, vol. 5091, pp. 406–415. Springer, Heidelberg (2008)
19. Koren, Y.: Factor in the neighbors: scalable and accurate collaborative filtering. ACM Trans. Knowl. Discov. Data (TKDD) **4**(1), 1 (2010)
20. Lippert, C., Huang, H., Weber, S.H., Tresp, V., Schubert, M., Kriegel, H.P.: Relation prediction in multi-relational domains using matrix factorization. In: Presented at the Workshop on Structured Input-Structured Output (NIPS 2008), Whistler, Canada (2008)

E-Government Research
and Intelligent Systems

Integrated Quality Assessment of Linked Thesauri for the Environment

Riccardo Albertoni[✉], Monica De Martino, and Alfonso Quarati

IMATI-CNR, Genoa, Italy
{albertoni,demartino,quarati}@ge.imati.cnr.it

Abstract. Thesauri usability, within a Spatial Data Infrastructure for the Environment, is pivotal for metadata compilation and data discovery. Thesauri effectiveness is affected by their quality. Diverse quality measures are available taking into account different facets, nevertheless an overall measure is needed whenever thesauri have to be compared in order to identify those to be improved for a proper reuse. The paper proposes a methodology for the quality assessment of linked thesauri aimed at providing an overall quality ranking. It provides a proof of concept of the Analytic Hierarchy Process adoption to the set of linked data thesauri deployed in the Thesaurus Framework for the Environment (LusTRE) developed within the EU funded project eENVplus.

Keywords: Environment · SKOS thesauri · Linked data · Quality · Analytic Hierarchy Process

1 Introduction

Different European policies and initiatives have been set up for the implementation of Spatial Data Infrastructures focusing on an international perspective aiming at supporting users from different countries sharing the same data sources. INSPIRE[1] is the European directive which pledges the EU member states to establish a Spatial Data Infrastructure for Europe to enable the sharing of environmental spatial information among public sector organizations and better facilitate public access to spatial information across Europe. It addresses 34 data themes needed for environmental applications with key components specified through technical implementation rules. SEIS[2] is the EC Communication towards a Shared Environmental Information System which sets out an approach to modernize and simplify the collection, exchange and use of the data and information required for the design, implementation and monitoring of environmental policy. Beside them, different EU funded projects (e.g. NutureSDI[3], eENVplus[4]) implement such initiatives to make them effective at different level by developing software services and tools in pilot testbeds.

---

[1] http://inspire.jrc.ec.europa.eu/.
[2] http://ec.europa.eu/environment/archives/seis/.
[3] http://www.nature-sdi.eu/.
[4] http://www.eenvplus.eu/.

© Springer International Publishing Switzerland 2016
A. Kő and E. Francesconi (Eds.): EGOVIS 2016, LNCS 9831, pp. 221–235, 2016.
DOI: 10.1007/978-3-319-44159-7_16

One of the key issues in data sharing, within a SDI, concerns with the multilingual and cultural barriers in the use and reuse of geographical data at global level. In the European context, multilingualism increases the complexity in the interoperability of data and the multicultural issues affect the sharing of geographic datasets provided by different multi-disciplinary communities. These issues require using geographic data in a standardised way and with a common nomenclature both in a multicultural and a multilingual context. Thesauri or controlled vocabularies are used to share standard technological and scientific terms of geographic data understandable by different user communities operating in the Environment domain. However, vocabularies are often made available for domain experts and cover only a very narrow knowledge area, they are mostly not translated in all EU languages and they embody different points of view. All these thesauri are precious and their join reusability within a Spatial Data Infrastructure, for metadata compilation and data discovery, is pivotal in order to provide a more effective description and to search data by keywords. The exploitation of linked data technologies allows making thesauri available not just as isolated data islands but as part of an interconnected federation of thesauri, referred to as Thesaurus Framework (TF).

As part of two sequential projects, the thematic network NatureSDI (Spatial Data Infrastructure for Nature Conservation) and CIP-PSP pilot projects eENVplus ("environmental services for advanced applications with-in INSPIRE"), a TF for the Environment, namely LusTRE[5], has been developed and exemplarily filled [1, 2]. LusTRE contains: (i) thesauri published as linked data [3, 4] to make them available to both humans and machines; (ii) interlinking between the thesauri and (iii) web services allowing to exploit the linked thesauri in third client application. Currently LusTRE grows in a quite exhaustive progress status and our activity is focusing on its maintenance phase, which concerns among the different tasks (e.g. inclusion of new vocabulary, new interlinking, server maintenance…) the study of the linked thesauri quality. The quality assessment of the linked thesauri is a crucial task for a TF manager who needs to identify those to be improved. Different quality dimensions have been defined in the linked data field [5] and others more specific for thesauri described through the Simple Knowledge Organization Systems (SKOS) model [6]. A critical issue is to combine all of them in order to compare the thesauri, facilitating decision maker to choice thesauri to be further improved.

The paper proposes a Multi Criteria Decision Making based methodology for the thesauri quality assessment, that we defined as the process aimed at supporting the decision maker (i.e. TF manager) in thesauri comparison based on the exploitation of an overall quality measure. The overall quality measure takes into account the subjective perceptions of the TF manager according to her needs. The Analytic Hierarchy Process (AHP) methodology [7] is adopted to capture both subjective and objective facets involved in the thesauri quality assessment and to provide a ranking of the assessed thesauri. The paper provides a proof of concept of the AHP adoption to the set of linked thesauri within the TF LusTRE. The thesauri quality assessment process has been carried out, on the basis of the quality measures assessed by applying the qSKOS tool [8], resulting in the overall ranking of the assessed thesauri.

---

[5] http://linkeddata.ge.imati.cnr.it/.

The paper is structured as following: Sect. 2 presents the TF LusTRE, Sect. 3 overviews related works and introduces the problem of assessing the quality of SKOS thesauri. Section 4 summarizes the approach and AHP process. Section 5 illustrates how AHP is used to supply an overall quality ranking of LusTRE thesauri. Section 6 concludes.

2 LusTRE a Framework of Linked Thesauri

LusTRE is the Linked Thesaurus fRamework for Environment developed in the EU projects NatureSDI and eENVplus. It is an innovative solution which aims to assemble various available thesauri for the Environment. It provides shared standards and scientific terms for a common understanding of environmental data among the different communities operating in the different field of the Environment.

The main component is a knowledge infrastructure of vocabularies, which interlinks different environmental domain vocabularies and offers access to them as one virtual integrated linked data source. The knowledge infrastructure can be exploited in client applications (e.g. metadata editor and geoportal) using a set of web services available in LusTRE. Morcover, an explorative tool allowing to browse and search for a concept within the knowledge infrastructure is also provided.

Currently the knowledge infrastructure of interlinked thesauri consists of a compilation of various thesauri (including EARTh [9] and ThIST) which are monolingual or bilingual and the interlinking between the concepts addressed by them. Thesauri are exposed as a collection of SKOS concept schemes, which provides lightweight semantics for thesaurus concepts. It includes vocabularies related to different INSPIRE data themes[6] such as Biodiversity, Habitats and Biotopes, Species Distribution, Biogeographical Regions, Protected Sites, Geology, Air Quality. Moreover, their concepts are linked with the concepts of other vocabularies uploaded in LusTRE's SPARQL end point (e.g. GEMET, AGROVOC) or exposed in the Linked Open Data Cloud (e.g. EuroVoc, DBpedia).

2.1 LusTRE Lifecycle

A multi-task approach has been applied to create LusTRE. In particular, its lifecycle involved the following tasks:

- Thesaurus selection. Selection and classification of existing vocabularies have been performed to identify the set of thesauri for the framework. Criteria concerning thesaurus "reusability" (i.e. license openness and compliance to Linked Data best practice) [10] and the coverage of the INSPIRE data theme have been considered.
- Thesaurus processing. The selected vocabularies have been processed in order to encode them in SKOS/RDF format. In-house procedures modifying the structure of

---

[6] http://inspire.ec.europa.eu/index.cfm/pageid/2/list/7.

the vocabularies and tools like LODrefine[7] have been applied to clean up the vocabularies.

- Thesaurus interlinking. Thesauri connections have been automatically generated using some tools (e.g. SILK[8]) and then validated by the domain expert communities. The interlinking is not aimed to connect each thesaurus to all the others. Connections between vocabularies should be created only where they are useful and sound, and anyhow completeness of interlinking is not always feasible considering terminologies that are independently developed and continuously evolving.
- Thesaurus publication. Thesauri and their interlinking have been made available on the web according to the Linked Data Best Practices using Virtuoso[9] as RDF store of the vocabularies. It also provides a SPARQL endpoint that can be used by semantic web literate users in order to directly perform SPARQL queries on LusTRE content.
- TF maintenance. It regards different activities: content updating, new thesauri, interlinking improvement, server maintenance, quality evaluation. TF is a living open environment and its exploitation to be effective must leverage on the consistency and accuracy of linked thesauri. In fact, modifications to the thesauri and their interlinking constantly occur, potentially affecting the quality of the framework. Anyway, we point out that the maintenance activity performed by the TF managers does not concern the improvement of the quality of the native thesaurus (e.g. coverage extension, documentation, …) which requires a domain knowledge pertaining to the thesaurus developer. TF manager deals with the technological quality issue related to the publication and management of thesauri as Linked Data, in particular analyzing those issues which can be solved mainly with automatic procedures without the specific knowledge of the thesaurus developer.

Currently, we are focusing on the TF maintenance task, in particular on the improvement of the quality of LusTRE's thesauri. From the point of view of the TF manager, it involves the analysis and comparison of the thesauri quality in order to identify those requiring overriding technical improvement.

3   Quality of Thesauri

3.1   Related Works

The Information Quality (IQ) problem [11] has been encountered in the Linked Data field of which SKOS thesauri are a particular case. Various proposals arose in these last years, addressing specific aspects of linked datasets quality and proposing specific sets of metrics and methodologies for their evaluation [12–16]. The work described in [5] is particular relevant as it provides a systematic survey on quality assessment proposals for linked data: it identifies 18 IQ dimensions, and classifies them into four major categories. An IQ metric is a procedure for measuring an information quality dimension. In

---

[7] https://github.com/sparkica/LODRefine.
[8] http://silkframework.org/.
[9] http://virtuoso.openlinksw.com/.

general, more than one metric may be supplied for assessing one dimension. The IQ assessment is the process of evaluating if a piece of information meets the information consumer's needs in a specific situation [17].

Looking at the problem of the quality of thesauri, the work presented in [18] suggests a range of abstract measurement constructs based on quality notions in thesaurus literature and inference from other related literature. The declared purpose of the measurement constructs (i.e. dimensions) is to support the evaluation approaches of thesauri but, as declared by authors, such constructs are solely based on theoretical analysis and they pointed out the necessity of operationalizing the measures and then refine them by application to real cases of thesauri. Moreover, the presented constructs do not address quality dimensions related to multilingual thesauri. The works in [19] extended [13] by proposing the linkset importing as a novel quality measure which estimates the completeness of dataset obtained by complementing SKOS thesauri with their skos:exactMatch related information. Such measure focused on easing multilingual issues such as incomplete language coverage, which affects many of the most popular SKOS thesauri.

One of the most complete related work about SKOS thesauri quality is provided in [6] that introduces a set of 26 quality issues, defined as computable functions exposing potential quality problems. By using the qSKOS tools [8] it analyses a corpus of 24 vocabularies, checking for their quality with respect to the 26 identified issues. The authors also applied the Skosify tool [20] to automatically correct a subset of those issues. Authors present several facets of the vocabulary quality assessment problem and supply useful observations, recommendations and best practices.

Analyzing the previous works, we notice that no explicit methodology has been supplied for assembling the measures resulting by the application of the various metrics, thus to obtaining an overall quality assessment of linked datasets.

3.2   Assessing the Overall Quality of SKOS Thesauri

In the following, we call thesauri quality assessment the process aimed at comparing a set of thesauri based on the exploitation of an overall quality measure.

Our aim is to present the Analytic Hierarchy Process (AHP), a well-founded decision making technique, as a useful means for supporting the thesauri quality assessment by supplying a ranking of the thesauri under evaluation. Such ranking is obtained by synthetizing for each thesaurus an overall score computed from the aggregation of several IQ dimensions. Often, the assessment of IQ dimensions is made under an "objective" perspective, without considering the "subjective" point of view of the expert. Dealing with subjectivity allows asserting the importance (priority) of some dimension with respect to another, or supply a judgment on dimensions that cannot quantitatively be measured (by a procedure) and required qualitatively assertion about their importance with respect to a given scenario.

Our proposal relies on the work [6] which provides a thorough discussion of quality issues that hinder SKOS vocabularies and supplies a framework for the automated assessment and correction of such issues. Those issues are grouped into three main categories, namely 'Labelling and Documentation issue', 'Structural issues' and 'Linked

Data issues'. We want to point out that grouping issues in categories may facilitate the emergence of higher level views of the quality dimensions, allowing to highlight possible trade-offs between alternative objectives.

Leveraging on the IQ issues of [6] avoided us to reinvent the wheel for what concern the definition of 'another set' of IQ dimensions. In fact, we are more interested in discussing how the AHP may be useful to address the thesauri quality assessment process and less to show the appropriateness of new IQ dimensions or metrics. Furthermore, we want to outline that the proposed approach, due to its generality, may be applied even if the set of dimensions was different or if the assessment and correction automatic tools should change.

4   MCDM Approach to Thesauri Quality Assessment

Due to the heterogeneity of the multiple IQ dimensions, the task of synthetizing an overall measure from the evaluation of the various dimensions is not, in principle, an easy one. In order to support such a "mixing apples with oranges" process, we have considered a well consolidated approach named Multi Criteria Decision Making (MCDM). MCDM techniques regard the analysis of a set of various (finite or infinite) alternatives, namely the decision space, described in term of multiple criteria, aimed at deriving the ones better performing respect to the goal of the planning process. Thousands of publications have been published to provide information about MCDM methods, their development and application in different fields [21].

MCDM can be usually classified into two broad categories: Multi-Attribute Decision Making (MADM) and Multi-Objective Decision Making (MODM). This distinction depends essentially by two characteristic of the decision problem at hand: the number of possible alternatives and whether we face a selection or a design problem. MODM studies decision problems in which the decision space is continuous, and an alternative can be found by solving a mathematical model with multiple objective functions, and (possibly) under specified constraints. MADM is concerned with the selection among a discrete (although potentially large) number of alternatives.

To evaluate each alternative and be able to compare it with others, the selection of criteria (aka attributes) is required to reflect alternative performance in meeting the objective. Criteria represent the different dimensions from which the alternatives can be viewed [22]. Each criterion must be measurable to assess how well a particular option is expected to perform in relation to the criterion. Criteria may be measured in cardinal numbers (e.g. price, number of drawbacks), some in binary terms (e.g. a tick indicates presence of a particular feature), or in qualitative terms (e.g. 'good', 'insufficient').

Amongst the most adopted MADM methods there are TOPSIS [23], SAW, AHP [7], and the ELECTRE family methods [24]. A useful classification helping decision makers in identifying the more suitable MADM technique, distinguishes: (a) Choice problem: the goal is to select a single alternative or to reduce the group of alternative to a subset of equivalent or incomparable alternatives; (b) Sorting problem: alternatives are sorted into ordered predefined categories; (c) Ranking problem: alternatives are ordered in a decreasing preference list; (d) Description problem: the goal is to help the description of alternatives and their consequences [25].

Based on the above mentioned decision problems classification, the comparison of thesauri, subject to the thesauri quality assessment, can exploit techniques supporting choice and/or ranking problems. As observed in [26] AHP is particularly useful for these kinds of problems. Furthermore, AHP ability of decomposing a problem in its elements (i.e. goal, criteria, sub-criteria and alternatives) and in structuring them as a hierarchy of different levels fits well with the description of the thesauri quality assessment problem as being characterized by grouping quality issues in distinct categories. Finally, the choice of adopting AHP is fostered by its impressive record of successes in a number of different applications fields [27].

The Analytic Hierarchy Process (AHP) supports decision-makers in structuring problem complexity and exercising judgment, allowing them to incorporate both objective and subjective considerations in the decision process [28]. As reported in Fig. 1, the AHP methodology involves the execution of six subsequent phases: (1) identifying the criteria that characterize the alternatives of the decision problem and organizing them as a hierarchy; (2) pairwise comparing criteria according to user preference and achieving weights derivation; (3) evaluating or gathering the performance of each alternative with respect to each criterion; (4) scaling of criteria; (5) synthetizing and ranking the alternatives; (6) selecting the high ranking alternative(s).

Fig. 1. AHP multi-phase process.

These phases are common to all possible application domains. In Sect. 5 we detail each AHP phase by discussing its adoption to the thesauri quality assessment process. In particular, we focus on the thesauri quality assessment application for the maintenance of a TF, exemplifying to the case of LusTRE's thesauri.

5 Thesauri Quality Assessment for LusTRE Maintenance

The TF LusTRE is a living environment, where new thesauri and interlinking can be added. Updating the interlinked thesauri may introduce various kinds of errors and thus change the overall quality of the framework. Based on these considerations, the quality assessment of the set of linked thesauri occurs during the TF maintenance and concerns the identification of those thesauri (and their interlinking) which majorly require to be fixed.

In the following, we discuss the application of the AHP phases to LusTRE for its maintenance, exemplifying our approach to its main linked thesauri. Although in principle AHP may be applied without the use of any software, MADM tools [29] greatly simplifies the decision maker activity allowing saving time and making the process more efficient. The availability of these tools allows to easily implementing the thesauri quality assessment process in a semi-automated way. We used the SuperDecisions[10] software that implements the AHP, as it granted us a free trial for one year.

5.1   Criteria Selection and Hierarchy Creation

This phase starts with the identification of a set of criteria affecting LusTRE's thesauri that, according to the decision maker, properly describe the decision problem at hand.

More specifically, of the 26 quality issues presented in [6], we consider just the ones relevant for the maintenance task, as reported in Table 1. In the following, we refer to them as issues or criteria. The criteria are grouped according to three categories: '1 Labelling and Documentation issues', '2 Structural issues' and '3 Linked Data issues'.

Table 1. Thesauri quality issues grouped by category. For each thesaurus absolute errors computed by qSKOS (left columns) and normalized scores (rights columns) are reported. (*) issue fixable with the Skosify tool.

	EARTh		ThIST		GEMET		EuroVoc		AGROVOC	
N° Authoritative Concepts	14352		34155		5257		6883		32323	
1 Labelling and Documentation issues										
1.1 Omitted invalid tags (*)	0	0	0	0	3	0,016	240	1	55	0,049
1.2 Incomplete language coverage	461	0,032	24055	0,705	904	0,172	5173	0,752	32310	11
1.3 Inconsistent prefLabel (*)	0	0	133	1	0	0	0	0	0	0
1.4 Disjoint label violation (*)	69	1	1	0,006	3	0,119	0	0	6	0,038
2 Structural issues										
2.1 Cyclic hierarchical relations (*)	0	0	9	1	0	0	0	0	3	0,352
2.2 Valueless associative relations	1124	1	2378	0,889	31	0,075	8	0,015	1671	0,66
2.3 Omitted top concept	1	0;003	1	0,001	1	0,009	139	1	0	0
2.4 Top concept having broader concept	0	0	0	0	0	0	0	0	4	1
2.5 Unidirectionally related concept (*)	0	0	39	0,001	0	0	15033	1	21351	0,302
2.6 Relational clashes (*)	61	1	98	0,675	2	0,089	1	0,034	79	0,575
2.7 Mapping clashes	0	0	5	0,296	0	0	0	0	16	1
3 Linked Data issues										
3.1 Missing In-links	8530	0,658	30838	1	471	0,099	4439	0,7143	29111	0,998
3.2 Missing Out-links	8530	0,659	30821	1	472	0,099	4442	0,715	29111	0,998
3.3 Broken links	39	0	178	0	206	0,002	120.790	1	160	0

In the maintenance task, the quality issues that can be fixed automatically are regard as important, while issues mentioned in [6] that intrinsically qualify the content of a thesaurus (e.g. 'Undocumented concept' and 'Overlapping labels') are not considered as they consist of editorial changes of which a framework manager is not usually in charge.

We have considered issues, which can be fixed by the Skosify tool (marked in Table 1 with an asterisk). Moreover, we have also considered the following issues: 'Valueless associative relations', 'Top concept having broader concept' and 'Mapping

---

[10] http://www.superdecisions.com/.

clashes' as the manager should try to fix these issues respectively by deleting the value-less, broader and mapping relations; 'Omitted top concept' as the manager can add omitted concepts as top concept; 'Incomplete language coverage' as the manager can ease this issue by exploiting translations of concepts imported from interlinked thesauri [19]. All the quality issues in the 'Linked Data issues' category are regarded relevant as the TF management includes the improvement of the interlinking between vocabularies in the TF and broken links should be deleted from the framework.

The selected criteria have been hierarchy organized as depicted in the tree of Fig. 2. Hierarchy organization helps the decision makers to organize a complex problem into its basic and simpler elements [30]. This decomposition activity sets the goal (i.e. thesauri quality assessment - abbreviated as TQA in Fig. 2) of the analysis to the top level of the hierarchy, i.e. in our case the selection of the thesaur(us/i) with higher quality.

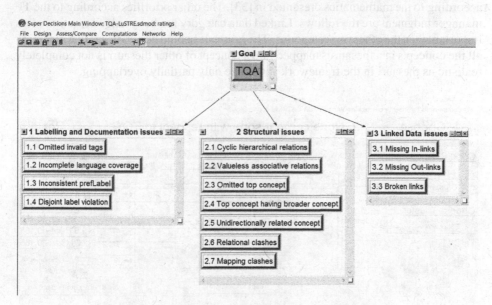

Fig. 2. Hierarchy creation through SuperDecisions.

5.2 Pairwise Comparison of Criteria and Weights Computation

Reciprocal paired comparisons allow expressing judgments on the relative importance of each criterion and to automatically linking them to a numerical fundamental scale of absolute numbers (in the integer interval 1–9) as defined by Saaty [31].

Operatively, the pairwise comparison made for each branch of each level, is mapped to square matrixes with the number of elements equal to the nodes at that branch. If an element X of the matrix is considered j times (with j an integer in the Saaty's scale) more important than an element Y, then it follows that Y is $1/j$ times as important as X. Based on the pairwise elicitation of relative importance of criteria given in matrix form, AHP allows estimating the criteria's weights. This can mainly be done using two methods: the logarithmic least squares method or the eigenvector method. The latter is advocated as more powerful as it allows dealing with inconsistencies that may arise from the pairwise elicitation process [32].

Considering the tree of Fig. 2 this phase requires to compare the elements of a 3×3 matrix (for the three issues categories), and of a 4×4, a 7×7 and a 3×3 matrix for the criteria at the leaves level. For instance, Fig. 3 shows the elicitation of priorities for the seven criteria of the '2 Structural issues' category, using SuperDecisions. The tool allows the insertion of priority in matrix form, however, as the inverse values are directly computed, just the triangular matrix has to be filled. Moreover, the priority of last criterion (i.e. '2.7 Mapping clashes') compared to the others is not explicitly given, as it can be computed by the values supplied in the other cells. In Fig. 3, '2.2 Valueless associative relations' and '2.3 Omitted top concept' are judged 2 times less important than the other issues of the category. The weights are automatically computed by SuperDecisions according to the mathematics presented in [33]. The other priorities according to the TF manager judgment are the follows: Linked data category has been judged two times less important than the other two categories. The rationale behind this choice is that assuming all the concepts in a thesaurus mapped into a concept of other thesauri is not completely realistic as thesauri in the framework should be only partially overlapping.

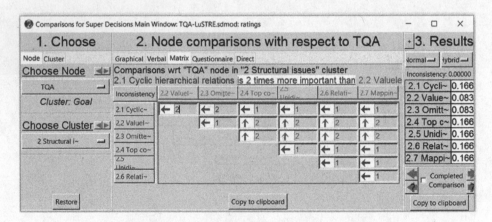

Fig. 3. Pairwise comparison and computation of relative weights given in (triangular) matrix form, for the '2 Structural issues' category, with SuperDecisions software.

5.3 Performance Evaluation

The third AHP phase requires the computation of performance values of each criterion C_j according to every thesaurus.

We gather these values by applying qSKOS directly to the five LusTRE thesauri, for what concerns the first two categories. As regards to Linked data issues category the In-links and Out-links issues has been worked out coherently with the definitions proposed in qSKOS, except that we have considered only intra-links, namely links involving only subjects and objects in LusTRE. This choice has been taken considering that our primary target is the quality assessment and the maintenance of LusTRE, and that SINDICE, the search engine qSKOS relies to retrieve In-links in the web of data, has been recently turned off.

5.4 Scaling Criteria

As performance values can be supplied in numeric, descriptive or categorical data, the scaling of criteria solves the problems of different ranges and different units of the performance values. The goal of scaling is to bring all criterion values into non-dimensional scores within the [0,1] interval, and thus make them comparable. However, before applying these phase, a pre-processing step has been required to make the actual performance quality values be ingested by the AHP tool.

This pre-processing is usually not necessary in decision scenarios that adopt AHP to compare alternatives such as, for instance when evaluating the price of goods, the air pollution caused by alternative producing plants, the horse power and energy consumption of vehicles and so on. However, in our case the performance values as computed by qSKOS are supplied as absolute number of errors for any given IQ issue and thesaurus, but the assessed thesauri have different size (i.e. different number of authoritative concepts). Thus prior to apply AHP normalization, such performance values have to be measured on a comparable scale or in other word their absolute values have to be relativized to the thesaurus size.

To this end we replaced the absolute performance value (i.e. #error$_{ij}$) for a criterion C_j given a thesaurus T_i, with the ratio:

$$P_{ij} = \#error_{ij}/\#authconcept(T_i) \tag{1}$$

Once all ratios are computed for each criterion and alternative, the actual AHP scaling phase may be applied. Saaty proposed different methods [34]. In particular, the so-called *Ideal* mode compares each performance value P_{ij} to a fixed benchmark. In its general application the ideal mode computes the score values $S(C_i)$ by dividing P_{ij} by the maximum value achieved for criterion C_i amongst all the alternatives. We therefore applied the following normalization formula to compute the score value S_{ij}:

$$S_{ij} = P_{ij}/max_j \quad \textit{iff } max_j \neq 0$$
$$S_{ij} = 0 \quad\quad \textit{iff } max_j = 0 \tag{2}$$

with max_j the maximum ratio for a given criterion C_j with respect to all thesauri (i.e. $max_j = max\{P_{ij}, i = 1,..,5\}$). The higher the error the greater the score achieved by a thesaurus for a given criterion, that will contribute to increase the ranking of the thesaurus when coupled with the computed weights. If for a criterion C_k, no error is reported for every thesaurus T_i, then $S_{ik} = 0$ for all i, while $S_{ij} = 1$ if $P_{ij} = max_j$. The scores obtained by applying (1) and (2) are reported in Table 1, rounded at the fourth decimal.

5.5   Synthesis and Ranking

Once scores have been computed for each criterion of each thesaurus, they are combined with the criteria weights derived from pairwise comparisons to determine an overall synthesis score for each alternative. This value is obtained by adding the products of each criterion score $S(C_i)$ with its associated weight w_i, (computed by SuperDecisions) across each branch of the hierarchy. This sum becomes the score value for the parent node directly above and the process is repeated at the next level of the hierarchy until the root node is reached. Based on this bottom-up process, SuperDecisions returns the ranking list of the five thesauri as shown in the histogram of Fig. 4, along with the resulting synthesis values. Higher synthesis scores mean more errors and higher ranks. The values of the first three thesauri are quite closer having all reported significant number of errors, while EARTh stands in the midst and GEMET, consistently with the few relative errors revealed by qSKOS, ranked last with about 10 % of the score of EuroVoc.

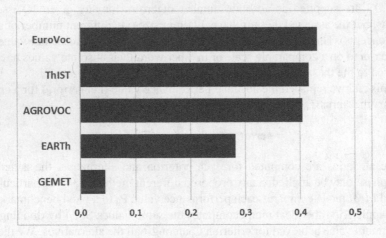

Fig. 4. Synthesis scores and ranking of the LusTRE thesauri.

5.6   Selection

The selection amongst the higher ranking thesauri, is the last AHP phase. It is made by the decision maker once the ranking list of the alternatives is returned. In the specific case of LusTRE maintenance, thesauri ranking reflects the amount of errors exposed thus higher ranking thesauri (i.e. EuroVoc, ThIST and AGROVOC) require to be fixed earlier than the lower ranking ones.

It is important to outline that the resultant ranking depends on the decisions of the TF manager concerning the priorities of the different criteria but it is also strongly affected by the actual performance (i.e. number of errors) of the thesauri. It is quite easy to see how the three first ranked thesauri often achieved higher values (i.e. normalized errors) in several criteria, while GEMET generally scores lower than the other four thesauri, almost for all criteria. Even changing the priorities, for instance equaling the priorities of the three category issues, does not significantly affect the ranks. This fact is partly explained by the small number of alternatives considered. This leaves few degrees of freedom to the possible change of the ranks, when coupled with the considerable differences of scores.

6 Conclusion

The paper proposes a methodology for the thesauri quality assessment supporting the comparison of environmental thesauri exposed as linked data. It exploits an overall quality measure based on the Analytic Hierarchy Process methodology, which takes into account both subjective and objective facets involved in the assessment process. The adoption of AHP to the set of linked thesauri deployed in the TF LusTRE developed within the EU funded project eENVplus provides a proof of concept of the proposed approach and as such, it can be replicated in wider different contexts.

References

1. Abecker, A., Albertoni R., De Martino, M., Podestà, P., Schnitter, K., Wössner, R.: Latest developments of the linked thesaurus framework for the environment (LusTRE). In: ENVIROINFO 2015 Conference, Copenhagen, Denmark (2015)
2. De Martino, M., Albertoni, R.: A multilingual/multicultural semantic-based approach to improve data sharing in a SDI for nature conservation. Int. J. Spat. Data Infrastruct. Res. **6**, 206–233 (2011)
3. Berners-Lee, T.: Linked data. http://www.w3.org/DesignIssues/LinkedData.html
4. Bizer, C., Heath, T., Berners-Lee, T.: Linked data - the story so far. Int. J. Semant. Web Inf. Syst. **5**(3), 1–22 (2009)
5. Zaveri, A., Rula, A., Maurino, A., Pietrobon, R., Lehmann, J., Auer, S.: Quality assessment for linked open data: a survey. Semant. Web J. **7**(1), 63–93 (2016)
6. Suominen, O., Mader, C.: Assessing and improving the quality of SKOS vocabularies. J. Data Semant. **3**, 47–73 (2013)
7. Saaty, T.L.: The Analytic Hierarchy Process. McGraw-Hill, New York (1980)
8. Mader, C., Haslhofer, B., Isaac, A.: Finding quality issues in SKOS vocabularies. In: Zaphiris, P., Buchanan, G., Rasmussen, E., Loizides, F. (eds.) TPDL 2012. LNCS, vol. 7489, pp. 222–233. Springer, Heidelberg (2012)
9. Albertoni, R., De Martino, M., Di Franco, S., De Santis, V., Plini, P.: EARTh: an environmental application reference thesaurus in the linked open data cloud. Semant. Web **5**(2), 165–171 (2014)
10. Albertoni, R., De Martino, M., Podestà, P.: Environmental thesauri under the lens of reusability. In: Kő, A., Francesconi, E. (eds.) EGOVIS 2014. LNCS, vol. 8650, pp. 222–236. Springer, Heidelberg (2014)
11. Batini, C., Scannapieco, M.: Data and Information Quality: Dimensions Principles and Techniques. Springer, Heidelberg (2016)
12. Guéret, C., Groth, P., Stadler, C., Lehmann, J.: Assessing linked data mappings using network measures. In: Simperl, E., Cimiano, P., Polleres, A., Corcho, O., Presutti, V. (eds.) ESWC 2012. LNCS, vol. 7295, pp. 87–102. Springer, Heidelberg (2012)

13. Albertoni, R. Gòmez-Pérez, A.: Assessing linkset quality for complementing third-party datasets. In: Joint EDBT/ICDT 2013 Workshops, pp. 52–59. ACM, New York (2013)
14. Kontokostas, D., Zaveri, A., Auer, S., Lehmann, J.: TripleCheckMate: a tool for crowdsourcing the quality assessment of linked data. In: 4th Conference on Knowledge Engineering and Semantic Web, St. Petersburg (2013)
15. Demartini, G., Difallah, D.E., Cudré-Mauroux, P.: Large-scale linked data integration using probabilistic reasoning and crowdsourcing. Int. J. Very Large Data Bases 22(5), 665–687 (2013)
16. Debattista, J., Lange, C. Sören, A.: LUZZU – A Framework for Linked Data Quality Assessment', CoRR abs/1412.3750. http://arxiv.org/abs/1412.3750
17. Bizer, C., Cyganiak, R.: Quality-driven information filtering using the WIQA policy framework. J. Web Semant. 7(1), 1–10 (2009)
18. Kless, D., Milton, S.: Towards quality measures for evaluating thesauri. In: Sánchez-Alonso, S., Athanasiadis, I.N. (eds.) MTSR 2010. CCIS, vol. 108, pp. 312–319. Springer, Heidelberg (2010)
19. Albertoni, R., De Martino, M., Podestà, P.: A linkset quality metric measuring multilingual gain in SKOS thesauri. In: 2nd Workshop on Linked Data Quality Co-located with 12th Extended Semantic Web Conference (ESWC 2015) (2015)
20. Suominen, O., Hyvönen, E.: Improving the quality of SKOS vocabularies with Skosify. In: ten Teije, A., Völker, J., Handschuh, S., Stuckenschmidt, H., d'Acquin, M., Nikolov, A., Aussenac-Gilles, N., Hernandez, N. (eds.) EKAW 2012. LNCS, vol. 7603, pp. 383–397. Springer, Heidelberg (2012)
21. Zavadskasa, E.K., Turskisa, Z., Kildienė, S.: State of art surveys of overviews on MCDM-MADM methods. Technol. Econ. Dev. Econ. 20(1), 165–179 (2014)
22. Triantaphyllou, E., Shu, B., Sanchez, S.N., Ray, T.: Multi-criteria decision making: an operations research approach. Encycl. Electr. Electron. Eng. 15, 175–186 (1998)
23. Hwang, C.L., Yoon, K.: Multiple Attribute Decision Making: Methods and Applications. Springer, New York (1981)
24. Roy, B.: Classement et choix en présence de points de vue multiples (la méthode ELECTRE). La Revue d'Informatique et de Recherche Opérationelle 8, 57–75 (1968)
25. Roy, B.: The optimisation problem formulation: criticism and overstepping. J. Oper. Res. Soc. 32(6), 427–436 (1981)
26. Ishizaka, A., Pearman, C., Nemery, P.: AHPSort: an AHP-based method for sorting problems. Int. J. Prod. Res. 50(17), 4767–4784 (2012)
27. Vaidyaa, O.S., Kumar, S.: Analytic hierarchy process: an overview of applications. Eur. J. Oper. Res. 169(1), 1–29 (2006)
28. Forman, E.H., Selly, M.A.: Decision by Objectives. http://professorforman.com/Decision ByObjectives/DBO.pdf
29. Mustajoki, J., Marttunen, M.: Comparison of multi-criteria decision analytical software: searching for ideas for developing a new eia-specific multi-criteria software. IMPERIA Project Report'. http://imperia.jyu.fi/tuotokset/Annex7.5.13ComparisonofMultiCriteriaDecisionAnaly ticalSoftware.pdf
30. Mesarovic, M.D., Macko, D.: Foundations for a Scientific Theory of Hierarchical Systems, pp. 29–50. American Elsevier, New York (1969). Hierarchical Structures
31. Saaty, T.L.: A scaling method for priorities in hierarchical structures. J. Math. Psychol. 15, 234–281 (1977)
32. Saaty, T.L., Vargas, L.: Comparison of eigenvalue, logarithmic least squares and least squares methods in estimating ratios. Math. Model. 5, 309–324 (1984)

33. Saaty, T.L.: The Fundamentals of Decision Making and Priority Theory with the Analytic Hierarchy Process. RWS Publications, Pittsburgh (2011)
34. Saaty, T.L., Vargas, G.: The seven pillars of the analytic hierarchy process. In: Saaty, T.L., Vargas, G. (eds.) Models, Methods, Concepts & Applications of the Analytic Hierarchy Process. International Series in Operations Research & Management Science, vol. 175, pp. 23–40. Springer, New York (2012)

Identifying the Main Problems in IT Auditing: A Comparison Between Unsupervised and Supervised Learning

Patrícia Maia[1]([⊠]), Leonardo Sales[1], and Rommel N. Carvalho[1,2]

[1] Department of Research and Strategic Information,
Brazilian Office of the Comptroller General, SAS, Quadra 01, Bloco A,
Edifício Darcy Ribeiro, Brasília, Distrito Federal, Brazil
{patricia.maia,leonardo.sales,rommel.carvalho}@cgu.gov.br
[2] Department of Computer Science, University of Brasília,
Campus Universitário Darcy Ribeiro, Brasília, Distrito Federal, Brazil
http://www.cgu.gov.br,
http://www.cic.unb.br

Abstract. One of the main challenges faced by the Brazilian Office of the Comptroller General (CGU) is applying consistent knowledge discovery tools and methodologies to learn from several years of auditing experience from hundreds of thousands of auditing reports with millions of pages it produced during these years. More specifically, we tackle the problem of identifying the most common topics in a context of Information Technology audits performed in Brazil since 2011. In order to tackle this problem, we compare two different approaches, supervised and unsupervised learning. On the one hand, the supervised learning approach generated a model that achieved around 73 % accuracy for seven categories using random forest. On the other hand, the unsupervised learning approach using Latent Dirichlet Allocation (LDA) generated a model with five topics, which was considered the best model based on the validation performed by the subject matter experts (SME) from CGU. Nevertheless, it is important to note that both approaches, although implemented independently, generated very similar topics. This also reinforces the success in identifying the main problems found during all these years of IT auditing at CGU using consistent and well-known knowledge discovery methods.

Keywords: LDA · Text mining · Classification · Auditing · IT · Topic modeling

1 Introduction

The Brazilian Office of the Comptroller General (CGU) is an agency responsible for, among other things, auditing all contracts and spending related to the federal budget from the Executive branch of the Brazilian Government.

© Springer International Publishing Switzerland 2016
A. Kő and E. Francesconi (Eds.): EGOVIS 2016, LNCS 9831, pp. 236–247, 2016.
DOI: 10.1007/978-3-319-44159-7_17

One of the main challenges faced by the CGU is applying consistent knowledge discovery tools and methodologies to learn from several years of auditing experience from hundreds of thousands of auditing reports with millions of pages it produced during these years.

The Audit and Inspection area is responsible for carrying out audits and inspection activities to check how public resources are being used. This task is carried out by CGU through the Federal Internal Control Secretariat, which is the unit in charge of evaluating the implementation of Federal Government budgets, inspecting the implementation of governmental programs, and auditing the management of federal public and private agencies and organizations, among other functions [13].

The result of conducted audits by CGU are stored in a report with all information about the scope, minister, program, findings, problems discovered, among others. This kind of report can be consulted in the Novo Ativa System. This system has all information about the audits conducted by CGU. However, all texts and information are stored without a well-defined categorization.

It is important to be able to retrieve more information from this data. For instance, what are the most common problems in the audits, or if the problems are different among regions of the country. Beyond that, the SFC wants to define a categorization for all kinds of problems found in reports and put this information in each new report that will be included in the system.

We try to solve the problem using two different approaches in parallel. One of them consisted in using a topic modeling technique to discover the main topics using LDA. The other approach used was classification. A small part of the data was manually classified and used to train a model in order to apply it to the remaining data. This paper will discuss both of them and compare the results.

The rest of this paper is organized as follows: Sect. 2 presents the related work. Section 3 describes our approach, divided in supervised and unsupervised learning. Finally, Sect. 4 presents the conclusion.

2 Related Work

Debasis [9] works with StackOverflow "linked questions" retrieval. Manual annotations, e.g., tags and links, of user generated content in community question answering forums and social media play an important role in making the content searchable. This work tries to reduce the manual effort by automatizing the search process to suggest a list of candidate documents to be linked to the new document, using topic models. The experiment shows that topic distributions results in a significant improvement in retrieval of the candidate set of related documents.

David [2] considered the problem of a user navigating an unfamiliar corpus of text documents where document metadata is limited or unavailable, the domain is specialized, and the user base is small. Their work proposed to augment standard keyword search with user feedback on latent topics. These topics are automatically learned from the corpus in an unsupervised manner and the users feedback is used to reformulate the original query. The model gives users the ability to provide feedback at the latent topic level.

Shinjee [16] proposed a unified topic model employs two LDA models, one for similar TV user grouping and the other for TV program recommendation. The unified model identifies the semantic relation between TV user groups and TV program description word groups more meaningful that the TV program recommendations usually made. Beyond that, the new model allows users with similar tastes can be grouped by topics and recommended as social communities. The unified model can make recommendations with results 6.5 % betters than just use topic models for TV users.

Sales [18] presents a supervised learning model to prevent default risk in public contracts in the Brazilian Government using Logistic Regression and Decision Trees Algorithms. Besides various databases related to public contracts in Brazil, like registry information of hired companies and operational capacity indicators, the model also used CGU audit findings to predict the "bad companies". This supervised model achieved an average accuracy of 64 %.

3   Experiment

The data available in the Novo Ativa System consists of approximately three hundred thousand findings. Finding is a significant fact reported by the designated civil servant during the auditing proceeding. Each of these findings has an key, year, resumed text, detailed text, kind of resource, government program, and location. The data was separated by kind of resource and we used IT resources for this research. We analyzed 2,500 findings related to different IT audits. The detail text range for these findings varied from 1 to 20 pages. The resumed text for each finding is around 2 or 3 lines.

Although we focused in IT audits, in future works we will apply the same methodology in other contexts, such as: education; health; among others.

The data was load in RStudio for pre-processing. In this stage we applied techniques for removing stopwords and low frequency words, changing upper to lower case letters, removing punctuation, accentuation, numbers, and white spaces. These techniques are common during the text mining process and are discussed in more detail in [3,8,10].

For implementing the techniques of text mining, we used the text mining framework provided by the TM package in R studio[1]. This package makes it possible to process, organize, transform, and analyze textual data.

The term-document matrix (TDM) was constructed using the Term Frequency - Inverse Document Frequency (TF-IDF) parameter. TDM is a matrix where the rows represent the words (terms) and the columns represent the documents. For more details in TDM and TF-IDF, see [4,14]. Several tests were implemented in this data using unigrams, bigrams, and trigrams in TDM. The bigrams and trigrams presented the best results [19].

---

[1] http://cran.r-project.org/web/packages/tm/index.html.

After some tests, with the help of the SME, we noticed that some words that remained in the model were not helpful in identifying the latent topic. Therefore, these words were included in the stopwords list.

3.1 Unsupervised Learning

After all the pre-processing, we work with an unsupervised learning, using LDA [4,20]. LDA is a topic modeling technique that consists in defining the most relevant terms in a topic, based in the distance and the proximity of the terms, given a number of topics. This technique calculates the probabilities of one document belonging to any of the topics. The topic with the highest probability will be the one in which the document will be designated.

First we defined 20 topics but some of them are very close, including overlaying sometimes. Then we tested several number of topics (20, 15, 12, 10, 7, 6, 5, and 4) and the best results were 5 topics. The results were demonstrated using the LDAvis[2], an R package for LDA visualization. In this kind of visualization, it is possible to see the most frequent topics, the proportion of topics in the set, and the proportion of the terms existing in a topic compared to the others. As shown in Fig. 1, each circle defines a topic and the size of this topic defines the proportion of this topic among all existing findings. The blue bars designs the 30 most frequent terms in all topics. The red bars show the most frequent terms in a specific topic. This plot was generated using 20 topics. As it is possible

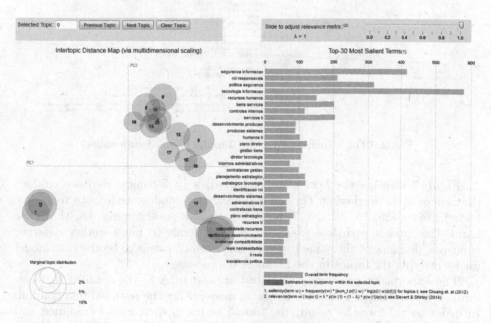

Fig. 1. LDA visualization with 20 topics (Color figure online)

---

[2] https://github.com/cpsievert/LDAvis.

see, this number is too big for this context because the circles are very close
or overlaying. This fact demonstrated that some topics have the same terms or
very close terms to define them. For this reason, we tried to modify the number
of topics and find the best model to define the findings being analyzed.

Figure 2 shows the same kind of visualization as in Fig. 1, but with 10
topics. The number of overlaying topics decreased and the distance between them
increased. These facts show that the model improved. However, even though this
model is better than the previous one, some topics are still overlaying such as
1 and 3, 6 and 8, 9 and 10, and 2 and 5. In an good model, there should have
no overlaying and topics should not be too close to each other. This means that
the topics are more likely to represent different concepts/domains.

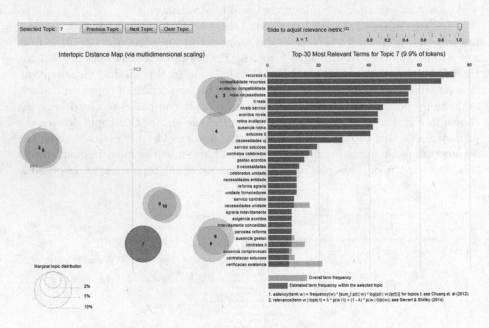

Fig. 2. LDA visualization with 10 topics (Color figure online)

Figure 3 displays the best result achieved, with 5 topics. Here we can see
that there is no overlaying. On the one hand, the models with more topics we
tested before (20, 15, 12, 10, 7, and 6) have some overlapping. On the other
hand, the models with less topics, such as 4, tends to put together different
concepts/domains in the same topic. In conclusion 5 seems to be the best model
for identifying the topics in the IT audit findings.

The experiment previously described applied LDA to the detailed text column. We also compared it with the same model using the resumed text column.
In order to validate the result, the top 15 terms in each model (resumed and
detailed text) were compared. Despite presenting similar terms, the detailed text
presented more consistent/similar words per topic than using the resumed text,
according to the SMEs.

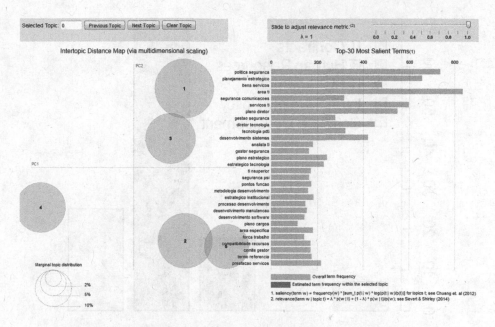

Fig. 3. LDA visualization with 5 topics

The topics found in the best model can be resumed as:

- Topic 1: Goods and services, contracts.
- Topic 2: Human resources, career
- Topic 3: Strategic planning, PDTI
- Topic 4: IT security, public security
- Topic 5: Software developing, function point

After selecting the best model, we can see one specific document and the probability of the topics inside it. LDA separates the clusters checking the frequency of words or terms in a document and comparing this frequency with the words or terms that is defined in each topic. In general, the documents have words that appear in different topics. Therefore, according to the frequency of these terms, it calculates the proportion that one document would have of belonging to each of the topics defined by the model. The LDA will choose the topic which presents the highest probability.

Figure 4 displays an example of probability distribution of topics inside a document. This document belongs to topic 3 because the terms of this topic are more frequent. Note, however, that the probabilities do not have to sum to 1.

Figure 5 illustrates an example based on part of the detailed text column after pre-processing. The terms present in each topic were highlighted with the colors of the topics they belong to. Looking at the colored text it is easy to see that this text belongs to topic 3 because the most predominant color is green (the color assigned to topic 3).

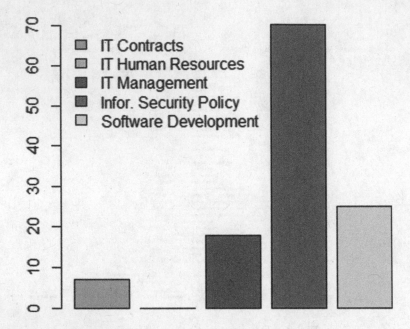

Fig. 4. Distribution of topics in a document

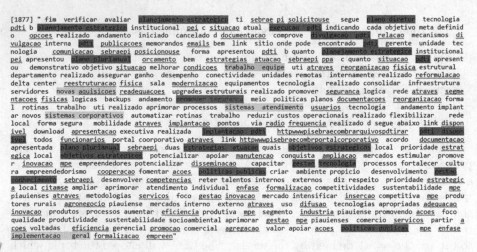

Fig. 5. Document with terms highlighted by topic (Color figure online)

3.2   Supervised Learning

In order to complement and validate the results of the topic modeling experiment described in Sect. 3.1, we built a supervised learning model, using a database previously classified by experts. This dataset was created from a sample of 335 records from the main database. This number represents 13.4 % of the registers and was calculated in order to allow a 95 % confidence level and a 5 % margin sampling error.

The field used to support the classification was the "detailed text". We emphasize that the categories were created without prior knowledge (by the experts) of the topics found in the previous approach.

The experts found eight categories of findings in the sample. Table 1 shows the distribution of these findings by category found.

The category "IT Management" involves noncompliance with the Brazilian standards that determine a minimum configuration of IT departments in government units. "IT Contracts" refers to problems found in IT procurement and hiring processes. "IT Human Resources" refers to failures in personnel policy established for the IT areas. "Information Security Policy" relates to the absence of clear rules of information security. "Software Development and Maintenance" involves problems like delays in the implementation of systems or the lack of use of the implemented system. "Internal Control" covers the problems in the process for assuring achievement of the IT department objectives. "Outsourcing" refers to specific contracts involving hiring IT personnel. "Not specified" is a category created to the registers where there is not enough terms to explain its meaning.

As shown in Table 1, there are too few registers in categories "Internal Control" and "Outsourcing". An alternative to get better results in machine learning processes is to join two or more categories (an example can be found in ALEJO [1]). At first, in this specific case we preferred to keep them in separate categories, as it is not so clear their relationship with other categories.

Table 1. Quantity of findings per category

Finding category	Quantity
IT Management	104
IT Contracts	72
IT Human Resources	42
Information Security Policy	41
Software Development and Maintenance	31
Internal Control	10
Outsourcing	9
Not specified	26
Total	335

After creating the labeled database we provided a transformation in the data by converting the field "detailed text" into a term frequency inverse document frequency (TF-IDF) vector. This vector represents a numerical statistic that increases proportionally to the number of times a word appears in a specific document, but is offset by the frequency of the word in the other documents [17].

We built the Machine Learning model using a Random Forest algorithm. This algorithm implements a Random Decision Forest, that is an ensemble learning technique for classification [7,11], that works by constructing a set of decision trees that depend on the values of a random vector sampled independently and with the same distribution of all trees in the forest [5].

In order to start the learning process we split the database into two subsets. The first (70 % of the registers) one was allocated to estimate and calibrate the model, using a 10-fold cross-validation process. This technique is commonly used to calibrate predictive models and involves partitioning the training data into ten subsets, performing the analysis on one subset and validating the analysis on the other subset. This process is repeated in multiple rounds of cross-validation using different partitions, in order to reduce variability. The second subset (30 % of the registers) was used as a test dataset.

The cross-validation process shows the set of trees in the Random Forest model that best fit the training data. After this step we got an accuracy [15] of 74.33 %, which means that on average 74.33 % of the records were classified correctly in the iterations. Another important indicator to measure the model efficiency is the Kappa index [6], which compares the overall accuracy with that obtained in each class, and is helpful to differentiate the prediction results from those that would be obtained randomly. We obtained a 0.67 score, considered "substantial" in accordance with the existing guidelines for the interpretation, as shows in Table 2 [12].

Table 2. Values of Kappa x levels of agreement

Value of Kappa	Level of agreement
Less than 0.01	Less than chance agreement
0.01–0.20	Slight agreement
0.21–0.40	Fair agreement
0.41–0.60	Moderate agreement
0.61–0.80	Substantial agreement
0.81–1.00	Almost perfect agreement

Applying the calibrated model in the test subset we got an accuracy of 73.27 % and a Kappa index of 0.66. It is common in such classification models to loose some prediction capability when comparing training and testing. Nevertheless the results were still very impressive and not statistically different than the results obtained during cross-validation.

A more accurate analysis of the errors shows us that most incorrect classifications occurred in "Internal Control" and "Outsourcing" categories. This result was expected, since these are the classes with few occurrences.

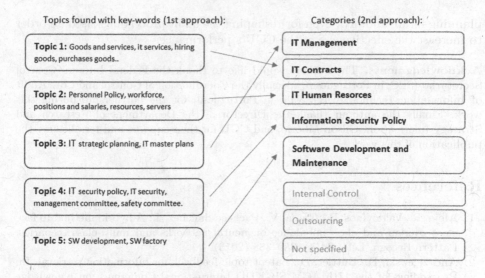

Fig. 6. Topic x categories

4   Conclusions

In this paper we investigated the IT audits of the Brazilian Office of Comptroller General. We applied a supervised (text classification) and unsupervised (LDA) approach. Both of them achieved very similar results.

Comparing both approaches, we can see a reasonable congruence between modeling topics (unsupervised) and the model learned from the manual classification by the specialist. In fact, the topics discovered in the first approach have high correlation with the manually identified classes used in the learning model. Figure 6 shows the correlation between the topics found (represented here by the most frequent words) and the classes defined in the supervised learning model.

As we can see, the five topics found in the best model using LDA were all represented in the classification model. The only classes that we could not related to the learned topics were the least frequent ("Outsourcing" and "Internal Controls"), probably because they represent only 5 % of the ratings. The reason for this is that the topic modeling presented better results using 5 topics, which meant that only the most representative categories of supervised model met correspondence.

This is the first study that analyzes CGU's audit reports using a well-known knowledge discovery methods. We believe that this study may be expanded to cover other types of audits (since here we covered only audits of IT resources). Another possible further development is to understand (*e.g.*, through a supervised learning model) the main problems that contribute to a finding being considered or classified as severe.

The great benefit of this work is the ability to learn from experience by using data mining techniques. A better understanding of the problems can be used for planning future audits or even for reshaping the audit proceedings used, in order to increase the effectiveness of the CGU's performance.

Acknowledgments. The authors would like to thank the Federal Internal Control Secretariat (SFC, in Portuguese), specially the Coordination of Control and Core Audit of Information Technology (GSNTI, in Portuguese) for the partnership during this work. Finally the authour thank the Director of the Department of Research and Strategy Information, Gilson Libório, and CGU for their support and for allowing the publication of this work.

References

1. Alejo, R., Valdovinos, R., Garca, V., Pacheco-Sanchez, J.: A hybrid method to face class overlap and class imbalance on neural networks and multi-class scenarios. Pattern Recogn. Lett. **34**(4), 380–388 (2013)
2. Andrzejewski, D., Buttler, D.: Latent topic feedback for information retrieval. In: Proceedings of the 17th ACM SIGKDD International Conference on Knowledge Discovery and Data Mining, pp. 600–608. ACM (2011)
3. Berry, M.W., Castellanos, M.: Survey of Text Mining II. Springer, New York (2008)
4. Blei, D.M., Ng, A.Y., Jordan, M.I.: Latent dirichlet allocation. J. Mach. Learn. Res. **3**, 993–1022 (2003)
5. Breiman, L.: Random forests. Mach. Learn. **45**(1), 5–32 (2001)
6. Carletta, J.: Assessing agreement on classification tasks: the kappa statistic. Comput. Linguist. **22**(2), 249–254 (1996)
7. Cheng, H., Yan, X., Han, J., Yu, P.S.: Direct discriminative pattern mining for effective classification. In: IEEE 24th International Conference on Data Engineering, ICDE 2008, pp. 169–178. IEEE (2008)
8. Sebastiani, F.: Machine learning in automated text categorization. ACM Comput. Surv. **34**, 1–47 (2002)
9. Ganguly, D., Jones, G.J.: Partially labeled supervised topic models for retrieving similar questions in CQA forums, pp. 161–170. ACM Press (2015)
10. Jurasfsky, D., Martin, J.H.: Speech and Language Processing. Prentice Hall, Upper Saddle River (1998). Stuart Russell and Peter Norvig
11. Korde, V.: Text classification and classifiers: a survey. Int. J. Artif. Intell. Appl. **3**(2), 85–99 (2012)
12. Landis, J.R., Koch, G.G.: The measurement of observer agreement for categorical data. Biometrics **33**(1), 159 (1977)
13. Maia, P., Carvalho, R.N., Ladeira, M., Rocha, H., Mendes, G.: Application of text mining techniques for classification of documents: a study of automation ofcomplaints screening in a Brazilian Federal Agency
14. Martins, C.A., Monard, M.C., Matsubara, E.T.: Reducing the dimensionality of bag-of-words text representation used by learning algorithms. In: Proceedings of the Third IASTED International Conference on Artificial Intelligence and Applications (AIA 2003), Benalmdena, Espanha, vol. 38 (2003)
15. Gordon, M., Kochen, M.: Recall-precision trade-off: a derivation (1988)
16. Pyo, S., Kim, E., kim, M.: LDA-based unified topic modeling for similar TV user-grouping and TV program recommendation. IEEE Trans. Cybern. **45**(8), 1476–1490 (2015)

17. Ramos, J.: Using TF-IDF to determine word relevance in document queries. In: Proceedings of the First Instructional Conference on Machine Learning (2003)
18. Sales, L.: Risk prevention of public procurement in the Brazilian government using credit scoring. OBEGEF working papers, OBEGEF - Observatrio de Economia e Gesto de Fraude (2013)
19. Tan, C.-M., Wang, Y.-F., Lee, C.-D.: The use of bigrams to enhance text categorization. Inf. Process. Manage. **38**(4), 529–546 (2002)
20. Wei, X., Croft, W.B.: LDA-based document models for ad-hoc retrieval. In: Proceedings of the 29th Annual International ACM SIGIR Conference on Research and Development in Information Retrieval, pp. 178–185. ACM (2006)

E-Government Cases - Data and Knowledge Management

Effective Biosecurity Knowledge Management: A Provenance Perspective

Qing Liu[✉], Yanfeng Shu, and Chris Peters

Software and Computational Systems, Data61, CSIRO, Hobart, Australia
{Q.Liu,Yanfeng.Shu,Chris.Peters}@data61.csiro.au

Abstract. Biosecurity covers a full range of issues, from identifying and combating threats internationally, to border and post-border protection, right down to identifying and controlling pests at the farm, food-chain and export levels. The effectiveness of a biosecurity system relies on its ability to convene, share and discuss sensitive, current and real-time information about possible threats as early as possible. However, in Australia, at the state border level, most of interstate sale related data is collected in paper-based systems and distributed in various forms. This greatly hinders the process of effective information access and decision making. Provenance describes history of result including people, process and source data. By capturing, integrating and analysing digitised provenance information with domain knowledge, biosecurity information systems could provide better capabilities to access and analyse information for proper decision making. In this work, we introduce our current development on building a near-real-time knowledge management system by working with one of the six state biosecurity agencies in Australia, including the design and implementation of a knowledge model and a workflow to capture provenance information, and some initial provenance analysis.

Keywords: Biosecurity · Provenance · Knowledge management

1 Introduction

Biosecurity is the protection of the economy, the environment, and human health from the negative impacts associated with entry, establishment or spread of exotic pests and diseases. It covers a full range of issues, from identifying and combating threats internationally, to border and post-border protection, right down to identifying and controlling pests at the farm, food-chain and export levels. The effectiveness of a biosecurity system relies on its ability to convene, share and discuss sensitive, current and real-time information about possible threats as early as possible. In addition, new and emerging issues including globalisation with increased movement of goods and people, greater trading opportunities and requirements, increased disease and pest incidents occurring overseas or interstate, potential threats of bioterrorism and many other factors need to be handled.

© Springer International Publishing Switzerland 2016
A. Kő and E. Francesconi (Eds.): EGOVIS 2016, LNCS 9831, pp. 251–260, 2016.
DOI: 10.1007/978-3-319-44159-7_18

This calls for a need to have near-real-time biosecurity information systems that could streamline the data collection and analysis process to ensure that decisions are made in a cost-effective manner. Although there are some systems available such as the National Livestock Identification System[1], Pests and Diseases Image Library[2], web-based systems for reporting suspected pests, diseases and weeds, these systems were designed primarily to target certain parts of the information process.

Given a biosecurity information system, one basic requirement is to be able to retrieve provenance information of a data product. Provenance is a record that describes people, data, and process involved in producing, influencing, or delivering a result. Captured provenance over time provides a rich source of information and generates a substantial body of knowledge that may be used in many ways: informational, data quality, audit trial, attribution etc. Typical provenance questions include who, when, where, what, why and how. With regard to the biosecurity domain, possible provenance questions include: what is the water resource of the farm? is the feed delivered in dedicated trucks? if not, where has the truck been prior to the delivery? does a particular plant to be imported meet a state quarantine requirement? is the chemical applied from authorised parties? etc.

By capturing, integrating and analysing digitised provenance information with biosecurity domain knowledge, a biosecurity information system could provide better capabilities to effectively identify risks, prioritise resources, evaluate and change policy, and monitor daily operations at all biosecurity levels. To build such an information system, it requires collection and integration of data from many sources (e.g. importer, exporter and grower information, chemical and treatment information, and certificates and state government quarantine policies) to ensure effective knowledge management through exploitation of integrated information.

We take a first step to build a biosecurity knowledge management system (BKMS) with provenance in the centre of design. Working with Biosecurity Tasmania, a state government agency who is responsible for the state border protection, we developed a knowledge model to capture our client's provenance requirements and a workflow system for provenance collection. BKMS collects and integrates various information required for importing products into Tasmania such as treatments and quarantine requirements to assist interstate sale procedure and decision making. In this work, We present our initial design and implementation.

The rest of the paper is organized as follows: Sect. 2 introduces the use case. The design of our knowledge model, the workflow and initial query analysis are described in Sect. 3. In Sect. 4, implementation details are presented. This is followed by discussion and conclusion.

---

[1] http://www.mla.com.au/Meat-safety-and-traceability/National-Livestock-Identification-System.

[2] http://www.padil.gov.au/.

2 Biosecurity Use Case Study

In this section, we first introduce the background, and then present our use case — the interstate sale procedure at the Tasmanian state border level.

2.1 Background

Australia is a federation consisting of six states, three federal territories and seven external territories. Restrictions apply to each state and territory for the movement of items to prevent or limit the spread of pests, diseases and weeds and safeguard Australian plant industries, related trade markets and the wider community from the impacts of pests and diseases. These restrictions operate under state and territory legislations. At the state border level, all fruits, vegetables, plant and plant products entering must be accompanied by certain documents such as Notice of Intention to import and approved Plant Health Documentation from the state of origin certifying that they meet the entry condition for the state of destiny.

Tasmania, as one of the six states, has a strong biosecurity culture shaped by its island nature and a long-standing export focus for its primary industries. One of the key goals of the Tasmanian Biosecurity policy is to minimise the threat to Tasmania's primary industries, natural environment and public health from disease and pest risks associated with plants and plant products brought into the State. In practice, this means that there are a large number of rules relating to the conditions of entry for a wide range of plants and plant products that are imported into Tasmania - these rules are known as 'Import Requirements', published in the *Plant Biosecurity Manual Tasmania* (PBMTas)[3]. The PBMTas is to help importers, exporters and the broader public understand the current requirements for the import and export of plants, plant products, and other prescribed matter authorised by the Plant Quarantine Act 1997 (Tasmania).

2.2 A Use Case of Biosecurity Interstate Sale Procedure

An interstate sale involves several sources and steps. Produces are packed by growers at farms. Consignors collect packed produces from farms, treat them according to the quarantine requirements of Tasmania and deliver all produces, called a consignment, to a carrier to the Melbourne port for transporting to Tasmania. Some produces may be re-packed and/or re-treated in Melbourne. A shipment arriving at the Tasmania port contains a certain number of consignments. Each consignment contains a number of produces. A fraction of these produces are inspected by Biosecurity Tasmania quarantine officers. If there is no quarantine concern, the consignment is released to the consignee to whom the consignment is sent. A consignment is said to be "contaminated" if it contains biosecurity risk materials. In this case, quarantine officers make the best possible decision that is within legislative parameters and can be justified.

---

[3] http://dpipwe.tas.gov.au/biosecurity/plant-biosecurity/plant-biosecurity-manual.

It is important for a consignor to understand the up-to-date quarantine requirements to import produces into Tasmania. There are two ways to find the information about the import requirements a produce must meet. The consignor can either refer to the PBMTas or search the online Tasmanian Biosecurity Import Requirements Database (TBIRD)[4] for the relevant import requirement. If fruits, vegetables, plants or plant produces are to be entered into Tasmania, the consignor needs to lodge a *Notice of Intention* (NOI) to import plants or plant products no later than 24 h prior to arrival in Tasmania by fax or email. Each NOI must be accompanied by approved Plant Health Documentation from the state of origin certifying that the produces meet the entry conditions for Tasmania. Tasmanian quarantine officers pre-examine the documents received and notify the consignor if documents are incomplete or inappropriate through email, fax and/or phone call.

For the above interstate sale procedure, there are several challenges for both consignors/consigneers and quarantine officers.

- In most cases, changes to import requirements are minor and will come into effect when the next edition of PBMTas is published. However, there may be occasions where changes need to come into effect immediately. In such cases, changes will be posted on the web, and consignors/consignees who refer to the PBMTas have to check the web to be aware of any such emergent declarations. It can be challenging for them to stay current with the latest regulations. If shipments are detained due to missing/fault certification, costly and time-consuming delays will occur, causing unnecessary stress and financial burdens for consignors/consignees.
- The interface between trade, travel and biosecurity is a challenging place for people who work there. Competing interests collide, risks change rapidly, information can be lacking or inconclusive, resources can be scarce, decisions must be made soon, and then made again. This stew of pressures means judging how best to control inbound movement for biosecurity purposes is demanding, even for a relatively small place like Tasmania [1]. Existing biosecurity system is paper-based and data is distributed in various forms. This greatly hinders the process of effective information access and decision making.

To address the above challenges, we take the first step in building a biosecurity knowledge management system in which provenance information is collected through quarantine interstate sale procedure. Furthermore, the system is able to integrate the latest published import requirements into the interstate sale procedure and suggests up-to-date import requirements and treatments required. Therefore, decisions for consignors/consignees and quarantine officers on what is the up-to-date import requirements can be made based on near real-time information. In the next section, we describe the design of the knowledge management system.

---

[4] http://imports.dpipwe.tas.gov.au/ImportRx.nsf.

3   Knowledge Management System Design

Figure 1 shows the main parts of a knowledge management system: knowledge model, provenance collection and provenance analysis. Knowledge model describes the provenance information as well as biosecurity domain knowledge (e.g. policies, chemicals and treatments). Provenance collection captures the interstate sale business procedure by the workflow system designed. Based on the collected information, various analysis can be done such as retrieval and comparison of provenance traces. In the following, we describe these parts in detail with respect to the interstate sale use case.

Fig. 1. The knowledge management system

3.1   Knowledge Model

The design is based upon a relational database model, taking advantage of the capability in relational database systems for querying based upon data values and enabling cross-dimension data retrieval and analysis. The information being modelled centres around the produces to be imported, including the descriptive information about produces such as their names, types and quantities, as well as the lineage information describing where they were produced, how they were treated, and when they were imported. Figure 2 shows portion of the model.

Within the model, each (imported) produce is associated with a Notice-Of-Intention (NOI) and a grower. A NOI is specified through importer information, as well as transportation information such as arrival date, port and means of transportation. Each NOI can be associated with multiple produces, and the same is true for each grower. In addition, each produce may need to satisfy an import requirement and have a Plant Health Assurance Certificate (PHAC) provided. Within the model, the certificate information of a PHAC is described through certificate details such as IP number and facility number, and information about consignor, consignee and reconsignee; each PHAC has a unique certificate number that can be linked to one or more treatments or produces. The treatments that can be represented in the model range from cold treatments to chemical treatments. For chemical treatments, the chemical used, its concentration, and treatment duration and temperature are specified.

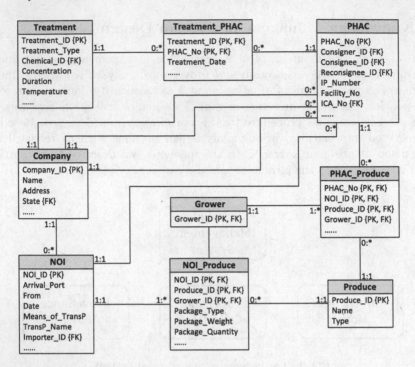

Fig. 2. Portion of the knowledge model. The primary key field for each table is designated with a PK label. Foreign keys are designated with a FK label. The lines between tables show relationships with cardinality indicated by numbers.

The knowledge model given in Fig. 2 only covers the information needed for describing provenance of an imported produce. In addition, it models the domain knowledge related to the interstate sale including state import requirements, their changes over time, and their relationships to interstate certification assurance (ICA) schemes.

3.2 Provenance Collection

The provenance information for the interstate sale use case is collected through a workflow. There are a lot of processes involved for the provenance collection but here, we only show a top-level view of the workflow in Fig. 3. It includes the following major steps:

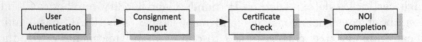

Fig. 3. A top-level view of the provenance collection workflow.

- User authentication: users log into the workflow system and indicate whether to work on an existing but possibly unfinished import application; for new users, registrations are needed.
- Consignment input: an import application involves deciding a consignment which refers to a combination of a consignor, a consignee, a possible re-consignee, and a set of produces to be imported and their growers. A new consignment input requires information of all these items. It is also possible to retrieve existing consignments for modification.
- Certificate check: for each produce in a consignment, its import requirements are suggested by the system according to the current quarantine requirements. Users follow the suggested requirements and provide the certificates and treatment details accordingly. If there is no correct certificate associated, the system recommends treatments and certificates required to users for action.
- NOI completion: once certificate or treatment details are provided, NOI transportation and importer details can be filled in, and the import application is ready for processing by quarantine officers.

3.3 Provenance Analysis

Through the above knowledge model and provenance collection process, many provenance questions could be answered. At the current stage, provenance analysis is mainly focussed on provenance information retrieval and summarisation. Such analyses may require linking multiple entities in the model. For example, to retrieve the produces that were imported in 2013 and had the treatment with the methyl bromide fumigation, it is necessary to link all the tables shown in Fig. 2 except Grower and Company.

4   Implementation

We developed BKMS by using MySQL[5] for data management of imported produces, and Camunda[6] for provenance data collection and analysis. Camunda is an open source Java based platform for workflow and business process automation. Based on Camunda, we constructed two workflows: one for provenance collection and one for provenance analysis. Both workflows are supported by the same database. In the following, we present some BKMS interfaces as examples to explain the provenance collection and analysis components.

Figure 4 shows one interface of the consignment input process. Through the interface, users can input produce details including their names, types, packages, quantities and growers. As the system stores the information of the growers entered earlier, users can choose to use an existing grower instead of creating a new one. The design minimizes input errors caused by users and guarantees the data consistency in the database.

---

[5] https://www.mysql.com/.
[6] https://camunda.com/.

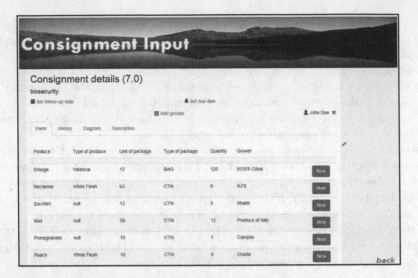

Fig. 4. Consignment details.

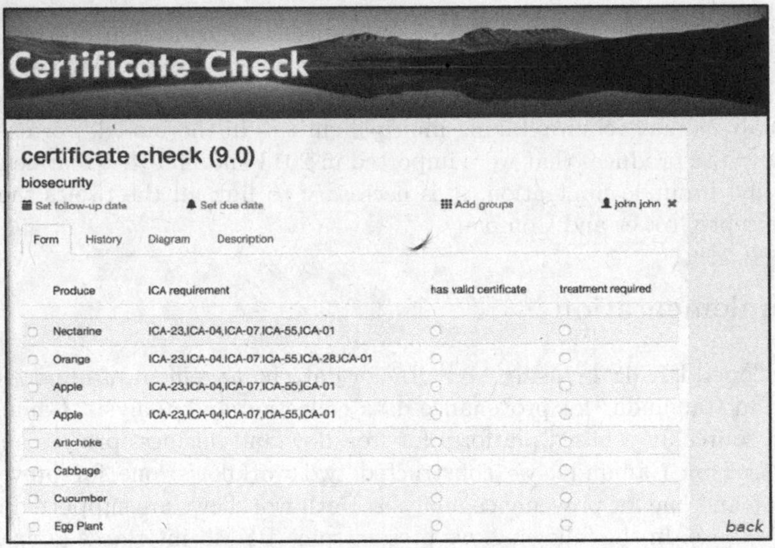

Fig. 5. Produce certificate requirements.

Figures 5 and 6 show two interfaces of the certificate check process, with the former giving a summary of certificate requirements of each produce, and the latter asking for treatment details. In Fig. 5, the certificates potentially required for a produce are listed in the second column. For example, for "Nectarine", the certificate that needs to be provided can be ICA-23 (Area or Property Freedom), ICA-04 (Fumigating with Methyl Bromide), ICA-07 (Cold Treatment),

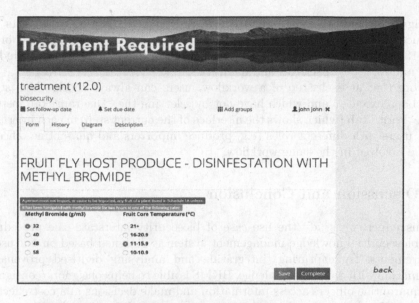

Fig. 6. Treatment details.

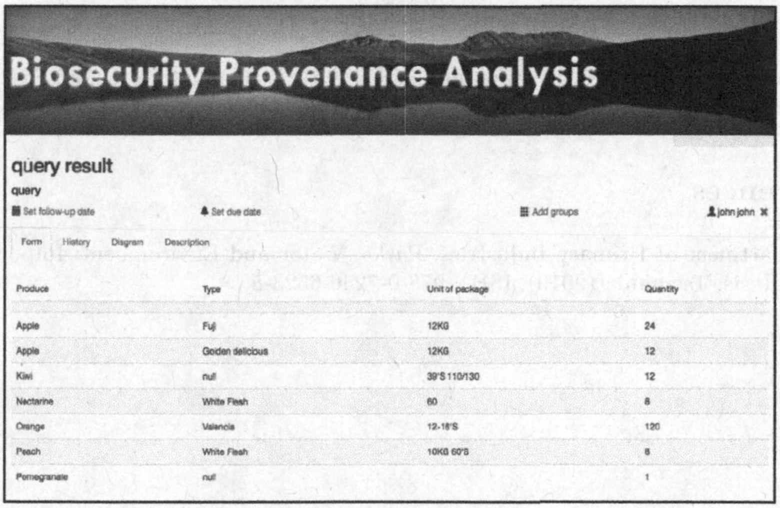

Fig. 7. Query result. .

ICA-55 (Irradiation Treatment), or ICA-01 (Dipping with Dimethoate or Fenthion). If one of these certificates is available, details of the certification and treatment need to be provided. Figure 6 shows the information needed for the methyl bromide treatment (ICA-04), which includes the concentration (the first column) and the temperature used (the second column).

Figure 7 shows a result interface of a provenance analysis, which lists the produces that satisfy the example query (i.e. the produces that were imported in 2013 and had the treatment with the methyl bromide fumigation), including their names, types, packages and quantities.

Note that at each step of a workflow, users can always check which steps have been executed and which have not by selecting the "Diagram" tab instead of the "Form" tab (which shows the interface of the current step) in each interface. Also, users with different roles (e.g. produce importers and quarantine officers) can be involved in the same workflow.

5   Discussion and Conclusion

In this paper, we study the use case of biosecurity interstate sale procedure. The biosecurity knowledge management system is designed based on our users' requirements. By capturing, integrating and analysing digitised provenance information with domain knowledge, BKMS is able to help consignors/consignees and quarantine officers access information and make decisions in a cost-effective manner. The system has been demonstrated and well received by Biosecurity Tasmania. Now we are working with them to enrich the knowledge model and address more advanced provenance questions.

Acknowledgments. We are grateful to Biosecurity Tasmania for providing us the use case and data and constructive discussion that helped us improve the system design.

References

1. Department of Primary Industries: Parks, Water and Environment: Import Risk Analysis, Tasmania (2010). ISBN 978-0-7246-6523-5

A Method of Inspecting and Applying Open Government Data in the Auditing Courts of Brazilian States

Walter Gonçalino da Silva Cruz[1], Cristiano Maciel[2(✉)],
Fernando B.M. de Castilho[2], and Natalina Namie Hirata Girata[1]

[1] Fundação de Apoio e Desenvolvimento da UFMT (Uniselva),
Tribunal de Contas do Estado de Mato Grosso (TCE-MT),
Av. Fernando Correia da Costa, Cuiabá, MT 2367, Brazil
walters@tce.mt.gov.br,
natalina@uniselva.tce.mt.gov.br
[2] Laboratório de Ambientes Virtuais Interativos (LAVI),
Instituto de Computação (IC), Universidade Federal de Mato Grosso (UFMT),
Av. Fernando Correia da Costa, Cuiabá, MT 2367, Brazil
cmaciel@ufmt.br, fernando@ic.ufmt.br

Abstract. This paper is aimed at conceiving and testing a method to inspect the level of adoption of policies regarding Open Government Data based on the analysis of the Audit Court's transparency portal of Brazilian states and the Federal District. The method establishes a score for public data of audit offices in the domains of People Management, Budget, Biddings and Contracts. We herein analyze the data from the State Audit Office of Brazil, and we discuss issues related to the method. We concluded that, despite the efforts of the audit offices, there is still a lot to do in order to reach a quality level of the public information according to the conceptual and legal devices audit offices are subject to.

Keywords: Open Government Data · State Audit Office · Transparency

1 Introduction

The possibility of providing tools that aid citizens to inspect and apply public resources, the need to monitor and assess services provided by our governments and, mainly, the transparency of accountability of public powers are reasons for investments in scientific research and development in the area of electronic government [10].

To provide support to the institutions and regulate issues relevant to information provision is the purpose of Brazilian Law n°. 12.527 of 16/05/2012, better known as the Law of Information Access (*LIA*) sanctioned on 18/11/2011 [1]. The LIA was an important step in the direction of public transparency and the consolidation of democracy, together with previous social control initiatives such as the Federal Government's Portal of Transparency (FGPT). According to the LIA and its ruling (Decree n°. 7.724 on 16/05/2012), "it is the duty of public organs and entities to promote, regardless of requests, the publication in places of easy access, in the ambit of

A. Kő and E. Francesconi (Eds.): EGOVIS 2016, LNCS 9831, pp. 261–275, 2016.
DOI: 10.1007/978-3-319-44159-7_19

its responsibilities, or information of a collective or general interest produced by them or which they are custodians of". This regulation establishes active transparency, that is, a minimum set of information must be made public in a proactive way by public organs or entities on official websites. Some Brazilian states also created their own legislation to reinforce the LIA. In Mato Grosso, Decree no. 1.973 of 25/10/2013 was created as an instrument of reinforcement of the LIA and which institutionalizes the Transparency Portal of the State Government.

However, for data published as a result of the requirements imposed by LIA to be considered Open Government Data they need to be reused or incorporated into other information systems created by third parties. Among other requirements, the data must be available in open format, able to be machine processed and be non-proprietary, as well as not being subject to any licensing restrictions or copyright [14]. This concept ensures the right of unrestricted access to the information, data and documents of public administrations and the LIA establishes, in article 8 para. 1, clauses I, II, III, IV and V, which sets of information must be compulsorily provided by the entities [1].

"Art. 8. "it is the duty of public organs and entities to promote, regardless of requests, the publication in places of easy access, in the ambit of its responsibilities, or information of a collective or general interest produced by them or which they are custodians of.
§ 1o When providing information as per the above, there must contain, at least:
I – records of the organization's responsibilities and structure, addresses and telephone numbers of its respective units and its public opening hours;
II – records of any sending or transfer of financial resources;
III – records of expenses;
IV – information relevant to bidding procedures, including the respective tenders and results as well as all the signed contracts;
V – general data for monitoring programs, actions, projects and work by organs and entities."

The benefits of this union between open data and public tools for using them are numerous. It is important that society as a whole knows how public administrations deal with their resources and how services are offered by providing graphical analysis, reports and charts with current data supplied by the public institutions and processed, aggregated and transformed into computer systems.

However, we need to assess the quality of the information provided as OGD in order to know the main obstacles to the mass and correct adoption of this public transparency policy. Such barriers can be found in the most diverse areas such as technology, socio-culture and even law, making it difficult to comply with the LIA and preventing public auditing for control or public action.

The State and Federal District Audit Courts, in Brazil, act as inspection organs of the local councils, chambers and other state entities. Almeida [2] brings a detailed approach to the tasks attributed to the Audit Courts in Brazil. Among them are inspector, sanctioner, consultative, normative and ombudsman [2]. The State Audit Courts have autonomy to pass judgement on subordinated municipal and state organs and apply fines to cases of mismanagement of public money.

But, what is the level of transparency of these organs given the Law of Information Access? To what extent are policies being adopted by these institutions considering principles of OGD? Faced with the above, the overall aim of this study is to conceive and test a method to inspect the level of adoption of policies regarding Open

Government Data – OGD based on the analysis of the Audit Court's transparency portal of Brazilian states and the Federal District.

The research conducted in this study has a quantitative approach by means of assessing the content of the transparency portals of State Audit Courts (*TCE*) Brazilian portals, and presents data in numbers and graphics as a ranking of the quality of the open data provided by these institutions. From the analysis of the quantitative data, information is collected in four categories: Personnel Management, Budgeting, Tenders and Contracts. This allows the qualification of the system improvements that are necessary. Overall, the study permits the verification of the method proposed in this research.

2 Theoretical Grounding

The theoretical grounding for this research comes mainly from the importance of transparency of the use of OGD and to explain it concepts, laws and principles as well as debating the role of IT in this process and the obstacles to information spread. Among these obstacles is the search for information quality, the legal aspects of open data reuse and the problems caused by the lack of licensing standardization for the use of public data. This framework is essential for discussion of the object of this study. We didn't intend to deeply analyze the eight fundamental principles of OGD. All we did was relating them to LIA.

Searching the internet, no studies were found that deal with the concepts of OGD and LIA in a related way and so we cannot have any other studies or methods to compare this one with directly. Recently, a survey was released by the Federal Public Ministry which set up the National Transparency Ranking [12]. The proposal was part of a national inspection campaign to fulfill the LIA as well as complementary laws 101/2000 and 131/2009 which also deal with the issue of the transparency of public data [12]. Faced with the above, it can be said that this research is original and understanding the method depends on the concepts presented in this section.

2.1 Transparency of Open Government Data

In recent decades, we have witnessed a variety of political, economic, social and cultural changes. And in the midst of these changes it is worth highlighting the evolution of Information and Communication Technology (ICT) resources in practically all spheres of knowledge. Castells [5] explains such evolution driven by the creation of a technological revolution in which the ICT artefacts provide social institutions with new capabilities allowing them to redefine and innovate their ways of acting using technological apparatus as the mainstay of executing public practices.

The Government is, without a doubt, one of the sectors that most utilizes the enormous potential of ICT, mainly on web platforms, to innovate and widen its actions. This movement is denominated as e-Gov. According to Rover and Galindo [13], electronic government has the aim of transforming the relationship between governments, citizens and companies above all in terms of its agility and transparency of process.

On this treadmill of technological revolution, the latent need appears to offer society greater transparency of government actions by means of OGD, the purpose of which is to overcome the information limitations imposed on users of public services in such a way as they can find, access and easily understand public data according to their needs.

According to Acar et al. [1], the concept of Open Government Data (OGD) includes the whole set of information produced, archived and distributed by government organizations, published on the internet in open and primary formats, of a non-proprietary, full, non-discriminatory, license-free nature and which is accessible to both citizens and computers. The eight fundamental principles of OGD[1], defined in 2007 by a working group of 30 people who met in California (USA), are: complete, primary, timely, accessible, machine processable, non-discriminatory access, non-proprietary format, license-free. Considering such principles is fundamental for an OGD strategy. This is why they are essential in the formulation of the method proposed in this research. Commenting on the purpose of making OGD available, Diniz [6] emphasizes that "the aim of making Open Government Data available is to overcome the existing limitations so that users of information on public services can easily find, access, understand and use public data according to their interests and convenience."

Beyond the challenge of making this data public for the whole population, there is a difficulty in making the data "readable" so that anyone can interpret them. As described in the second principle of open government data, the data must be provided in its primary form in the highest possible level of granularity possible. This is the challenge for IT professionals who need to use all the available technology to develop systems that will consume this range of information in its rawest form and present it in a clear and easy to understand way.

2.2   The Role of Information Technology

It is relatively easy to describe the importance of IT to democracy in the digital era. Just providing data in its raw state does not meet the principles of transparency since it is necessary for society to understand this information in a simple and precise way. To Madnick et al. [9] the ICT resources, especially the internet, favor the availability of ever greater volumes of data. Such data are generated, stored, processed and used for businesses aiming to deliver to organizations the most relevant information extracted from the available data both internally and externally. In this universe of information overload, one of the challenges that is ever greater for IT professionals is the creation of tools and mechanisms, with the intention of ensuring that an institution's data is of the highest quality, enables the organization to use it to improve its business processes, improve its decision-making and create strategic advantages [9].

Moreover, transforming raw data into easily viewed and understood information contributes to spreading the transparency of government actions and aids society in monitoring public assets and combating corruption and bad resource management.

---

[1] http://dados.gov.br/dados-abertos/.

2.3   The Obstacles to Information Dissemination

The massification of the LIA and consequently of OGD faces obstacles in the areas of technology, law and socio-culture. In each of these areas, the challenge is to find solutions that enable the loosening bureaucratic and operational blocks to allow the dissemination of public information.

In the technological context, there are a variety of problems that make the process of spreading government data a tough job. We highlight some of them: the low quality of data made available; the non-compliance with the laws and principles of open data; the frequency of information updates leaves a lot to desire; and the lack of information maintenance. Michener et al. [11] state in their research on the application of LIA that: The right of access to public information, granted constitutional status, does not only face significant disparities in relation to its practical realization, but it also encounters situations where public organs apply it in a discriminatory fashion.

In the legal ambit, there is a lack of standardization of licenses for the use of information made available by means of the LIA, since the law is not explicit about the rights and responsibilities for data use and reuse, leaving a gap for institutions to adopt non-standardized and questionable terms of use and which in some cases make it impractical for third parties to proliferate the data.

Civil society in general creates another difficulty for the LIA by its lack of action, by its passiveness in relation to the public sector and by its lack of knowledge of all aspects of the LIA and its potential benefit in terms of inspection and control of public administration. This socio-cultural obstacle deserves some investment and education in transparency is one of the challenges for modern society [10].

3   The Method

This sections aims to explain how the research method was developed and in which way it was applied, touching on the research stages and detailing the point distribution in the categories assessed. Following the eight principles of OGD is the basis of the point calculation in each of the categories. Therefore, the greater the compliancy of the information collected with the OGD principles, the higher the resulting score when the method is applied.

The research is focused in collecting, assessing and scoring the open data in four information categories: personnel management, budgeting, tenders and contracts. The choice of the categories was based on a survey made with the portals of some Audit Courts of the largest Brazilian states (in terms of population) during the process of creating the Transparency Portal of the Audit Court of Mato Grosso, of which one of the authors of this study was an analyst responsible for its development.

At the time, one of the tasks completed by the team was to analyze the transparency portals of Audit Courts of a number of States to define the most common and relevant categories for the publication of data as well as assessing the strong and weak points of each website and the portal's usability. All of this survey served as the basis for the development of a new version of the Transparency Portal for the Audit Court of Mato Grosso in the first quarter of 2012 [16]. Transparency Portal is the term commonly used by public entities for the designation of an internet page specifically created for public accountability [17].

The categories selected for this study are in accordance with the determination of Article 8, paragraph one of the LIA, which presents a minimum set of information to be made available and, therefore, to be present in practically all transparency portals of all state and Federal District Audit Courts. Since the categories are directly related to public spending, the proposal is for all of them to have the same weighting in the final score for the purpose of the ranking which goes from 0 to 100. See Table 1.

Table 1. Points per category of open data

#	Category	Description	Maximum Score
1	Personnel Management	List of servants (permanent, commissioned and outsourced) and table of salaries per position or function	25 points
2	Budgeting	Detailed information on the organ's revenue and expenses.	25 points
3	Tenders	Data on the pricing records, public competition, price taking and invitations.	25 points
4	Contracts	Information on the contracts signed with private companies.	25 points
Total applicable points			**100 points**

To reach the score of each category, the data collected was matched with the eight OGD principles. For greater clarity in the scoring of the principles and to prevent subjective judging of the scores to be given to each of them, this methodology is guided by the proposal in Table 2 of classifying the points according to the criteria stated in each of the categories.

After adding up the points for meeting the OGD principles, the next step is to calculate the percentage obtained and subtract that percentage from the maximum score available for each category, which is 25 points. For example, if in a particular category 60 % of the points is obtained according to the OGD principles, then the calculation is 60 % of 25 points resulting in 15 points. This formula is applied to all the other categories and the final result is the total of the scores obtained.

Table 3 shows the formula and scoring per information category and the final score:

The first step to reach the final score of an institution is to calculate the score for each of the four categories. The points per category are calculated by multiplying the maximum score possible in one category (25) by the result of dividing the points obtained from meeting the OGD principles by 8 (the total number of principles).

Table 2. Points per criteria by OGD principles – methodology table of points

Principle	Category	Observed criteria	Points
Complete	Personnel management	List of permanent servants	0,25
		List of commissioned servants	0,25
		List of outsourced servants	0,25
		Table of salaries per position or function	0,25
	Budgeting	Expenses report	0,50
		Revenue report	0,50
	Tenders	Open bids (face to face or electronic)	0,25
		Price taking	0,25
		Competitions	0,25
		Invitations	0,25
	Contracts	Information on creditors	0,25
		Object of the contract	0,25
		Period of validity	0,25
		Contract value	0,25
Primary	All	Non-aggregated data	1,00
Timely	All	Data available up to 30 days	1,00
Accessible	All	Direct access through a browser	0,50
		No need for additional software to access information	0,50
Processible	All	Data structured to allow automated processing	1,00
Non-discriminatory access	All	Access permitted with no need for registration of identification	1,00
Non-proprietary format	All	Data available in open format	1,00
License-free	All	Free for sharing or redistribution	0,50
		Free for adaptation	0,50

The final result of this survey will be a ranking from 0 to 100 of the level of adoption of the OGD policy by the Audit Courts of all states and the Federal District according to the Final Score obtained by each court.

Here is a practical example: imagine that we have obtained a score of 5.5 from the observance of the OGD principles in Table 2 for data collected in the Budgeting category of one particular Audit Court. Now we apply the formula described in Table 3 to calculate the category score:

$$\text{Points per Category} - \text{Budgeting} = 25 \times (5.5 \div 8)$$
$$\text{Points per Category} - \text{Budgeting} = 25 \times 0.68$$
$$\text{Points per Category} - \text{Budgeting} = 17.18$$

Table 3. The calculation formula and scoring per information category and the final score

Description	Calculation formula
Points per category	$PCn = 25 \times (PP \div TP)$
Final score	$FS = PC1 + PC2 + PC3 + PC4$

PC = Points per category, PP = Points per compliance
with the OGD principles, TP = Total of the OGD
principles (8), FS = Final Score

Now, let's suppose that the points for the categories of Personnel Management, Tenders and Contracts are **14.81, 21.4** and **8.9**, respectively. Then, the final score is:

$$\text{Final Score} = 17.18 + 14.81 + 21.4 + 8.9 / \text{Final Score} = 62.29$$

In this example, the Audit Court assessed would have a score of 62.29 out of a possible maximum of 100. The overall ranking will be ordered according to the final score in decreasing order and the higher the score the better the position at the end of the study. To verify the method, we opted to analyze the transparency portals of the Mato Grosso State Audit Court, in this article, as an example.

4   Method Application

This section presents the proposed verification method for the application to the Audit Courts' portals. The portals were accessed between 22/12/2014 and 21/01/2015, with data taken from this period, although the period is not itself a factor for the assessment of the method, acting only as an indication for the courts to assess their own systems. The method was applied to each of the courts, where an independent set of data for each institution was kept in the research. For this article, the excerpt presented is from the Audit Court of Mato Grosso[2], used to demonstrate the method. Then, the overall ranking of TCE Brazilian portals is shown.

4.1   The Audit Court of the State of Mato Grosso

The TCE-MT (Audit Court of the State of Mato Grosso) was ranked second among the Audit Courts in the Center-west region and seventh in the National Ranking with 50.78 points (above the national average of 42.28 points).

Table 4 shows the points for the Personnel Management category for the TCE-MT. During the visit to the institution's Transparency Portal it was not possible to locate the list of outsourced servants. Also, the data in this category were available from the portal in PDF format (a proprietary format and dependent on additional software to be accessed) and was non-structured, which makes automatic information processing unviable. The lack of a license of use also impacted negatively on the category score.

---

[2] http://www.tce.mt.gov.br.

Table 4. TCE/MT - The result of the personnel management category

PERSONNEL MANAGEMENT (A)		
OGD PRINCIPLE	OBSERVED CRITERIA	POINTS
Complete	List of permanent servants	0,25
	List of commissioned servants	0,25
	List of outsourced servants	0,00
	Table of salaries per position or function	0,25
Primary	Non-aggregated data	1,00
Timely	Data made available in up to a maximum of 30 days	1,00
Accessible	Direct access through a browser	0,50
	No need for additional software to access information	0,00
Processible	Data structured to allow automated processing	0,00
Non-discriminatory access	Access permitted with no need for registration of identification	1,00
Non-proprietary format	Data available in open format	0,00
License-free	Free for sharing or redistribution	0,00
	Free for adaptation	0,00
TOTAL POINTS ACHIEVED WITHIN THE OGD PRINCIPLES		4,25
FINAL CATEGORY SCORE		13,28

Table 5. TCE/MT -The result of the budgeting category

BUDGETING (B)		
OGD PRINCIPLE	OBSERVED CRITERIA	POINTS
Complete	Expenses report	0,50
	Revenue report	0,00
Primary	Non-aggregated data	1,00
Timely	Data made available in up to a maximum of 30 days	1,00
Accessible	Direct access through a browser	0,50
	No need for additional software to access information	0,50
Processible	Data structured to allow automated processing	0,00
Non-discriminatory access	Access permitted with no need for registration of identification	1,00
Non-proprietary format	Data available in open format	1,00
License-free	Free for sharing or redistribution	0,00
	Free for adaptation	0,00
TOTAL POINTS ACHIEVED WITHIN THE OGD PRINCIPLES		5,50
FINAL CATEGORY SCORE		17,19

In the Budgeting category, the data were considered to be incomplete due to the lack of a revenue report. As can be seen in Table 5, the lack of a license for use and the non-structured data also impacted on the score. In the Tenders category, the lowest score for the TCE-MT, the negative points were due to a lack of license, the need for additional software to access the information due to the use of a proprietary format, the use of aggregated data (high granularity) and a difficulty in automatic processing due to the data not being available in a minimally structured way. The details of the points achieved in this category can be seen in Table 6. Table 7 shows the low score in the Contracts category for the TCE-MT, in which it obtained the lowest score of all the categories assessed for the institution. Of the thirteen criteria assessed in this category, only five were satisfactorily met.

According to the final score for the Audit Court of Mato Grosso, by adding up the points obtained in the four categories, the final score for the TCE-MT was 50,70. The Contracts category (9.38 points) and Tenders (10.94 points) need to better meet the OGD requirements since they did not achieve half of the maximum score possible (25 points). In the categories of Personnel Management (13.28 points) and Budgeting (17.19 points) better scores were achieved which are above the national average for these respective categories (11.83 and 12.5 points respectively). With this score, the TCE-MT was ranked as 7th. Based on these proposals, the TCE-MT portal has been adjusted.

Table 6. TCE/MT - The result of the tenders category

TENDERS (C)		
OGD PRINCIPLE	OBSERVED CRITERIA	POINTS
Complete	Open bids (presential or electronic)	0,25
	Price taking	0,25
	Competitions	0,25
	Invitations	0,25
Primary	Non-aggregated data	0,00
Timely	Data made available in up to a maximum of 30 days	1,00
Accessible	Direct access through a browser	0,50
	No need for additional software to access information	0,00
Processible	Data structured to allow automated processing	0,00
Non-discriminatory access	Access permitted with no need for registration of identification	1,00
Non-proprietary format	Data available in open format	0,00
License-free	Free for sharing or redistribution	0,00
	Free for adaptation	0,00
TOTAL POINTS ACHIEVED WITHIN THE OGD PRINCIPLES		3,50
FINAL CATEGORY SCORE		10,94

Table 7. TCE/MT - The result of the tenders category

CONTRACTS (D)		
OGD PRINCIPLE	OBSERVED CRITERIA	POINTS
Complete	Information on creditors	0,25
	Object of the contract	0,25
	Period of validity	0,00
	Contract value	0,00
Primary	Non-aggregated data	0,00
Timely	Data made available in up to a maximum of 30 days	1,00
Accessible	Direct access through a browser	0,50
	No need for additional software to access information	0,00
Processible	Data structured to allow automated processing	0,00
Non-discriminatory access	Access permitted with no need for registration of identification	1,00
Non-proprietary format	Data available in open format	0,00
License-free	Free for sharing or redistribution	0,00
	Free for adaptation	0,00
TOTAL POINTS ACHIEVED WITHIN THE OGD PRINCIPLES		3,00
FINAL CATEGORY SCORE		9,38

4.2 Overall Performance

Graph 1 shows the ranking with the final scores of each of the Audit Courts assessed in the research. The highest number of points indicate greater compliance with the general aspects of OGD, whilst the lowest scores show a greater deficiency in meeting the OGD principles.

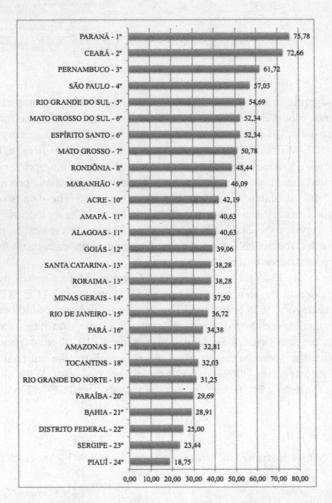

Graph 1. The overall research results

As can be seen in the overall ranking (Graph 1), the Audit Court of the State of Paraná achieved the best score (75.78 points of a maximum of 100), with the highest number of points coming in the Personnel Management, Budgeting and Contracts categories which achieved 21.09, 21.88 and 21.88 points respectively, followed by the Audit Court of the State of Ceara (72.66 points). Among the Audit Courts that performed least well in this survey are those from the states of Piauí, in last position with a

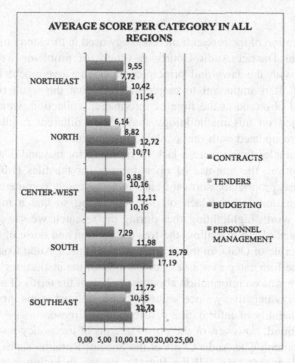

Graph 2. Average score per category in all regions.

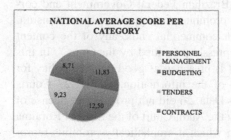

Graph 3. National average score

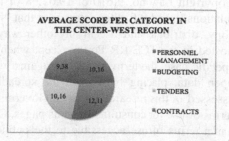

Graph 4. Center-west region Average

score of just 18.75 points, just behind Sergipe (23.44 points) and the Federal District (25.0 points). Overall, the average score was 42.28 points with only ten entities getting a score above this and seventeen others scoring less than the average (Graph 2).

Graphs 3 and 4 show the national and center-west region averages of the points distribution over the four categories assessed. In this case, the Brazilian states are according to the distribution of the State Audit Courts.

4.3 Discussion

During the application of the research methodology used in this study together with the State and Federal District Audit Courts, a variety of problems were detected of non-compliance with the laws and principles of Open Government Data in all the entities surveyed. It is important to emphasize here that the result of this research reflects what was observed at the time of information collection, which suggest that new surveys based on this methodology may obtain different results as the Audit Courts' portals are updated with the available information.

The main obstacles found were a lack of licensing for use and distribution of the available information, the non-use of open formats for the files (which creates the requirement to use proprietary software and, in some cases, commercial software to access the information and the lack of data structuring so that it may be machine processed). It is worth highlighting that during the research we saw a lack of clear policies for licenses of use that allow the free distribution and reuse of the data, which is the eighth principle of OGD. In this criteria, none of the 27 Audit Courts managed to score in any of the four categories assessed. On most of the institutions' portals, during the research, there was no information about the policy of the terms of use. This lack of information impacts negatively since without clearly defined terms there is no way to know about the legality of information distribution and reuse.

A case was found, however, of the use of a terms of use policy restricting the free distribution of content. The Audit Court of the State of Roraima states on its page the terms of use policy that says "all the Portal contents, including system data, texts, photographs, audio, video, images and graphic elements, besides the TCE-RR logo, are copyrighted and have their intellectual property reserved, as established by the Copyright Law no. 9.610 of 19.02.98 of the Brazilian Federal Government and correlations". And it further determines that "it is prohibited to reproduce, store, transmit, copy, distribute and use in any other way for commercial ends, any of the content hosted in the TCE-RR Portal except when expressly permitted by the court.". In this specific case, the terms of use go against what is preached as good practice policy for open data, placing barriers to the spreading of the information. Of the 27 Courts assessed in this research on Open Government Data, 26 did not provide any license of terms of use for consultation on its pages. Only the Audit Court of the State of Roraima has a terms of use accessible to the public in which it emphatically prohibits reproduction, storage, transmission, copying, distribution or any other form of use for commercial ends. It is worth highlighting that these terms apply to the whole portal and its respective content and not just the specific content.

Another non-compliance common among the Audit Courts in relation to the OGD principles is in relation to the formats of the files used which impede machine processing. The use of documents in the Portable Document Format (PDF) is a common practice on the transparency portals of all the organs assessed and despite being proprietary, it is considered an open format by the maker itself. However, PDF files are generated from other documents and do not allow modifications, as well as making processing difficult if not impossible since they are binary file formats and need software or a set of specific libraries in order to be visualized. Of the Audit Courts assessed, only those in the States of Ceará, Paraná, Rio Grande do Sul, Rondônia and São Paulo achieved points in at least one of the categories on the issue of processible data by using other formats such as eXtensible Markup Language – XML and Comma Separated Values – CSV.

5   Conclusions

The LIA is an important reinforcement of the democratization process by allowing society to inspect and demand institutions to make use of public resources. However, in its coverage, the law only requires that there be accountability but does not define the rules in terms of the format of the data. As a result, there is a variety of non-standardized information that cannot be machine processed or simply depends on proprietary software in order to access the content. Besides, the lack of terms of use and licensing of the available content places in risk the legality of the distribution and reuse of the data.

The policy of OGD is an alternative to solving the gaps in the LIA as it defines clear laws and principles to be followed so as to allow public data to be effectively considered open and so that it can be used in applications developed by society and freely distributed thus offering new perspectives on the efficiency of public administration.

In the light of these issues, this is what this research proposes. As an overall objective of this study a method was conceived and tested as a way of inspecting the level of adoption of Open Government Data – OGD policies based on the analysis of the Audit Court's transparency portal of Brazilian states and the Federal District. With the application of this method, it was found that there is much progress to be made so that public data transparency does in fact become OGD.

Among the 27 Audit Courts involved in the research, the average score was just 42.28 and this number is an indicator that these institutions need to be more attentive to the principles of Open Government Data. Just fulfilling the requirements of the LIA does not ensure that the OGD policies are being fulfilled too. It is necessary for the organs to try to only serve the citizen/inspector of public spending, but also serve those who want to use this information for the development of computer applications that will help to strengthen checks and accompany public administration on the part of society.

The final result of this survey shows that there is much to do to advance the culture of Open Government Data. In this sense, it is beneficial to have methods such as this one that allow systematization of the court's work by means of software developed within the scope of existing legislation and the principles that rule over important concepts in the area of technology.

This study can be used as the basis for the elaboration of future work which could provide a wider understanding of the adoption of OGD policies in the Brazilian government. Among the suggestions for improvement, we cite the application of the method to other government organs in the executive, legislative and judiciary powers; the inclusion of new categories for research in the areas of healthcare, public security and education; the increase of criteria assessed for the OGD principles.

Another suggestion that could lead to improvement in the quality of data transparency in public entity administration in relation to OGD is the creation of a portal dedicated to registering and periodically updating the ranking of the scores obtained by the public organs assessed by means of this methodology. This portal would have the aim of keeping society and the government institutions themselves informed of the level of adoption of OGD policies and instigating society to demand improvements and great attention on the part of the public organs in terms of the quality of information provided.

Also, with the publication of the recent survey by the Federal Public Ministry [12], a comparative study can be made between the results of that assessment and this one since they were both from similar periods and/or, especially, compare the two methods so as to propose improvements to the method described in this article.

The method presented can be useful for state and municipal governments which can assess if their transparency portals are in accordance with the LIA and the OGD principles. Also, it may act as an example to other government organs that wish to adapt the method to specific cases.

Acknowledgements. The authors thank the TCE_MT for is supports in performing this research, the UFMT by means of the Specialization in Web System Engineering and the UNI-SELVA Foundation for the support given through the agreement between these three organs.

References

1. Acar, S., Alonso, J.M., Novak, K.: Improving access to government through better use of the Web. W3C Interest Group, vol. 12 (2009)
2. de Almeida, G.C.: O papel dos Tribunais de Contas no Brasil (2005). http://jus.com.br/artigos/7487/o-papel-dos-tribunais-de-contas-no-brasil. Accessed 12 Dec 2014
3. Brasil. Lei no. 12.527, 18 Novembro 2011. http://www.planaltogov.br/ccivil_03/_ato2011-2014/2011/lei/l12527.htm. Accessed 15 Jan 2015
4. Brasil. Lei no. 9.610, 19 Fevereiro 1998. Altera, atualiza e consolida a legislação sobre direitos autorais e dá outras providências. Diário Oficial [da República Federativa do Brasil], Brasília, 20 Fevereiro 1998. http://www.dou.gov.br/materias/do1/do1legleg19980220180939_001.htm
5. Castells, M.: A Sociedade em Rede: A era da Informação: Economia, Sociedade e Cultura, vol. 1, 698p, 6th edn. Paz e Terra, São Paulo (2011)
6. Diniz, V.: Congresso Consad de Administração Pública, Brasília, vol. 3 (2010). http://migre.me/iJ9cK. Accessed 2 Apr 2014
7. Eaves, D.: The Three Laws of Open Government Data (2009). http://eaves.ca/2009/09/30/three-law-of-open-government-data/. Accessed 20 Nov 2015
8. Germano, C.E., Takaoka, H.: Uma análise das dimensões da qualidade de dados abertos em projetos de dados governamentais abertos. In: Congresso CONSAD de Gestão Pública, Brasília, vol. 5 (2012). http://migre.me/opv5X. Accessed 16 Nov 2014
9. Madnick, S.E., Wang, R.Y., Lee, Y.E., Hongwei, Z.: Overview and framework for data and information quality research. ACM J. Data Inf. Qual. 1, 1–22 (2009)
10. Maciel, C., Cappelli, C., Slaviero, C., Garcia, A.C.B.: Technologies for popular participation: a research agenda. In: Proceedings of the 17th International Digital Government Research Conference on Digital Government Research, June 2016, pp. 202–211. ACM (2016)

11. Michener, G., Moncau, L.F.M., Velasco, R.: Estado Brasileiro e Transparência: Avaliando a aplicação da Lei de Acesso à Informação. In: Seminário de Avaliação Nacional de Transparência Governamental, vol. 1, p. 14. Pesquisa, Rio de Janeiro (2014)
12. MPF. Ministério Público Federal, Ranking Nacional da Transparência. http://www.rankingdatransparencia.mpf.mp.br. Accessed 20 Dec 2015
13. Rover, J.A., Galindo, F.: O governo eletrônico e suas múltiplas facetas. Lefis série, vol. 10, 345p. Univ. de Zaragoza, Zaragoza (2010)
14. W3C Brasil. Melhorando o acesso ao governo com o melhor uso da web. http://www.w3c.br/divulgacao/pdf/gov-web.pdf. Accessed 18 Jan 2015
15. Wang, R., Strong, D.: Beyond accuracy: What data quality means to data consumers. J. Manage. Inf. Syst. **12**(4), 5–33 (1996)
16. Girata, N.N.H., Maciel, C.: eGov website evolution study within strategic planning. In: Proceedings of the 15th Annual International Conference on Digital Government Research, June 2014, pp. 69–78. ACM (2014)
17. de Oliveira, L.K.B., Maciel, C.: Transparency and social control via the citizen's portal: a case study with the use of triangulation. In: Kő, A., Leitner, C., Leitold, H., Prosser, A. (eds.) EDEM 2013 and EGOVIS 2013. LNCS, vol. 8061, pp. 112–124. Springer, Heidelberg (2013)

Electronic Document Certification Service: An Enabler of e-Government Uptake in Hungary

Péter József Kiss[✉], József Károly Kiss, and Gábor Klimkó

MTA Information Technology Foundation, Budapest, Hungary
mtaita@t-online.hu

Abstract. Binding electronic documents to persons are usually achieved by using electronic signatures that are created off-line. It is argued that this approach hinders both the widespread usage and the long-term applicability of e-government services. In order to enable e-government uptake, a new on-line electronic document service is to be offered in Hungary. The legal background for the new service was laid down by the Hungarian counterpart of the Regulation 910/2014 of the European Parliament and of the Council.

Keywords: Electronic document certification · Electronic signature · Trust service · Public key infrastructure

1 Introduction

Binding electronic documents to natural and legal persons as legal statements is a necessary basic precondition of conducting business by electronic means within public administration. The traditional way of binding an electronic document to a physical person is the creation of an electronic signature on the document. The legal basis of this procedure in the European Union was the Directive 1999/93/EC of the European Parliament and of the Council of 13 December 1999 on a Community framework for electronic signature. In Hungary, the Act XXXV of 2001 on electronic signature based on Directive 1999/93/EC sets the scene in legal sense. Detailed legal rules are described – among others – in Government decree 78/2010.(III.25.) on the use of electronic signatures in public administration and on specific rules for electronic communication and in Government decree 85/2012.(IV.21.) on the detailed rules conducting business with government by electronic means.

Directive 1999/93/EC introduced the concept of qualified certificates and secure signature creation devices (SSCDs). The creation of an electronic signature using these means was intended to have basically the same legal power in relation to data in electronic form as in a handwritten signature on paper-based data.

For the purposes of this paper we shall distinguish between the legal concept of electronic signature and the technical concept of digital signature. Note that this differentiation might be sometimes confusing as ETSI technical standards also use the term electronic signature which is "essentially the equivalent of a hand-written signature".

The technological basis of creating an electronic signature is the implementation and usage of a Public Key Infrastructure (PKI) [1, 2]. In a PKI each individual has a private

A. Kő and E. Francesconi (Eds.): EGOVIS 2016, LNCS 9831, pp. 276–286, 2016.
DOI: 10.1007/978-3-319-44159-7_20

(cryptographic) key that is accessible exclusively by its owner and also a public key. An electronic document can be digitally signed by using the private key and the digital signature on a document can be verified by using the public key. The PKI model relies on three parties, as

- the person who digitally signs the electronic document. This person owns the private key that is necessary for the creation of the digital signature;
- the person who verifies the digital signature on an electronic document by using the certificate that contains the public key of the signing person. This way the binding of the electronic document to its issuing individual is assured, and
- the certification authority (CA) that certifies that the data that is necessary for verifying the digital signature (i.e., the public key) is bound to a specific person. In practice, the certification authority also provides the hardware device that physically creates the digital signature. The certification authority does not participate in the process of digital signing of the document.

The PKI model is originally based on off-line creation of digital signatures. That is, the creation of a digital signature on an electronic document is done by a hardware device owned by the signing person and there is no need for an internet connection at all. The private key that is necessary for the creation of the digital signature is usually stored on a smart card. Access to the internet is required, but is not compulsory for verifying a digital signature, that is the verification of the validity of the certificate and its binding to the person concerned. The on-line verification of a certificate could be accomplished by using the Certification Revocation List (CRL) of the respective certification authority or by using the Online Certification Status Protocol (OCSP).

Digital timestamping is a service based on a PKI where the hash code of an electronic document and the creation date of the timestamp go together as a document is digitally signed by a timestamping authority. Note that "digital signature", standardized by IETF and ETSI [3] is an umbrella term with various technical meanings. A digitally signed document is often stored in XML Advanced Electronic Signature (XAdES) format and there are a number of XAdES variations as

- the basic digital signature XAdES-BES;
- the digital signature XAdES-T in which a timestamp field is added to protect against repudiation;
- the digital signature XAdES-X-L that includes the validation data for those situations where the validation data are not stored elsewhere for the long term and
- the digital signature XAdES-A that includes additional time-stamps for archiving signatures in a way that they are protected if the cryptographic data becomes weak [3].

Electronic documents in Portable Document Format (PDF) can also be digitally signed according to the PDF Advanced Electronic Signatures (PAdES) standard [4].

There are European countries, such as Austria [5], Belgium [6], Estonia [7] and Portugal [8], where large scale e-government initiatives were based on using smartcards and PKI. The uptake of the smartcard-based e-government services, however, did not meet the previous expectations.

One of the reasons for falling behind the initial ambitious targets in e-government penetration is probably the disparate development trends in information technology that no one expected. The widespread use of personal computers that was dominant at the end of the last century in the developed world was soon replaced first by portable computers and later by tablets and smartphones. It is curious that this phenomenon as a barrier to widespread adoption of e-government services has not been scrutinized in the otherwise really far-reaching literature [9].

In this paper we shall deal with only with physical persons as a client of public administration. In Hungary currently there are different methods of binding an electronic document to a physical person as

(a) an electronic document with a qualified electronic signature (that is, created with a qualified certificate and an SSCD) is full documentary evidence;

(b) according to the Government decrees mentioned in the introduction, in certain specific cases an electronic document with an advanced electronic signature that can be verified with a qualified certificate is also full documentary evidence and

(c) in a limited circle of cases (e.g. electronic submission of income tax forms) electronic documents, that are uploaded through the so-called Client Gate to the Central System, are bound to the uploading person [10, 11]. The Client Gate is an electronic service that is bound to a physical person who is required to register personally. Users of the Client Gate authenticate themselves by a username/password mechanism; uploaded documents are digitally timestamped by the Central System.

These methods differ in their level of security. The use of qualified signatures is fairly expensive, that is why legislation made it possible to use more risky methods where the consequences of an abuse are relatively modest.

The usage of the qualified electronic signature did not gain ground at all in Hungary due to the cumbersome use and ancillary expenses of the digital signature technology. Use of Client Gate became widespread only because its use was made compulsory by the law in certain cases [12]. Then the increasing use of new types of personal computing devices diminished the uptake, therefore new methods are needed in order to make possible the widespread use of e-government services.

From the legal point of view the Regulation 910/2014 of the European Parliament and of the Council on electronic identification and trust services for electronic transactions in the internal market and repealing Directive 1999/93/EC came in handy. Due to the legal harmonization obligation of Hungary the Act CCXXII of 2015 on electronic administration and the general rules of trust services as constituted, opened the possibility of introducing new methods of binding physical persons to electronic documents. We are going to elaborate the main principles of such a new binding method.

2   Problems with the Off-Line Creation of Electronic Signature

The traditional model of off-line creation of electronic signatures is based on certain assumptions that hinder both its widespread usage and its long-term applicability.

When the reliability of an electronic document is in question, three factors should be scrutinized

- the trustworthiness of the person who verifies or certifies the document,
- the reliability of the environment where the verification or certification happens and
- the reliability of the media that contains the electronic document.

Note that one can draw an analogy between electronic authentication of a client and binding an electronic document to a client of public administration. For the purposes of electronic authentication of a client typically three independent factors are distinguished as,

- the client has it (inherence factor, e.g. his fingerprint);
- the client knows it (knowledge factor, e.g., her password) and
- the client possesses it (possession factor, e.g. a smartcard)

For example, when a person is authenticated at the border by checking his biometric passport then the checking border guard, the checking environment where the reader is and the chip containing the biometric data can be considered reliable, too.

In the traditional model it is assumed that all the three factors are reliable. Clear supporting evidence of this statement is that the certificate policy of the CA requires that only the physical persons who registered will create electronic signatures exclusively in a reliable environment. It is different, however, to require something and to enforce the requirements.

It is inherently problematic to assume that only the registered person himself will use a device (usually a smartcard) that contains the data to be used for the creation of the digital signature. The law in Hungary requires that a new company should be registered by a lawyer only by electronic means, where the use of a qualified electronic signature is required. However, it can happen that the lawyer passes his SSCD smartcard with his PIN code to his secretary even though this way the secretary could make a legal disclaimer in another affair, too.

If we have a closer look on the assumption that a registered person himself will use the device that contains the private key, traditionally the risk of stealing and copying the device is taken into consideration. In fact, this approach led to the concept of SSCD as a countermeasure to this risk. There is, however, the risk that an unauthorized person uses the device. In this case the unauthorized person should know the PIN code and temporarily should possess the device. It is relatively easy to commit such a crime at a workplace. PIN codes can be captured by mobile phones, smartcards are easy to steal. This fundamentally undermines the basic belief in the reliability of the aforementioned three factors (person, environment, media). If, for example, an electronic document on a loan has a qualified electronic signature on it then it is presumed by the law that the registered person created it. If the signature happened to be created by an unauthorized person then the burden of proof is on the person who doubts it.

The use of home computers also raises serious doubts on the reliability of the environment where the digital signature is created. According to market surveys, a significant ratio of home computer users do not have up-to-date virus protection and even if they happened to have that, it still does not guarantee complete defense against a cyber-attack.

The practice has shown that the use of such an environment and device that can be claimed to be reliable is so cumbersome, that clients do not use those. In summary, traditional methods are based on assumptions that simply do not hold. We need a better solution.

3 A New Method of Binding Electronic Documents to Persons

The new method is still based on a PKI but the creation of digital signatures will be arranged differently. The starting point of the new model lies in the exploitation of the new possibilities offered by advances in information technology. Today the geographical coverage of networks with high bandwidth is (or will be) almost complete in the developed world and as a consequence, the condition "always on" can be met or will be met in the near future. In Hungary the plan is to have broadband access in each household by 2018. This circumstance supports an on-line document certification service for clients.

3.1 The Concept of Central On-Line Document Certification

There are two distinguishing features of the new method.

1. Binding the document to a natural person is done via a central on-line certification service (by the Central Certification Agent, CCA). The document will be signed with a XAdES-A type signature.
2. The person who uses the service will have immediate and periodical electronic notification on the certification events occurring on his behalf. The certified document could be sent back to the client who requested the service.

From the legal point of view, the CCA is a trust service according to Regulation 910/2014 of the European Parliament and the Council on electronic identification and trust services for electronic transactions in the internal market and repeals Directive 1999/93/EC. Being a trust service, the CCA is required to have an information security management system in place and a respective audit.

The CCA places a digital signature either on the document itself or on the hashcode of the document according to the request of the client. The digitally signed document is given back to the client. The communication channel between the user and CAA should be defended, that is both during the uploading of the document to be digitally signed and the downloading which should also be encoded.

The CCA service will be available for smartphones, too, that are used widely today. A further advantage of the CCA is that stronger computing capacity can be used as opposed to an average computing device. Therefore longer keys can be used for the creation of the digital signature that makes it possible for a longer period of validity of the electronic document.

Users of the CCA services will be required to register themselves personally before using the service in order to prevent or make it difficult to be abused This is the same security technique that is used to bind qualified certificates to users.

Immediate notification, however, is a new guarantee element of the method. The client is expected to specify an electronic address and a channel through which he will be notified when a certification on his behalf is made. The client will also have access to the certified document. The new method cannot completely exclude possible abuses but as the client will have a notification, then in a case where an unauthorized certification request was sent, they could act as necessary.

The periodical notification is another guarantee element. This practice is known in the banking sector as monthly notifications. The periodical notification compensates for the risk of the diversion of the immediate notification – an immediate SMS, or e-mail can be forged or deleted if somebody has access to the communication channel. Periodical notifications are to be sent regularly even if there was no event. Periodical notifications are to be certified by the service, too, which makes them protected.

Figure 1 summarizes the basic processing logic of the central on-line electronic document certification.

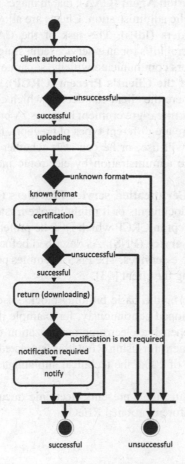

Fig. 1. Basic processing logic of the electronic document certification service.

Verification of a certified electronic document is done in the same manner as it would happen with an electronically signed document.

3.2   Electronic Document Certification Processing in Detail

To describe the processing logic of the electronic document certification service in more detail we need to understand the concept of Regulated Electronic e-government Services (REeGS). Act CCXXII of 2015 on electronic administration and the general rules of trust services, describes the specific REeGS, some of which should be provided by the Hungarian state, and others can be offered by the market players. There is a dedicated authority that supervises and gives permission for working the providers of a REeGS. The electronic document certification service itself is a REeGS.

The electronic document certification service builds upon the following REeGS

- **the Central Authentication Agent (CAA)**, that manages the electronic authentication of the clients of public administration. Clients are allowed to use the services of different Identity Providers (IdPs). The task of the CAA is to hide away the complexity of using several IdPs for an e-service requesting a client's authentication, that is, e-service providers communicate with the separate IdPs via the CAA [13]
- **the Central Register of the Client's Precept (CRCP).** A precept (or officially a disposition) is a way where the client can declare which communication channel is to be used during conducting e-government business. A precept is a legal statement given by the client. There are different types of precepts, for example the client can declare which IdPs he will use; or he can state whether he is willing to conduct business with the public administration by electronic means for certain types of cases [13].
- **electronic Document Certification service Providers (DCPs).** The CCA might itself certify electronic documents or it might invoke trusted third party DCPs. The client might have a precept in CRCP which DCP he prefers to use.
- **the Periodical Notice Service (PNS).** As described before the PNS provides feedback on the use of public e-services. The PNS assembles periodical reports based on logs of events concerning the client [13].

REeGS are designed to be the basic building blocks of e-government services in Hungary. REeGS are developed continuously, for example the CRCP and CAA were developed in the "Comprehensive electronic authorization of clients" (EKOP-2.3.8) project. The legal environment for using REeGS was created in Act CCXXII of 2015 and its precursor Act CXL of 2004, the technical implementation of the REeGS is an ongoing activity.

The sequence diagram in Fig. 2 presents electronic document certification taking place with the help of the aforementioned REeGSs.

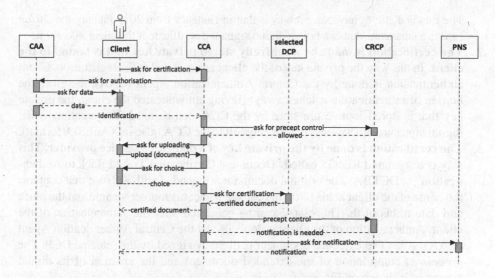

Fig. 2. Processing logic of the electronic document certification service with REeGS.

3.3 Resorting the Electronic Document Certification Service

In order to enable the quick introduction of the on-line electronic document certification service, three ways of using the new service are to be offered.

1. **The certification is done with the client's private key, which is on an SSCD possessed by him.** The document is uploaded to CCA and the client is expected to select a preferred DCP. The CCA sends the document to the selected DCP that computes its hashcode and transmits it forward to the client. The hashcode of the document will be digitally signed on his SSCD, the result is sent back to the selected DCP that creates the full document with XAdES-A type digital signature. The digitally signed document is to be sent to the CCA. This process is shown in Fig. 3.

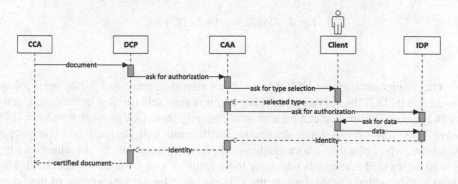

Fig. 3. Certification with the client's owned SSCD.

The raison d'etre to have such a way is that in Hungary from 2016 January the citizen card is a smartcard that can hold a digital signature certificate if the client asks for it.

2. **The certification is made by a centrally stored private key that is bound to the client.** In this way the private key of the client is generated at the registration. Client authentication is done by the Central Authentication Agent (CAA), therefore the burden of authenticating is taken away. Having authenticated the client, the private key that is stored in a secure store by the CCA, can be used. The creation of the digital signature otherwise is completely left to the CCA (also in XAdES-A format).

3. **The certification is done by the private key of a dedicated service provider.** This way is a separated REeGS called "Document Certification Traced Back to Authentication" or DCTBA. The original document is extended with a clause that contains the name of the client at his birth; his current name; his mother's name and the place and date of his birth. This clause can be generated after the authentication of the client. Authentication of the client is done also by the Central Authentication Agent (CAA). After The extended document is digitally signed by the selected DCP. The process of compilation of the extended document and the creation of its digital signature is shown on Fig. 4.

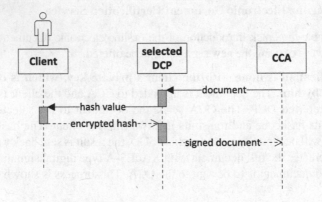

Fig. 4. Certification by the DCTBA.

The implementation of DCTBA has been started already and it has been partly finished. The DCTBA service is working and it is available for files in Portable Document Format. The service can be accessed currently from Government Windows [14] only. This way of electronic document certification will be used in Government Windows, where electronic documents are filled out by the client, by the administrator, as well as scanned documents which are to be certified, that are bound to the client. The client can be authenticated through the Client Gate. The implementation of the other two ways of using the electronic document certification services are under planning.

4 Conclusion

In this paper we pointed out assumptions behind the currently used off-line methods of binding electronic documents to physical persons in Hungary. These assumptions hinder and make impossible the take-up of e-government services. We described briefly a new on-line way of binding electronic documents to physical persons. A distinguishing feature of the model is notification of the certification events. Periodical and case-by-case notification guarantees that the client is aware of all certification events run on his behalf.

From the legal point of view Act CCXXII of 2015 on electronic administration and the general rules of trust services, that is the corresponding Hungarian part to the Regulation 910/2014 of the European Parliament and of the Council on electronic identification and trust services for electronic transactions in the internal market and repealing Directive 1999/93/EC, builds the legal background for the implementation of the new service. Three ways of using the new service were shown, amongst them the development of the Document Certification Traced Back to Authentication was started. This service is to be offered soon in the Government Windows.

Internal processing of the clients' cases can be completely done by electronic means by the time the DCTBA service is available. The client is expected to bring his paper-based evidence that is required by the law in order to administer his case to the Government Window. The public servant will scan these documents and fill out the necessary form then the client can see all the electronic documents, including the form and the scanned documents and verify them as his own by using DCBTA. From this point on the public administration has the complete documentation of the case in electronic format which is certified and should be legally accepted by all concerned Hungarian entities. This approach makes unnecessary the usage of qualified electronic signatures and this way results in significant cost savings. A similar service is offered to public servants where they are able to make their own electronic documents be certified without using (personal) qualified electronic signatures, too.

The electronic document certification service also will make it possible to bind electronic documents to home users. If the client is able to compile the documentation of his case including the scanned versions of the supporting paper based evidence with the help of CCA, he will be able to start case processing.

References

1. Richard, K.D. et al.: Introduction to Public Key Technology and the Federal PKI Infrastructure (NIST SP 800-32). National Institute of Standards and Technology (2001)
2. Buchanan, J.A., Karatsiolis, E., Wiesmaier, A.: Introduction to Public Key Infrastructures. Springer, Heidelberg (2013)
3. ETSI: Electronic Signatures and Infrastructures (ESI); XML Advanced Electronic Signatures (XAdES). ETSI TS 101 903 V1.4.2 (2010-12) (2010)
4. ETSI: Electronic Signatures and Infrastructures (ESI); PAdES digital signatures; ETSI TS 119 142-1 V1.0.1 (2015-07) (2015)

5. Aichholzer, G., Strauß, S.: Electronic identity management in e-government 2.0: exploring a system innovation exemplified by Austria. Inf. Polity **15**(1–2), 139–152 (2010)
6. Mariën, I., Audenhove, L.: The Belgian e-ID and its complex path to implementation and innovational change. Identity Inf. Soc. **3**(1), 27–41 (2010)
7. Martens, T.: Electronic identity management in Estonia between market and state governance. Identity Inf. Soc. **3**(1), 213–233 (2010)
8. Vasconcelos, A.: The Portuguese Interoperability Framework applied to the Portuguese Citizen Card Project, presented at the OECD Workshop on Digital Identity Management (IDM), 9 May 2007 (2007). http://www.oecd.org/dataoecd/36/9/38573902.pdf
9. Savoldelli, A., Codagnone, C., Misuraca, G.: Understanding the e-government paradox: learning from literature and practice on barriers to adoption. Gov. Inf. Quart. **31**, S63–S71 (2014)
10. European Commission: eGovernment in Hungary, Edition 16.0 (2014). https://joinup.ec.europa.eu/elibrary/factsheet/egovernment-hungary-april-2014-v160
11. OECD: OECD e-Government Studies: Hungary 2007. OECD Publishing, Paris (2007). doi:http://dx.doi.org/10.1787/9789264030527-en
12. Harindranath, G.: ICT in a transition economy: the case of Hungary. J. Glob. Inf. Technol. Manage. **11**(4), 33–55 (2008). doi:http://dx.doi.org/10.1080/1097198X.2008.10856478
13. Kiss, J.K., Kiss, P.J., Klimkó, G.: Towards a Model of Client-Driven Access to Public e-Services. In: Kö, A., Francesconi, E. (eds.) EGOVIS 2015. LNCS, vol. 9265, pp. 117–131. Springer, Heidelberg (2015)
14. OECD: Public Governance Reviews. Hungary: Towards a Strategic State Approach (2015). http://www.oecd.org/publications/hungary-towards-a-strategic-state-approach-9789264213555-en.htm

Identity Management in E-Government

Implementing Advanced Electronic Signature by Public Digital Identity System (SPID)

Francesco Buccafurri[✉], Lidia Fotia, and Gianluca Lax

DIIES, University Mediterranea of Reggio Calabria, Via Graziella,
Località Feo di Vito, 89122 Reggio Calabria, Italy
{bucca,lidia.fotia,lax}@unirc.it

Abstract. Advanced electronic signature is a form of signature recognized by EU legislation, which does not include the heaviest features of qualified electronic signature (i.e., qualified PKI certificates and qualified signature creation devices). The massive adoption of advanced electronic signature strictly depends on how solutions are easy, usable, and little invasive for citizens. In this paper, we propose a new advanced electronic signature protocol that relies on a public system for the management of the digital identity. Our proposal aims at implementing an effective synergy between the two mechanisms to provide the citizen with a unique, uniform, portable, and effective tool applicable to both peer authentication and document signature. The solution is designed for the Italian Public Digital Identity System (SPID), but it is easily extensible to any identity management system compliant with the EU regulatory environment (i.e., eIDAS).

1 Introduction

Digital signature is obtained by applying a series of cryptographic operations on the document to sign, based on the use of asymmetric cryptography and hash functions. The purpose of digital signature is to guarantee authentication and integrity of the signed document.

The European Union (EU) and the United States (US) have adopted legislation to recognize when electronic signatures (in principle not based on cryptography) are legally enforceable. Whereas the US regulatory framework [4] provides a large definition of electronic signature (often called e-signature) that comprises signatures made using various technologies, the EU legislation establishes some minimum security levels in the signature processes and could be also extrapolated to other countries or regions [1]. This directive makes a distinction between simple e-signatures, advanced e-signatures and qualified e-signatures. The standard for the e-signature with automatic legal value is public-key-encryption-based qualified electronic signature, which enforces the utilization of qualified PKI certificates and qualified signature creation devices (like smart cards or HSM-services in case of remote signature).

Qualified e-signature has become a crucial component of any digitalization process, in which we require that exchanged documents have a full legal validity.

A. Kő and E. Francesconi (Eds.): EGOVIS 2016, LNCS 9831, pp. 289–303, 2016.
DOI: 10.1007/978-3-319-44159-7_21

But the role of electronic signatures is important not only in the public sector. Indeed, we expect that also in transactions between citizens and companies the use of e-signature will always be increasing in the next future. However, in this process, there are some aspects to take into account. In particular, if we think of using qualified e-signature, we must consider the cost of the devices and the invasiveness of the operations related to signing, verification, registration and certificate management.

For this reason, EU has adopted an act [5] that fosters the use of the advanced e-signature, for which no qualification of certificates and devices is required. The new regulatory framework states that the advanced e-signature has automatic legal value if applied to closed domains, such as document exchange between registered citizens and municipal public offices. For an advanced electronic signature, we just have to fulfil the following properties: (1) it is uniquely linked to the signatory, (2) it is capable of identifying the signatory, (3) it is created using means that the signatory can maintain under his sole control, and (4) it is linked to the data to which it relates in such a manner that any subsequent change of the data is detectable [1]. No requirement about devices and certificates is given.

The addressed problem relies on the fact that identity management and signature are different matters, but our attempt is to implement an effective synergy between the two mechanisms to provide the citizen with a unique, uniform, portable, and effective tool, applicable to both peer authentication and document signature. For this purpose, we propose a new advanced e-signature protocol which relies on a public system for the management of the digital identity.

The identity management system considered in this work is the Italian Public Digital Identity System (SPID) [7,17]. SPID is compliant with the EU regulatory environment called eIDAS [3], aimed at implementing electronic identification and trust services to enable secure and seamless electronic interactions between businesses, citizens and public authorities. In SPID, public and private entities, accredited by "The Agency for Digital Italy" [2], can offer services of electronic identification for citizens and businesses. The providers of such services have to ensure a suitable procedure for the initial identification and have to implement the authentication of citizens to service providers. SPID is based on the technical specifications accepted in Europe and adopted by projects as Stork and Stork2 [36,40]. According to the requirements of eIDAS, from July 1, 2016, SPID will be recognized and accepted by all other EU Member States.

A good point of our solution is that we do not require any change of SPID, so that the adoption of our solution appears both realistic and effective. The paper is organized as follows. In the next Section, we survey the related work of the recent literature. In Sect. 3, we recall some background notions. In Sect. 4, the SPID framework is presented. In Sect. 5, we present our solution to implement an advanced electronic signature in SPID. Then, in Sect. 6, we analyze the security of this protocol. Finally, in Sect. 7, we draw our conclusions.

2   Related Work

In this section, we contextualize our paper in the literature, with respect to the two topics, authentication and signature, which are the most related to our proposal.

Let us start with electronic identification, authentication and trust services (eIDAS). In [27], the authors present the main principles of eIDAS and analyze whether these principles are a positive evolution from the currently existing legal framework for electronic seals, time stamping, electronic document acceptability, electronic delivery and web site authentication. However, the authors demonstrate that the European Commission may have moved too hastily in drafting this proposal, resulting in a number of unclarities, inconsistencies and ambiguities. Massacci et al. [32] discuss potential security and privacy issues related to electronic IDs and trust service providers, and proposes recommendations for the eIDAS draft based on the innovative technological contributions of EU Trust and Security Programme projects. Also, in [26], the authors describe eIDAS and the three UE projects related to it (Stork, Stork 2.0 and FutureID). In particular, they analyze whether eIDAS provides requirements that need to be implemented in the FutureID infrastructure. For this purpose, the description of eIDAS and the analysis of its main requirements for technical developers are in general relevant to the development of online identification and authentication schemes. Buchmann et al. [20] discuss the adaption of the upcoming eIDAS standard towards trusted banking transactions and outline resulting security and privacy enhancements. In particular, they extend the eIDAS standard by biometric authenticated transactions which not only boost user convenience, trust and confidence towards eBanking and eBusiness, but suggest to integrate state-of-the-art privacy compliant biometric technologies into the security ecosystem. As a result, they demonstrate that eIDAS is highly suitable for banking transactions since it is solely based on security protocols and infrastructure which have been for more than ten years proven secure in the civil aviation domain. In [17], the authors propose a modification of SPID to allow user authentication by preserving the anonymity of the identity provider that grants the authentication credentials in such a way that information leakage about the customers of identity providers is fully prevented. To the best of our knowledge, our proposal is the first attempt to exploit SPID for the generation of document signature. The problem of the information leakage derived from the expression of opinions in social networks is dealt with in [12–15]. A recent survey on attacks and vulnerability of digital signature is provided in [30].

Concerning the generation of signature document, there exist in the literature several proposals. Conditional signatures were originally introduced by Lee et al. [31] to implement fair exchange of digital signatures in untrusted environments and do not require the card to have a user interface or any special peripheral (like Clarke et al. [24]). Berta et al. [9] propose a method to generate, instead of an ordinary signature, a conditional signature such that it is guaranteed that the condition can not become true before a certain amount of time has passed. This should leave time for the user to move to a trusted terminal for checking the signatures generated by the card and to enforce that the conditions of the fake signatures can ever become true. Since this approach requires the smart card to know the current time but most smart cards have no internal clock, it could be acquired from a secure time servers as described in Berta et al. [10]. Moreover, this proposal requires the user to store every signed message, because this message has to be checked later by means of a trusted terminal. Since it may be infeasible for C to store large message, this problem can be solved by outsourcing the logging function to an external logserver. Therefore, even though the required hardware is the standard one, a trusted third party is required.

Electronic signature is a data structure that contains some information that must be linked to the signature, like the digital certificate, the cryptographic algorithms or the time at which the signature was generated. International standardization organizations have defined many formats of electronic signatures that include basic forms of electronic signature (ES-BES) and advanced electronic signatures (AdES) [21, 37]. AdES formats that include additional validation information allow a relying party to obtain a higher assurance respecting the validity of the certificate used during the signature creation. Therefore, these formats intend to support the verification stage, but do not positively affect the reliability of the creation stage.

Weak signature [38] was introduced to solve a problem (Verifiable Secret Sharing [23]) motivated by a question of general multi-party secure computation in the unconditional setting (network of untappable channels). They provide a form of authentication for which the on-line participation of a third party is needed. The weak signature scheme relies on the presence of an on-line trusted server that participates in the creation of every signature, and also participates whenever a signed message holder wishes to prove to anyone that a signature is valid. This trusted server stores and retrieves information received from the signing agency and the message holder, and computes certain linear combinations of values it receives.

Another signature scheme in the unconditional setting was introduced by Chaum and Roijakkers [22]. It satisfies a stronger set of conditions than Rabin's Information Checking Protocol, at a great increase in communication cost.

Visual cryptography [35] is a type of cryptographic scheme which can decode concealed images without any cryptographic computation. Naor et al. [34] suggest a number of transparency-based methods for visual authentication and identification, and give rigorous analysis of their security. [33] presents human-friendly identification schemes such that a human prover knowing a secret key in his brain is asked a visual question by a verifier, which then checks if an answer sent from the prover matches the question with respect to the key. Ateniese et al. [8] propose a visual cryptography scheme for a set of participants to encode a secret image into many secondary images in such a way that any participant receives one secondary image and only qualified subsets of participants can "visually" recover the secret image, but non-qualified sets of participants have no information, in an information theoretical sense, on the original image. This scheme does not require the participants to perform any cryptographic computation.

The problem of generating e-signature not using public key cryptography has been dealt with in [16,18]. In [19], the authors propose a protocol conceived for closed domains of users, such as the case of document exchanges between citizens and municipal public offices or private companies and employees. The signature functions are spread out over the popular social network Twitter, making the implementation of this solution scalable and easy to apply.

From the point of view of signature, our proposal has the great advantage of not requiring the use of cryptography or dedicated devices and is fully compatible with the current SPID system. Moreover, the user load can be considered very limited if compared to visual cryptography and conditional signature.

3   Background

In this section, we present the technical detail necessary to understand our proposal, which regards the digital signature and the PKCS#7 format of the cryptographic envelope.

Digital signature [16]. The digital signature mechanism relies on a public key infrastructure enabling the binding of public keys with user identities by means of a trusted third party, the Certification Authority. Each user owns two keys, a private key and a public one. The private key is kept secret and the public one is made public. The first step of the signature generation process is the computation, on the document to be signed, of a cryptographic hash function, typically SHA-256. The result is called *digest* of the document. The properties of the hash function guarantee that the digest can substitute the original document in the signature generation process as the probability of having two distinct documents producing the same digest is negligible. Moreover, the problem of finding a document with digest equal to that of another given document is unfeasible, so that an attacker cannot corrupt a signed document without the digest changes. The digest is computed on the PC by the signature software (typically supplied by the certification authority) and sent to the smart card embedding the private key of an asymmetric cryptographic cipher, typically RSA. The smart card is then enabled by the user (typically by inserting a secret PIN) to encrypt the digest with the private key, thus producing the digital signature. This is sent from the smart card to the signature software running on the PC to produce the cryptographic envelope, which can be encoded in several formats, such as PKCS#7 [29], CMS [28], CAdES [37], XAdES [25] or pdf [39]. The cryptographic envelope typically contains at least the document, the signature, and the certificate of the signer. Given a cryptographic envelope B, the verification of the signature on the document contained in B is done by: (i) computing the digest I of the document D, (ii) computing J as the result of the decryption of the signature with the public key of the subscriber (included in the certificate), and (iii) checking that the decrypted digest J coincides with the computed digest I. The verification is completed by checking recursively also validity, trustworthiness, and non-revocation of the certificate.

The PKCS#7 Format. PKCS#7 [29] supports several different content types: data, signed data, enveloped data, signed-and-enveloped data, digested data, and encrypted data [11]. The data content type represents a sequence of bytes. The encrypted-data content type consists of encrypted content of any type. The digested-data content type consists of content of any type and a message digest of the content. The signed-data content type consists of content of any type and encrypted message digests of the content for zero or more signers and it is used to represent digital signatures. The enveloped-data content type is intended to represent digital envelopes, combining encrypted data sent to one or more recipients and the information (the content-encryption keys) needed by each recipient in order to decrypt the content. Finally, the signed-and-enveloped-data content type represents digital envelopes providing data with "double encryption", i.e. an encryption with a signer's private key followed by an encryption with the content-encryption key. Any of the content types defined in PKCS#7 can be enveloped for any number of recipients and signed by any number of signers in parallel. The signed-data content type is intended to be used for digital signatures, and it constitutes the basis upon the cryptographic message is built. Such a content type consists of (i) a given content of any of the types defined in PKCS#7 and, for each signer, (ii) both an encrypted message digest of the content (i.e. of the document) representing the signer's digital signature on the content, and (iii) other signer-specific information (concerning, for example, certificates and certificate-revocation lists). Additional information can be signed in order to authenticate attributes other than the content, such as the signing time.

4   The SPID Framework

In this section, we present the Public Digital Identity System (SPID) framework and the technical details necessary to understand our proposal. SPID is an open system allowing public and private accredited entities to offer services of electronic identification for citizens and businesses. The actors of SPID use the Security Assertion Markup Language (SAML) for communication [6]. SAML is an XML-based, open-standard data format for exchanging authentication and authorization data between an identity provider and a service provider. It uses security tokens containing assertions to pass information and enables web-based authentication and authorization scenarios including cross-domain single sign-on, which helps reduce the administrative overhead of distributing multiple authentication tokens to the user. Short SAML messages are carried directly in the URL query string of an HTTP GET request. Due to the limit of URL length, longer messages are transmitted via HTTP POST Binding. Although SAML allows the use of SSL or TLS for the communications, in SPID, it is mandatory the use of TLS.

The stakeholders of SPID are:

1. *Users*, physical or legal people using SPID to authenticate. Each user can be associated with one or more SPID IDs.

2. *Identity Providers*, which create and manage SPID IDs. They are private or public subjects certified by a trusted third party.
3. *Service Providers*, public or private organizations providing a service to authorized users.
4. A *Trusted Third Party (TTP)*, which guarantees the standard levels of security required by SPID and certifies the involved entities (e.g., in Italy it is "The Agency for Digital Italy").
5. *Attribute Authority*, which certifies a particular set of attributes (such as possession of a degree, membership of a professional body, etc.) relating to a user who owns a digital identity.

To obtain an ID, a user must be registered to one of the *Identity Providers*, which is responsible of the verification of the user identity before issuing the ID and the security credentials. Observe that different levels of sophistication are allowed for security credentials. This derives from the need to have a technologically neutral model, which fits the technological evolution without continuous remodeling.

When a user needs to access a service given by a *Service Provider*, the authentication mechanism illustrated in Fig. 1 is carried out. First, the user using a browser (`User Agent`) sends to *Service Provider* a request for accessing the service (Step 1). Then, *Service Provider* replies to `User Agent` with an authentication request to be forwarded to *Identity Provider* (Step 2). The authentication request `AuthnRequest` is defined as:

Definition 1. `AuthnRequest` is a message that contains the following fields:

- an unique attribute `ID`. This is generally obtained by a combination of origin and timestamp, such as ID = Assertion-uuidae7136e4-0118-18d8-999d-cff934ae63db;
- an attribute `Version`, which indicates the version of SAML of the message;
- an attribute `IssueInstant`, which specifies the instant at which the request was issued;
- an attribute `Destination`, the address to which the request is sent;
- an attribute `ForceAuthn`, which specifies the authentication level required;
- an attribute `AssertionConsumerServiceIndex`, a positional index that allows to obtain by another element the URL to which the response is sent;
- an optional attribute `AssertionConsumerServiceURL`, which is the URL of the destination of the response message (i.e., the URL of *Service Provider*);
- an optional attribute `ProtocolBinding`, a URI that identifies the binding (GET or POST) to be used to forward the response message;
- an optional attribute `AttributeConsumingServiceIndex`, which specifies the attributes that must be present in the assertion;
- an optional element ⟨`Subject`⟩, which indicates the person seeking the authentication;
- an element ⟨`Issuer`⟩, the unique identifier of the *Service Provider*;
- an element ⟨`NameIDPolicy`⟩, which defines the name identifier formats supported by the *Identity Provider*;

- an optional element ⟨Conditions⟩, which specifies the time of validity;
- an element ⟨RequestedAuthnContext⟩, which indicates the robustness of the required credentials;
- an optional element ⟨Signature⟩, the *Service Provider* signature on the request (only in the case of HTTP POST binding).

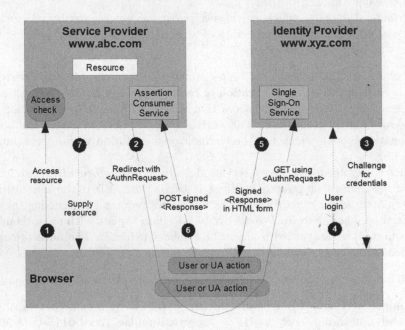

Fig. 1. Data flow during an authentication request in SPID.

If the received request is valid, *Identity Provider* performs a challenge authentication with the user (Steps 3 and 4). In case of successful user authentication, *Identity Provider* prepares the *Assertion* containing the statement of user authentication for *Service Provider*. The Assertion is defined as:

Definition 2. Assertion contains the following fields:

- an unique attribute ID. This is generally obtained by a combination of origin and timestamp, such as ID = Assertion-uuidae7136e4-0118-18d8-999d-cff934ae63db;
- an attribute Version, which indicates the version of SAML of the message;
- an attribute IssueInstant, which specifies the instant at which the request was issued;
- an element ⟨Subject⟩. It identifies the authenticated user and must hold:

- an element ⟨SubjectConfirmation⟩, which contains:
- an attribute InResponseTo, which refers to ID of the corresponding AuthnRequest;

- an element ⟨Issuer⟩, which specifies the EntityID of *Identity Provider*;
- an element ⟨Conditions⟩, which defines the temporal range of validity;
- an element ⟨AuthStatement⟩, which is the description of the authentication's context;
- an element ⟨AttributeStatement⟩, which contains the SPID identification code of the authenticated user;
- an element ⟨Signature⟩, the *Identity Provider* signature on the assertion.

Now, *Identity Provider* returns to User Agent the message Response containing Assertion (Step 5), which is forwarded to the *Service Provider* via HTTP POST Binding (see Step 6). The message Response is defined as:

Definition 3. Response contains the following fields:

- an unique attribute ID;
- an attribute Version, which indicates the version of SAML of the message;
- an attribute IssueInstant, which specifies the instant at which the request was issued;
- an attribute InResponceTo, containing the value of the attribute ID of AuthnRequest;
- an attribute Destination, the URI to which the response has to be sent;
- an element ⟨Status⟩, which specifies the outcome of the request (e.g., success);
- an element ⟨Issuer⟩, which reports the EntityID of *Identity Provider*;
- an element ⟨Assertion⟩, as defined in Definition 2.
- an optional element ⟨Signature⟩, the *Identity Provider* signature (only in the case of HTTP POST binding).

5   SPID-Based Signature

In this section, we describe how to modify the SPID protocol described in Sect. 4 to enable the generation of electronic signature based on SPID, which allows us to be aware of the identity of the person who created the document and to ensure that this document has not been altered since that person created it.

Differently from digital signature, a SPID-based signature does not relies on certification authority, asymmetric cryptography, or signature device, and this is the main advantage of such a solution.

We describe how a SPID-based signature works by referring to the application scenario illustrated in Fig. 1. In our proposal, the role of *Service Provider* is played by a trusted third party that ensures the standard levels of security required by digital signature. We call *Signature Provider* this entity.

The solution here proposed allows the signature of a document and the verification of a signature. These two procedures are described in the following.

Signature generation. To generate the signature of a document, the user connects to the web site of *Signature Provider* and sends the document to sign together with his SPID identification code. Then, *Signature Provider* computes the digest by using a cryptographic hash function (typically, SHA-256) and creates an `AuthnRequest`. The structure of this message is the same described in Definition 1: all information are the same as of a standard SPID request, except the value of the attribute ID, which is the document digest (we recall that in the standard SPID protocol, ID is a random number). The `AuthnRequest` message is sent back to the user to be forwarded to *Identity Provider* (as Step 2 of Fig. 1). If `AuthnRequest` is valid, *Identity Provider* performs a challenge authentication with the user as in the Steps 3 and 4 of the SPID system and, in case it successes, *Identity Provider* prepares the *Assertion*. In particular, the attribute `InResponseTo` of ⟨SubjectConfirmationData⟩ contained in the element ⟨Subject⟩ is set to the value of the attribute ID of `AuthnRequest`, which corresponds to the digest of the document to be signed. This establishes a linkage between the `Assertion` and its corresponding `AuthnRequest`. In our case, the `Assertion` represents the signature of the document created by the *Identity Provider*. At this point, *Identity Provider* returns the message `Response` containing `Assertion`, which is forwarded to the *Signature Provider* (Steps 5 and 6).

Once the *Signature generation* is completed, *Signature Provider* creates the cryptographic envelope, which enables the possibility to distribute signed documents. In this phase, all information necessary to validate the signature has to be inserted into a cryptographic envelope, whose structure needs to be defined. In our proposal, the format for exchanging data between the providers is SAML [6]. The XML structure we designed for our cryptographic envelope resembles the structure of PKCS#7 [29] and is constructed as follows:

Definition 4. `Cryptographic Envelope` is signed by the *Identity Provider* and contains the following fields:

- an attribute `Version`, which gives a syntax version number for compatibility with future revisions of the document;
- an attribute `Content`, which is the document signed;
- an attribute `DigestAlgorithms`, which indicates the message-digest algorithm under which the content is digested for the signer;
- an final element ⟨SignatureAssertion⟩, which is composed of fields whose values are extracted from the `Assertion`:

- an unique attribute `Digest`. Its value is equal to the attribute `InResponseTo` of `Assertion`, which corresponds to the digest of the document;
- an attribute `Timestamp`. Its value is equal to the attribute `IssueInstant`, which specifies the instant at which the document was issued;
- an element ⟨Owner⟩. This value is taken from ⟨Subject⟩ and indicates the signer;

- an element ⟨SPIDcode⟩. This value is extracted from the element AttributeStatement, which contains the SPID identification code of the user;
- an element ⟨Issuer⟩. This is the same as ⟨Issuer⟩, which specifies the EntityID of *Identity Provider*;
- an element ⟨SPIDsignature⟩. This is the same as ⟨Signature⟩, which is the *Identity Provider* signature on the document.

Once *Cryptographic Envelope* is completed, *Signature Provider* sends it to the user (Step 7).

The procedure allowing any entity to verify authenticity and integrity of a document signed by the SPID system is described in the following.

Signature verification. Any user who wants to verify a signature needs to have the corresponding cryptographic envelope. First, the integrity and authenticity of the cryptographic envelope is checked, to ensure that it is genuine and has been issued by an identity provider.

Then, the verifier extracts from the attribute Content of the cryptographic envelope the document whose signature has to be validated. Then, he computes the document digest II using the cryptographic function referred by the attribute DigestAlgorithms and compares H with the digest contained in the field Digest. If these do not mach, the integrity of the document has been compromised. Otherwise, the document is genuine. Concerning the authenticity of the document, the information about the identity of the signer is available by the element Owner of ⟨SignatureAssertion⟩.

6 Security Analysis

This section is devoted to the analysis of the features provided by SPID-based signature and to prove its robustness against real-life attacks. The analysis is based on the following assumptions. The first one is that *Identity Providers* and *Signature Providers* are trusted third parties, so that they cannot create fraudulent digital content. The second assumption is that the communication between the stakeholders is secure (for example, we can assume that TLS is adopted, as required in SPID). The third one is that SPID-authentication credentials of users are secret and cannot be known by any attacker.

The security properties supplied by the SPID-based signature are discussed in the following.

Document Authenticity. SPID-based signature allows us to be aware of the identity of the signer of the document. Indeed, the system releases for each user an identification code that identifies the user unambiguously and uniquely. This code is inserted in the element ⟨SPIDcode⟩ of the Cryptographic Envelope. Moreover, the message contains the element ⟨Owner⟩, which refers to the signer of the document and this gives us the possibility to know signer identity.

Document Integrity. At the end of the signature, the document digest has been inserted in the `SignatureAssertion`. Any change of the document produces a change of the digest so that a difference between the value of the attribute `Digest` of the `Cryptographic Envelope` and the digest of the altered document detects such an attack.

Non repudiation. This property ensures that a signer cannot at a later time deny having signed a document. A user could attempt to repudiate a signature claiming that another user signed that document. However, as identity providers are assumed to be trusted (Assumption 1) and SPID-authentication credentials are maintained secret (Assumption 3), so that the assertion signed by the identity provider guarantees that such a signature has been produced by that user.

Signature Timestamp. It is a pleasant feature to have a timestamp stating when the signature is made. In the digital signature, this value is provided by a trusted third party. In our case, the signature timestamp is directly provided by SPID. The `Cryptographic Envelope` contains the attribute `Timestamp`, which specifies the instant at which the signature was issued.

Revocation. It is the procedure carried out to withdraw the trust in a user and thus inhibit him to sign other document. In the digital signature, a certificate authority (CA) generates a certificate that is valid for a specific amount of time. In some cases, it is necessary that CA revokes the certificate. After one or more certificates have been revoked, the CA generates a certificate revocation list (CRL) that can be checked during the authentication process. In our case, the identity provider invalidates SPID code of the user and, from that moment, he cannot longer sign any documents. Observe that, the signatures generated before the revocation continue to be valid because the presence of that assertion signed by an identity provider ensures that the signature has been done before the revocation.

Impersonation. By impersonation, an attacker simulates to be the victim of that attack. This can be done or by logging in SPID with the victim's credentials or by registering a SPID account with the identity of the victim. The first attempt is contrasted because victim's credentials are secret and cannot be known be the adversary (Assumption 3). As far as the second attempt, SPID does not create an account if it has not verified the person's identity. Indeed, the user must physically go to an identity provider and submits some document to be identified securely. Only after this procedure, SPID releases an identification code.

7   Conclusion

In this paper, we proposed a new advanced electronic signature protocol by relying on the Italian public system for the management of the digital identity named SPID. The aim of our proposal is to design a solution that can appear suitable for a massive adoption of advanced electronic signature, once public identity management systems will become fully adopted in EU. This is in fact a process already in place, thanks to the new European regulatory environment called eIDAS. Indeed, although our solution is designed for the Italian Public Digital Identity System (SPID), it can be easily extended to any identity management system compliant with eIDAS. The security analysis performed in our study shows that our solution is compliant with the notion of advanced electronic signature and, further, that it is robust against possible attacks, being thus a solution with real applicability.

Acknowledgments. This work has been partially supported by the Program "Programma Operativo Nazionale Ricerca e Competitività" 2007–2013, Distretto Tecnologico CyberSecurity funded by the Italian Ministry of Education, University and Research.

References

1. Directive 99/93/CEE. http://eur-lex.europa.eu/legal-content/EN/ALL/;jsessionid=TCsMT1yBQ965GRJTMG9GnFDxQqYP1W7Y1LFLLkwsmjvWRy1Q15FJ!527097711?uri=CELEX:31999L0093
2. Agency for Digital Italy (AgID) (2015). http://www.agid.gov.it/
3. Electronic identification and trust services (eIDAS) (2015). http://ec.europa.eu/dgs/connect/en/content/electronic-identification-and-trust-services-eidas-regulatory-environment-and-beyond
4. Electronic Signatures in Global and National Commerce Act (2015). http://www.gpo.gov/fdsys/pkg/PLAW-106publ229/html/PLAW-106publ229.htm
5. On Electronic Identification and Trust Services for Electronic Transactions inthe Internal Market and Repealing Directive 1999/93/EC (2015). http://eur-lex.europa.eu/legal-content/EN/TXT/?uri=uriserv:OJ.L_.2014.257.01.0073.01.ENG
6. Security Assertion Markup Language (SAML) (2015). http://it.wikipedia.org/wiki/Security_Assertion_Markup_Language
7. SPID-Agenzia per l'Italia Digitale (2015). http://www.agid.gov.it/sites/default/files/regole_tecniche/spid_regole_tecniche_v0_1.pdf
8. Ateniese, G., Blundo, C., De Santis, A., Stinson, D.R.: Constructions and bounds for visual cryptography. In: Meyer auf der Heide, F., Monien, B. (eds.) ICALP 1996. LNCS, vol. 1099, pp. 416–428. Springer, Heidelberg (1996)
9. Berta, I.Z., Buttyán, L., Vajda, I.: Mitigating the untrusted terminal problem using conditional signatures. In: Proceedings of International Conference on Information Technology: Coding and Computing, ITCC 2004, vol. 1, pp. 12–16. IEEE (2004)
10. Berta, I.Z., Vajda, I.: Documents from malicious terminals. In: Microtechnologies for the New Millennium 2003, pp. 325–336. International Society for Optics and Photonics (2003)
11. Buccafurri, F., Caminiti, G., Lax, G.: Fortifying the dalì attack on digital signature. In: Proceedings of the 2nd International Conference on Security of Information and Networks, pp. 278–287. ACM (2009)
12. Buccafurri, F., Fotia, L., Lax, G.: Allowing continuous evaluation of citizen opinions through social networks. In: Kő, A., Leitner, C., Leitold, H., Prosser, A. (eds.) EDEM 2012 and EGOVIS 2012. LNCS, vol. 7452, pp. 242–253. Springer, Heidelberg (2012)

13. Buccafurri, F., Fotia, L., Lax, G.: Privacy-preserving resource evaluation in social networks. In: 2012 Tenth Annual International Conference on Privacy, Security and Trust (PST), pp. 51–58. IEEE (2012)

14. Buccafurri, F., Fotia, L., Lax, G.: Allowing non-identifying information disclosure in citizen opinion evaluation. In: Kő, A., Leitner, C., Leitold, H., Prosser, A. (eds.) EDEM 2013 and EGOVIS 2013. LNCS, vol. 8061, pp. 241–254. Springer, Heidelberg (2013)

15. Buccafurri, F., Fotia, L., Lax, G.: Allowing privacy-preserving analysis of social network likes. In: 2013 Eleventh Annual International Conference on Privacy, Security and Trust (PST), pp. 36–43. IEEE (2013)

16. Buccafurri, F., Fotia, L., Lax, G.: Social signature: signing by tweeting. In: Kő, A., Francesconi, E. (eds.) EGOVIS 2014. LNCS, vol. 8650, pp. 1–14. Springer, Heidelberg (2014)

17. Buccafurri, F., Fotia, L., Lax, G., Mammoliti, R.: Enhancing Public Digital Identity System (SPID) to prevent information leakage. In: Kö, A., Francesconi, E. (eds.) EGOVIS 2015. LNCS, vol. 9265, pp. 57–70. Springer, Heidelberg (2015)

18. Buccafurri, F., Lax, G., Fotia, L., Nicolazzo, S., Nocera, A.: A lightweight electronic signature scheme using twitter. In: Proceedings of 23rd Italian Symposium on Advanced Database Systems (SEBD 2015), Gaeta, Italy (2015)

19. Buccafurri, F., Lax, G., Fotia, L., Nicolazzo, S., Nocera, A.: A new approach for electronic signature. In: Proceedings of 2nd ICISSP 2016 Roma, Italy (2016)

20. Buchmann, N., Rathgeb, C., Baier, H., Busch, C.: Towards electronic identification and trusted services for biometric authenticated transactions in the Single Euro Payments Area. In: Preneel, B., Ikonomou, D. (eds.) APF 2014. LNCS, vol. 8450, pp. 172–190. Springer, Heidelberg (2014)

21. Centner, M.: XML Advanced Electronic Signatures (XAdES). Citeseer (2003)

22. Chaum, D., Roijakkers, S.: Unconditionally-secure digital signatures. In: Advances in Cryptology-CRYPT0 1990, pp. 206–214. Springer, Heidelberg (1991)

23. Chor, B., Goldwasser, S., Micali, S., Awerbuch, B.: Verifiable secret sharing and achieving simultaneity in the presence of faults. In: 26th Annual Symposium on Foundations of Computer Science, 1985, pp. 383–395. IEEE (1985)

24. Clarke, D., Gassend, B., Kotwal, T., Burnside, M., van Dijk, M., Devadas, S., Rivest, R.L.: The untrusted computer problem and camera-based authentication. In: Mattern, F., Naghshineh, M. (eds.) PERVASIVE 2002. LNCS, vol. 2414, pp. 114–124. Springer, Heidelberg (2002)

25. Cruellas, J.C., Karlinger, G., Pinkas, D., Ross, J.: XML advanced electronic signatures (XAdES). World Wide Web Consortium, Note NOTE-XAdES-20030220 (2003)

26. Cuijpers, C., Schroers, J.: eIDAS as guideline for the development of a pan European eID framework in FutureID. In: Open Identity Summit 2014, vol. 237, pp. 23–38 (2014)

27. Dumortier, J., Vandezande, N.: Critical Observations on the Proposed Regulation for Electronic Identification and Trust Services for Electronic Transactions in the Internal Market. ICRI Research Paper, vol. 9 (2012)

28. Housley, R.: Cryptographic message syntax (1999)

29. Kaliski, B.: Pkcs# 7: Cryptographic message syntax version 1.5 (1998)

30. Lax, G., Buccafurri, F., Caminiti, G.: Digital document signing: vulnerabilities and solutions. Inf. Secur. J. Global Perspect. **24**(1–3), 1–14 (2015)

31. Lee, B., Kim, K.: Fair exchange of digital signatures using conditional signature. In: Symposium on Cryptography and Information Security, pp. 179–184 (2002)

32. Massacci, F., Gadyatskaya, O.: How to get better EID and Trust Services by leveraging eIDAS legislation on EU funded research results (2013)
33. Matsumoto, T.: Human-computer cryptography: an attempt. J. Comput. Secur. **6**(3), 129–149 (1998)
34. Naor, M., Pinkas, B.: Visual authentication and identification. In: Kaliski Jr., B.S. (ed.) CRYPTO 1997. LNCS, vol. 1294, pp. 322–336. Springer, Heidelberg (1997)
35. Naor, M., Shamir, A.: Visual cryptography. In: Santis, A. (ed.) EUROCRYPT 1994. LNCS, vol. 950, pp. 1–12. Springer, Heidelberg (1995)
36. Navarro, V.A., Gumbau, J., Santapau, P., Marzal, A.: Stork project results: Pan-European eID interoperability demonstrated (2011)
37. Pinkas, D., Pope, N., Ross, J.: CMS advanced electronic signatures (cades). IETF Request for Comments, vol. 5126 (2008)
38. Rabin, T.: Robust sharing of secrets when the dealer is honest or cheating. J. ACM (JACM) **41**(6), 1089–1109 (1994)
39. Taft, E., Pravetz, J., Zilles, S., Masinter, L.: The application/pdf media type. Internet proposed standard RFC, vol. 3778 (2004)
40. Wessels, B.: Identification and the practices of identity and privacy in everyday digital communication. doi:10.1177/1461444812450679 (2012). New Media & Society

Digital Signatures Workflows in Alfresco

Patrícia R. Sousa[1]([✉]), Pedro Faria[2], Manuel E. Correia[1], João S. Resende[1], and Luís Antunes[1]

[1] Department of Computer Science, Faculty of Science,
University of Porto, Porto, Portugal
patriciarvsousa@gmail.com, jsresende8@gmail.com,
{mcc,lfa}@dcc.fc.up.pt
[2] HealthySystems, Porto, Portugal
pedro.faria.80@gmail.com

Abstract. There are some obstacles, towards a paperless office. One of them is the collection of signatures, since nearly half of all documents are printed for the sole purpose of collecting them. Digital signatures can have the same legal evidential validity as handwritten signatures, provided they are based on certificates issued by accredited certification authorities and the associated private keys are stored on tamper proof token security devices like smart cards. In this article, we propose a platform for secure digital signature workflow management that integrates secure token based digital signatures with the Enterprise Content Management *Alfresco*, where each user can associate a set of smart cards to his account. The documents can then be signed with the citizen card or other smart card that has digital signatures capabilities. We have implemented an *Alfresco* module that allows us to explore several workflow techniques to implement real task secure digital signatures workflows, as people for example do when they pass a paper document between various departments to be signed. Since all users can see the current state of the documents being signed during the entire signage process, important security properties like system trust are preserved. We also describe an external validation web service, that provides a way for users to validate signed documents. The validation service then shows to the user important document security properties like timestamps, certificates attributes and highlights the document integrity in face of the digital signatures that have been collected in the workflows defined by our module in *Alfresco*.

Keywords: Digital signatures · Workflow management · Digital citizen card · Business Process Management · Alfresco

1 Introduction

Documents which are in printed format have been used for many years, such as books, papers, forms, contracts and any related materials [1]. Nowadays, there are a lot of reasons why people might choose to paperless environments, including reduction of the environmental harm of paper consumption and the economic cost of paper production, print, transfer and storage. Digital environments

© Springer International Publishing Switzerland 2016
A. Kő and E. Francesconi (Eds.): EGOVIS 2016, LNCS 9831, pp. 304–318, 2016.
DOI: 10.1007/978-3-319-44159-7_22

release people or companies of the location and physical constraints of paper and provide better support for updating, archiving, and searching of documents [2].

With the evolution of Information technology and computer systems, the documents have been managed by computer-based document management systems. A Document Management System (DMS) can be defined as a computer system that is used to store, manage, and retrieve electronic/digital documents on a closed client/server architecture network [3]. However, DMS were interested in the file and storage/indexing/retrieval mechanisms to allow the user to classify and retrieve documents. They were initially concerned only with the file as a container. But, as market needs changed, the DMS focus shifted from file management to content management. For example, if we have a Web site, it is composed of HTML, XML, or ASP pages that need to be managed. So, the name of the system was changed to Enterprise Content Management (ECM) [4].

According to the authors of [5,6] going paperless is convicted to failure soon. Despite of many efforts which have been done to consume less paper, companies still use large amounts of paper. There are some obstacles towards a paperless office such as: read on screen is difficult for some people especially mid aged people it was not that easy to adapt to computer and Internet, who don't like to read on monitors and prefer to read in paper; the risk of losing data and document due to software or hardware failure; the people has fear because despite electronic storage be safer than having data on paper, some people do not trust the authenticity or security of online tools. Signatures is another obstacle towards a paperless office and according to the authors of [7] nearly half of all documents are printed for the sole purpose of adding signatures, so, we want to focus on a solution to this.

There are two methods of transforming a company into paperless office. One of the methods is by automating the processes that normally use paper as an essential tool. There are several technologies to make this: enterprise data automation software, used to integrate forms and data with systems that processes them; form technology, used to design various types of forms; databases device used to replace the function of a filing cabinet, i.e., data is made into digital form and then stored in a database with sufficient security technology; digital signature allow evidence of signature in digital form. Papers are generally used as business evidences. This is required in business transactions to generate legal binding between two or more parties and workflow platforms technology that is a processes flow of an office. Normally, paper documents are used to transfer a data to other departments so that it can continue doing what is needed next (for example, one document is transferred to other department to be signed). This flow of work can be documented and transferred in digital form, using the workflow platforms. The second method of transforming a company into paperless office is data storage transformation. In a general office, the data is normally stored and protected in a filing cabinet. This turns out to fill offices full of useless paper. Using the "Paperless Office" technology, all this data can be transformed to a digital form very easily. Some of the tools available to support this process: Scanners, book copiers, photo scanners, fax to Portable Document Format (PDF) converter and more. One of the most important tools are ECM systems [8]. This two methods of transforming a company into paperless office leads us to a solution that could combine the technologies to automate processes that typically use the paper an essential tool, with a tool to store digital information, for example a ECM system as stated above.

The work detailed in this paper aims to provide companies a way to be able to automate their processes signatures to avoid transferring a printed data between departments. This type of transferring can result in loss of important documents or falsification of documents/signatures using printed paper. We want that companies to be able to involve several people in the automated process of signatures, safely in a ECM system. This leads companies to also benefit from a printed paper reduction and reduction of the loss of important documents because documents are online, this way. We will focus in integrating a digital signatures systems with a ECM system. This allows users to sign documents in a document manager, so users can also save their documents online, digitally. We take advantage of the workflow feature that some ECM systems have. Thus, we provide users a way to create a workflow signatures in a ECM system, so, multiple users can sign the same document for example, and all can see the state of the document. We provide a secure way to users sign documents, through a smart card (citizen card, for example).

The next chapters of the paper are organized as it follows: Related Work, Electronic Signature vs Digital Signature, Cryptography Concepts, Smart Cards, Alfresco and workflows, Implementation and Conclusions.

2   Related Work

In the following sections we present an overview of a set of systems comparing their features. As our goal is to integrate these two systems, we also present an overview what there is in that direction that is, digital signature systems (with or without workflows) integrated with an ECM and an overview of the features. To compare the different ECM systems analysed and choose the best ECM system

Table 1. Comparison of DMS/ECM systems - (E-Enterprise Version, C-Community Version)

	Alfresco C	Alfresco E	Nuxeo	DocuWare	eFileCabinet
Open Source	LGPLv3	-	LGPLv2.1	-	-
Add-ons	✓	✓	✓	✓	✓
Workflows	✓	✓	✓	✓	✓
PDF support	✓	✓	✓	✓	✓
Txt/binary support	✓	✓	✓	✓	✓
Users/Groups support	✓	✓	✓	✓	✓
Digital signatures	-	-	-	-	-
Electronic signatures	-	-	-	✓	✓
Record management	-	✓	✓	✓	-

to use, we decided to do a comparative table with the main features that we need in the system. Based on [9–11], we construct the following Table 1:

-	LogicalDOC C	LogicalDOC E
Open source	LGPLv2.1	-
Add-ons	✓	✓
Workflows	-	✓
PDF support	✓	✓
Txt/binary support	✓	✓
Users/Groups support	✓	✓
Digital signatures	-	✓
Electronic signatures	-	-
Record management	-	✓

We analyse some systems that are the most popular ECM. We're interested in open-source systems as well as we can have full control over the system and can create free add-ons, we also have security guarantees seeing the system code and adapt it to all our needs [12]. We also analysed some non open source because they could have some features that we want, so, we must consider whether we are adding something new to the market or if already exists. Within the non open source, we try to see those in which there have signatures or workflows, that are our principal focus. To select the open-source ECM, we look for systems that have workflows, so *LogicalDOC community* is not an option. Among others, *Alfresco community* and *Nuxeo community* the choice was more complicated, but beyond Alfresco has more users, it also has much more online communities, more tutorials and help documents.

To compare the different digital signature workflow systems analysed and see features that can be added to improve what already exists in the market, we decided to do a comparative table with the some features (Table 2):

It is important to know if this type of software has support to physical technology like USB tokens, smart cards or mobile for example. There are some type of workflow: Individual Workflow (only one person), Sequential Workflow (follows a defined order), Parallel Workflow (any order allowed) or Group Workflow (the system allow the creation of groups of registered users). The validation of all signatures is a feature of the system that validates a document with multiple signatures and gives information about them.

In this table we can see the principal features of the independent systems that can be integrated in the *Alfresco* and of the add-ons of *Alfresco*. We can compare the principal features that we need in our system. The difference of independent system and add-ons is that the add-ons are designed for work within *Alfresco* only, however, independent systems works without *Alfresco* providing the signature functionality and can be integrated into *Alfresco*.

Table 2. Comparison of digital signature workflow systems

	SecuredSigning	SigningHub	DocuSign
Open source	-	-	-
Cryptography technology	X.509	X.509	X.509
Physical technology	-	Smart Card and Mobile	Smart Card
Individual workflow	✓	✓	✓
Parallel workflow	✓	✓	✓
Sequential workflow	-	✓	✓
Group workflow	-	-	-
Validation of all signatures	✓	✓	✓

We now proceed to compare some these systems by the following Tables 3 and 4:

With this investigation, we can see that the most popular independent systems / add-ons have most of the features that interest to us and can help us to

Table 3. Independent digital signature systems for *Alfresco*

	CoSign	DocuSign
Open source	-	-
Crypt. technology	X.509	X.509
Psychical technology	-	Smart Card
Workflow ready/independent	✓	✓
Workflow *Alfresco*	-	-
One signature	✓	✓
Multiple signatures	✓	✓
Validation	-	-

Table 4. Add-ons for *Alfresco*

	Zylk	E.Roux	Toolkit	CounterSign	Sinekarta	Dig. Legale
Open Source	✓	✓	✓	✓	✓	-
Crypt. technology	X.509	X.509	X.509	X.509	X.509	X.509
Psychical technology	✓	-	-	✓	✓	-
Workflow signatures	-	✓	-	✓	-	-
One signature	✓	✓	✓	✓	✓	✓
Multiple signatures	✓	-	-	✓	-	✓
Validation	✓	-	-	✓	✓	-

see what we can improve on the market and that does not exist in the market to we can introduce a new idea.

3 Electronic Signature vs. Digital Signature

These two concepts are often confused by people in general. However, a digital signature is an electronic signature but the reverse is not the case. Electronic signature is easy to implement, because a simply typed name can serve as one. Therefore, this type of signature has many problems to maintaining integrity and security, as there is nothing to prevent one person from typing another persons name. Due to this reality, electronic signatures is an insecure way of signing documentation. Electronic signatures are vulnerable to copying and tampering, making forgery easy. There are some examples of electronic signature such as, the scanned image of the person ink signature, the signature with a digital pen, a typed name, a signature at the bottom of an email, a biometric hand-signature, a video signature or a click in an "I agree" check box. The main point is that an electronic signature is any "mark" made by the person to confirm their review/approval of the document [13].

In the case of the digital signature, this is a mathematical scheme for demonstrating the authenticity of a document. A valid digital signature gives a recipient reason to believe that the message was created by a known sender and the message was not altered during the transport. Therefore, this sender cannot deny having sent the message, that ensures authentication, non-repudiation and integrity. Digital signatures comply laws and regulations. This helps organisations ensure signer authenticity, data integrity, and the verifiability of signed electronic documents. Any changes made after the document has been signed invalidate the signature, thereby protecting against signature forgery and information tampering [14]. According to Portuguese law [15], electronic signatures have the same evidential validity as handwritten signatures, provided they are based on certificates issued by accredited certification entities. They are called digital signatures.

Nonetheless, electronic signature can be combined with a digital signature and gain legal value. It is important, today, generate a digital signature by deriving a signature key from human biometrics. Biometrics is the science of using digital technologies to identify a human being based on the individuals unique measurable biological characteristics [16]. With an electronic biometric signature, users can see his handwritten signature in the document and this is an important feature for usability. It is important to have this complement in a signature system because users have a connection in past with the signatures on the paper and users are more comfortable if they can see his usual handwritten signature on the document.

Thus, we now proceed to describe some sections about a digital signatures: cryptography concepts related to digital signatures, digital signature scheme and the different types of digital signatures.

3.1   Cryptography Concepts

Digital signatures use a public and private key pair that are usually purchased by a sender and issued by a Certificate Authority (CA). A key pair are mathematically related because a message encrypted with a private key can only be decrypted with a public key. So, a sender uses his private key to sign a document and the recipient uses the senders public key and the signature to confirm the authenticity of the document. The private key is received by a person and remains secret. This key is not to be distributed to anyone other than the private key owner. The public key, can be made available for anyone and can be found by accessing a CA public database. CA is a trusted third party who verifies the identity of the person requesting the key pair and can be created through a PKI [17]. According to the authors of [18], "a PKI is a set of hardware, software, people, policies and procedures needed to create, manage, store, distribute and revoke digital certificates (also called public key certificate) based on public-key cryptography. PKI is an arrangement that binds public keys with respective user identities by means of a CA".

3.2   Digital Signature Scheme

A digital signature scheme provides a cryptographic analogue of handwritten signatures that provides much strong security guarantees. In many countries, digital signatures is a powerful tool and are accepted as legally binding. This scheme is used by a signer and a set of verifiers. A signature scheme consists of three probabilistic, polynomial-time algorithms (Gen, $Sign$, $Vrfy$) along with an associated message space $M = M_k$. The signer starts by running some randomised key-generation algorithm Gen to produce a pair of keys (pk,sk), where pk is the signers public key and sk is the singers private key (also called secret key). The security parameter k is implicit in both pk and sk. For security parameter k, the signing algorithm $Sign$ (possible randomised) takes as input a private key sk and a message $m \in M_k$ and takes as output a signature $\sigma \leftarrow Sign_{sk}(m)$. If $m \notin M_k$, the signature algorithm outputs $\perp$. For security parameter k, the verification algorithm $Vrfy$ takes an input a public key pk, a message $m \in M_k$ and a signature σ. The output produces a bit, with $b = 1$ that means "accepted" and $b = 0$ that means "reject". This is written as b:= $Vrfy_{pk}(m, \sigma)$. If $m \notin M_k$, the verification algorithm return "reject" [19].

In summary, a digital signature is composed of a unique digital certificate for each signer; a private key which only the signer can use to sign and a public key which allows anyone to validate the signature. Signers can include, in digital signatures, for example their name, date, time stamp, their reasons for signing and also can include graphical signatures.

3.3   Types of Digital Signatures

Public Key Cryptography Standards (PKCS#7) is a standard defined by RSA (Rivest-Shamir-Adleman cryptosystem) describing a general syntax for data to which cryptography may be applied, such as digital signatures. PKCS#7 supports some different content types: data, signed data, enveloped data, signed-and-enveloped data, digested data, and encrypted data. Beyond PKCS#7, there are other formats to encode the cryptographic messages, that are been proposed to improve security and interoperability [20]. There are some types of digital signatures. Comparing two standards, XML Advanced Electronic Signatures (XAdES) and CMS Advanced Electronic Signatures (CAdES), that serve the purpose of digitally signing any type of data using qualified certificates. Both of the standards allow the storage of attributes such as the Multipurpose Internet Mail Extensions (MIME) type of the data to be signed, signing time, for example [21]. XAdES is based on CAdES but required the syntax of eXtensible Markup Language (XML). XAdES introduces the attribute DataObjectFormat to describe the encoding format of the signed data. PDF Advanced Electronic Signature (PAdES) is a proprietary format for digital signatures in a PDF documents where a PDF can be seen as two compartments house. The first contains the PDF document to be signed and the second contains the information required by digital signatures, like, user's certificate, the encrypted digest (Digital Signature Algorithm (DSA) and RSA are supported). In PAdES, it's possible to sign more than just the document such as, time stamp obtained from a trusted server, a graphical signature, the system and the software application the user. This kind of signature has some strong advantage in terms of resistance to ambiguous-presentation attacks [20].

4   Smart Cards

Security solutions based only in software are not safe and are very vulnerable to some attacks. The reason for this lack in security is the conventional storage media use to store certificate and private key are not secure.

Hardware security modules (HSM) are an important security issue of the modern computer networks. Their principal purposes consists on increasing the overall system security and accelerating cryptographic functions. Smart cards can be seen as an example of an HSM that provides a secure and portable way to securely manage cryptographic keys and corresponding X.509 digital certificates, in a PKI context. Smart cards enhances the PKI security through an extra authentication level ("something you have") and with fact that cryptographic keys generated on the card never leave the card. PKI smart cards can provide most main security functions in modern information systems: authentication (X.509 digital certificate), confidentiality (based on asymmetric private key), data integrity (digital signature) and non-repudiation (digital signature by asymmetric key generated and stored on the card) [22].

5   *Alfresco* and Workflows

An example of an open source ECM system is *Alfresco*. This system incorporates the major applications of ECM: documents, images, Web contents, records, and digital assets management. *Alfresco* system stands out in its services and controls that manage the content and features. The most important features of this system are the workflows, versions control, metadata management and search.

For a business, for example, this system has the most important features to support the content requirements of a number of business critical processes and uses. Office work, search and discover is supported by the document management tools. The businesses also needs workflow management capabilities that includes case management, review and approval. The creation and refinement of content and documents are supported by the collaboration applications. The scalable Web content management services support the delivery and deployment of content from the enterprise to its customers. One of the most benefits of this system is the capability of record management, that provides an affordable means to capture and preserve records based upon government-approved standards. The standards-based platform also provides access to applications that use these standards, such as publishing, image, and email management [9].

For a developer, the system has a benefit, the add-ons. They can develop an *Alfresco* add-on to improve the capabilities of an *Alfresco* product. The developers can make, for example, integrations with external systems, package customisations and system administration tools.

For creation of a business process more efficient, adaptive and effective to accomplish business tasks, Business Process Management (BPM) provides methods and techniques for this [23]. One of the biggest tools of the ECM *Alfresco* are the support to the Business Process Model and Notation (BPMN) and workflows. BPMN is used to modelling notations for designing business processes, consists of to represent the business workflow. BPMN solutions are framework used to develop, deploy, monitor and optimise multiple types of process automation applications, including processes that involve both systems and people like workflows.

Workflow can be seen as a task that has a initial and final state. An workflow handles approvals and prioritises the order documents are presented. The decisions of workflow are based on predefined rules developed by system owners [4].

6   Implementation

In this section, we describe the technical implementation of the proposed integration of digital signature with an ECM, in this case, *Alfresco*. We took the fact that this ECM has support for BPM and workflows to integrate digital signatures in a workflow where people could define who signs a specific document.

We focus on the signatures in PDF documents. We implement the signature in this type of a document because, as we can see in the Types of Digital Signatures subsection, this kind of signature is more resistant to attacks. One interested property is the time stamps. Timestamping is the process of securely keeping track of the creation and modification time of a document. No one, not even owner of the document, should be able to change it once has been recorded. That way, integrity is ensured. The timestamp is obtained from a trusted external server to have the guarantee that the service we are using is not changing the timestamps [24]. This can be considered as the stamps made by a notary in a paper.

We used smart cards to provide a way to users sign safely, quickly and provide mobility, as described in Smart Cards section.

As *Alfresco* allows add-ons, we took advantage of this feature and we integrate all the process to signing a document as one module/add-on that can be integrated in the *Alfresco*.

In the Fig. 1, we can see an example of our workflow process:

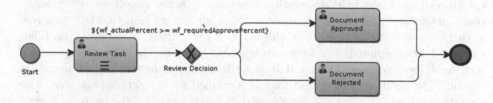

Fig. 1. BPMN

In this diagram, we can see that we have a circle that represent the state that indicates the start of your business process. Then, we have a user task that should be used when human interaction is required for the business process, for example, when details are to be filled or verified by a human. The review decision is represented by an exclusive gateway, that is used when we want to proceed with one path from the multiple paths defined. So, we can compare the exclusive gateway to an if-else statement of the programming concept. In this review decision, we can define a condition, that if it's true, the document is approved through the user task, otherwise the document is rejected trough other user task. In the two cases, we advance for the final state that represents the end of the business process.

We have three types of workflows as talked in the Related Work section. One of the workflows, users can sign in parallel, i.e., can sign in any order. The other workflow, users have to sign with a specific order, for example, first signs employed X, and only when X signs, employed Y can sign and in the final the director of the company accepts the task. The last workflow, a group of users can sign in parallel. Alfresco has a feature that allows the creation of user groups, so, we can associate a group to the workflow, without the need to associate one person at a time.

This diagram represents the BPMN that we create for this work. In the initial state, we have a form that we can choose the title of the workflow ($bpm\_workflowDescription$), a due date ($bpm\_workflowDueDate$), a priority ($bpm\_workflowPriority$), the reviewers ($bpm\_assignees$) that we want to sign a specific document (or more than one document $packageItems$) and the required approval percentage ($wf\_requiredApprovePercent$), i.e., the percentage of people that have to sign the document for workflow can be approved by the owner of that workflow. We have a possibility of send an email to the reviewers that are attached to the workflow with the link of the task to review and with the link(s) of the document(s) attached to the workflow too ($bpm\_sendEMailNotifications$).

When the workflow is started, is created in the document(s) attached to the workflow, one signature field for each reviewer attached to the workflow. Each field has the corresponding user name of the reviewer who will sign this field. After the initial state, the review task consists in send a task, to each reviewer attached to the workflow, for the reviewer sign and therefore accept the task. If the user reject the task, then it does not agree with the document, therefore, does not sign. To review the task, a form is displayed to the reviewers, with the info of the task: title/description (*message*), owner (*taskOwner*), priority (*bpm_priority*), due date (*bpm_duedate*) and identifier (*bpm_taskId*); progress with the status of the task (*bpm_status*): not yet started, in progress, on hold, cancelled or completed; the items attached to the task (*packageItems*) and a comment (*bpm_comment*) that if it is written, is put in the digital signature reason. The result of the review task is identified by $wf\_reviewOutcome$. The signature is made through the citizen card. When the user hit the button "Accept and Sign" is shown a pinpad to insert the signature PIN. When the signature is placed in the document, in addition to the signature of the reason it is placed in the same field the name of the person who signed the document and the date and time.

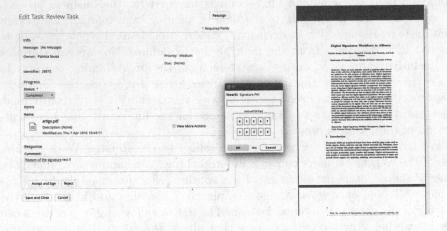

Fig. 2. Example of a signature page

Digitally signed by PATRÍCIA RAQUEL VIEIRA SOUSA
Date: 2016.05.10 17:16:43 WEST
Reason: Reason of the signature test !!

Fig. 3. Example of a signature

After this, the condition $\$wf\_actualPercent >= wf\_requiredApprove Percent$ is tested for the review decision. The $wf\_actualPercent$ is the percentage of reviewers that sign and accept the document and the $wf\_requiredApprovePercent$ is the required approval percent, filled on the form, previously described in this section. If the condition is true, then the document(s) can be approved by the workflow owner.

Algorithm 1. Count percentage of reviewers that approve the document

---

1: **if** $task.getVariableLocal('wf\_reviewOutcome') ==' Approve'$ **then**
2:     $newApprovedCount := wf\_approveCount + 1;$
3:     $newApprovedPercentage := (newApprovedCount/wf\_reviewerCount) * 100;$
4:     $execution.setVariable('wf\_approveCount', newApprovedCount);$
5:     $execution.setVariable('wf\_actualPercent', newApprovedPercentage);$
6: **end if**

The Algorithm 1 is called whenever a user approves a task. After this, the owner ends the workflow through a form, even if it is approved or rejected and can do a comment to the workflow. The form has info of the workflow: title/description, owner, priority, due date and identifier; progress with the status of the task: with the same choose status then the task review form; the information of outcome: number of reviewers, reviewers who approved, required approval percentage and actual approval percentage; the items attached to the task and a comment that owner can put in the workflow.

As the signatures are made with the citizen card, each user has to associate the card to their user profile. The system makes a check if that card already belongs to someone else profile, for security reasons. If the user has no smart card in the profile, when the user tries to sign a document through a workflow, it's required to associate the citizen card to their profile. To facilitate the use of the service, we have another way of association of the card to the profile. The users can associate the card without leaving the current workflow task through a button that makes the direct association of the smart card to the user profile.

In addition to the citizen card, we decided to also give the possibility of users associate other smart cards to their profile, instead of only citizen card. If the users work in a hospital, they can associate their hospital card profile. So they can, for example, sign hospital internal documents with the hospital card and human resources documents with the citizen card. It gives the possibility of the person to choose which card you want to use to sign the documents.

One of the other biggest capacity of our system is the provision of information about the signature fields for each document. Through an action button, which is one of Alfresco capabilities, that calls an external web service we offer the user the possibility to validate the document and which fields that are already signed and if the signatures are valid.

We decide to make a external web service to validate the signatures because, for example, if we have a customer, Alfresco and the validation service, the customer wants to ensure that the document signing is being properly assessed on your product. To make sure that the validation is done correctly, the validation service has to includes a signature in your answer that the customer can validate and have the security that Alfresco is not changing any validation response.

The information that web service returns is the number of revisions, the number of fields, the status (empty, partial or full) and the number of signed fields. For each field the information is the name of the field, if it is signed. If it is signed we have the information if the signature cover all the document, if it has been revised, date, the certificate of the citizen card, the integrity of the signature and the response that web service gives (valid or not) is stored on the validation variable, then in the client side, we test the conditions again and we compare this variable, so, we can see if the result by the server is correct.

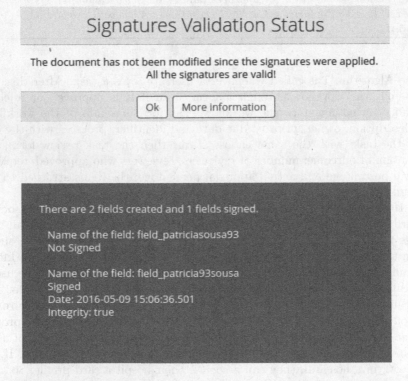

Fig. 4. Pop-ups example with signatures validation status and more information of validation

We can see in the Fig. 4 the pop-ups that we use to show the information to the client. The first pop-up is showed when the user clicks on the "Verify Document" in a specific document, if the document has been modified since the signatures were applied and therefore, if the signatures are valid or not. With "More information" button, we can see an example, on the second pop-up, of the information that is showed. We give the information of the number of fields that exists on the document, how many fields are signed, the name of the fields and if each field are signed. For the signed fields, we show which is the date/time and the integrity of the field.

7 Conclusions

When a paper document passes between multiple departments, the document can be falsified or tampered with. With this system, as already mentioned, import security properties are preserved, like system trust, since all users can see the current state of the documents being signed during the entire signage process, it's possible to verify the document at any time and see the modifications in real time. The digital signatures perverse too the security properties integrity, authenticity and non-repudiation. This all together, is an advance in paperless technology, since the signatures in addition to being integrated into a workflow, the signatures workflow are integrated in an enterprise content management, in this case, *Alfresco*. Thus, everyone can access the documents at any time and anywhere. This system will avoid the print of the paper for the purpose of the signatures and will contribute for the environment. This will be important not only to avoid the paper as well as to prevent damage to the paper using pens for example, but also avoid the use of printers and scanners to print and scan the papers that have the signatures.

8 Future Work

This investigation will enable to integrate, in the future, other forms of signatures beyond the smart cards, such as an yubikeys with a certificate to be using to sign, for example.

This system only allows digital signatures in a PDF file therefore, as a future work, we plan to add electronic signatures and biometric signatures and give the user option to choose between different types of signatures. It is also desirable to implement the signatures for other types of document that not only PDF such as XML, for example.

References

1. Asili, H., Tanriover, O.O.: Comparison of document management systems by meta modelling and workforce centric tuning measures. arXiv preprint 1–2(2014). arXiv:1403.3131
2. Plimmer, B., Apperley, M., Work, M.P.: Making paperless work 2007. In: Proceedings of the 8th ACM SIGCHI New Zealand Chapter's International Conference on Computer-Human Interaction: Design Centered HCI, pp. 1–2. ACM (2007)
3. Zantout, H., Marir, F.: Document management systems from current capabilities towards intelligent information retrieval: an overview. Int. J. Inf. Manag. **19**(6), 471–484 (1999)
4. Intergraph. Enterprise Content Management (ECM) Overview. Copyright Intergraph Corporation, pp. 4–5 (2010)

5. Vesali, M.: Paperless Office. Business Consulting Master. Hochschule Furtwangen University, pp. 1–7 (2012)
6. Sellen, A.J., Harper, R.H.: The Myth of the Paperless Office, pp. 17–18. MIT Press, Cambridge (2001)
7. ALA's Legal Management. http://www.arx.com/files/uploads/2014/11/CoSign_ALA_Legal%20Management.jpg. Accessed 13 Mar 2016
8. Nye, J.: Issues and disadvantages of moving to a paperless office. Issues, pp. 4–6 (2009)
9. Caruana, D., Newton, J., Farman, M., Uzquiano, M., Roast, K.: Professional Alfresco - Practical Solutions for Enterprise Content Management, pp. 39–42. Wiley, New York (2010)
10. Maass, W., Kowatsch, T. (eds.): Semantic Technologies in Content Management Systems - Trends, Applications and Evaluations, 1st edn. Springer, Heidelberg (2012)
11. LogicalDOC - Product features. www.logicaldoc.com/product/features.html. Accessed 13 Mar 2016
12. Nikoi, E., Boateng, K.: Collaborative communication processes and decision making in organisations. In: Advances in Human Resources Management and Organisational Development. IGI Global, pp. 51–54 (2013)
13. Aalberts, B.P., van Der Hof, S.: Digital signature blindness analysis of legislative approaches to electronic authentication. EDI L. Rev. **7**, 7–8 (2000)
14. Luppicini, R.: Evolving Issues Surrounding Technoethics and Society in the Digital Age, pp. 186–187. IGI Global, Hershey (2014)
15. Decreto-Lei n. 290-D, 99, de 2 de Agosto. https://dre.pt/application/dir/pdf1sdip/1999/08/178A01/00020011.pdf. Accessed 13 Mar 2016
16. Jo, J.-G., Seo, J.-W., Lee, H.-W.: Biometric digital signature key generation and cryptography communication based on fingerprint. In: Preparata, F.P., Fang, Q. (eds.) FAW 2007. LNCS, vol. 4613, pp. 38–49. Springer, Heidelberg (2007)
17. Stern, J.E.: The electronic signatures in global and national commerce act. Berkeley Technol. Law J. JSTOR. **16**, 394–396 (2001)
18. Xenitellis, S.: The Open-source PKI Book. Open CA Team, pp. 34–35 (2000)
19. Katz, J.: Digital Signatures. Springer, Heidelberg (2010)
20. Gorelik, S., Lyaper, V., Bershadskaya, L., Buccafurri, F.: Breaking the barriers of e-participation: the experience of russian digital office development. In: Kő, A., Francesconi, E. (eds.) EGOVIS 2014. LNCS, vol. 8650, pp. 173–186. Springer, Heidelberg (2014)
21. Gonçalves, J.P.B., Cidadão, C.: Autenticação de Papéis do Cidadão. Lisbon Technical University (2010)
22. Marković, M., Savić, Z., Kovaĉević, B.: Secure mobile health systems: principles and solutions. In: Istepanian, R.S.H., Laxminarayan, S., Pattichis, C.S. (eds.) M-Health, pp. 81–106. Springer, New York (2006)
23. Laliwala, Z., Mansuri, I.: Activiti 5. x Business Process Management Beginner's Guide. Packt Publishing Ltd., Birmingham, pp. 26–27 (2014)
24. Boonmee, C., Chatchumsai, R., Boonmee, S.: Development of electronic correspondence letter time-stamping service using oasis digital signature services. In: The Proceedings of the 11th European Conference on EGovernment. Faculty of Administration, University of Ljubljana, Ljubljana, Slovenia. Academic Conferences Limited, pp. 3–4 (2011)

Author Index

Printed in the United States
by Baker & Taylor Publisher Services